Social Science and Historical Perspectives

"Eller's book is a logically structured and highly readable overview of the key tenets of various social science disciplines."
—Wendy Rouse, San José State University, USA

This accessible book introduces the story of "social science," with coverage of history, politics, economics, sociology, psychology, anthropology, and geography.

Key questions include:

- How and why did the social sciences originate and differentiate?
- How are they related to older traditions that have defined Western civilization?
- What is the unique perspective or "way of knowing" of each social science?
- What are the challenges—and alternatives—to the social sciences as they stand in the twenty-first century?

Eller explains the origin, evolution, methods, and main figures in each discipline, as well as the literature, concepts, and theories. The chapters also feature a range of contemporary examples, with consideration given to how the disciplines address present-day issues.

Jack David Eller is Associate Professor (Emeritus) of Anthropology at the Community College of Denver, USA. An experienced teacher and author, his other books for Routledge include *Cultural Anthropology: Global Forces, Local Lives* (third edition, 2016), *Cultural Anthropology: 101* (2015), *Culture and Diversity in the United States* (2015), and *Introducing Anthropology of Religion* (second edition, 2014).

T0398173

Social Science and Historical Perspectives

Society, Science, and Ways of Knowing

Jack David Eller

Routledge
Taylor & Francis Group

LONDON AND NEW YORK

First published 2017
by Routledge
2 Park Square, Milton Park, Abingdon, Oxon OX14 4RN

and by Routledge
711 Third Avenue, New York, NY 10017

Routledge is an imprint of the Taylor & Francis Group, an informa business

© 2017 Jack David Eller

British Library Cataloguing in Publication Data
A catalogue record for this book is available from the British Library

Library of Congress Cataloging-in-Publication Data
Names: Eller, Jack David, 1959– author.
Title: Social science and historical perspectives: society, science,
and ways of knowing/Jack David Eller.
Description: First Edition. | New York: Routledge, 2016. |
Includes bibliographical references.
Identifiers: LCCN 2016007405| ISBN 9781138675803
(hardback: alk. paper) | ISBN 9781138675797 (pbk.: alk.
paper) | ISBN 9781315560434 (ebook)
Subjects: LCSH: Social sciences—History.
Classification: LCC H51 .E45 2016 | DDC 300—dc23
LC record available at http://lccn.loc.gov/2016007405

ISBN: 978-1-138-67580-3 (hbk)
ISBN: 978-1-138-67579-7 (pbk)
ISBN: 978-1-315-56043-4 (ebk)

Typeset in Sabon
by Florence Production Ltd, Stoodleigh, Devon
Printed and bound by CPI Group (UK) Ltd, Croydon, CR0 4YY

Contents

Introduction

Imagine that you were a car salesperson. You could be very successful at selling cars without any knowledge of how cars are manufactured, or how they work internally, or how they were invented in the first place. However, you might be curious to know more about the history and technology of cars, or you might hope someday to own your own car dealership or auto manufacturing plant. You might even have an idea for a better car or an alternative to cars.

Now imagine that you were not a purveyor of cars but of information, that is, a teacher. You could be very successful at teaching information without any real knowledge of how information is made, or how information works, or how the things we know or the particular ways that we organize and transmit information were invented in the first place. However, you might be curious to know more about the history and function of knowledge, or you might hope someday to be a school administrator or to open your own school. You might even have an idea about a better way to teach or run a school or an alternative to existing knowledge- or school-systems.

This book is about the knowledge that we have and teach in what we call the "social sciences." Social sciences are either a sub-type of science or a parallel field to the "natural sciences." They are also typically distinguished from, but also related to, the "humanities." Finally, "social studies" is a particular condensed and simplified version of (some of) the social sciences.

This book is not a presentation on methods for teaching the social sciences or social studies to any particular set of students. There are many books on social science teaching methods. This book is also not a survey of a specific social science, although it does discuss each of the major conventional social sciences. Texts providing "introduction to sociology" or "general psychology," etc. are readily available, and entire college courses serve to introduce students and future practitioners to the various disciplines.

This book does something more unusual, indeed rare, and there are few college courses that attempt precisely what we will attempt here. The best way to think of the project at hand is "sociology of knowledge," that is, the social organization of knowledge-making and knowledge-transmitting.

Knowledge, after all, does not grow on trees, and humans do not simply "find" knowledge lying about in the world around them. Humans have to not only discover but *construct* knowledge; at the very least, we must put facts together to draw conclusions and arrive at generalizations. But we must also perform certain actions to acquire facts and establish standards for *what counts as a fact*. One common action in science is the "experiment," but as we will see soon, not all sciences perform experiments, and experiments are not the only path to scientific knowledge.

Even more than gathering facts and spinning them into generalizations and conclusions (often and ideally "laws"), humans must organize themselves in some way to produce and disseminate knowledge. One familiar way to organize the production of knowledge is the research laboratory. One familiar way to transmit knowledge is the classroom and the academic discipline and department; another is scholarly writing. But these are only the beginning of an incredibly complex and controversial knowledge-construction process.

Obviously, different sciences and disciplines know different things. Indeed, each science and discipline was invented for the purpose of knowing different things. So each is a particular body of knowledge. But much more, each is a particular *way of knowing*. Each has its own language or terminology, its own questions, its own methods, its own literature, and its own disciplinary history. Each is a specific, though not isolated, "knowledge community," and, as scholars often complain, members of one knowledge community tend not to read the work or even talk to the members of other communities. Sometimes, the differences in language and questions make it difficult to talk to each other, and the burden of mastering and keeping up with one's own field leaves little time to follow the developments in other fields.

Science is a very powerful way of knowing. An interesting and important question is whether science is the *only* way of knowing. There are those who insist that only scientific knowledge *is* knowledge; we can, for instance, know scientific things about music or art, but music and art themselves contain and convey no knowledge. Others counter that music, art, literature, and perhaps religion have their own knowledge and their own unique and valuable ways of knowing.

Still more narrowly, there are also those who contend that only the natural sciences produce knowledge, in the form of theories and laws. Such people may reject the "social sciences" as poor imitations of "real" or "hard" science. Or social scientists may try to make their disciplines more "scientific" to meet the high standards of "hard" science. Others, though, may insist that social sciences do not have to copy natural sciences in language or method, arguing instead that the subject of social sciences (human beings and social action) is so different from the subject of natural sciences (matter and physical processes) that the social sciences demand their own approach.

Then there are those who assert that science is itself not a universal but a culturally-specific way of knowing. In particular, they contend that science is a Western or European way of knowing, one that discounts non-Western knowledge, whether that is knowledge from other civilizations (for instance, Asian, Indian, or Middle Eastern) or from the world's many indigenous peoples. Critics accuse Western science of dismissing these other bodies of knowledge and ways of knowing as non-scientific, as "traditional" at best and as mythological or false at worst. Non-Westerners and indigenous people often answer science's complaint by reminding us that science, despite its many successes, has also had some profoundly negative effects on the natural and social world.

Finally, there are those who say that the current way of organizing knowledge—the contemporary academic disciplines, the existing school and university systems, and the traditions of article writing and book publication—are not the best way to construct and transmit knowledge. They may call for new research and information-sharing methods, perhaps using the Internet and technology or social networking media. They may urge the use of non-textual forms of knowledge such as video and photography. They may recommend more collaborative work, between practitioners of the same discipline, practitioners of different disciplines, or even members of different cultures and civilizations. At the extreme, they may challenge us to rethink existing disciplinary boundaries altogether, proposing new transdisciplinary ways of knowing or even the dismantling and reinvention of disciplines and institutions altogether.

While an ambitious project, the reinvention of the social sciences is not as preposterous at it sounds at first hearing. The truth is, as we will stress in this book, *the social sciences were invented very recently*, which means (1) that they have not always existed in their present form and therefore (2) that they need not always exist in their present form. In fact, we know that virtually all organizations and institutions are in an almost continuous cycle of self-examination and self-invention these days. Organizations and institutions are encouraged and required to assess themselves, to reconsider their policies and processes, to "think outside the box" and to incorporate perspectives from often neglected and invisible constituencies like subordinated races, ethnicities, languages, genders, religions, age groups, and so on. In other words, just because we have done things a certain way in the past—whether "we" are a business, a school, a country, or an academic discipline—does not mean that we must continue to do things that way.

Features of the Book

This book contains nine chapters, each of the middle seven chapters dedicated to one of the conventional social sciences. (Note that not all scholars agree on which fields count as "social sciences," and different colleges and universities arrange their departments differently.) We begin with a chapter exploring more deeply the construction of social knowledge and the recent invention of the contemporary social sciences, and we end with a chapter considering challenges to the received order of social science—and of science itself—in the form of alternative ways of knowing.

Each of the discipline-specific chapters includes a variety of kinds of information about that discipline. Key professional organizations and journals are listed, and the history of the discipline is discussed. The major figures who shaped the discipline into its current form are presented, as well as the central theoretical schools of thought and, when appropriate, the diverse "careers" offered within that discipline. The current predominant concepts and methods of the field are also described.

Readers will note that some thinkers have been foundational to more than one discipline, like Karl Marx or Adam Smith. Further, all current Western social sciences owe a debt to ancient thinkers like Plato and Aristotle, and these social sciences all emerged out of a common tradition of philosophy and theology, which marked them and still marks them today. Indeed, it will become clear that a driving concern, beyond merely learning true things and acquiring practical tools for managing society, has been *morality*, that is, conceiving and creating the "good person" and the "good society."

In addition to the presentations on each discipline, the chapters offer a comparative perspective on a specific significant social issue, in order to convey how the various disciplines think differently about any single issue. The issue chosen here is terrorism, but hopefully readers will quickly see how the diverse perspectives can be applied to any social topic and how each perspective brings something unique and valuable to the analysis, which in combination give us the most complete possible understanding of the matter. Finally, the volume includes a list of key terms and a bibliography of references cited.

My hope is that, through this text, readers will come to better understand how the knowledge that they read in textbooks and hear in lectures—and that they themselves are called upon to preserve and transmit as teachers, as parents, or simply as citizens—is invented. And since knowledge is invented, or constructed as we social scientists like to say, then there are inevitable disagreements about that knowledge—about what is true, what is important, and about how it should be used. And since knowledge is invented, including the very boundaries between different kinds or fields of knowledge, it can always be reinvented. The reader him/herself may, in fact hopefully will, find him/herself engaged in precisely this negotiation and reinvention of knowledge and of knowledge disciplines and knowledge institutions in the future.

Key Terms

a priori
prior to experience; self-evident and necessary, even without empirical data

agency
the capacity to participate in society or history as a creative actor, rather than as a passive product or victim; the possession of intelligence or will or "intentionality" (the ability to act on your own intentions)

agnotology
the practices and tactics used by individuals and institutions to obscure or misrepresent knowledge for the purpose of breeding doubt and ignorance

collective memory
also known as social memory and first discussed in detail by Maurice Halbwachs, a follower of Émile Durkheim, the notion that a society possesses, perpetuates, and sometimes invents memories for its members, stored in various social practices like documents, stories, memorials, and of course the curriculum and canon

cultural relativism
the position that a society or an historical era can only be accurately understood in terms of (relative to) its own concepts, beliefs, and values

discourse
the language or ways of speaking (and therefore of thinking and acting) in a particular society, historical era, or academic discipline. Also sometimes described as a "discursive regime"

embodiment
the notion that culture is not merely "ideas" but is enacted in and through the body; social categories (like gender or race) are experienced through the body, "performed" with the body, and "inscribed" on the body; culture is not just thought but felt and lived

enskilment	the acquisition of practical "know-how" in addition to, or instead of, "factual" or "propositional" knowledge; skill in this sense often is not expressed in words and sometimes cannot be expressed in words
epistemic culture	according to Karin Knorr Cetina, the arrangements and mechanisms, which, in a given field, make up *how we know what we know*; the people, practices, and institutions that create and warrant knowledge—the premier knowledge institution being science
epistemology	the philosophical study of the nature of knowledge (i.e. how we know)
expert knowledge	greater or deeper knowledge of a subject usually resulting from training and experience and commonly conferring power and prestige
hermeneutics	practices of interpretation: at least, that interpretation is a problematic process; at the extreme, that all "facts" must be interpreted or are interpretations
indigenous knowledge	the things that native or indigenous peoples know, and more importantly the *ways in which they know*, based on unique local concepts, terms, values, practices, and institutions
normative	a statement that establishes, is based on, or implies a judgment or preferred standard of behavior (a "norm"); research that proposes or argues what should be, rather than that describes what is
positivism	the position that knowledge involves the accumulation of facts, and therefore that better knowledge means more and better facts
postmodernism	as formulated by Jean-Francois Lyotard and others (like Jean Baudrillard), the contemporary cultural moment and experience in which "truth" breaks down, "grand narratives" are no longer believed, "progress" is no longer assured if even possible, and in which perspective and subjectivity, emotion and irrationality, images (rather than words), and fragmented and reassembled experiences dominate

practice
: the analysis and description of what members of a group or society actually do, as opposed to the abstractions that we call "culture" or "social structure"; practice is informed by culture and occurs within a social structure, but it is not pre-determined by those forces, instead depending on skilful and creative performance in social situations

reductionism
: the practice of explaining a phenomenon in terms of (that is, reducing it to) some lower-level phenomenon (e.g. claiming to explain "life" in purely physical or chemical terms, or society in purely psychological terms)

representation
: the choices and strategies concerning how to communicate or convey a set of information (for example, as a narrative or story, as "raw data" or mere facts, as equations and graphs, as pictures, etc.

social construction
: the idea that humans create and perpetuate their social reality through culturally-informed interaction

social reproduction
: the practices in a society that "reproduce" an existing community or society, that is, that perpetuate its relationships, institutions, beliefs and values, and inequalities

sociology of knowledge
: the study of the social processes and practices by which knowledge is created, distributed, institutionalized, disseminated, and used

structure of scientific revolutions
: according to Thomas Kuhn, the idea that science does not proceed in a straight line, getting better and better "facts" and "theories," but that scientific thinking jumps from one "paradigm" to another—each paradigm being a different way of thinking and talking about the world

1 What is Social Science?

Key organizations

National Social Science Association (www.nssa.us)
Consortium of Social Science Associations (www.cossa.org)
Academy of Social Sciences (www.acss.org.uk)
Social Science History Association (www.ssha.org)

Key journals

Contemporary Social Science
National Social Science Journal
Social Science History

Society is our immediate everyday reality, yet we understand no more of it merely by virtue of living in it than we understand of physiology by virtue of our inescapable presence as living bodies. The history of [social science] has been a long and arduous effort to become aware of things hidden or taken for granted: things we did not know existed—other societies in distant places and times, whose ways of life make us wonder about the naturalness of our own; things we know of only distortedly—the experiences of social classes and cultures other than our own; the realities of remote sectors of our own social structure, from inside the police patrol car to behind the closed doors of the politician and the priest; things right around us unreflectingly accepted—the network of invisible rules and institutions that govern our behavior and populate our thought, seemingly as immutable as the physical landscape but in reality as flimsy as a child's pantomime.

(Collins and Makowsky 1993: 1)

Humans always and everywhere have lived in societies, but they have not always taken the existence or nature of society as a mystery to be pondered, let alone a question to be systematically investigated. In fact, for the majority of societies throughout history, and arguably for a majority of people today, society is opaque and taken for granted, in need of no analysis and sometimes beyond questioning. To be sure, people may wonder how to make a better life for themselves, but they typically do so within the familiar constraints of their society, without asking why their society exists in the first place or whether that society could be managed or fundamentally altered.

Society has always been there (in fact, many non-human animals also live in societies), but the scientific study of society is a remarkably new enterprise. "Social science," or perhaps more accurately "the social sciences" (because they are multiple and relatively distinct) were only invented in anything resembling their modern form in the mid-1800s, and they only reached their current form in the early 1900s. They certainly have much older roots, which is an important fact, but nobody was doing sociology or anthropology or psychology until very recently.

More, a discipline like history or psychology or anthropology is not just a body of facts to know. It is *a specific way of knowing*, in a number of senses. First, somebody had to divide knowledge into "historical knowledge" and "psychological knowledge," and "anthropological knowledge" etc. Then each discipline must discover—or construct—its knowledge, based on its particular interests and questions, its terminology and theories, and its methods and tools. Further, each discipline must enshrine its knowledge— and its territory or "turf," if you will—in specific institutional forms and perpetuate those institutions over generations. Social scientists refer to this process of the creation, perpetuation, transmission, and institutionalization of their own knowledge, and that of other sciences and of informal non-scientific knowledge, as the *social construction of knowledge*.

Before we can discuss how each social science constructs knowledge in its own distinctive way, we must first understand how knowledge is constructed in whatever field or domain—social science, natural science, or non-science. It may turn out, in the final analysis, that it is less proper to speak of knowledge than of diverse *knowledges*, each constructed by its own knowledge-practices and knowledge-traditions.

The Sociology of Knowledge

Knowledge, and even its building block, namely "the fact," is not so much found as made; the very word "fact" actually derives from the Latin *factum* for "something done" (more basically from the verb *facere* or "to do"). We might define a fact as a true statement, but such a definition begs the question of what is true and how we know it.

As science marched along allegedly discovering more facts, scholars began to notice that our knowledge is not as factual or objective as we tend to think. Sociologist Karl Mannheim was one of the first to suggest a social approach to knowledge, including knowledge that is not about society. For

Mannheim and the early sociology of knowledge, the fundamental question was "how the social location of individuals and groups shapes their knowledge" (Swidler and Arditi 1994: 305).

One of the early topics for Mannheim was the relation between knowledge and age or generation. In a 1923 essay, he urged us to consider that one's generation profoundly affects one's individual knowledge, because the individuals who occupy a generation share "a common location in the social and historical process" and therefore "a specific range of potential experience" (1952: 292). People of the same age, having lived through the same events, have in common "possible modes of thought, experience, feeling, and action" (292), resulting in what he called "the 'stratification of experience'" (297), virtually guaranteeing that members of a society would not possess the same knowledge, perspectives, and attitudes.

The sociology of knowledge has grown since its first days, and Swidler and Arditi asserted that the "new sociology of knowledge" that emerged by the 1990s was interested in the more general question of "how kinds of social organization make whole orderings of knowledge possible"; further, it investigated all sorts of knowledge, "political and religious ideologies as well as science and everyday life, cultural and organizational discourses along with formal and informal types of knowledge" (1994: 306). Ultimately, it expanded "the field of study from an examination of the contents of knowledge to the investigation of forms and practices of knowledge" (304).

Teachers are especially aware of the social-knowledge function of schools and of themselves as agents of social knowledge. In a series of publications from the 1970s to the 1990s, Basil Bernstein studied the social processes of educational knowledge. Central to his analysis is the notion of the school as a "social classifier," of both people and knowledge, through the three "common message systems" built into the school institution, which make it "an agency of socialization and allocation" to produce and reproduce social differences and boundaries (Bernstein 1975: 199).

The first of the three message systems is the *curriculum* or the "contents" of education. Someone must select, from among all of the possible things to know, the things that are worth knowing and appropriate for the level of the knower. We also refer to this as the "canon," the body of information that "counts as" knowledge, that has been officially sanctioned for knowing and therefore for teaching. The canon of literature in America, for instance, contains Shakespeare and Dickens and other prominent authors; it does not contain Danielle Steele or James Patterson. In history, too, choices must be made about which events to include and exclude, how to emphasize them, and how to interpret them. There is no objective or non-social way to make such decisions, and they are therefore ripe for disagreement and controversy (see Chapter 2).

The second message system is *pedagogy* or teaching methods. Any academic institution, and any individual teacher, must decide how to teach, whether to encourage rote memorization or critical thinking, whether to employ textual or visual materials, whether to promote group work or individual work, what kinds of homework to assign, and so on. Finally, Bernstein listed *evaluation* as the third message system, including "testing" but also all of the other ways in which teachers evaluate students—and teachers are evaluated by administrators and parents.

Taking his thinking further, Bernstein identified two dimensions of the organization of knowledge itself. The first was *classification*, by which he meant the boundaries between subject areas in the curriculum, for instance, how firmly we separate math from history from art. These borders might be weak or strong. The second was *frame*, a variable of pedagogy, referring to teaching practices such as the degree of control that the teacher exercises over the learning process (e.g. the order and timing of activities). When classification and frame are both strong, Bernstein suggested that learning operates on the "collection code," meaning that areas of knowledge are kept neatly apart and study is highly specialized, with loyalty to a subject expected by professionals (that is, a person becomes *a* psychologist or *a* sociologist). In the "integrated code," when classification and frame are weak, subject-boundaries are porous, individuals and ideas can move across or between disciplines and perspectives, and students and professionals are freer to create, combine, and question knowledge.

Expert Knowledge

Knowledge is not only socially constructed but also socially distributed. Different individuals, groups, and communities within a society know different things or know things at different depths. One of the most important distinctions in the knowledge distribution, especially in regard to science, is that between the "expert" and the novice or merely the average member of society. Of course, experts exist not only in the natural and social sciences but in every walk of life, from music and law to sewing and sports.

According to Marissa McBride and Mark Burgman, expert knowledge is

> what qualified individuals know as a result of their technical practices, training, and experience. It may include recalled facts or evidence, inferences made by the expert on the basis of "hard facts" in response to new or undocumented situations, and integration of disparate sources in conceptual models to address system-level issues. . . . Experts are usually identified on the basis of qualifications, training, experience, professional memberships, and peer recognition.
>
> (2012: 13)

Expert knowledge is often "domain specific," that is, limited to a specific subject area, but it can also be more general and integrative, crossing subject boundaries.

Construction of Knowledge in Early Childhood: Kindergarten as Boot Camp

"Student" is a specific social role, and elementary school is one location or site of social knowledge. No one is born knowing how to be a student, but it is a role that must be learned early and securely. Harry Gracey (1968) characterized the first year of formal schooling, kindergarten, as a kind of "boot camp" for future schooling and future life, in which the new recruit to the educational system had to master the basic skills of a student. Indeed, he claimed that kindergarten existed to teach the student role and its standard repertoire of behaviors and attitudes more than to teach any particular information. Conducting field observations inside kindergarten classrooms, Gracey determined that most of the teachers' energies were dedicated to training young children in "school routines," which were drilled into the students as surely as any military routines into a new soldier. Among the resources utilized by teachers were the physical structure of the classroom, with its different spaces and functions, and the social structure of interaction, with its timed and organized activities. Spontaneity had to be replaced with discipline, and one of the primary characteristics of this discipline was its arbitrary quality: teachers started and ended activities at their own time, and most of these activities were literally meaningless to the students. Gracey mentioned routines like pledging allegiance to the flag, which young students did not understand (and often garbled), as examples of routine for routine's sake, but much of the "academic" experience was equally capricious, such as learning particular facts about foreign countries. The point of much of the activity in the kindergarten classroom—and in classrooms throughout secondary and even higher education—consisted of tasks assigned by the teacher and performed by the students simply *because* they were assigned. The "meaning" of the work to the students was often the fact that the students had to do it. But there was one other meaning to these routine tasks: once the students graduated from and left the school institution, they would find themselves increasingly in institutions (like the workplace) where they were expected to conform to routines imposed by authorities that had little meaning or sense for them. Thus, Gracey concluded that kindergarten "can be seen as preparing children not only for participation in the organization and structures of large modern school systems, but also for a lifetime of employment in the large-scale organizations and offices of modern society" (1968: 71).

Expert knowledge of this sort is obviously social in a number of ways, with several crucial social consequences. For instance, as already mentioned, the initial source of much expert knowledge is education, which depends on schools, teachers (themselves ideally experts in a subject and in teaching methods), and textbooks (ideally written by experts). In other cases, the acquisition of expertise involves learning techniques from a "master" of those skills. Brian Moeran (2014), for instance, describes his apprenticeship in Japanese pottery, during which he acquired expert knowledge in multiple aspects of the art, from selecting clays to heating the kiln to shaping the designs and even displaying and selling the wares. Further, experts often work in groups, and those groups may establish specialized sites of practice (like the laboratory) and professional organizations including guilds, unions, and academic departments. Experts commonly if not normally act as masters and trainers for the next generation of experts, transmitting their expert knowledge and shaping the subjectivity (the thoughts and feelings) of novices.

Experts provide services for the wider society. At the very least, they serve as repositories of knowledge which other members of society do not have but which they can call upon; a good example is the "expert witness" in court trials. Experts can apply their knowledge to answer specific questions or render judgments. Experts of course can and often do produce new knowledge, from scientific discoveries to technological breakthroughs. Individuals who are recognized for possessing expert knowledge enjoy a certain prestige and power, although not without some resistance (see later discussion): experts are often paid well for their expertise, and ordinary people often defer to and obey the recommendations of experts, even outside their area of expertise. Albert Einstein's celebrated genius lent gravitas to his views on war and nuclear weapons.

Finally, in an attempt to quantify expert knowledge, Marie-Line Germain also suggested a number of social or personality qualities about the expert in addition to the obvious intellectual and technical competencies. To be sure, in her sixteen-item Generalized Expertise Measure (2006), the expert has knowledge and education, symbolized by formal credentials, but s/he is also "charismatic," "self-assured," "self-confident," and "outgoing."

Power and Practice

Bernstein's conceptualization of educational knowledge together with the sociology of expert knowledge raises issues of power and of practice. One of the most influential thinkers of the late twentieth century, Michel Foucault, stressed the *techniques of power* by which individuals, groups, institutions, and societies shape the knowledge and actions of others. Such techniques certainly include curriculum, pedagogy, and evaluation but also include more subtle tactics such as labeling and less subtle tactics such as punishment and physical constraint. Each particular social site or institution, from the school to the mental hospital, has its own repertoire of techniques of power (schools after all have detention and formerly had paddling), and such techniques for Foucault are also forms of knowledge. As the saying goes, knowledge is power, and also power is knowledge, and, as Swidler and Arditi put it, "New forms of knowledge also create new sites where power can be applied (and where resistance can form)" (1994: 315). For example, new economic knowledge can be applied to public policy and government, and those who hold such knowledge can establish organizations to exercise their knowledge-power (like think tanks) and control access to their organizations (through credentialing or admissions and membership qualifications).

Foucault was thus very interested in how the techniques of power and knowledge change over time and how they become "regimes of truth." Foucault referred to the knowledge/power system of any given society or historical period as a *discursive regime* or an *episteme*, the ancient Greek term for knowledge. An episteme is not only what people in a time or place know but *what it is literally possible to know or think*. It is the very limits of the knowable or thinkable for an individual or society, usually unconscious but definitely learned and definitely evolving over time. For instance, at one time the notion of germs as the cause of disease was unthinkable; for most of us today, spirit possession or witchcraft as the cause of disease is unthinkable.

As discussed earlier, expert knowledge is a particularly powerful type of knowledge, but even among experts—and certainly among the general public—much knowledge "remains informal, primarily because it is typically not documented and remains tacit until its expression is demanded in specific applications" (Perera, Drew, and Johnson 2012: 4). Many social scientists have since pursued the notion that much of what we call "knowledge" is less a matter of explicit cognitive or verbal information than of practical skills and learned intuitions—more inscribed in the body (we literally sometimes refer to "muscle memory") than processed by the mind. Moeran's research and experience in Japanese pottery is again an illustrative example: master potters typically do not "teach" in the familiar and formal sense but instead force the apprentice to observe (often for months or years) and then to emulate, absorbing the skills and abilities of the master—a process that we call *enskilment*—by doing.

Jean Piaget was among the first to notice that children develop their knowledge of the world through physically interacting with objects and people. In his model of "genetic epistemology," children at various levels of maturity construct embodied (sensory-motor-cognitive) strategies or *schemas* for understanding the world, such as that liquid poured from one container to another retains its volume. The systematic mistakes of judgment that children make at different ages, which indicate what they can and cannot think about (e.g. object permanence or conservation of matter, not to mention morality and other people's feelings). Pierre Bourdieu borrowed the term "habitus" from earlier sociologist Marcel Mauss to name this acquired but largely unconscious embodied knowledge that makes social action possible. In his famous *Outline of a Theory of Practice*, he defined habitus as "systems of durable, transposable dispositions, structured structures pre-disposed to function as structuring structures, that is, as principles of the generation and structuring of practices and representations" (1977: 72). To make a difficult idea somewhat simpler, Bourdieu considered knowledge to be less about facts and more about "skills" that individuals possess and use more or less masterfully to act in society. John Scahill (1993) suggested that Bourdieu meant "outlooks, opinions, and embodied phenomena such as deportment, posture, ways of walking, sitting, spitting, blowing the nose, and so forth." A valuable example of Bourdieu's thinking is the question of "taste," as he wrote in his 1984 *Distinction*. From foods to clothing to music to art, humans learn "taste," which is a form of social knowledge. More-over, in line with Mannheim, the tastes that we acquire reflect not only our society but our position or location in society—our gender, class, age, and such.

As all of these streams of thought suggest, some of our most profound knowledge is informal if not unconscious. Social scientists from Antonio Gramsci to Harold Garfinkel have focused on informal, sometimes even invisible, forms of knowledge/power, the most pervasive of which Gramsci called *hegemony*. Like Foucault, Gramsci saw much knowledge/power as utterly taken for granted, as even more than common sense but as the very horizon of the thinkable. It is the knowledge and perspective of a particular society—or a particular group or class within society—made "natural." Garfinkel, the inventor of the approach called ethnomethodology, examined the multiple small, everyday knowledge and skills that members of society exercise in their interactions, from taking turns and participating in conversations to (most famously) standing in elevators.

The Contestation of Knowledge and the Pursuit of Ignorance

The process of acquiring knowledge and submitting to those with knowledge (the "experts") is not automatic or passive. There is sometimes disagreement about who actually is an expert, and experts frequently disagree with each other (this is why there are commonly competing "schools of thought" or "theoretical schools" within a science or discipline). Matters of interest and power can intercede in matters of knowledge. It is often assumed that all people are honest brokers in the pursuit of knowledge and truth. A sociological approach to knowledge suggests, to the contrary, that knowledge or truth may be to the benefit of some individuals, groups, institutions, or societies and not others. Undoubtedly, people can sincerely disagree on the facts and/or their ramifications. From some social positions, though, not knowing the facts—*or not letting others know the facts*—might be desirable or advantageous. People can even argue over what the facts are.

Science is often portrayed as a steady march from non-knowing to knowing; ignorance is thus the simple absence of knowledge. But there are many alternatives to full knowing, including secrets, silence, and active suppression of knowledge. An exciting and important new field of *agnotology* has emerged lately to study these processes. Derived from the roots *a-* for "no/without" and *gnosis* for "knowledge," agnotology is the investigation of the causes and effects of ignorance or knowledgelessness. Robert Proctor, for one, has insisted that ignorance is not merely the absence of knowledge, but is a social product as much as knowledge is, often by means of the same techniques of power. Ignorance may be our native or default condition (before we know, we do not know), or it may be a result of losing knowledge (e.g. by forgetting), but it can also be "a deliberately engineered and *strategic ploy* (or active construct)" (2008: 3).

Some knowledge-claims contradict, threaten, or undermine cherished knowledge, belief, values, or interests. Obviously, if cigarette smoking is dangerous for human health, admitting that fact goes against the interests of tobacco companies. Corporations that do not want to curtail their polluting ways, or consumers who do not want to forfeit their lifestyle, may resist the science of climate change (global warming). Supporters of abstinence-only programs may dismiss evidence that such programs fail or actually backfire. And people who subscribe to a creationist view of life would understandably contest the facts of evolution.

David Michaels (2008) has quite critically researched how corporations and governments traffic in ignorance in his *Doubt is Their Product: How Industry's Assault on Science Threatens Your Health*. Discussing tobacco, occupational health standards, and illegal drugs among other subjects, Michaels identifies some of the motivations and strategies for "manufacturing uncertainty" among the public. He and others have warned about the practice of using industry- or government-hired "experts" to disseminate disinformation, while attacking the credibility of reputable scientists. The tobacco industry, he reports, went so far as to publish its own "scientific journal" called *Tobacco and Health Research* to refute evidence of the harmful effects of smoking.

Among the other tactics employed in what we might call *agnomancy* or the conjuring of ignorance, are accusations of conspiracy ("the scientists are trying to fool you"), selective picking of evidence, censorship, and encouraging doubt or insisting that doubt exists ("scientists do not agree" or "the evidence is inconclusive"). Probably the most sophisticated treatment of ignorance is Michael Smithson's *Ignorance and Uncertainty: Emerging Paradigms*, in which he explained that ignorance can be much more than mere absence of or uncertainty about knowledge. He argued that there are two subtypes of ignorance—error and irrelevance. Instances of irrelevance include those claims that are off-topic, undecidable, or taboo. Under errors, there is distortion and incompleteness, as follows:

- distortion
    1. confusion
    2. inaccuracy

- incompleteness
    1. absence
    2. uncertainty
        a. probability
        b. ambiguity
        c. vagueness (including fuzziness and nonspecificity)

(1989: 9)

Obviously then, ignorance, like knowledge, is more diverse and more intentional and motivated than we might think. It is important to bear this idea in mind as we proceed through the book.

Social Construction of Scientific Knowledge

Turning to science, three widely-held assumptions about knowledge are that:

- scientific knowledge inexorably "progresses," that is, each day science has more and better knowledge than the day before;
- scientific knowledge is superior to other forms of (or spurious claimants to) knowledge because of its "method"; and
- scientists are particularly conscious of both.

The notion that science (or any pursuit of knowledge) is simply a matter of getting more and better facts is called (and often condemned as) *positivism*. From the position of positivism, knowledge equals facts. However, social scientists and philosophers of science have become crucially aware that science is not and cannot be the pre-social search for facts, that the "scientific method" is neither as distinct from ordinary knowing as scientists tend to believe nor that it is used as singularly as they believe, and that science does not progress in a straight line as much as we believe.

Ludwik Fleck: Thought Collectives and Scientific Facts

Among the first scientists to ponder how scientific facts come to be was Ludwik Fleck, whose 1935 *Genesis and Development of a Scientific Fact* was overshadowed by the work of Thomas Kuhn (see p. 11) thirty years later. Writing from his experience with research on syphilis (specifically the development of the Wasserman test), Fleck noticed that scientific discovery was not a straightforward asocial process. Rather, essential for the production of knowledge are what he called "thought-collectives" and "thought styles." Thought, he asserted, is always a social or collective activity: people do not know in isolation but as members of a community of thought or thought-collective, that is, a collection of people who share ideas through their social and intellectual interaction. Thought-collectives exist outside of science too, but a team of scientists and members of a scientific discipline or profession definitely constitute a thought-collective.

Every thought-collective or knowledge community also has its distinctive thought style. Like any style in any human endeavor, a scientific thought style

> consists of a certain mood and of the performance by which it is realized. A mood has two closely connected aspects: readiness both for selective feeling and for correspondingly directed action. It creates the expressions appropriate to it, such as religion, science, art, customs, or war, depending in each case on the prevalence of certain collective motives and the collective means applied. We can therefore *define thought style as [the readiness for] directed perception, with corresponding mental and objective assimilation of what has been so perceived*. It is characterized by common features in the problems of interest to a thought collective, by the judgment which the thought collective considers evident, and by the methods which it applies as a means of cognition. The thought style may also be accompanied by a technical and literary style characteristics of the given system of knowledge.
>
> (Fleck 1979: 99)

Among the ingredients of a thought-style are what Fleck called "pre-ideas," those ways of thinking that predate knowledge—often inherited from long ago—and shape how we think and know about specific scientific topics today.

Fleck's conclusion was that scientific knowledge, even the scientific "fact," is not an absolute, eternal, and presocial thing. Any scientific fact is a *historical and social* achievement, the history of which can be investigated (100), and as an accomplished fact or bit of knowledge it is always "a supplement, development, or transformation of the thought style" of a practicing thought collective (92).

Thomas Kuhn: Paradigms and Scientific Revolutions

Thomas Kuhn's 1962 book *The Structure of Scientific Revolutions* is a much better-known analysis of the scientific process. Noticing that the path of scientific knowledge from, say, Aristotle to Newton to Einstein is not a straight one—not just a matter of accumulating more facts—Kuhn posited that scientific "progress" was actually a series of "revolutions" or changes of fundamental worldview. A scientific revolution or change of scientific worldview is, in Kuhn's words, a shift of *paradigm*.

A paradigm for Kuhn is more than a theory; it is the context of ideas that makes a theory possible and sensible. At any given moment, scientists, he asserted, operate within a particular paradigm. A paradigm is a model of reality at the fundamental scale, shared ideas about what kinds of things exist and their qualities and characteristics. Even more, a paradigm carries with it a set of methods and practices, including tools and instruments: if you think, for instance, that there are microscopic organisms in the world, then a microscope is a necessary technology for knowing them. Likewise, if you are an alchemist then you have "methods" for turning lead into gold, and if you are an astrologer, you have tools and methods for charting and reading horoscopes.

Even more, each paradigm is distinguished by its own unique questions and problems. That is, if a particular scientific paradigm holds that light is a wave, then its specific questions will involve the wavelength of light, etc.; if the paradigm holds that light is a particle, then the question of the mass of the particle is important. But if light is a wave, then the mass of light is not only unimportant but unthinkable. At the deepest level, each paradigm has or is a "language" or terminology: alchemists and modern chemists, or psychoanalysts and experimental psychologists, literally do not speak the same language. (By extension, psychologists do not speak the same language as anthropologists or geographers, and none of them speak the same language as artists, philosophers, or theologians.)

Most of the time, Kuhn reasoned, scientists work within their established paradigm, doing what he called "normal science," defined as "research firmly based on one or more past scientific achievements, achievements that some particular scientific community acknowledged for a time as supplying the foundation for its further practice" (1970: 10). Doing normal science means solving the problems that the paradigm poses, perfecting the measurements that the paradigm has already made, and adding new knowledge within the existing paradigm. In this sense, normal science is actually rather conservative: "No part of the aim of normal science is to call forth new sorts of phenomena; indeed those that will not fit the box are often not seen at all" (24) or if seen may be thrown out as exceptions or experimental errors.

However, sometimes scientists inadvertently encounter phenomena that cannot be easily accommodated in the reigning paradigm, like the discovery of X-rays. On other occasions, exceptions and anomalies pile up until the old paradigm becomes shaky. What happens then is a "paradigm shift": someone, often a young scientist who is not completely socialized into and committed to the inherited paradigm, offers a new view. The best example is Albert Einstein, who radically re-envisioned the universe as not Newtonian flat space but as a curved time-space continuum. When the old parad-igm becomes untenable, there is a struggle between new competing parad-igms, until the evidence (at least for a time) settles the question in favor of one of the rival new paradigms. We can then say that a paradigm shift has occurred.

One crucial aspect of science is that when a new paradigm triumphs, the old one as well as its rivals are typically discarded. (By contrast, religions, philosophies, and social science theories tend to multiply rather than substitute.) As Kuhn expressed it, defeated paradigms "disappear to a very considerable extent and then apparently once and for all" (17). A second significant effect is that the new paradigm launches a different project of normal science, now solving the problems and answering the questions raised by the new models, theories, instruments, and language.

The consequence for science, and for us in this book, is that holders of a paradigm constitute a Fleckian thought-collective and are often intellectually and even emotionally committed to their paradigm. They talk to each other, work together, and found institutions on and for the paradigm, from scientific organizations to training facilities. And they often do not—and cannot—talk to holders of other paradigms. At least to a certain extent, the differences between paradigms "are both necessary and irreconcilable" (103). The gap between paradigms is not just a difference of opinion; it is a difference of language and even of facts themselves. "The proponents of competing paradigms are always at least slightly at cross-purposes. Neither side will grant all the non-empirical assumptions that the other needs in order to make its case" (148), which may lead to actual disagreements about what the facts are or what the facts mean. It is fair to say that, more than being unable to talk to each other, radically different paradigms cannot even quite argue with each other, their realities being so incompatible. In the end, "there can be no scientifically or empirically neutral system of language or concepts" (146). Again like Mannheim and others contended, where you stand affects what you see, even in science.

Since the seminal work of Kuhn, historians, sociologists, and philosophers have explored how scientists actually do science and *how they produce scientific knowledge*. This often entails conducting observations of scientists at work in their laboratories. One of the most famous studies is Bruno Latour's *Science in Action: How to Follow Scientists and Engineers Through Society*. Observing the process rather than the product of science (what we might awkwardly call "sciencing"), Latour insisted that we "study science *in action* and not ready-made science or technology; to do so, we either arrive before the facts and machines are blackboxed [that is, before the knowledge-production processes become invisible] or we follow the controversies that reopen them" (1987: 258). He concluded that humans and their technology interact in a complex network of relationships and "a gamut of weaker and stronger associations; thus understanding *what* facts and machines are, is the same task as understanding *who* the people are" (259). At bottom, then, the trail of science "is in a large part the history of the resources scattered along networks to accelerate the mobility, faithfulness, combination and cohesion of traces that make action at a distance possible" (259). That is, individual scientists do not make knowledge, and machines alone do not make knowledge, and certainly facts themselves do not make knowledge, but knowledge is a contested product of human-machine-fact interaction.

Karin Knorr-Cetina: Epistemic Cultures

Developing the insights of Kuhn, Latour, and others, Karin Knorr-Cetina insisted that different sciences or even different subfields within a science function as discrete knowledge communities. Knorr-Cetina introduced the term *epistemic culture* to refer to

> those amalgams of arrangements and mechanisms—bonded through affinity, necessity, and historical coincidence—which, in a given field, make up *how we know what we know*. Epistemic cultures are cultures that create and warrant knowledge, and the premier knowledge institution throughout the world is, still, science.
>
> (1999: 1)

Comparing the work of high-energy physicists with that of molecular biologists, she debunked the common conception that different sciences or specialties within a science all follow the same scientific method, that is, that there is one single universal version of science. Instead, close inspection "reveals the fragmentation of contemporary science; it displays different architectures of empirical approaches, specific constructions of the referent, particular ontologies of instruments, and different social machines. In other words, it brings out the *diversity* of epistemic cultures. This *disunifies* the sciences" (3). She thus falsified the presumption that "there is only one kind of knowledge, only one science, and only one scientific method" (3)—which would hypothetically also have to be applied to human behavior and social systems. In other words, as we will discuss shortly, social scientists have often been told and convinced that they must adopt the same epistemic culture as natural scientists. However, if Knorr-Cetina is correct, the natural scientists do not even share a single epistemic culture; physicists have theirs, biologists have theirs, and presumably chemists and astronomers, etc. have theirs. It would make sense, then, that social science would have an appropriate epistemic culture of its own and that each social science (history, psychology, political science, and so forth)—and maybe even each sub-discipline (clinical psychology versus experimental psychology, or cultural anthropology versus physical anthropology)—would have a disciplinary epistemic culture all its own.

The Idea of Social Science

As we said at the outset, humans have always had society, but we have not always had a systematic study of society (any more than we have had a systematic study of the human body even though we have always had

---

The Pluralism of Scientific Methods

Taken together, the work of Fleck, Kuhn, Knorr-Cetina, and others indicates that there is no such single thing as "science" and no single "scientific method." Within different sciences, different methods (including different instruments) are appropriate and necessary, and the tendency to view physics and/or math as the paradigm of all sciences is inaccurate. For instance, in their *A History of Chemistry* (1997), Bernadette Bensaude-Vincent and Isabelle Stengers posited that chemistry has a distinctly different and underappreciated history and way of thinking. In his magisterial *Styles of Scientific Thinking in the European Tradition* (1994), Alistair Crombie identified six different scientific styles—postulation, experimentation, hypothetical modeling, taxonomy, statistical analysis, and historical derivation. Later, Ian Hacking (2002) added the "laboratory" style and explained that each style creates its own knowledge and even its own objects of knowledge and is "self-authenticating" (i.e. contains its own standards of validation). Unlike Kuhn's paradigms, however, these styles can communicate with each other, and any one science may use multiple methods, just as non-sciences may also use these methods.

---

bodies). And even when humans first began to ponder society, they did not do so in a "scientific" way, since science as we know it did not yet exist.

For most of human history, our institutions and practices (language, government, religion, gender roles, etc.) were taken to be either natural or supernatural. If natural, then our way of life was just "the way it had to be"; there was nothing in particular to understand and certainly nothing to change. If supernatural, then the conclusion was much the same: our way of life was given to us by non-human agents (spirits, ancestors, gods), and knowledge of this supernatural authorship of our society was sufficient; it was definitely beyond human capacity to change—or even fully know—society.

From either of these positions, there was little to learn about society—and virtually nothing to learn about other societies. Being "good" meant basically obeying your society's rules and fulfilling your nature- or supernature-given obligations. To the best of our knowledge, the first people to speculate about society, and to consider their own and other (even imaginary or possible) societies, were the ancients, especially the Greeks. This general rumination about human life and social organization is called today, and was called then, philosophy, from the Greek *sophia* for "wisdom" and

---

St. Augustine: Strive Not for Knowledge

Some major religious thinkers have actively discouraged human curiosity and the pursuit of knowledge. In his seminal *Confessions* (Book Ten, Chapter 35, section 54), St. Augustine wrote, "in addition to the fleshly appetite which strives for the gratification of all senses and pleasures—in which its slaves perish because they separate themselves from thee [God]—there is also a certain vain and curious longing in the soul, rooted in the same bodily senses, which is cloaked under the name of knowledge and learning; not having pleasure in the flesh, but striving for new experiences through the flesh. This longing—since its origin is our appetite for learning, and since the sight is the chief of our senses in the acquisition of knowledge—is called in the divine language 'the lust of the eyes.'"

---

philo- for "love." The philosopher was the person who sought wisdom, usually for its own sake, rather than accepting the popular or traditional views about things. The assumption, expressed best by Plato in his renowned Parable of the Cave, was that we are often ignorant of or blind to truth and wisdom, literally taking shadows and lies for reality.

The social sciences as we know them, however, had not yet been invented, and even terms, which were in use at the time, such as "history," "politics," "economics," and "geography" tended to have different meanings than they have in the modern social sciences. This is why the box below depicts some

---

The Modern Social Sciences

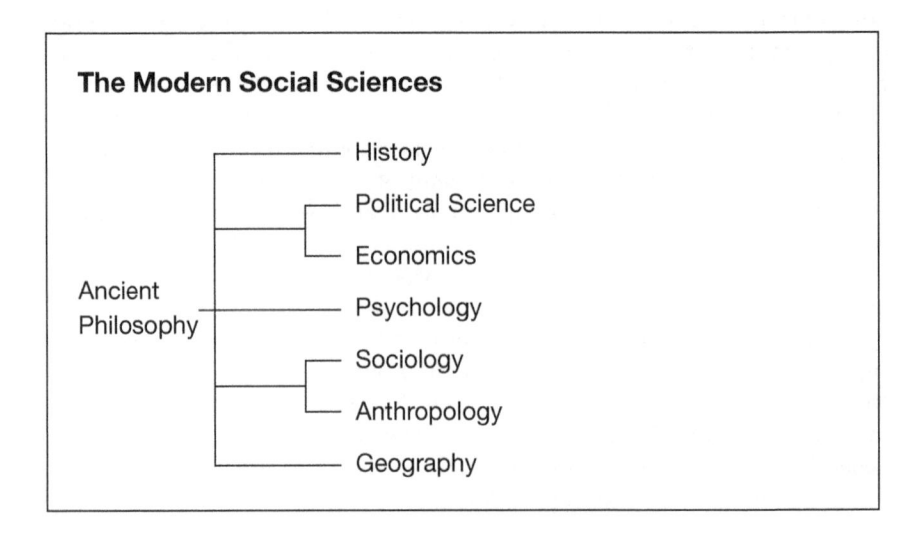

of the contemporary social sciences having an ancient pedigree and others having a much more recent origin. It also depicts political science and economics as developing out of a common background, as well as sociology and anthropology sharing common roots.

The Science in Social Science

In a leading textbook on the social sciences, John and Erna Perry say that the

> purpose of the social sciences is to study systematically all aspects of the human condition and of human behavior, using a methodology borrowed from the physical sciences wherever possible. This insistence on systematic and methodical study is what distinguishes the social sciences from philosophy, art, and literature, which also comment and reflect on all facets of the human condition.
>
> (2012: 2)

Philosophers and artists might take exception to those remarks, and physical scientists might dispute them; even social scientists themselves might object. And as we have seen, since the physical or natural sciences do not actually have a single methodology or epistemology, the assessment is highly problematic.

So the first question to confront is why the social sciences—at least in name and often in practice—have attempted to be "scientific" in ways that, say, philosophy and art have not. Part of the answer, of course, as Alfred Schutz reasoned, is that the natural sciences "have brought about such magnificent results" (1954: 257), and there can be no doubt that science has achieved great things and answered many previously unanswered (and even unasked) questions. In both empirical knowledge and technical application, there really are signs of progress—more productive factories, safer cars, faster computers, and such. Because of its spectacular accomplishments in solving problems and clearing away the debris of myth and falsehood, Schutz saw that it was easy to conclude that the practices of natural science "are the only scientific ones and that they alone, therefore, have to be applied in their entirety to the study of human affairs. Failure to do so, it has been maintained, prevented the social sciences from developing systems of explanatory theory comparable in precision to those offered by the natural sciences" (257).

It is fair to say that science enjoys a high reputation for most people, and in the modern world it is prestigious to be "scientific" and dubious to be "unscientific." Consider, for example, how a certain brand of religion dons the mantle of "creation science." Calling one's activity "science," or ideally actually doing it "scientifically," lends an aura of legitimacy. In the strongest interpretation, knowledge is either scientific *or it is not knowledge at all.*

So, to be "scientific" has so far largely meant to be like the natural sciences, which are the "real" and the most successful sciences. Yet curiously Theodore Porter and Dorothy Ross, in the introduction to their edited volume on the history of the social sciences, contended that "theology had a better claim to the status of science during the Middle Ages than did the study of living things, or even the study of matter in motion" (2003: 3). It is worth remembering that "science" is simply the Latin word for knowledge (*scientia*, from *scire*, "to know"), and little was actually known about the material (or social) world until surprisingly recently.

In fact, the word science was not immediately applied to the new study of material and biological phenomena, which was first called "natural philosophy" or "natural history" or "experimental physics." Porter and Ross taught that it was only around the year 1800 that science "emerged as the standard name for the organized pursuit of knowledge," and since the social sciences were born in the same era, "it was not immoderate for inchoate fields like sociology, anthropology, or statistics to march under the same banner" (3–4). On the flip side, the "modern practice of attacking fields of inquiry by denying their scientific credentials was uncommon until late in the nineteenth century, and it remains more plausible in English than in most other languages" (4).

What is it exactly that makes science scientific? As Knorr-Cetina insisted, it is not a single universal method or epistemic culture; nor, as Kuhn proved, is it linear progress. It is also not experimentation and laboratories, since some bona fide sciences do not and cannot use them (like astronomy), and there are also legitimate scientific fields like theoretical physics that work without laboratories or experiments.

The philosopher of science Karl Popper argued influentially that science is unique among thought-systems because it offers propositions that can be *tested and falsified*. If a statement is not testable and potentially falsifiable, it is by definition not scientific (we could say that it is no better than a guess, since how could we ever know if we are wrong?).

Fundamentally, science as it has developed in the modern era is characterized by two key concepts—*law* and *cause*. Science clearly pursues the discovery of facts, but facts are part of a much more ambitious project, to identify and specify the "laws of nature." A law in science (as opposed to politics and jurisprudence) is a description, ideally in mathematical form, of the operation of a phenomenon or a relation between phenomena. It is a statement of regularity. The best example is the "law of gravity," which states that the force of gravity, F, equals the product of the masses of two bodies times the gravitational constant, divided by the square of the distance between them. With this precise equation, we can predict the gravitational force between any two objects and use that prediction to generate other knowledge and to make practical applications (like space flight).

"Cause" in science refers to the necessary (and ideally mathematically specifiable) relationship between two variables or events, such that if one,

A, occurs then the other, *B*, will occur. Although there are arguably other kinds of causes, the most basic and "scientific" causal relationship can be stated simply, *If A, then B*. Such causal knowledge can also be used to generate new knowledge (e.g. what happens if *A* does not occur?) and to design applications and to control phenomena (e.g. if we do not want *B*, do not allow *A*).

It is a simplification, but a useful one, to view science as the enterprise that searches for facts in order to discover laws and causes. Further, the value of laws and causes is the capacity *to predict and control* future events and phenomena. In the process, science dispels preconceptions and errors about how things work and how things are related.

Early social thinkers like Auguste Comte (1798–1857), who coined the term "sociology" (see Chapter 6), very much aspired to a science of society. In his *The Course of Positive Philosophy*, published serially between 1830 and 1842, Comte explained that "the first characteristic of the Positive Philosophy"—what would come to be called social science—"is that it regards all phenomena as subjected to invariable natural laws. Our business is . . . to pursue an accurate discovery of these Laws, with a view to reducing them to the smallest possible number" (1855: 28). John Stuart Mill, an eminent scholar in his own right and an admirer of Comte, endorsed his colleague's project "to 'remedy' the 'backward state of the moral sciences' by 'applying to them the methods of physical sciences, duly extended and generalized'" (Porter and Ross 2003: 1).

What Comte and many later social scientists envisioned was literally a "Social Physics," and he believed that he had made a significant contribution to the formation of a physical science of society by discovering the "law of human progress," namely, that "the human mind, by its nature, employs in its progress three methods of philosophizing, the character of which is essentially different, and even radically opposed: viz, the theological method, the metaphysical, and the positive" (1855: 25). By "positive" he meant positivism in the sense described earlier, that is, based on facts rather than beliefs and faith (theological) or philosophical speculation (metaphysical).

Is Natural Science the Best Model for Social Science?

One of the other great founders of modern social science, Émile Durkheim (1858–1917), was also committed to the notion of the "social fact" (see Chapter 6), which he conceived as independent of biology or psychology, shared within a society, and exerting an external pressure on the individual. Nevertheless, many scholars have questioned the appropriateness of natural science as a template for social science. Alfred Schutz objected to modeling social science after natural science on the grounds that "there is a basic difference in the structure of the social world and the world of nature"; for one thing, as he said in slightly difficult language, "the social sciences are idiographic, characterized by individualizing conceptualization and seeking

The Return of Social Physics

While the notion of social physics might sound quaint or even misguided, it has reappeared in the twenty-first century, aided by the possibilities of massive data-collection offered by computer technology. In his 2014 book actually titled *Social Physics: How Good Ideas Spread—The Lessons from a New Science*, Alex Pentland correctly observes that, although we occupy society, we still do not really understand society, and clearly do not control it. Worse but true, our present "ways of understanding and managing the world were forged in a statelier, less connected time. Our current conception of society was born in the late 1700s during the Enlightenment and crystallized into its current form during the first half of the twentieth century" (2014: 2). Indeed, Comte and others whom we will meet in future chapters were the makers of this stately social theory. Instead of these old outdated models, Pentland proposes a new social physics, which will be

> a quantitative social science that describes reliable, mathematical connections between information and idea flow on the one hand and people's behavior on the other. Social physics helps us understand how ideas flow from person to person through the mechanism of social learning and how this flow of ideas ends up shaping the norms, productivity, and creative output of our companies, cities, and societies. It enables us to predict the productivity of small groups, of departments within companies, and even of entire cities. It also helps us tune communication networks so that we can reliably make better decisions and become more productive.
>
> (4)

Pentland declares that the dream of scientific social knowledge that affords us prediction and control is within reach finally because the "engine that drives social physics is big data: the newly ubiquitous digital data now available about all aspects of human life. Social physics functions by analyzing patterns of human experience and idea exchange within the digital bread crumbs we all leave behind us as we move through the world—call records, credit card transactions, and GPS location fixes, among others" (8). Sifting through this data, which he calls "reality mining," will expose "micropatterns" of human activity that were previously invisible and perhaps unimaginable. In short, and not to be flippant, better social knowledge—indeed, a true social science—only needs more facts. A sign of the growth of this perspective is three new academic journals, *Journal of Big Data*, *Big Data & Society*, and *International Journal of Big Data Intelligence*.

singular assertory propositions, whereas the natural sciences are nomothetic, characterized by generalizing conceptualization and seeking general apodictic [certain, necessary] propositions" (257).

In plainer and more contemporary language, it can be argued that social sciences call for a different methodology—one that might not exactly qualify as "scientific" (at least by natural science standards)—because the subject matter of natural science and social science are so different. Experts these days use the term *agency* to express this difference. Agency is the capacity to have subjectivity, will, or desire; an agent has its/his/her own perspective and intentions. Agents have "personality," feelings, and perhaps above all else, *meanings*. As Schutz said firmly, "The world of nature as explored by the natural scientist does not 'mean' anything to the molecules, atoms, and electrons therein" (266). Nor do atoms want or will anything.

As another founding figure of the social sciences, Max Weber, recognized in his aptly-named *On the Methodology of the Social Sciences*, in an essay first published in 1904, humans do not merely or ordinarily act *because of* some prior condition but *in order to* attain some future condition. That is, human behavior cannot be explained so much in terms of "cause" as in terms of "ends" or "purposes," so any "serious reflection about the ultimate elements of meaningful human conduct is oriented primarily in terms of the categories 'end' and 'means.' We desire something concretely either 'for its own sake' or as a means of achieving something else which is more highly desired" (1949: 52).

What this signifies is that "cause," a precious term for natural science, may not be the right term for social science. Since an atom or gravity or electricity has no agency (at least in the scientific worldview; see Chapter 9), any behavior of these phenomena can be (and theoretically can only be) explained in terms of cause. They have no intentions or meanings of their own. The same is not true of human beings.

Even more, since an atom has no agency, every atom in the same circumstances exposed to the same conditions should behave the same (within the limits of the "uncertainty principle"). This is also not true of human beings. Therefore, generalizability—that is, *law*—is not as easy to apply, if applicable at all, to human behavior. First, each individual human has his or her own perspectives, meanings, and reasons; two different people in the same circumstances may not behave the same. "All knowledge of cultural reality," Weber concluded, "is always knowledge from *particular points of view*" (81); thus the social scientist has a double burden, to describe and explain the action *and* to describe and explain the *particular points of view* of the human actors.

Second, the human social world is infinitely more complex than the physical world, if only because each individual has his/her own perspective, not to mention the myriad and diverse rules, roles, groups, and institutions within which they live and act. Justifiably, Weber asked, "how is the *causal explanation* of an *individual* fact possible—since a *description* of even the smallest slice of reality can never be exhaustive?" (78).

Third, since human actors have their individual (yet socially constructed and shared) perspectives and reasons, and since human action and society are infinitely complex, much if not most human action is not replicable. That is, the specific conjuncture of individuals and circumstances may only happen once. This makes generalization almost impossible. We might, for instance, investigate what happened to the Roman Empire and what individual Romans did in the past, but to generalize those actions and events to other times and places, let alone to all times and places (as Comte attempted to do) is absurdly difficult. Add to that problem the fact that many social phenomena cannot be observed at all (e.g. those that occurred in the past), and social science faces unparalleled challenges as science.

Therefore, Weber judged that the ultimate "presupposition of every *cultural science*" lies not in collecting brute social facts, and definitely not in judging any society better or more valuable than another, "but rather in the fact that we are *cultural beings*, endowed with the capacity and the will to take a deliberate attitude towards the world, and to lend it *significance*. Whatever this significance may be, it will lead us to judge certain phenomena of human existence in its light and to respond to them as being (positively or negatively) meaningful" (81).

A half-century later, Peter Winch, contemplating "the idea of a social science," proposed that the central concept in human behavior is the *rule* rather the law or the cause. A rule (or we might say a norm), according to Winch, is a meaningful guide for action and therefore a commitment to act in a certain way, based on prior knowledge (whether that is tradition, education, or personal experience): "all behavior which is meaningful (and therefore all specifically human behavior) is *ipso facto* rule-governed" (2003: 51–2). To explain his point, Winch employed an analogy that has become very common in the social sciences—the analogy between social rules and the grammar of a language:

> In learning to write English there are a number of fairly cut-and-dried grammatical rules which one acquires. . . . In terms of correct grammar one does not have a choice between writing 'they were' and 'they was': if one can write grammatically the question of which of these expressions one should use just does not arise. But this is not the only kind of thing one learns; one also learns to follow certain stylistic canons, and these, while they guide the way in which one writes, do not *dictate* that one should write in one way rather than another. Hence people can have individual literary styles but, within certain limits, can write only correct grammar or incorrect grammar. But it would plainly be mistaken to conclude from this that literary style is not governed by any rules at all.
>
> (53)

These social rules or norms account for the regularity that we see in human action. Yet, the rules can never specify every possible action, which relates to Bourdieu's concept of *habitus*: *habitus* is learned skills and dispositions, like grammar, that allow us to produce an infinite array of original actions (and utterances). That is why he called it a structured structure that operates as a structuring structure: our knowledge, skills, and dispositions are structured by prior action and then structure—but never determine—subsequent action.

But since human action is never completely determined, it cannot be reliably predicted. As Winch added,

> sometimes even if O knows with certainty the rule which N is following, he cannot predict with any certainty what N will do: where, namely, the question arises of *what is involved* in following that rule, e.g. in circumstances markedly different from any in which it has previously been applied. The rule here does not specify any determinate outcome to the situation, though it does limit the range of possible alternatives; it is made determinate for the future by the choice of one of these alternatives and the rejection of the others—until such time as it again becomes necessary to interpret the rule in the light of yet new conditions.
>
> (92)

In short, Winch insisted "that the central concepts which belong to our understanding of social life are incompatible with concepts central to the activity of scientific prediction" (94).

In a filmed interview, the Noble-prize winning physicist Richard Feynman called social science "a kind of pseudo-science" because social scientists "do not do science" although "they follow the forms" of science (www.youtube.com/watch?v=HtMX_0jDsrw). He granted that they collect data, but "they don't get any laws." "They sit at a typewriter and make up all this stuff." "I might be quite wrong," he confessed, "maybe they do know all these things, but I don't think so" because "I know what it means to know something."

Inventing the Social Sciences

Somewhere between Richard Feynman's condescension and Durkheim's nineteenth-century ambition for a study of society "that is objective, specific, and methodical" (1982: 35) reside today's social sciences. As mentioned several times already, most of these disciplines are quite new, although they all have deep roots in Western civilization, and they surely did not evolve spontaneously. They are instead the end-results of sustained efforts to create and perpetuate distinct intellectual spaces—to separate the social sciences from other previous and contemporary scholarly undertakings and to separate each social science from the others.

While there were no familiar social sciences in the ancient world, there was teaching and writing, under the general rubric of philosophy. Much of philosophy speculated on the natural world, asking what matter was composed of and how it changed or moved; Pythagoras led a school of thought examining numbers and mathematics (although in a mystical way). Closer to social science were the political and social searchings of Socrates and Plato. Socrates was an itinerant teacher who wrote nothing (and was tried and sentenced to death for his impious questions). Plato, like other successful intellectuals of his time, opened a teaching institution, the Academy around 387 BCE, which lasted for nearly a thousand years until shuttered by the Christian Roman Emperor Justinian I in 529 CE.

Plato's Academy was exclusive and closed to the public but did not charge tuition or fees. Neither did it have formal teachers and students or a set curriculum. Instead, at least in Plato's lifetime, the master would pose questions or problems to the junior members of the club, which were studied and debated. Occasional lectures were given, but more commonly participants engaged in the "dialectical" method of give and take, argument and counter-argument. Philosophical topics were the main fare of the Academy, although mathematics was also discussed, as well as subjects that would be considered scientific today, such as the motion of the planets.

Aristotle codified much of ancient knowledge in a series of writings in the fourth century BCE, on politics, ethics, poetics, metaphysics, and nature; we will encounter many of Aristotle's contributions in the following chapters. As indicated by Justinian's closure of the Academy, such free inquiry fell out of favor in the Christian-Roman era, and learning settled into two channels— a repetition of Aristotle's teachings and, of course, Christian theology. The questions that scholars pondered for a thousand years in Europe focused on proof of God's existence, speculations on God's nature, expositions of Christian belief, and interpretation of Christian literature.

A new form of education began to emerge in the early second millennium, modeled after Islamic universities. The oldest continuously-functioning university in Europe, the University of Bologna, was opened in 1088; in this and similar institutions, students "sought out eminent scholars and after learning everything the teacher could offer, received a prized certificate. Bolognese masters charged students what they thought the traffic would bear and collected their fees" (Byrd 2001: 2). The medieval university, however, "had no campus," and "each master made his own arrangements for renting lecture halls" (3). These early universities mostly offered training in professions such as law, medicine, and theology.

In the late medieval period, and especially during the Renaissance, subject-areas referred to as the "liberal arts" were added to the university curriculum. As the name suggests, the liberal arts were somewhat freer of Church authority, freer from specific professional careers, and intended to generate freer minds. In the standard medieval curriculum, the liberal arts consisted of seven disciplines divided into two sets:

- *Trivium*, a collection of three verbal arts including grammar, rhetoric (the art of persuasion or public speaking), and dialectics or logic
- *Quadrivium*, an assortment of four technical subjects including arithmetic, astronomy, geometry, and music.

Universities, of course, continued to offer degrees in the professions.

As much of ancient philosophy had done, the university curriculum and wider Christian education was especially committed to "moral" matters. By "moral" we mean morality both in the familiar and narrow sense (e.g. sexual chastity, marital fidelity) and in the widest sense of the formation of the "good person" and the "good society." Indeed, it could be argued persuasively that education then (and now) was largely dedicated to the construction of moral persons and the establishment and stability of moral society.

As we will see in the later chapters, around the 1600s recognizable political and social philosophy began to appear, in the works of René Descartes (1596–1650), Thomas Hobbes (1588–1679), Francis Bacon (1561–1626), Blaise Pascal (1623–62), Baruch Spinoza (1632–1704), and John Locke (1632–1702), to name but a few of these "Enlightenment" thinkers. Significantly, a timeline of philosophers or social scientists usually shows a yawning gap between the ancient era and the Enlightenment, as if no original thinking was happening at all.

These intellectual figures and those to come in the 1700s and 1800s were products of turbulent social forces in their own lives and societies. Religious turmoil caused by the Protestant Reformation and the subsequent religious wars; colonialism and the discovery of many previously owned lands and peoples; the emergence of capitalism and dramatic changes in work and wealth; urbanization; political upheavals and revolutions; and of course industrialization and the many changes that it wrought on society must be understood as the backdrop against which social sciences were born.

Much of this incipient social science had a distinctly practical purpose. The area of "political economy" promised ways to better understand and manage national economies and promote national wealth. History, as we will see in the next chapter, served a useful function in creating national identity and national pride. Later, sociology would promise tools to direct the forces of social change, anthropology would provide useful information for administering global empires, and geography would prove to be a valuable resource for global trade and war.

It was not immediately apparent what the new emerging social sciences would be or even what they would be called. Porter and Ross reminded us that in the English-speaking world, " 'sciences of man,' 'moral sciences,' 'moral and political sciences,' 'behavioral sciences,' and 'human sciences' have been among [the] predecessors and competitors" of social science (2003: 1). Meanwhile, in France by the late 1700s the terms *sciences morales et politiques* were in use, and later the word *Geisteswissenschaften* or "spirit/mind-science/knowledge" was introduced in German. Many of these names indicate more clearly than the phrase "social science" that "such studies had a moral and spiritual character, quite unlike the sciences of nature" (1).

It was also uncertain in the initial stages of social science whether there would be one unified social science or multiple discrete social sciences. "For a time, it seemed possible that social knowledge would not require such synthetic labels" as sociology and economics and psychology and anthropology, "because it would be united in a single field" (2). In France in particular, this single field was conceived as the *sciences humaines* (human sciences) or the *sciences de l'homme* (the sciences of man).

But the specialization inherent in the modern era would triumph over the budding unified social science, partly because each discipline had to carve an intellectual and administrative space for itself. "Political economy" thus split into political science and economics. Psychology largely grew out of medicine, both neurology and the clinical treatment of "mental illness." Sociology, most explicitly in the case of Durkheim, struggled to separate itself from both philosophy and psychology, and anthropology wrestled against history.

The bigger point here is that, just as knowledge in general (or ignorance) is socially constructed, so specific fields of knowledge are and must be socially constructed. It took and takes concerted effort to formulate and professionalize a new science or academic field, to differentiate it from other previous and concurrent fields. The first thing that such an effort requires is some energetic champions, some early heroes and founding fathers. Students of the various social sciences learn about these heroic founders, such as Adam Smith and David Ricardo in economics, Émile Durkheim and Max Weber in sociology, or Franz Boas and Bronislaw Malinowski in anthropology. Some deeply influential figures like Thomas Hobbes, Karl Marx, Immanuel Kant, and even Durkheim and Weber straddle disciplinary boundaries.

These founding fathers (almost all of them male) set the central questions of the embryonic fields, as well as their distinct methods. Recall, for instance, how both Durkheim and Weber tried to formulate the correct methods for social science. Such individuals tended to gather a coterie of followers around them, acting as the mentor (like Plato) to train the next generation of practitioners. Often charismatic persons, their influence cannot be left to charisma alone. Instead, for a discipline to survive and flourish, it must be institutionalized, turned into enduring forms that give the discipline its boundaries, its characteristics, and its means of self-replication. Among the standard techniques of disciplinary institutionalization are:

- academic departments and teaching chairs
- journals and newsletters
- professional organizations
- national, international, and local conferences
- research institutes
- debates and controversies
- funding sources (grants, prizes, and sponsorships)
- a literature, consisting of all of the previous writings of members
- textbooks
- in the twenty-first century, websites, blogs, online courses, and more.

As a result of strategic and successful implementation of these means, the familiar standardized social sciences crystallized in the late 1800s and early 1900s, but not without disagreement and contention. Those disagreements and contentions persist today, as specialists seek to redefine their disciplines, expand or contract their boundaries, cross disciplinary lines, invent new disciplines, and/or secede from the existing social sciences—or from the family of "social science"—altogether. Porter and Ross indicated, for instance, that some psychologists prefer to think of their field as closer to natural science (e.g. biology) than to social science. Similarly, economics cannot "be described straightforwardly as a social science, and economists often claim a higher standing for their field" (2003: 2). Meanwhile, historical processes have often left strange bedfellows uncomfortably within the same disciplines and departments, such as cultural anthropology, physical anthropology, and archaeology under "anthropology." And, as further proof of the constructed and contingent nature of social sciences, not all colleges and universities agree on how to organize them: where I went to college, anthropology and sociology were grouped in a single department, but my graduate school housed cultural anthropology in a separate department from archaeology, and we cultural anthropologists literally had no interaction with the archaeologists.

As we will see as we proceed through the chapters of this book, the social sciences share an epistemic culture that distinguishes them from the humanities and the natural sciences. Further, each social science discipline has its unique epistemic culture (sometimes more than one, separating subdisciplines, theoretical schools, and various "careers" within the discipline) distinguishing it from the others. Each social science also has its particular "biography" or disciplinary history, sharing some elements with some other disciplines while claiming other elements as unique to itself. All of the social sciences significantly bear the mark of the wider civilization—Western, Christian civilization—in and from which they were born. Finally, as we will consider in the final chapter, each social science, and social science as a whole, *and even science itself*, has undergone and is undergoing diverse challenges from other fields and from other societies and civilizations to rethink and reinvent itself once again.

From Social Sciences to Social Studies

"Social science" is a moniker worn in higher education and in professional research. At the elementary and secondary school level, it is uncommon to find explicit coursework or literature in sociology or anthropology or psychology, etc. Instead, a condensed and simplified version of social knowledge dubbed "social studies" is characteristic of the lower curriculum. "Social studies" borrows widely from the various social sciences to teach grade-appropriate social knowledge. Indeed, the National Council for the Social Studies has defined social studies as the integrated study of the social sciences and humanities to promote civic competence. Within the school program, social studies provides coordinate, systematic study drawing upon such disciplines as anthropology, archaeology, economics, geography, history, law, philosophy, political science, psychology, religion, and sociology, as well as appropriate content from the humanities, mathematics, and natural science. The primary purpose of social studies is to help young people develop the ability to make informed and reasoned decisions for the public good as citizens of a culturally diverse, democratic society in an interdependent world.

(Task Force of the National Council
for the Social Studies 1994: 3)

Further, the same organization has promulgated ten central themes for social studies, including culture; time, continuity, and change; people, places, and environments; individual development and identity; individuals, groups, and institutions; power, authority, and governance; production, distribution, and consumption; science, technology, and society; global connections; and civic ideals and practices.

2 Historical Thinking

According to the familiar story, George Washington visited the Philadelphia tailor shop of Betsy Ross in 1776 as part of a congressional flag committee. However, there is no record in any document of any such committee, and Washington, as a commanding general but not a member of Congress, would not likely have been involved in such a party. Further, the Flag Resolution describing the new flag was not adopted until 1777. "Virtually every historian who has studied the issue believes that Betsy Ross did not sew the first American flag" (Leepson 2006: 39). This particular bit of storytelling owes its origin to Ross' grandson, William Canby, who in 1870 presented an essay to the Historical Society of Pennsylvania called "The History of the Flag of the United States." Canby (1870) confessed that no concrete evidence supported the Ross tale, but he advanced the dubious, if not dangerous, claim that the "next and the last resort then of the historian (the printed and the written record being silent) is tradition"; surely, he argued, a family tradition "uncontradicted by the written record, stands unimpeachable, quite as reliable and often more so, than the books." Subsequently he provided the now-canonical legend (in his own words: "Let us now return to our Legend") of Betsy Ross and the first flag. But such a lovely fable still needs assistance, which it got from Ross' descendants, who made and sold "Betsy Ross flags," as well as from an 1873 article in *Harper's New Monthly Magazine* essentially repeating Canby's version uncritically. And the legend grew: the latter article's author, H. K. W. Wilcox, added the assertion that Ross became the supplier of flags for the country—a boast that not even Canby had made. Another pillar of the lore was a book by Canby's nephew Lloyd Balderson, *The Evolution of the American Flag*, restating Canby's material. Other aid came from the Betsy Ross Memorial Association, the movement to preserve the Betsy Ross House (which may actually be at the wrong address), and Charles Weisberger's evocative but historically inaccurate 1893 painting *Birth of Our Nation's Flag*, reprinted "in school textbooks for years, deceiving generations of unsuspecting students" (Ayres 2000: 212).

Did Betsy Ross sew the first American flag? We usually say, "Time will tell" or "History will be the judge." But which time? And how does history determine its judgments? Many other events are still more obscure: What really happened on the "first Thanksgiving"? Why did the Roman Empire fall? Did the Chinese visit America before Columbus? Was the invasion of Iraq in 2003 a good idea?

It can hardly be disputed that events occurred in the past and that those events occurred in some chronological order. But "history" is more than just the facts of the past, and it is certainly more than "just one thing after another." History is also a narrative—a story that assembles facts in some meaningful way—and an evaluation. History is not merely "what happened" but what we (choose to) remember and what it means for us today. And history is always and unavoidably *somebody's* history or a narrative *told from someone's point of view*. It would seem that there is no such thing as "objective" or neutral history.

Yet more, humans have not always "done history": we have obviously always had a past, but we have not always thought "historically." As we will soon see, even when humans began to collect and write historical accounts, the prime concern was not necessarily to "get the facts right." History has many uses, only one of which is factual knowledge.

Historian E. P. Thompson once asked, "Why should men care to preserve the record of history at all?" According to Antonis Liakos, Thompson's answer was that "the past should be rescued in order to provide alternative ways of seeing things, as well as possible new values for the future" (2007: 46). That opinion raises two other questions, though: why should we seek alternative ways of seeing things, and how does the past offer new values for the future?

History Before "History"

If history is the chronicle of human actions, then what is *prehistory*? Modern historians, because of their methods and their theoretical commitments, tend

Ancient Sumerian "History"

As in Egypt and elsewhere, chronicles of the past were largely records of—and tributes to—the kings, often claiming a divine origin for the royal line. One example of such a king list from Sumer reads:

> After the kingship descended from heaven, the kingship was in Eridug. In Eridug, Alulim became king; he ruled for 28,800 years. Alaljar ruled for 36,000 years. Two kings; they ruled for 64,800 years. Then Eridug fell and the kingship was taken to Bad-tibira. In Bad-tibira, En-men-lu-ana ruled for 43,200 years. En-men-gal-ana ruled for 28,800 years. Dumuzid, the shepherd, ruled for 36,000 years. Three kings; they ruled for 108,000 years. Then Bad-tibira fell (?) and the kingship was taken to Larag. In Larag, En-sipad-zid-ana ruled for 28,800 years. One king; he ruled for 28,800 years. Then Larag fell (?) and the kingship was taken to Zimbir. In Zimbir, En-men-dur-ana became king; he ruled for 21,000 years. One king; he ruled for 21,000 years. Then Zimbir fell (?) and the kingship was taken to Curuppag. In Curuppag, Ubara-Tutu became king; he ruled for 18,600 years. One king; he ruled for 18,600 years. In 5 cities 8 kings; they ruled for 241,200 years. Then the flood swept over.
>
> (http://web.archive.org/web/2001060-5223010/
> http://www-etcsl.orient.ox.ac.uk/section2/tr211.htm)

The "histories" of Sumer also tended not to distinguish history from legend or religion, and they were hardly disinterested accounts of the past. Some of these documents were laments for the defeat or destruction of great cities and kingdoms, as in these first few lines from the lament for Sumer and Urim:

> To overturn the appointed times, to obliterate the divine plans, the storms gather to strike like a flood.
>
> An, Enlil, Enki and Ninhursaja [Mesopotamian gods] have decided its fate—to overturn the divine powers of Sumer, to lock up the favorable reign in its home, to destroy the city, to destroy the house, to destroy the cattle-pen, to level the sheepfold; that the cattle should not stand in the pen, that the sheep should not multiply in the fold, that watercourses should carry brackish water, that weeds should grow in the fertile fields, that mourning plants should grow in the open country; that the mother should not seek out her child, that the father should not say 'O my dear wife!', that

> the junior wife should take no joy in his embrace, that the young child should not grow vigorous on his knee, that the wet-nurse should not sing lullabies; to change the location of kingship, to defile the seeking of oracles, to take kingship away from the Land, to cast the eye of the storm on all the land, to obliterate the divine plans by the order of An and Enlil.

to regard "history" as the period commencing with the advent of writing. "History" then is what we can know of the past from written records. But humans lived long before "history," so most of human history is "prehistoric." Sometimes those many millennia are left to the archaeologists (see Chapter 7).

Even when humans began to write, some four to five thousand years ago, their writings on the past did not quite qualify as "history" in the contemporary sense of the term. For one thing, records typically only documented kings or the significant occurrences during the reign of various kings. As an example, the famous Palermo Stone from ancient Egypt (probably around 2300 BCE) consists of a list of pharaohs and a chronology of memorable events while each was on the throne. These "royal annals" preserved data on wars, construction, religious festivals, and Nile River floods (see e.g. Wilkinson 2000). In the view of François Hartog, these Egyptians were not doing "history": "instead of expressing an interest in the past, they exhibit a desire for eternity, but a material one or a petrified one"—and it is noteworthy that they were focused only on themselves, since as "far as they looked into the past, the Egyptians didn't see anybody but themselves and the gods" (2000: 385).

The case in Mesopotamia was the same if not more stark. Once a unified monarchy was established, rulers hired "scribes to write its history, thereby legitimating its power in the present. This historiography was a royal history (only kings made history), a monumental one (making itself visible especially through enormous inscriptions), and an exclusive one (held in the hands of a caste of intellectuals, masters of writing)" (385).

The same is the case with other ancient chroniclers. Ancient books from the Hindu Vedas to the Hebrew scriptures mixed history with theology to create documents of national memory and supernatural activity. But, "although the Bible is infused throughout by the demands of remembrance, it never displays any curiosity for the past as such. The principal danger was to forget the ancestors' experiences and no longer believe in their truth. To quote Y. H. Yerushalmi: Israel 'receives the order to become a dynasty of priests and a holy nation: nowhere is it suggested that it would become a nation of historians'" (Hartog 2000: 385). And nowhere in the ancient world was it suggested that people should seek alternative views or new values.

The Invention of History

Scholars today typically consider the Greeks to be the inventors of history, and in order to understand the rise of historical thinking we must once again consider the purpose of knowledge. We can distinguish a variety of kinds of "historical knowledge," from the royal chronicles just discussed to religious myths and national epic poetry to "history" in the familiar sense. All of these forms preserve memories and "the past" in their own way. Royal lists are obviously intended to legitimate the power of specific kings and dynasties. Myths anchor and strengthen belief and provide guidelines for ritual and moral behavior. Epic poetry celebrates the achievements of nations (great victories at war, etc.) toward the goal of national integration and pride. In all three of these genres, humans and the gods are often co-actors.

Among the ancient Greeks, Homer was the transitional figure from myth and epic to history. His tales of the Trojan War, the *Iliad* and the *Odyssey*, allegedly report on a historical event—what Hartog calls "the 'axial' event at the edge of history" (388). But "the Homeric epic is in no way history" (389), not only because it is still poetry rendered in verse but because "factuality" is not its main interest. Likewise, humans and gods still interact; indeed, gods ultimately direct the action, intervening in the Greeks' wars. The first words of the first book of the *Iliad* make our point:

> Sing, O Goddess ["Muse" in some translations], the anger of Achilles, son of Peleus, that brought countless ills upon the Achaeans. Many a brave soul did it send hurrying down to Hades, and many a hero did it yield a pretty to dogs and vultures, for so were the counsels of Jove fulfilled from the day on which the son of Atreus, king of men, and great Achilles, first fell out with one another.
>
> And which of the gods was it that set them on to quarrel? It was the son of Jove and Leto; for he was angry with the king and sent a pestilence upon the host to plague the people, because the son of Atreus has dishonored Chryses his priest.
>
> (classics.mit.edu/Homer/iliad.1.i.html)

Here, as Hartog suggested, is the work of the poet or bard, that "master of glory (*kleos*), a dispenser of immortal encomia to the heroes who died gloriously" (394). And ultimately it is not the human witness but the goddess or muse who tells the story.

Herodotus, Thucydides, and the Ancient Tradition of History

If Homer (perhaps a fictitious author) was still a poet and bard, Herodotus was a historian, if only because he applied the term "history" to his work. More importantly, gone are the gods and the muse in Herodotus; what we have now is a man writing about men for men. Indeed, the first paragraph of his book *The Histories*, probably composed around 440 BCE, reads:

"Herodotus of Halicarnassus, his *Researches* are here set down to preserve the memory of the past by putting on record the astonishing achievements both of our own and of other peoples, and more particularly, to show how they came into conflict" (1972: 41).

As Herodotus' introduction indicates, he regarded his own work not as "history" in the modern sense but rather more generally as "research" or "inquiry." Indeed, the verb *historein* in Greek meant to narrate or to inquire—that is, to tell what one has seen or learned—derived from *histor* for an observer, a judge, or a wise man, one who knows and sees and who knows because he sees. This is why Hartog concluded that "Herodotus is neither bard nor even *histor*; he *historei* (investigates). He does not . . . benefit from the divine vision of the bard. He has only *historie*, a certain form of inquiry, which is the first step in historiographical practice. . . . The historian, acting on no authority but his own, intends from now on to 'go forward with his account, and speak of small and great cities alike. For many states that were once great have now become small'" (394).

Perusing Herodotus' researches, it is quite clear that it consists of more (and perhaps also less) than history. It is a report on all that he has witnessed during his travels, with sections on foreign customs (such as the Egyptian treatment of animals), monuments, natural environments, myths and hearsay, and anything that an attentive voyager might pick up along the way. He does not systematically strive to separate the speculative, the mythical, and the factual.

Thucydides had a narrower and more modern focus. Written very soon after Herodotus (around 431 BCE), his *History of the Peloponnesian War* was an account of one of the defining conflicts of the ancient Greek era. It begins much as Herodotus' book begins, with an identification of the individual man behind the account:

> Thucydides, an Athenian, wrote the history of the war between the Peloponnesians and the Athenians, beginning at the moment that it broke out, and believing that it would be a great war and more worthy of relation than any that had preceded it.
>
> (classics.mit.edu/Thucydides/pelopwar.1.first.html)

Note that Thucydides was an Athenian, in fact an Athenian general, yet most critics laud the neutrality in his reporting.

One of the more remarkable facets of his record of the war are the speeches of important characters that he preserved. One wonders, though, how he could have been present at all of these occasions and how he could have remembered them so accurately. Interestingly, he addressed this matter early in the project:

> With reference to the speeches in this history, some were delivered before the war began, others while it was going on; some I heard myself, others

I got from various quarters; it was in all cases difficult to carry them word for word in one's memory, *so my habit has been to make the speakers say what was in my opinion demanded of them by the various occasions, of course adhering as closely as possible to the general sense of what they really said* [emphasis added].

This confession raises the very important issue of the authenticity and veracity of historical data, including its sources and the standards that historians apply to evaluate it. We will return to this question shortly, but Thucydides was not unaware of the problem, writing that, "with reference to the narrative of events, far from permitting myself to derive it from the first source that came to hand, I did not even trust my own impressions, but it rests partly on what I saw myself, partly on what others saw for me, the accuracy of the report being always tried by the most severe and detailed tests possible."

Some Key Greco-Roman History-Writers

After Herodotus and Thucydides, history-writing—including biography—became an established genre in Greco-Roman culture. In addition to the *Annales Maximi*, records of magistrates and important events kept by the Pontifex Maximus of Rome, among the many accomplished historians and their works were:

Callistenes: ten-volume history of Greece and *The Deeds of Alexander*

Timaeus of Tauronmenius: forty-book *The Histories* covering Greece from its origins to the first Punic war

Polybius: *The Histories* recounting the rise of the Roman Republic

Cato the Elder: seven-book *Origines* on the history of Rome and other Italian states

Livy: *Ab Urbe Condita Libri* (Books from the Foundation of the City), on the first days of Rome until his own time

Julius Caesar: *The Gallic Wars*, *The Civil Wars*, and *The African Wars*, among others

Seneca the Elder: a lost history of Rome from the civil wars to his own life

Tacitus: *The Annals* and *The Histories*, on the Roman emperors from 14 to 70 CE

The Rise of Modern History

It is apparent that the tradition of writing "histories" was well established by the classical era, whether these were researches into particular great men, great events, or great civilizations. Also, writing of this sort was not exclusive to the Western world. China also had its own *The Classic of History*, prepared in the sixth century BCE and spanning nearly two thousand years of early Chinese history (although some of its documents and sources are believed to have been invented long after the facts and to incorporate later biases and perspectives). Islam too developed a historical tradition, as in the work of Ibn Khaldun (1332–1406), whose *Muqqadimah* not only investigated the past but also attempted to set some standards for the methodology and philosophy of history.

As recognized in the previous chapter, the writing of history went largely dark for more than a thousand years in the West, partly because of the breakdown of central government and literacy during the Middle Ages and partly because Christianity was firmly convinced that history was about to end at any moment. History was only revived in the early modern period, first through speculative accounts of the origins of society or government and then through (almost equally speculative) efforts to formulate a universal human history.

Before proceeding, it is worth noting one other genre for imagining alternative ways of living and new values for the future—*utopian* literature. Utopia, literally meaning "no place," is associated most closely with Thomas More's *Utopia* published in 1516. However, his was neither the first nor the last piece of utopian writing, envisioning another (and typically better) society while tacitly critiquing the current society. Plato's *Republic* is also a utopian social model, which we will discuss in the next chapter.

Utopian writings like More's fiction frequently presented themselves as if they were not fiction at all. Rather, they were often offered as if they were eye-witness accounts of the discovery of other, happier societies, perhaps on an island somewhere. (Other utopian stories, like Jonathan Swift's *Gulliver's Travels*, were obviously fictional and satirical.) Similar to More's island of Utopia, Johann Valentin Andreae and Tommaso Campanella described their ideal worlds in the 1619 *Christianopolis* and the 1623 *Civitas Solis*, respectively. Thereafter, utopian writing became a common practice, from Samuel Butler's 1872 *Erewhon* to Edward Bellamy's 1888 *Looking Backward* (placing the perfect society in another time instead of in another place) to H. G. Wells' 1905 *A Modern Utopia*. By the twentieth century, however, much of the optimism of early thinkers had waned, and authors began to imagine "dystopias" or "bad places" such as Yevgeny Zamyatin's 1921 *We*, Aldous Huxley's 1932 *Brave New World*, and George Orwell's 1949 *1984*.

Utopian thinking shares certain characteristics and goals with historical thinking, but Liakos believed that they are different, even antithetical.

In early utopian novels "there was no place for history. Utopias resisted, escaped from, and introduced a suspension of history. History in utopia was absent and considered an obsolete adviser" (2000: 28). History, for utopians, "was bound to tradition, not to the self-shaping human" (28) who emerged from Renaissance and Enlightenment culture. Utopian authors, and others committed to social progress, "considered history as the useless burden of the past" (29).

For modern historical thinking to emerge, "history" had to be emancipated from both utopia and religion with its eschatological (end-of-time) views. "This transformation," this invention of history, "required the prerequisite of conceiving society as an ontological concept, detached from the presence of God, autonomous, and grounded in human needs" (31). In a word, history had to become a "thing" that could be studied on its own terms, just as society was becoming a "thing," an ontological reality, both of which could be understood in terms of universal laws.

What is History the History *Of*?

If history is a thing to be known, then the obvious question is what kind of a thing it is. That is, what is history *about*—if history is a story, whose or what's story is it?

In the early 1700s, Christianity offered an answer, when Johann Albrecht Bengel (1687–1752) coined the term *Heilsgeschichte* or "salvation history." From the perspective of *Heilsgeschichte*, the Bible is "an account of God's working out divine salvation in human history"; interestingly, this perspective replaced the understanding of scripture as the source of doctrine, in which the Bible stands "as a history of God's redemptive plan" (Grenz, Guretzki, and Nordling 1999). In the words of Hans Frei, the "saving facts" of Christianity are "real and historical but not in an ordinary way that would open them up to religiously neutral verification" (1974: 180).

At least one construction of *Heilsgeschichte* (see Figure 2.1) contemplates history as a series of stages, from the original "problem" (human sinfulness and the Fall of Adam and Eve) to the "promised solution" (the Hebrew covenant) to the attempted solution (the history of ancient Israel, with its prophets and sacrifices) to the accomplished solution (the life and death of Jesus) and the solution realized (in the formation of the Church). Why, of course, the twelve hundred years of attempted solution did not work is not explained.

Whether or not one subscribes to this particular interpretation of history, it does provide a "plot" for disparate events. It was not the only possible or actual interpretation of history, though. A different and influential theory was posited by Johann Herder (1744–1803), for instance in his *Ideas for the Philosophy of History of Humanity* written between 1784 and 1791. Herder believed that humanity as a species was on a mission of progress, of higher development and achievement, but that the agent of this

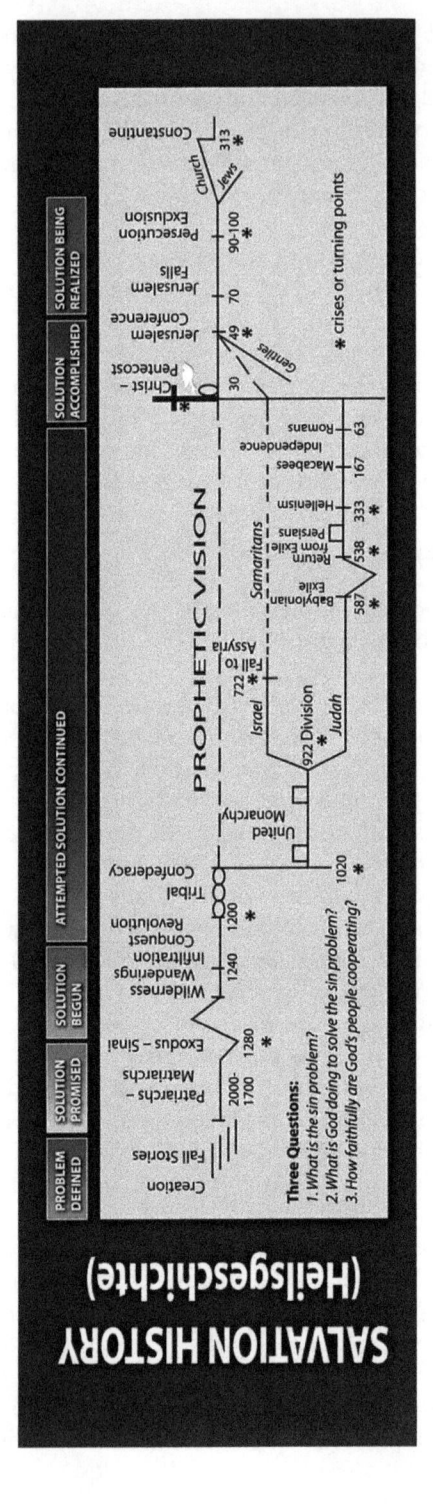

Figure 2.1 *Heilsgeshichte*: History as God's Plan for Salvation

Source: Biblical Literature Course at Hesston College, Texas. Created by Marion Bontrager. © Hesston College.

development was not humanity as a whole nor the individual but an intermediate level, *the group*. Specifically, the active group of history was the *national group* or *nation*. This is because each nation, he argued, is an "organic unit," a "national organism" with its own unique and natural qualities and genius, its own special culture and language, even its own national soul. Herder used such phrases as *Nationalgeist* (national spirit), *Seele des Volks* (soul of the folk/people), *Geist der Nation* (spirit of the nation), and *Geist des Volks* (spirit of the folk/people) to capture this national peculiarity which was, to him, "inexpressible." Being that the "natural and the national were synonymous in Herder's mind" (Ergang 1931: 95) he perceived the nation as the ineffable yet rightful unit of mankind: "Every nationality is one people, having its own national culture as well as its language," claimed Herder (quoted in Ergang: 88).

In this view, individuals are de-emphasized as basically incarnations of the national spirit, cells in the national body. Being a natural unit, "the group becomes a single being, an individuality, a personality," in which "culture" is the national personality, the group mind. The bearers of this culture, and even more so the authors or creators of this culture, the "individual prophets, writers, artists or poets are but the means employed by the national soul to give expression to a national religion, a national language, or a national literature" (87). Being natural and distinct, national culture and the nation should be cultivated, unfettered by artificial rules and undisturbed by foreign influences; to do otherwise would be to defy nature's plan and to interfere with the natural processes of human development.

Herder's point of view would prove very useful for building modern national states and identities, as we will see throughout this book. It is worth pausing here to appreciate that the nineteenth century was particularly noteworthy for research into "national histories" and "national cultures," finding (or inventing) a number of national chronicles. Among the most famous are the *Kalevala* of the Finns, the *Epic of Sundiata* of the African Malinke, the *Book of Vlas* of the Russians, the *Epic of Manas* of the Kyrgyz, and the *Mahavamsa* of the Sinhalese. Some of these works naturally have earlier sources, and much older examples exist, including the *Mahabharata* of India and Virgil's *Aeneid* of Rome. Scholars also set out to collect and preserve the culture or folklore of various nations, where the genius of the folk was allegedly stored. Such folkloristic expeditions became the precursors of modern social research, inventing "cultures" and "societies" along the way.

A different approach was the "universal history," placing all of human past achievement in a single narrative—often, still, with a nationalistic slant. A prime example is Marquis de Condorcet's 1796 *Outlines of an Historical View of the Progress of the Human Mind*. In this project, Condorcet, a proud Frenchman writing in the era of the French Revolution, divided human history into ten stages, to be precise:

1. Humans united into tribal hordes
2. Pastoralism and the agricultural state
3. Invention of writing
4. Greece to the age of Alexander, and the division of the sciences
5. Decline of the sciences
6. Decline of learning and its restoration around the time of the Crusades (1100–1200 CE)
7. First progress of the sciences, from the end of the Dark Ages to the invention of printing
8. Sciences and philosophy freed from authority and tradition
9. Descartes to the French Revolution
10. Future progress of mankind

In this plan, France plays a pivotal role, with French philosophy and French politics representing the high point in human social and intellectual development. No doubt the future progress of mankind will be in the French mold.

Hegel and the Philosophy of History

One of the most prominent thinkers on the nature of history—on what is "going on" in history—is Georg W. F. Hegel (1770–1831). In his 1837 *The Philosophy of History* Hegel spelled out his theory of what history was about. Hegel's philosophy is complex and not easy to summarize, but in a word, the active force in human history is not exactly the individual nor the nation nor the species but the Idea. For him, all of reality was the actualization, the coming-to-be-real, of the Idea. When the Idea takes the form of matter or space, it is "nature," and when it takes the form of time, it is "spirit" (*Geist*, the same term used by Herder). The movement or development of spirit over time, then, is history.

   "Spirit" here should not be confused with the Christian sense of spirit (or the holy spirit), if only because Hegel's spirit is not initially fully realized or self-aware. Indeed, history is the increasing self-awareness of *Geist*, which requires humanity as its vehicle or manifestation. Thus, history is the unfolding or the working-out of spirit, its march toward self-fulfillment. The "plot" of this story is the progress of freedom. Again, individual humans cannot embody spirit or advance its self-knowledge and ultimate freedom alone; humans achieve this goal collectively, in the organized political society or the "state." "The state is the divine Idea, as it exists on earth," Hegel asserted. Individuals reach their fullest development in the state (a notion similar to Plato's and Aristotle's thinking; see Chapter 3), and the state is like the body of spirit, coming increasingly to know itself and to act rationally. In summary, the progress of the Idea or spirit toward self-consciousness *is* human history.

Hegel also asserted that the path of the Idea or spirit progresses through stages, which are the historical societies or civilizations, from Mesopotamia to Greece and Rome to the Renaissance and presumably to nineteenth-century Germany. Each of these historical formations is a particular *Volksgeist* or *Zeitgeist* (spirit of the people/time). And, just as each state or civilization embodies the spirit, so occasionally a specific person like Julius Caesar or Napoleon embodies his state and his time.

This claim leads to the concept of "the great man," envisioned by Hegel but more fully elaborated by Thomas Carlyle in his 1841 *On Heroes, Hero-Worship, and the Heroic in History*. "Universal history," Carlyle wrote,

> the history of what man has accomplished in this world, is at bottom the History of the Great Men who worked here. They were the leaders of men, these great ones; the modellers, patterns, and in a wide sense creators, of whatsoever the general mass of men contrived to do or to attain; all things that we see standing accomplished in the world are properly the outer material result, the practical realization and embodiment, of Thoughts that dwelt in the Great Men sent into the world: the soul of the whole world's history, it may justly be considered, were the history of these.
>
> (1906: 1)

As evidence Carlyle gave chapters on Mohammad, Dante and Shakespeare, Martin Luther, Jean-Jacques Rousseau and such "men of letters," and Oliver Cromwell and Napoleon—"our last Great Man!"

Karl Marx: Class as History's Actor

"The history of all hitherto existing society is the history of class struggles," declared Karl Marx in the first section of his 1847 *Manifesto of the Communist Party*. No great man for Marx, since each person was the product of his or her particular historical period. Neither the nation nor the state—or certainly not God—was the prime move of history. The state was too recent an invention; the nation, along with other collectivities such as race and religion, was at best a thing of the past and at worst a lingering source of "false consciousness." For Marx, what mattered in the past, and what promised or threatened to act in the present, was class.

Much more will be said about Marx in the coming two chapters; his work is essential for both politics and economics. As a historian, Marx is important for envisioning history as a series of "social formations" (specific historical societies) each resting solidly on its material/economic base. So, Marx's historical theory is a broader social theory. And what distinguishes each society or social formation in history is its particular internal relations. There has always been a distinction, and a struggle, between intra-society groups, going back to the master-slave relationship of ancient (and too often modern) societies. When the lower and dominated group attains self-consciousness and acts *as* a group, it throws off the dominant group and destroys that particular social arrangement. A new social formation arises, inevitably with its own internal differentiation and inequalities, say, the patricians and plebeians of Roman society, or the lords and serfs of medieval feudal society, or the masters and apprentices of the High Middle Ages.

As can be seen, the contrasting and struggling groups or classes are separated by their material or economic conditions. Indeed, it is these material or economic conditions that create classes and that drive history. Hence, Marx's theory of history is called *historical materialism*, the totally anti-Hegelian notion that it is not ideas but human actions that provide the motor of history; practical issues of land ownership, labor, wealth, and such forces define the classes and influence (even determine) thought and behavior. In his time, industrialization had bred a new urban capitalist social formation with two sharply differentiated classes—the capital-owning bourgeoisie and the labor-selling proletarians. The proletarians possessed nothing that could produce wealth; they were thus forced to trade their time and energy for money. The bourgeoisie, owning the means of production (land, factories, etc.) dominated not only the class structure but the culture of society, including its beliefs and values.

However, for Marx (as for many historically-minded scholars) his model of history not only described the past but predicted the future. When the workers of the world united, as they surely would—dispensing with divisive identities like nationality, race, or religion—they would throw off the bourgeoisie and build a classless society, which would literally be the end of history. Without class inequalities, there would be no fuel for further historical change. But all of this would depend on workers recognizing themselves as and only as workers, that is, achieving class consciousness. (For Marx, this might and hopefully would occur spontaneously, as workers gained an almost Hegelian self-awareness, while for Marxists like Lenin it might or would require the leadership of an avant-garde, a great man or a party of great men—like Lenin himself!)

Contemporary Historical Thinking

Whether one accepts nations, classes, great individuals, or ideas as driving history, by the mid- to late-nineteenth century, history as we know it today was coming into shape. Indeed, as Leopold von Ranke, author of the 1883 *Weltgeschichte* (World History) pronounced, "history writing, as a reaction to philosophy, needed to become a distinct discipline" (Liakos 2007: 37). And this new discipline, with its roots in the ancient world, would inevitably be shaped by two other forces of the 1800s—evolutionary theory and natural science, especially biology. Thus, society could be thought of—and studied like—an organism, one that had internal "life processes" and that grew and changed over time through a series of "stages" or "phases," which equated to the distinct eras or periods of history.

Furthermore, the professional discipline of history did not appear accidentally; it was also the product of another nineteenth-century force, mentioned earlier. As historian Patrick Geary opined, "Modern history was born in the nineteenth century, conceived and developed as an instrument of European nationalism" (2002: 15). That is, history as a discipline was not only produced by Western societies of the 1800s but produced those societies.

The real history of the nations that populated Europe in the early Middle Ages begins not in the sixth century but in the eighteenth. This is not to deny that people living in the distant past had a sense of nation or collective identity. But the past two centuries of intellectual activity and political confrontation have so utterly changed the ways we think about social and political groups that we cannot pretend to provide an "objective" view of early medieval social categories, unencumbered by this recent past.(15)

Geary might be understood to say that we construct or invent our past and that as we do so we construct or invent our present and future.

> George Orwell in his dystopian novel *1984* presciently wrote, "He who controls the past controls the future. He who controls the present controls the past."

This consciousness of history, this learned habit of historical thinking, could be taken further. In the opinion of nineteenth-century *historicism*, and even of earlier historical thinkers like Giambattista Vico (1668–1744), any person, society, or era can only be understood in its historical context, and even when we look back at the past, we can only see it through the eyes of today. To say this most adamantly, "the human mind knows no other reality than history" (Iggers 1995: 130), because "all human ideas and values are historically conditioned and subject to change" (133). From this perspective, we are inescapably historical beings.

At any rate, a "scientific" discipline of history cannot rest on the details of past societies but tries to derive generalities (even "laws") active across the past—and presumably operating in the present. For instance, Edward Gibbon might ask in *The History of the Decline and Fall of the Roman Empire* (published in six volumes between 1776 and 1789) what caused Rome to collapse, but more interesting and important is why *any* civilization—including our own—would collapse.

Significantly, by the early 1900s, especially after the First World War (1914–18), much of the optimism about progress and positivism (better knowledge through more facts) had faded in the face of multiple disappointments.

In the field of history, this ethos is reflected in Oswald Spengler's *The Decline of the West* (published between 1918 and 1923), the title of which suggests the pessimism of which many have accused it. "Is there a logic of history?" Spengler wondered on the first page of the introduction:

> Is there, beyond all the casual and incalculable elements of the separate events, something that we may call a metaphysical structure of historic humanity, something that is essentially independent of the outward forms—social, spiritual, and political—which we see so clearly. . . . Does world-history present to the seeing eye certain grand traits, again and again, with sufficient constancy to justify certain conclusions. . . . Is it possible to find in life itself—for human history is the sum of mighty life-courses which already have had to be endowed with ego and personality . . .—a series of stages which must be traversed, and traversed moreover in an ordered and obligatory sequence? . . . In short, is all history founded upon general biographic archetypes?
>
> (1926: 3)

Spengler's answer was yes, for by examining eight separate civilizations—Babylonian, Egyptian, Chinese, Indian, Mayan/Aztec, Greco-Roman, Arabian, and Western—he concluded that a civilization has a life cycle like any living being. During the course of centuries, it proceeds from birth to growth and creativity to maturity and rigidity and inexorably to decline. Whether the senescence of a society is due to war, environmental degradation, the failure of leadership and confidence, or sheer exhaustion, a new young civilization awaits the opportunity to begin its life story.

From 1934 to 1961 Arnold Toynbee took the global analysis of history further yet, comparing more than two dozen civilizations, "arrested civilizations," and "aborted civilizations" from ancient to modern times. Like Spengler and Gibbon before him, he concluded that history is the tale of the organic rise and fall of societies, each great civilization arising in response to some social or environmental challenge. The source and energy of a civilization, then, is its creativity, which is the result of the actions of a "creative minority" of the population.

Sooner or later, though, this creative minority becomes conservative and defensive, turning into a "dominant minority" that imposes its will on the majority, stifling creativity and change. This marks the beginning of the decay and decline of the civilization, leading to the formation of a "universal state" that wants to guard its past achievements but suffocates its future.

> First the Dominant Minority attempts to hold by force—against all right and reason—a position of inherited privilege which it has ceased to merit; and then the Proletariat repays injustice with resentment, fear with hate, and violence with violence when it executes its acts of secession. Yet the whole movement ends in positive acts of creation—and this on

the part of all the actors in the tragedy of disintegration. The Dominant Minority creates a universal state, the Internal Proletariat a universal church, and the External Proletariat a bevy of barbarian war-bands.

(Toynbee 1946: 369)

Crucial to the future of the civilization is this "internal proletariat," which, as for Marx, is the agent of social change. Indeed, Toynbee contended that a number of responses to decline are possible, including "archaism" (clinging to and idealizing the past), "futurism" (idealizing the not-yet of society), "detachment" (disengaging from the problems of the present), and most positively "transcendence," inventing a new response, such as a new religion, which is the creative act at the leading edge of a new civilization and a new historical moment.

Doing History Today: Historical Research, Historical Writing

Two things are hopefully clear by now. First, history is not the mere past but *our knowledge of the past*, which depends crucially upon our sources, our methods, and our interests. Second, history—or rather, "historical thinking"—depends crucially upon what R. G. Collingwood (1946) called persuasively "the idea of history," that is, the idea that there is such a thing as "history" that we can and should know. Precisely what this "history" is and what it is trying to tell us have been argued over the centuries, as we have just surveyed. No matter what theory or approach we adopt, though, Collingwood is correct in assessing that since the dawn of the modern age "mankind has acquired a new habit of thinking historically" (1946: 232).

Collingwood also warned us against a naïve notion of history, as something that is accessible to the historian "because it exists ready made in the ready-made statements of his authorities" (234). Instead, he insisted that history was a construction of the historian, an act of the imagination:

> The historian's picture of his subject, whether that subject be a sequence of events or a past state of things, thus appears as a web of imaginative construction stretched between certain fixed points provided by the statements of his authorities; and if these points are frequent enough and the threads spun from each to the next are constructed with due care, always by the *a priori* imagination and never by merely arbitrary fancy, the whole picture is constantly verified by appeal to these data, and runs little risk of losing touch with the reality which its represents.
>
> (242)

Ultimately, in answer to the question, "Of what can there be historical knowledge?" he posited, "Of that which can be re-enacted in the historian's mind" (282), which led him to proclaim that historical knowledge "has for its proper object thought: not things thought about, but the act of thinking itself" (305).

This realization alone would force us to consider how historians "know" the past and how they *represent* the past to us, ordinarily in the form of written descriptions. And our consideration of historical knowledge must confront three problems: what historians want to know, how they know it, and how they write their knowledge.

George Santayana is widely recognized for saying, "Those who cannot remember the past are condemned to repeat it." It might equally be granted that those who remember the past are often eager to repeat it—except to change its outcome in their favor.

What is Historical Knowledge?

History, as we stipulated at the outset, is not just "what happened in the past" and certainly not just a chronological list of facts and events. But it is fascinating to recognize that, despite the centuries of theorizing on the nature of history, historians almost never explain what they mean by history or historical knowledge in their popular or textbook writing. It seems to be taken for granted that we all know what history is and what historians want (and want us) to know.

In their textbook for elementary social studies teachers, John Hoge, Thomas Lucey, and Laura Pinto (2013) identify some of the key concepts for constructing and interpreting historical knowledge (they do similar treatments for the other social sciences). Fundamental to historical thinking naturally is chronological order or sequence. That hardly exhausts the historical perspective, though. One of the key concepts in history is *periodization* or the specification of distinct periods or eras in history. This is the historical version of the general scientific project of *typology* or *taxonomy*, that is, classifying and naming the different "kinds of things" that exist within their domain of knowledge. Just as biologists classify living organisms into plants and animals (which is overly simplistic) or into vertebrates and invertebrates, so historians attempt to distinguish between epochs or civilizations and to describe the features of the various categories, such as "ancient" or "medieval" or "Renaissance."

All typologies, including chronologies or periodizations, face a number of challenges. First, the real world is more complicated—and more "analog" or continuous—than any typology can express. A typology is always and necessarily a simplification, even an idealization. That is, "ideal types" may reside in the thinker's mind but seldom exist in the real world. Second and therefore, historians do not all agree on where to draw the lines between

Research Topics in History

A fine way to take the pulse of a discipline is to peruse the topics that professionals are publishing in current journals. A number of social sciences publish an *Annual Review* journal, and for those that do, the article titles will be featured in the forthcoming chapters. There is no annual review of history, but the articles in the recent issues of three prominent history journals include:

The Journal of American History, June 2016
"'Swarms of Negroes Comeing about My Door': Black Christianity in Early Dutch and English North America"
"Reunion and Reconciliation, Reviewed and Reconsidered" (post-Civil War)
"'This Thing Has Ceased to be a Joke': The Veterans of Future Wars and the Meanings of Political Satire in the 1930s"
"William Worthy's Passport: Travel Restrictions and the Cold War Struggle for Civil and Human Rights"

The American Historical Review, June 2016
"After Death, Her Face Turned White: Blackness, Whiteness, and Sanctity in the Early Modern Hispanic World"
"Entangled States: The Translocal Repercussions of Rural Pacification in China, 1869–1873"
"Baltimore Teaches, Göttingen Learns: Cooperation, Competition, and the Research University"
"Capturing the Moment, Picturing History: Photographs of the Liberation of Paris"

The Historical Journal, June 2016
"The Cannibal Cavalier: Sir Thomas Lunsford and the Fashioning of the Royalist Archetype"
"1666 and London's Fire History: A Re-evaluation"
"Hobbes's Publisher and the Political Business of Enlightenment"
"Protestantism, Colonization, and the New England Company in Restoration Politics"
"The Mutiny and the Merchants"
"The Electoral Dynamics of Conservatism, 1885–1910: 'Negative Unionism' Reconsidered
"Italy's Informal Imperialism in Tianjin During the Liberal Epoch, 1902–1922"

> "'Sanders of the River, Still the Best Job for a British Boy': Recruitment to the Colonial Administrative Service at the End of Empire"
> "At the Nation-State's Edge: Centre-Periphery Relations in Post-1947 South Asia"
> "Britain and the Politics of Ceylon, 1948–1961"

various historical periods: when did the Renaissance begin and end, when did the modern era begin, and so on? Third and worst of all, these familiar categories and labels may not be and frequently are not applicable to all societies or civilizations: did Chinese or Islamic civilization experience a "dark age" or a "renaissance," and if so, did they experience it at the same time and in the same way as Europe?

According to Hoge, Lucey, and Pinto, historians are also crucially concerned with the *decisions and actions of people* in their chronological context, that is, how circumstances at a given point in time provide the *antecedent conditions* for human decisions and actions. This is not equivalent to a "great man" model of history, although it is most likely true that the decisions and actions of some individuals shape history more than others. But there is always the question of the consequences of these "turning points" in history and of alternative decisions and actions that people may have made: what if Julius Caesar had not invaded Rome, or what if Adolf Hitler had not chosen to attack the Soviet Union? Additionally, since no one person or event, or even country or civilization, determines history alone, they stress the question of multiple causation, the particular conjuncture of individuals, circumstances, and forces that shaped any moment in time.

Finally, Hoge, Lucey, and Pinto propose that historians are interested both in *change and in continuity*. To be sure, historians care about directions, patterns, and rates of change, but history is also about endurance: Rome eventually fell but only after persisting for a thousand years in one form or another. More, a civilization may give rise to other related civilizations, as the Roman Republic did to the Roman Empire and subsequently the Byzantine and Holy Roman Empires. Historians have argued that dreams of the Roman Empire motivated later actors from Napoleon to Hitler, and the way that the Roman Empire was divided left scars on Europe that are still visible today. Historians' curiosity about beliefs, traditions, and institutions thus shades into the territories of other social sciences, such as political science, economics, sociology, and anthropology.

How Historians Construct Knowledge: Historical Research Methods

Perusing history books and textbooks, one notices that historians seldom discuss *how they know* what they are presenting; instead, they present (their) history as if it were obvious, objective, and settled. In their *A Thinker's Guide to Historical Thinking*, Meg Gorzycki and Linda Elder say that "despite the fact that students are required to 'study history,' *they are usually not taught how to think like a historian.* Learning 'history' often means memorizing

---

The Problems with History, according to Gorzycki and Elder

History is not a linear thread from the past to the present and it is not a science. But historians must deal with a large number and variety of scientific questions. Historians must also make scores of critical decisions to maintain the integrity of a narrative. They must determine the credibility of sources, make inferences based on evidence, interpret information and testimony, assign priority to evidence and accounts, evaluate assertions, and construct appropriate questions. They must perceive relationships between variables in order to explain correlation or cause and effect. They must evaluate the relevance of evidence and assertions, identify implications of conclusions and opinions, assess the role of social and geographic contexts in events, provide insights into motives, and interpret the significance of events, ideas, individuals, institutions, beliefs, and experiences. And they must explain what value their historical knowledge and perspective brings to contemporary conflicts and problem solving.

Since historians 're-construct' the past by assembling existing evidence and interpreting it, the logic of history is based largely on the power of inference. We cannot physically go back in time. So we understand historical events by proxy. We attempt to construct a reasonable representation of what actually occurred. Denied the opportunity to be an eye-witness to most historical events and the privilege of knowing the subtle and hidden motives of human agents, the historian must weave a tapestry that represents a picture of the past sturdy enough to withstand the test of reasonable doubt given the evidence. Yet the 'facts' themselves are often merely an illusion. Historians must often interpret events from the past even when missing information relevant to that interpretation can never be retrieved. And they must recognize that the information available to them (and presented as facts) may well have been fabricated or distorted in keeping with a certain view of the world.

(13)

names, dates, and events rather than learning to think in scholarly ways about the past or about historical narratives" (2011: 13). This is all the more surprising and disappointing because historians have thought long and hard about their own thinking.

Whether or not history is a science, it generally cannot apply the standard scientific method of experimentation, nor does it even have access in most cases to direct observation. And whether or not, as Collingwood believed, history depends on imagination, it is still guided by facts. The question, then, is how historians gather facts and how they evaluate those facts.

The most basic problem in historical research is sources. As already mentioned, "history" is almost synonymous with "document," so historians tend to privilege written records (some, as we noted, claim that "history" only begins with the advent of writing; before that time, social scientists can only do archaeology). One issue with sources is naturally that they are often totally unavailable: many written documents have been lost, and many events were never documented in the first place. Sometimes the documents are written in obscure or untranslated languages.

All sorts of materials can serve as historical sources. The most desirable are "primary sources," records kept at the time of the events. There are also previous histories: for example, today's historians of the Peloponnesian war or of ancient Rome can refer to histories written by Thucydides or Julius Caesar. Historians can turn to more informal sources, such as letters and diaries, as well as to military, hospital, or police records if they exist. For more recent events, they may collect oral histories from living witnesses.

Then of course there are the matters of authenticity and trustworthiness. On more than a few occasions, documents have literally been forged and passed off as if they were old. In other cases, copying errors or editorial changes have entered the documents. Even authentic records can embed the biases of the writers, as when a partisan on one side writes about a war. We must also understand that documents in the past were not always written with the intention of factuality; sometimes they were hortatory (urging a certain course of action), sometimes apologetic (defending a person, institution, or belief).

For these reasons, historians engage in "source criticism," interrogating the validity of their sources. Gilbert Garraghan (1946) specified six questions that a historian should ask about his/her sources:

1. When was the source produced, that is, can it be dated?
2. Where was it produced?
3. By whom was it produced, that is, can we identify its author?
4. How was it produced, for instance, what were *its* sources, and was it produced soon or long after the events it describes?
5. What was the original form in which it was produced, and can we trace it from its origin to the version in hand (the question of "provenance")?
6. What is its value and credibility as evidence?

These questions or criteria are usually referred to as *external criticism*, that is, inquiry into facts outside the document (e.g. where it came from and how it came to be). Historians may then attempt *internal criticism*, judging the contents of the document itself. Researchers may use specific phraseology or references in the document to determine its age and credibility; often it can be determined that a document is an anachronism, written or edited at a later time. They must inspect the data for bias, believability, and consistency and compare it to other records of the events, if possible. They must be attentive to the fact that previous eras did not follow modern standards of authenticity: it was common to borrow sections from older texts, reassign authorship, or modify texts freely. When historians encounter contradictory information on the past, or discordant versions of events, they must carefully weigh the different data.

As historians assess their material, they must also be ever vigilant against their own biases and against the problem of "presentism," that is, of viewing

Fighting about the Facts of History

In 2010, the Texas Board of Education approved new history standards for the state's schools. According to a *New York Times* article, there were no historians on the board or consulted during the deliberations, but board members endorsed a version of American history "stressing the superiority of American capitalism, questioning the Founding Fathers' commitment to a purely secular government and presenting Republican political philosophies in a more positive light" (McKinley 2010). Other changes included revising the information about the civil rights movement to mention "the violent philosophy of the Black Panthers" along with the nonviolence of Martin Luther King, Jr. and adding commentary on the "unintended consequences" of liberal policies like "the Great Society legislation [combatting poverty and creating Medicare], affirmative action, and Title IX legislation [promoting gender equality in school sports]." Perhaps most controversially, the curriculum emphasized white contributions to American history and downplayed the role of other races. "Efforts by Hispanic board members to include more Latino figures as role models for the state's large Hispanic population were consistently defeated, prompting one member, Mary Helen Berlanga, to storm out of a meeting late Thursday night, saying, 'They can just pretend this is a white America and Hispanics don't exist.'" She accused the board of "rewriting history, not only of Texas but of the United States and the world."

the past through today's eyes or of imposing contemporary beliefs, values, or interests on that past.

This is not the only or most pernicious example of rewriting history. There is, for instance, a persistent camp of "Holocaust deniers," who, according to the United States Holocaust Memorial Museum (www.ushmm. org) "ignore the overwhelming evidence of the event and insist that the Holocaust"—the murder of millions of Jews by Nazi Germany—"is a myth, invented by the Allies, the Soviet Communists, and the Jews for their own ends." These ends include "to extract huge payments in restitution from Germany and to justify the establishment of the State of Israel." On the question of historical documentation, "Some Holocaust deniers argue that, since there is neither a single document that outlines the Holocaust nor a sign document from Hitler ordering the Holocaust, the Holocaust itself is a hoax." At the same time, anti-Semites are not above perpetrating their own hoax, such as the widely-distributed but fraudulent *Protocols of the Elders of Zion*, allegedly laying out the plan for global Jewish domination. Elsewhere, pseudohistories abound, from Masonic conspiracies to Ice Age civilizations to "DaVinci code" cover-ups.

Historiography: Writing History

Assuming that the historian has performed all of the tasks just described, now s/he must select, organize, and interpret the material and produce some kind of secondary document—that is, turn it into a "history." This raises the further issue of *historiography* or "the study of the way history has been and is written—the history of historical writing. . . . When you study 'historiography' you do not study the events of the past directly, but the changing interpretations of those events in the works of individual historians" (Furay and Salevouris 2009: 223).

Historians, like all social scientists and indeed like all authors, have their discipline-specific literary traditions; these are part of the paradigm or epistemic culture of history. They, like all researchers, also write for different audiences. Hoge, Lucey, and Pinto mention three different genres of historical writing—academic, textbook, and popular. Academic history is written for other scholars; it usually has the highest level of scholarship (for instance, the most footnotes) and engages most closely with the literature and theories in the field. Textbook history is written for students, at various levels from elementary school to university. Its style and contents are less sophisticated. Popular history is written for the general public, in a style accessible to the average reader, and generally does not delve into theoretical questions or disciplinary debates.

Textbooks are an especially interesting and important genre, because they transmit knowledge and ways of thinking to the next generation. In a 2004 review of history textbooks for the American Textbook Council, however,

Gilbert Sewall found a number of shortcomings with current world history texts. Among the criticisms of current world history books were

- bad writing and fragmented narrative, with trendy additions like cartoons and the overuse of sidebars "which often feature mere trivia" (14)
- instructional confusion, with " 'impenetrable' lessons and exercises" (15)

Fact and Feel in Historical Writing

History writers sometimes chose a stolid, even dry, courtroom approach to historiography—the facts, all the facts, and nothing but the facts. At worst, history could be reduced to a bulletpoint chronological list of events (although no historian writes that way). However, some historians have attempted a different approach, transforming the facts of the past into an account that conveys the lived quality of that time. While this is no doubt an act of some historical imagination, it makes for a deeper and more human view of the past. One representative text is Jan Huizinga's *The Waning of the Middle Ages*, subtitled *A Study of the Forms of Life, Thought, and Art in France and the Netherlands in the Dawn of the Renaissance*. Huizinga's description of the feel of life in the late Middle Ages begins:

> To the world when it was half a thousand years younger, the outlines of all things seemed more clearly marked than to us. The contrast between suffering and joy, between adversity and happiness, appeared more striking. All experience had yet to the minds of men the directness and absoluteness of the pleasure and pain of child-life. Every event, every action, was still embodied in expressive and solemn forms, which raised them to the dignity of a ritual. . . . Calamities and indigence were more afflicting than at present; it was more difficult to guard against them, and to find solace. Illness and health presented a more striking contrast, the cold and darkness of winter were more real evils. . . . Then, again, all things in life were of a proud or cruel publicity. Lepers sounded their rattles, and went about in processions, beggars exhibited their deformity and their misery in churches. Every order and estate, every rank and profession, was distinguished by its costume
>
> (1954: 9)

- persistent presentism, such as applying "contemporary standards of social justice to the past" (19)
- the loss of diversity: textbooks tend to perpetuate a Western bias and "resort to obscure, inconsequential, and even fictive subject matter to satisfy countless 'diversity' demands" (19). Coverage of Islam and Africa is particularly inadequate, where "deliberate omissions and deceptive content are the rule, not the exception" (19).

A major part of the problem, he deems, is the textbook publishing system, dominated by a few (as few as four) major publishers and driven by a few large-population states (like Texas) that dictate what textbook writers write—and what all American students read. In the final analysis, on

> subjects ranging from Africa to terrorism, the nation's leading world history textbooks provide unreliable, often scanty information and provide poorly constructed activities. In doing so, these textbooks foster ignorance of geopolitics and deprive students of authentic global understanding. Publishers could and should be providing high school teachers and students with cheaper, smaller, more legible volumes, stripping trivia and superfluity from current volumes.
>
> (4)

Whether or not Huizinga's account is "factually true," it certainly helps us avoid presentism by perceiving a radically different social reality than our own.

The Future of History

The past is not what it used to be. The past lives for us through our knowledge of the past, and that knowledge depends on our sources, our methods, and ultimately our present-day concerns and interests. The "facts" of history are indubitably what they are, but, as we insisted in the first chapter, the "facts" and our knowledge are not identical.

Because our knowledge of the facts of history changes, along with our current interests and values, it is necessary and healthy from time to time to revisit our historical knowledge and revise it. *Historical revisionism* is the re-examination and critique of our prevailing knowledge of the past, in the light of new data or new perspectives. As such, it is a highly legitimate and even essential activity. In other cases (and it can always be argued), historical revisionism is opportunistic tampering with historical knowledge. Opponents of the Texas Board of Education's actions would certainly accuse them of such. A more extraordinary example of historical revisionism is the Conservative Bible Project (conservapedia.com/Conservative_Bible_Project), in which partisans are literally retranslating the Bible to reflect modern conservative agendas, based on the charge that the existing translations are biased toward liberal ideas.

In the worst of cases, historical revisionism is an instance of the agnomancy discussed in the previous chapter, using dubious or even forged sources, circular reasoning, intentional misinterpretations, and cooked statistics to promote a prejudiced point of view. In other cases, though, historical revisionism is welcome and overdue. One often-cited illustration of desirable revision of historical knowledge is the work of Patricia Limerick, who shook up the history of the American West in her 1987 *The Legacy of Conquest: The Unbroken Past of the American West* and 2000 *Something in the Soil: Legacies and Reckoning in the New West*.

A specific angle of new historical thinking is to move away from the "great men" and even from the classes and nations that animated traditional historical writing and to focus instead on the ordinary people, especially the people whose voices have been lost or suppressed in conventional historiography. A champion of this approach was Howard Zinn, whose 1980 *A People's History of the United States* explored history from the perspective of Native Americans, African slaves, the poor, women, Hispanics, and various conquered parts of the American empire (Hawaii, Guam, and Puerto Rico, for instance). Many previously silent or silenced groups have taken to writing their own histories, from Native Americans to gays and lesbians.

This altered interest is consistent with a general reorientation of history and social sciences toward "the everyday" rather than the big events like wars. An influential example of this focus on ordinary life, in addition to Huizinga's study of the late Middle Ages above, is Fernand Braudel's *Civilization and Capitalism, 15th-18th Century, Volume I: The Structure of Everyday Life*. Writing on such topics as food, drink, houses, clothes, and fashion, Braudel insisted that

> The ways people eat, dress, or lodge, at the different levels of that society, are never a matter of indifference. And these snapshots can also point out contrasts and disparities between one society and another which are not all superficial. It is fascinating, and I do not think pointless to try and reassemble these imageries.
>
> (1981: 29)

Surely the best of history writing tells us more than "what happened" but what it was like to be a human in other times and places.

Disciplinary Study #1: The History of Terrorism

True to its disciplinary paradigm or epistemic culture, historical thinking about terrorism stresses continuity and change, periodization, and antecedent conditions, individual decisions, and alternative paths. For instance, while most modern citizens are rightfully concerned about twenty-first century terrorism, they are often unaware that it is not unique to the twenty-first century. Terrorism, in the sense of using violence to frighten people and governments into changing their policies and behavior, has probably existed as long as there have been governments and policies, although the forms have surely altered over the years.

One of the oldest recognized versions of terrorism is the ancient *sicarii* or Zealots of Roman-occupied Jerusalem. In the first century CE, to resist Roman rule and the imposition of foreign religious practices, extremist Israelites would assassinate Romans, as well as Jewish collaborators, with the short sword or dagger (the *sicari*) that gave them their name. Striking in crowded places in broad daylight, the point was to instill fear in Romans and complicit Jews and hopefully drive both from their homeland.

The very word "assassin" derives from another famous group of frightening killers. The original Assassins or *Hashshashin* were a sect of Nizari Ismali Shi'ite Muslims in the eleventh and twelfth centuries who struck individually at enemy leaders. Certain to be captured and killed themselves, since they waited impassively with their victim, their skills and their single-mindedness inspired dread, like terrorists today.

Other warriors like the Romans or the Mongols used terror to weaken and persuade their opponents. Placing severed heads on spikes or displaying execution victims on crosses was intended to scare and dishearten those who might resist. But "terror" first became a formal tactic and policy during the French Revolution of the 1790s, when the revolutionary government employed *terroire* to enforce its rule and impose its image of a good and just society. The guillotine, the classical symbol and tool of the 1793–94 Reign of Terror, literally carried the inscription "The Justice of the People." In his campaign to create the ideal French society, Maximilien Robespierre accepted no limit on the means that revolutionaries might use against the counter-revolutionaries and "enemies of the people." A colleague of Robespierre named Anacharsis Cloots, declared that the "orthodoxy of the cult of equality must inspire in us a holy dread. . . . Let us devote a civic hatred to all these denigrators of the universal republic: I look upon them as the executioners of the human race," and Robespierre himself is quoted as saying:

> If the spring of popular government in time of peace is virtue, the springs of popular government in revolution are at once virtue and terror: virtue, without which terror is fatal; terror, without which virtue is powerless. Terror is nothing other than justice, severe, inflexible; it is therefore an emanation of virtue; it is not so much a special principle as it is a consequence of the general principle of democracy applied to our country's most urgent needs.

> (Halsall 1997)

Following in the philosophical footsteps of the French revolutionaries, the nineteenth century was a century of terrorism. Targets, tactics, and causes all evolved, with perpetrators singling out political leaders for assassination.

Over those decades, often inspired by radical doctrines (especially leftist ones that were anti-government and/or pro-working- or lower-classes), activists killed three presidents of the United States (Abraham Lincoln in 1865, James Garfield in 1881, and William McKinley in 1901), as well as heads of state in France, Spain, Italy, and Russia (Tsar Alexander II in 1881).

In his periodization of terrorism from the nineteenth century to the late twentieth century, David Rapoport divided those years into four periods or "waves" of violence. A wave, he reasoned, "is a cycle of activity in a given time period—a cycle characterized by expansion and contraction phases" (2004: 47). As he further explained, a wave "is composed of organizations, but waves and organizations have very different life rhythms. . . . When a wave's energy cannot inspire new organizations, the wave disappears. Resistance, political concessions, and changes in the perceptions of generations are critical factors in explaining the disappearance" (48).

The first of these waves, indeed in his reckoning the "first global or truly international terrorist experience in history" (47), was the nineteenth-century "anarchist" phase. It has been associated with the *philosophy of the bomb* and the *propaganda of the deed*, because actors often seemed to believe in nothing more than destruction and used their violence to make a political point (see Chapter 3). No clearer statement of its (anti)philosophy could be imagined than Nechayev's "Catechism of a Revolutionary," in which he advised that a revolutionary has no other interest or attachment than revolution. Since the revolutionary "has broken all the bonds which tie him to the social order and the civilized world," then he "knows only one science: the science of destruction." He hates the established world, and between him and that world is "a relentless and irreconcilable war to the death."

"For him, there exists only one pleasure, one consolation, one reward, one satisfaction—the success of the revolution. Night and day he must have but one thought, one aim—merciless destruction."

He is the very definition of the fanatic.

The second wave, following the end of World War I in 1918, was the nationalist and ant-colonial wave. Encouraged now to struggle against occupying colonial forces in the non-Western world (Africa, Asia, the Middle East) and for the formation of independent national states in Europe (Ireland, Cyprus, "greater Germany"),

> Second-wave strategy sought to eliminate the police—a government's eyes and ears—first, through systematic assassinations of officers and/or their families. The military units replacing them, second-wave proponents reasoned, would prove too clumsy to cope without producing counter-atrocities that would increase social support for the cause. If the process of atrocities and counter-atrocities were well-planned, it could favor those perceived to be weak and without alternatives.

(54)

Hence a common feature of second-wave terrorism was "guerrilla-like (hit and run) actions against troops" (54).

The third "New Left" wave, emerging mid-century, was significantly stimulated by the Vietnam war and involved many organizations like "the American Weather Underground, the West German Red Army Faction, the Italian Red Brigades, the Japanese Red Army, and the French *Action Directe* [that] saw themselves as vanguards for the Third World masses" (56). In regard to tactics, " 'Theatrical targets,' comparable to those of the first wave, replaced the second wave's military targets. International hijacking is one example. Terrorists understood that some foreign landing fields were accessible," although high-profile kidnappings and assassinations continued (57).

The fourth wave, associated with the late twentieth century, was the "religious wave." Although it is hardly alone, "Islam is at the heart of the wave" (61), with its too common suicide bombing. However, Rapoport notes that other religions, from Sikhism in India to Buddhism in Sri Lanka to Christianity in the United States (the latter in the guise of Christian Identity movements and anti-abortion activists) have been involved in acts of terrorism.

Alarmingly, Jeffrey Kaplan thinks that a new, fifth wave of terrorism is upon us. Calling it a "new tribalism," Kaplan maintains that the fifth wave "is at its core a deeply religious quest for the creation of an immediate terrestrial utopia peopled by new men and new women uncontaminated by the ways of the old world" (2010: 71). The examples he offers are the Lord's Resistance Army in Uganda and the Janjaweed in Sudan; a more global example would be ISIS/Islamic State. In every case, "all are victims: victims and perpetrators alike are swept along by the swift current of apocalyptic violence that deforms the lives of both victim and perpetrator, transforming both utterly" (183).

Specifically, he asserts that fifth-wave terrorists subscribe to the view of a "golden age" in which they will literally eradicate history and start the world over again. They believe that they can and will inaugurate the perfect, pure society, and nothing will stand in their way. Because any dissenter is an "enemy of the people" and of their imagined ideal regime, fifth-wave organizations "kill with impunity, and often kill for the sake of killing (not something commonly associated with terrorism). If a Fifth-Wave group gains power, the result is invariably genocidal violence" (49).

3 Science of Politics

Key organizations

American Political Science Association (www.apsanet.org)
Political Studies Association (www.psa.ac.uk)
International Political Science Association (www.ipsa.org)

Key journals

The American Political Science Review
The British Journal of Politics and International Relations
Perspectives on Politics
Journal of Comparative Politics

Citizenship is one of the prime benefits (and burdens: citizens are expected to obey laws, pay taxes, and serve in the military) of modern countries. However, citizenship is a relatively new idea even in Western countries, where not long ago residents were "subjects" rather than citizens, and in other places citizenship is conceived differently if at all. Thomas Janoski contends that Chinese citizenship is shaped by Confucianism, which stresses communitarianism over individualism and obligations over rights; since the Communist revolution in 1949, citizenship has further been constrained by one-party government. Not surprisingly, then, "the idea of 'citizen' with rights and obligations is somewhat new to people in China" (2014: 371). To measure its progress, Janoski separates citizenship into three areas of rights—legal, political, and social. Legal rights involve the rule of law (e.g. effective and impartial courts, trustworthy police, etc.), property rights, freedom of speech, and religious freedom, among others. Political rights include citizens' ability to participate in the political process, such as voting. In both of these areas, Janoski finds China falling far short of countries like the United States and Canada and lower than Russia and Indonesia. In the realm of social rights,

China does much better: citizens can expect housing, health care, education, and pensions from the government. In fact, Janoski opines that "it is a characteristic of communist societies to provide decent social rights while neglecting political and legal rights" (379). He predicts that, as China develops economically, the country "could develop stronger citizenship rights, with the execption that political rights will develop very slowly and citizen obligations (e.g. promoting economic growth and social harmony) will be stronger" (382).

Political science is different in a number of ways from history and other social sciences. First of all, it is the only social science with "science" in its name. This aspiration to scientificity is supported by empirical and statistical research of a sort not associated with history but more common in economics and psychology and, to an extent, sociology. Finally, unlike history, but similar to economics (and in some cases psychology), political scientists may be involved both in the study of politics and *the practice of politics*, that is, in making policy and in getting political candidates elected. Political science is not an exact science (any more than is economics), since political scientists do not always get their candidate elected or make effective policy, but political science (like economics) is an area where scholarship and practice—even partisanship—overlap.

The Ancient Origins of Political Science

As we said of history, humans have always and everywhere had politics, but political science is new. In fact, political science is newer than history as an intellectual activity and an academic discipline, since it did not differentiate from "political economy"—or from "statecraft and practical advice to rulers"—until quite recently.

When most people think of "politics," they envision governments, elections, laws, courts, police, etc. that is, the formal political institutions characteristic of complex modern societies. However, it is important to understand from the outset that formal political institutions are a novel invention, dating back maybe five or six thousand years. Before that time, society did not lack politics, but neither did it contain discrete and formal institutions like kings or court systems. Earlier and more informal means of politics included headmen (individuals who led small bands of hunters and gatherers) and chiefs; additionally, as in contemporary societies, people exercised political power over each other through public opinion and personal reward and punishment. Last but not least, politics was not then (nor is it now) entirely distinguished from kinship or religion. The term "politics" derives from the ancient Greek word *polis*, which referred to a city or a central- ized society, in the Greek case an independent city-state. As such, it did not quite imply "government" in the modern sense so much as living in organized, stable, and virtuous groups. When Aristotle declared that humans were "political" beings, he meant that we are the kinds of beings who can, should, and ideally do live in such orderly groups. We achieve our highest individual and collective development and happiness in organized political societies.

Prior to Aristotle's essential work on politics, other Greek philosophers pondered the nature of political life and compared the political systems of various Greek city-states. The city-states or *poleis* (plural of *polis*) were in the habit of writing constitutions, and scholars studied and evaluated the differences between them, as Aristotle for instance did in his *On the Lacedaemonian Constitution* around 340 BCE. The Greeks used the word *politeia* to designate a constitution or a particular form of government, or yet more generally "the conditions and rights of the citizen, citizenship" (Liddell and Scott 1940). For the Greeks, "politics" was what the citizen of the city did; it was participation in the city's public life.

Plato wrote a number of important works on politics, such as his *Laws* and *Statesman*. In *Laws* his characters debate such questions as divine law and revelation, natural law, and education in relation to the law, citing Athenian and Spartan constitutions as examples. In *Statesman* (literally *Politikos*), he strived to define the statesman or ruler and to decide what kind of knowledge a ruler should possess. Plato is probably most remembered, though, for his *Republic* (*Politieia* in the original Greek) in which he interrogated the concept of justice and offered a description of his ideal society. Not only in his utopian republic or political system would a philosopher or wise man be king, but society would be rigidly structured, with "Guardians" to maintain the peace and order and each level or role of society carefully organized. Significantly for our purposes, Plato explored the kinds of knowledge and training that citizens should receive—not only factual education but exposure to particular salutary kinds of physical exercise, music, and even poetry—and the very difference between true knowledge and mere opinion, tradition, or illusion (in his famous Parable of the Cave).

Aristotle was the most systematic ancient thinker on the subject of politics, as on most social and scientific subjects. Among his most important works on politics were *Nichomachean Ethics* and of course *Politics*. The former is crucial to consider in our discussion because he, like others before and since, deeply associated politics, the participation in a stable and happy society, with morality and ethics, or "virtue" as he preferred to say. In that book (section 1099B30), he explained that the "end [or goal] of politics is the best of ends; and the main concern of politics is to engender a certain character in the citizens and to make them good and disposed to perform noble actions." Well-practiced politics not only produced virtuous societies but also virtuous people.

Key then as today to the practice of good politics was the form of government, and Aristotle weighed the various known types of government and constitution to judge which were good or bad. He measured six systems in terms of *power* (that is, who or how many have power) and *interest* (that is, whose interests are served). We could rightly call this a first step toward a science of politics, since one of the essential acts of science is classification.

Aristotle's Six Forms of Government

Monarchy = rule by one in the interest of all
Aristocracy = rule by a few (the *aristos* or the "excellent ones") in the
   interest of all
Polity = rule by many in the interest of all
Tyranny = rule by one in the interests of one (himself)
Oligarchy = rule by a few in the interest of a few (themselves)
Democracy = rule by many in the interest of the many (the majority,
   themselves)

Perhaps surprisingly to us today, Aristotle considered the first three types —monarchy, aristocracy, and polity—to be good or valid political systems, since the overall public interest was (allegedly) served by them. Like other thinkers including Plato, Aristotle was leery of democracy, which was often condemned as "the tyranny of the majority." The key point here is that in his analysis "it is less important to have equal participation in the process of decision making than it is to have equality reflected in the results of the decision arrived at" (Grigsby 2009: 83). It might be wishful thinking on Aristotle's part, however, that the monarch or aristocrat governs in the best interests of the people.

Curiously, while most of the political institutions of the West derive from Roman government, Roman political thinking is much less important to us than Greek. "Explicit theorizing was not a Roman characteristic" because "Rome was a society used to accepting authority," according to Thomas Wiedemann (2005: 517); Romans are remembered as doers rather than thinkers. "Theoretical speculation of the kind which had developed in the fifth century BC," as later by Plato and Aristotle, was "frowned upon, and even explicitly rejected as Greek"; in particular, "constitutional analysis was of little interest to them" (521). Yet there were some noteworthy political thinkers, like Cicero (106–43 BCE), whose *De Officiis* defended the assassination of Julius Caesar within a broader discussion of power and justice. He also composed *De Re Publica* (literally, "On the Public Thing"), arguing that the society or commonwealth belonged to the people who appointed representatives or magistrates to manage it for them, as well as *De Legibus* ("On the Laws"). Other Roman writers on politics included Seneca and Pliny, although Miriam Griffin insists that "Seneca showed no interest in political theory and restricted the *moralis pars philosophiae* [moral philosophy] to individual ethics" (2005: 532). The lesson here is that one can have great political success without having great political thought.

Medieval and Early Modern Political Thought

The European "dark ages" present us with another gap in the line of social thinkers. From the fall of the Roman Empire (fifth century CE) until the Renaissance around 1500, centralized political authority broke down in Western Europe, and political thinking was largely submerged in Christian theology. Petty kingdoms squabbled with each other, monarchs eventually inventing the concept of "divine right of kings" to provide religious justification for their rule.

Two important thinkers of the era, spanning almost a thousand years, were Augustine of Hippo (354–430), also known as St. Augustine, and Thomas Aquinas (1225–74), also known as St. Thomas. Both were predictably more interested in theological than political issues, but Augustine's *City of God* (full title *De Civitate Dei Contra Paganos* or "The City of God Against Pagans"), written after the sack of Rome by the Visigoths in 410, essentially separated the worldly pursuit of politics from the spiritual pursuit of religion. Augustine first defended Christianity against the charge that it was responsible for the decline of Rome; then he turned to a theological history of man-made and imperfect governments (the City of the World) and future realization of the perfect Kingdom, the "New Jerusalem" (the City of God).

Aquinas, who is best known for his magnum opus *Summa Theologica* organizing and defending Christian doctrine, is arguably most valuable to Western history for re-introducing Aristotelian thinking. He also expounded on the concept of "natural law," which fundamentally conjoined law, nature, and religion, with God as the source of eternal law. Aquinas echoed Aristotle by saying that humanity is inherently a social or political species (a "civic and social animal") and that politics or society originates in human nature.

Both Augustine and Aquinas might be most noteworthy for their comments on one particular political problem, that is, violence. After the early days of Christian pacifism, Christianity found itself in possession of an empire that it had to rule and protect—and expand. Thus, Christian rulers and soldiers needed to develop a theory that justified war in religious terms. These two thinkers contributed to the theory of "just war" which held that war was legitimate on a number of conditions, such as when it was declared by a legitimate authority, had a just cause, used just means, and obeyed various just regulations (such as a formal declaration of war and the safeguard of civilians and prisoners from harm). Augustine, for instance, argued that war was entirely consistent with Christian values: while the Christian "law of love" forbids them to harm or kill even in self-defense, "the law of love itself obliges Christians to come to the aid of others and so justifies the use of force that inflicts harm on malefactors" (Regan 1996: 17).

They also worked out a concept of "just persecution" by which the Church could impose force, even torture, on non-believers and heretics. Aquinas agreed with Augustine that Christians could and should persecute heretics, since deliberate religious error was a sort of perjury (giving false testimony about God), only infinitely worse than ordinary perjury. Perjury was a crime, so heresy and nonconformist belief was a much graver crime. Therefore, persecution of the heretic was a matter of criminal justice, and like all criminals the guilty "by right . . . can be put to death and despoiled of their possessions by the secular [authorities], even if they do not corrupt others, for they are blasphemers against God, because they observe a false faith. Thus they can be justly punished more than those accused of high treason" (quoted in Levy 1993: 52). Note that both men wanted to leave the dirty work of violence to the secular government, although religion authorized and condoned it.

Simultaneously, the Muslim world was developing political thinking of its own, based on the model of Muhammad (570–632) as a law-giver and civil authority. Much of the *Qur'an* and the *Hadith* consists of rulings made by Muhammad—and/or given by God/Allah—on mundane subjects such as property or inheritance. Lists of political philosophers of the Middle Ages typically include Muslim scholars like Ibn Rushd (1126–98), known in the West as Averroes, Ibn Taymiyyah (1263–1328), and Ibn Khaldun (1332–1406).

A specific genre of political writing found in the Muslim world (but not exclusively there) was advice to the righteous ruler or "the mirror for the prince." Kings were usually encouraged to govern in accordance with the teachings of Islam and with *maslahah* or "public interest" or "common good." In such guidebooks as Ibn Zafar al-Siqilli's *The Just Prince*, Mauizah I Jahangiri's *Advice on the Art of Governance*, and Nizam al-Mulk's *Book of Government*, certain themes appeared again and again, such as religion of course, the "just king" who makes decisions with his people in mind, the king who lives a personal life of virtue and family values, and the notion that nature is "both a reality (i.e., the landscapes and topography of princely action) and an analogy or metaphor for princely fortune or political rule" (Blaydes, Grimmer, and McQueen 2013: 19).

Such princely handbooks and practical political advice have a long history in Christian Europe too, including John of Salisbury's *Policratus*, Ptolemy of Lucca's *On the Government of Rulers*, and Erasmus' *Education of a Christian Prince*.

Standing at the threshold of the medieval mirror for princes and modern political theory is Niccolo Machiavelli's *The Prince*. Written in 1512–13 and published in 1532, Machiavelli (1469–1527) offered his counsel to the rulers of Florence, Italy, advising them how they might best exercise and maximize their political power. As Grigsby describes his instruction:

> *The Prince* recommends that states are most effective at maximizing their power if organized along the following lines. If possible, *states should use cultural traditions and long-standing folkways to justify their use of power*. If a state needs to attack an enemy, it is best to use religious

Excerpts from Sa'di's *Treatise on Advice to Kings*, 1257–58

Kings who attend to their subjects are, in fact, guardians of their own state and status because the kings' justice, grace, and fairness result in security and harmony among his subjects, breed civil prosperity, and boost productivity.

One of the chief qualities of the kings should be that, in their nightly solitude, they beg at the Almighty's doorsill, while during the day they resume their statesmanship.

Among the most important tasks of the State is the construction of mosques, houses of dervishes, bridges, water reservoirs, and roadside wells.

The king should incessantly attend to the weak and the aged, to widows, orphans, the needy, and strangers. As advised by the sages, the king who does not care for his subjects is not worthy of the name of master, and his mastery will not last.

Generosity when your expenses exceed revenue is blameworthy; squandering and stinginess are equally culpable. Find the path in between.

Benevolence and noblesse oblige have limits: too much clemency may empower the wicked and kindle their avarice. Earning a reputation for magnanimity does not imply tolerating the transgressors' injustice. The wise do not find such tolerance virtuous, only fatuous.

Generosity is praiseworthy as long as it does not weaken state power. Reducing state expenditures is prudent as long as the soldiers and state servants do not suffer financially.

or cultural symbols to legitimize the attack. Attack, but claim the attack is consistent with God's will, for example. This will win support for the state's actions. In addition, when a state seeks to expand its territory, it may be useful to colonize new territories in order to control them. In colonizing a territory, the state should move its own people into the land and confiscate land from the conquered population. Through these actions, the conquered population will be rendered too powerless to resist the state. Conquered peoples will suffer from such actions, but this is not necessarily bad. The suffering can be very useful, for it can serve as a visible warning of how the state can crush people at will.

(2009: 89, emphasis added)

As for Machiavelli's most infamous advice, which earned his style the term "Machiavellian," he admonished his prince to use the people's love and fear against them—but to exploit fear when love did not get the job done:

> a state must not allow its own populations to grow powerful enough to threaten the state itself. Thus, Machiavelli justifies state action to weaken economic classes to prevent them from becoming powerful rivals of state officials, and he also suggests that states keep their general population in fear. In a revealing discussion of whether it is better for states to be hated, feared, or loved by their own people, Machiavelli decides that fear is the optimum basis for ruling.
>
> (2009: 89)

The Origins of Modern Political Thought

The formation of modern political thought (although not quite yet "political science") happened at the same time and therefore in the same circumstances as the formation of modern historical (and other social scientific) thinking. The time was the Enlightenment of the 1600s and 1700s, and the circumstances were global colonialism and empire, the integration of modern states and the attendant nationalism, and dizzying social change. All of these forces were linked in the Protestant Reformation, which forever split European Christendom into (at first extremely hostile) religious camps, contributed to national identity and competition, and spread with colonialism. In England, which established its own national Protestant Church (the Church of England or the Anglican Church) in 1534, the political and religious struggle, together with the emergence of a British trading empire, led to one of the signature moments in political theory.

Charles I, king of England from 1625, one of the last "divine right" kings, and for many of his Protestant subjects too tolerant of the Catholics, found himself embroiled in a civil war in 1642, ending in his defeat, conviction, and execution in 1649. And not only did the English people kill their God-appointed king, but they abolished the God-appointed office of king completely (until 1660). In the midst of this turmoil, Thomas Hobbes (1588–1679) wrote his *Leviathan* (full title *Leviathan or the Matter, Form, and Power of a Commonwealth Ecclesiastical and Civil*) in 1651. This book is exceedingly important not only for its political analysis but for its historical and psychological claims as well.

"Hobbes sought to discover rational principles for the construction of a civil polity that would not be subject to destruction from within," specifically by a civil war like the one fought in his lifetime (Lloyd and Sreedhar 2014). In order to make his argument, he first provided an account of human nature and of social history. Thus the first part of his book is entitled "Of Man," with chapters on the senses, the imagination, speech, reason, the passions, the virtues, and indeed knowledge or "the several subjects of knowledge."

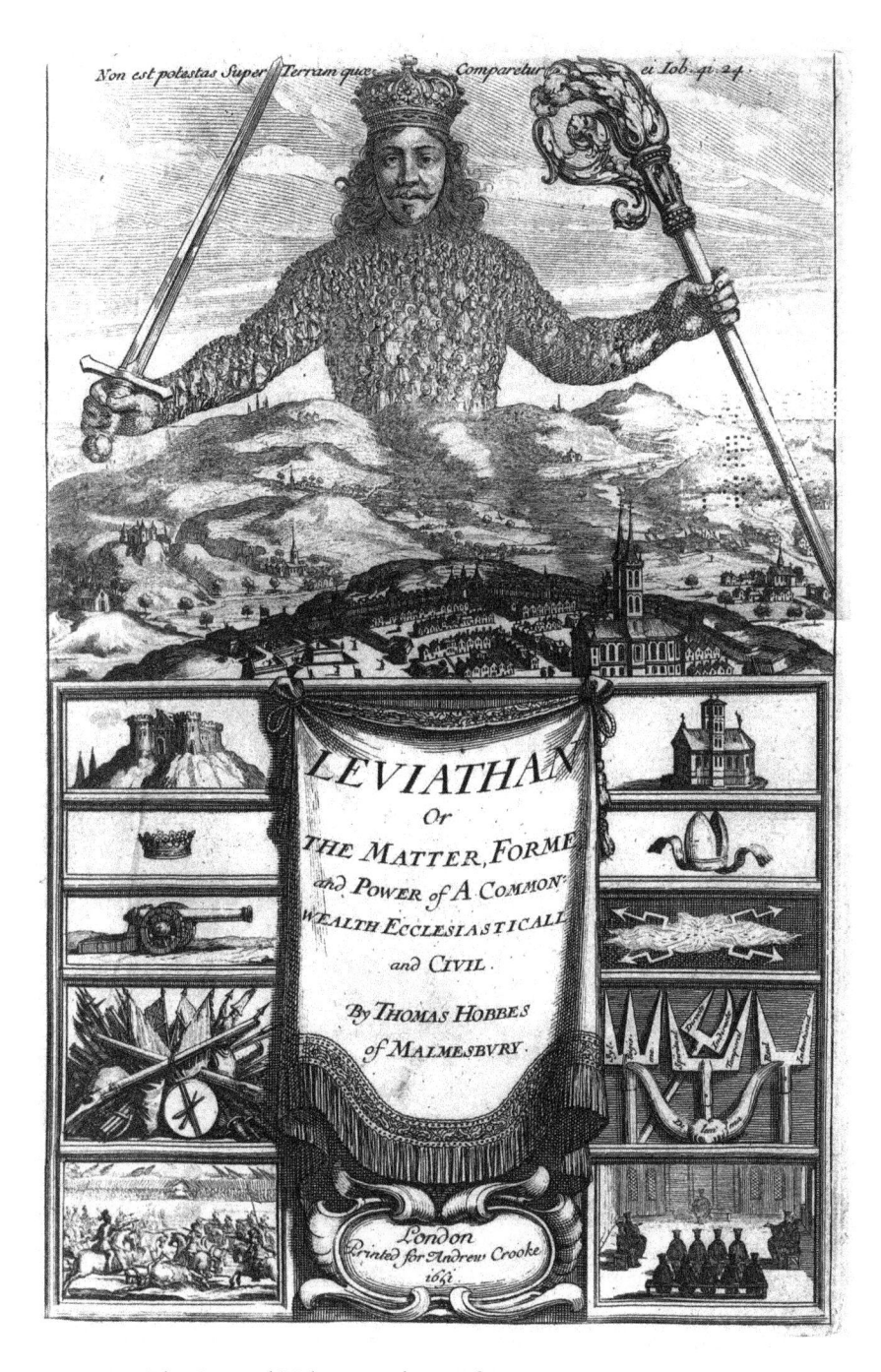

Figure 3.1 The Original Title Page of *Leviathan*

The origin of all knowledge, he contended, was the senses or perceptions, which are themselves caused by the physical body. Sense-perception of course leaves mental traces, and this "memory of many things, is called experience," and imagination is "only of those things which have been formerly perceived by sense, either all at once, or by parts at several times" (Hobbes 1651: 12). He also proposed a theory of knowledge, asserting that:

> There are of knowledge two kinds, whereof one is knowledge of fact; the other, knowledge of the consequences of one affirmation to another. The former is nothing else but sense and memory, and is absolute knowledge; as when we see a fact doing, or remember it done; and this is the knowledge required in a witness. The latter is called science, and is conditional; as when we know that: if the figure shown be a circle, then any straight line through the center shall divide it into two equal parts. And this is the knowledge required in a philosopher; that is to say, of him that pretends to reasoning.
>
> The register of knowledge of fact is called history, whereof there be two sorts: one called natural history; which is the history of such facts, or effects of Nature, as have no dependence on man's will; such as are the histories of metals, plants, animals, regions, and the like. The other is civil history, which is the history of the voluntary actions of men in Commonwealths.
>
> The registers of science are such books as contain the demonstrations of consequences of one affirmation to another; and are commonly called books of philosophy; whereof the sorts are many, according to the diversity of the matter.
>
> (51–2)

At this point he suggested an outline of the sciences—for him synonymous with philosophy—including mathematics, astronomy, geography, mechanics, physics, ethics, logic, poetry, and finally politics or "civil philosophy." The subject-matter of civil philosophy was the "consequences from the institution of Commonwealths, to the rights, and duties of the body politic, or sovereign" and the "consequences from the same, to the duty and right of the subjects" (53).

Hobbes is most remembered for his speculation on how political society came to be in the first place. He argued that in humanity's first days there was no such thing as society (by which he meant the institutions of government or the commonwealth). There were only individual humans living in "a state of nature." Hobbes' view of human nature now becomes critical, and it was a dark view: humans are naturally selfish and competitive, such that "if any two men desire the same thing, which nevertheless they cannot both enjoy, they become enemies; and . . . endeavor to destroy or subdue one another" (76). As such, the natural and original condition of humans was "a war as is of every man against every man" (77). In that condition, there is no place for industry, because the fruit thereof is uncertain: and consequently no culture of the earth; no navigation, nor use of the commodities that may be imported by sea; no commodious building; no instruments of moving or removing such things as require much force; no knowledge of the face of the earth; no account of time; no arts, no letters; no society; and which is worst of all, continual fear, and danger of violent death; and the life of man, *solitary, poor, nasty, brutish, and short.*

(78, emphasis added)

Hobbes saw only one solution to this problem of endless squabbling, which was the establishment of an overwhelmingly power government, an "absolute political authority" (Lloyd and Sreedhar 2014)—a leviathan—to which citizens submit and which they promise not to overthrow. Thus, he believed that he proved the necessary relationship "between political obedience and peace" (Lloyd and Sreedhar 2014).

Jean-Jacques Rousseau and the Social Contract

Fascinatingly, almost exactly a century later the French philosopher Jean-Jacques Rousseau (1712–78) argued the precise opposite conclusion from the same general premise. Living in a very different context than Hobbes—one not with too little king but with too much king—in his 1762 *Of the Social Contract, or Principles of Political Right*—Rousseau pronounced that society or government was not the solution but the problem. He agreed with Hobbes that humans had initially lived in a state of nature, but this nature was peaceful, equal, and above all *free*. These free individuals, in order to secure their freedoms, entered into an agreement, a "social contract," to build "a form of association which will defend and protect with the whole common force the person and goods of each associate, and in which each, while uniting himself with all, may still obey himself alone, and remain as free as before" (1923: 10). If the people should choose to enthrone a king, so be it, but that king's powers are not absolute, nor are they God-given. They are given by humans and contingent upon the happiness of those humans. These established powers are often abused—Rousseau opened his book with the line, "Man is born free; and everywhere he is in chains" (2)—but citizens have the right and the duty to throw off such chains and modify or discard their old social contract.

John Locke and Classical Liberalism

If anything, John Locke (1632–1704) is even more immediately important for contemporary Western politics than Hobbes or Rousseau. In his seminal 1690 *Two Treatises of Government*, he joined Rousseau in maintaining "that men are by nature free and equal against claims that God had made all people naturally subject to a monarch" (Tuckness 2012). In fact, Locke's book is a disputation with the forgotten Robert Filmer, whose position is presented in the first treatise, namely, that the adventures of Adam and Eve introduced the first sovereignty into the human world (Adam's sovereignty over nature, Eve, and his offspring), which sovereignty was conveyed to kings as an inheritance from Adam.

Locke responded in the second treatise, "Concerning the True Original Extent and the End of Civil Government," invoking the notion of "state of nature" like Hobbes and Rousseau. Humanity's natural state, he asserted, was "a state of perfect freedom to order their actions, and dispose of their possessions and persons as they think fit, within the bounds of the law of Nature, without asking leave or depending upon the will of any other man" (chapter II, section 4). As this passage illustrates, a key to Locke's theory of past and future governments was "natural law" or "the law of nature," which also conferred on humans certain "natural rights." Very importantly, natural law was not the same thing as divine law: God's law could only be known from revelation, while natural law could be known directly by reason. Also, some of God's law, like items of the Torah/Old Testament law, were not mandatory for all times and peoples, while natural law was universal. Natural law even became the standard for judging and interpreting religion. At any rate, natural law included certain natural rights, qualities or entitlements of rational humans that were "inalienable," that is, that could not be stripped from them (at least not rightfully) by any political authority; these natural rights included the right of life, of liberty, of property, and of the freedom to pursue happiness. Any king or government that threatened these rights was acting against nature and reason and could be opposed on the basis of nature and reason.

In short, Locke argued the foundations of what has come to be called *classical liberalism*, the position that freedom is the first virtue of society and that a limited government is the best guarantee of that freedom. A number of fundamental political, psychological, and moral implications flow from this position:

- "The individual is more important than the state and becomes a citizen of the state only through consent.
- The individual is rational and capable of making his or her own decisions; this makes the individual capable of autonomy and self-government.
- Progress is possible in political affairs, so change is not to be feared.
- State power should be limited.
- Economic inequality is not necessarily bad.
- Economic freedom (individual freedom to make economic choices) is more important than economic equality."

(Grigsby 2009: 100)

An Exercise in Social Contract and Classical Liberalism: The U.S. Declaration of Independence

The United States is an intentional product of Rousseau's and Locke's liberal-contractual thinking. The Constitution is the binding contract establishing political institutions and powers, but it is the Declaration of Independence that makes the liberal case for the right to create a new social contract:

> When in the Course of human events, it becomes necessary for one people to dissolve the political bands which have connected them with another, and to assume among the powers of the earth, the separate and equal station to which the Laws of Nature and of Nature's God entitle them, a decent respect to the opinions of mankind requires that they should declare the causes which impel them to the separation.
>
> We hold these truths to be self-evident, that all men are created equal, that they are endowed by their Creator with certain un-alienable Rights, that among these are Life, Liberty and the pursuit of Happiness.—That to secure these rights, Governments are instituted among Men, deriving their just powers from the consent of the governed,—That whenever any Form of Government becomes destructive of these ends, it is the Right of the People to alter or to abolish it, and to institute new Government, laying its foundation on such principles and organizing its powers in such form, as to them shall seem most likely to effect their Safety and Happiness. Prudence, indeed, will dictate that Governments long established should not be changed for light and transient causes; and accordingly all experience hath shewn, that mankind are more disposed to suffer, while evils are sufferable, than to right themselves by abolishing the forms to which they are accustomed. But when a long train of abuses and usurpations, pursuing invariably the same Object evinces a design to reduce them under absolute Despotism, it is their right, it is their duty, to throw off such Government, and to provide new Guards for their future security.

The other great ancestor of classical liberalism, Adam Smith, will be discussed in the next chapter.

Edmund Burke and Classical Conservatism

Liberalism then and today suggests changes to the established order, but those living through the convulsions of the French Revolution in the late 1700s were often alarmed at the ramifications of abrupt change. One was Edmund Burke (1729–97), a British intellectual and politician. Like most scholars of his era, he cannot be pigeon-holed into one academic category: he was a philosopher, historian, and political thinker, publishing *A Philosophical Enquiry into the Origin of our Ideas of the Sublime and Beautiful* in 1757, *An Abridgement of English History* between 1757 and 1762, and most importantly for our purposes *Reflections on the Revolution in France* in 1790.

Reflecting not only on the current revolution in France but the just-concluded revolution in America and the "Glorious Revolution" in his own country in 1688, he adopted a position contrary to that of Locke, emphasizing the theory of "just war" in the 1688 event (which was brought about peacefully anyhow), which he interpreted as inherently *unrevolutionary*: "The Revolution was made to preserve our *ancient*, indisputable laws and liberties, and that *ancient* constitution of government which is our only security for law and liberty" (26). Burke argued that the rights of Englishmen did not flow from "abstract principles" and universal reason but were specifically "the rights of Englishmen, and ... a patrimony derived from their forefathers" (27). In other words, the political thoughts and institutions of England were a product of English *history* rather than of ahistorical nature or reason.

It follows that the idea of throwing off government and providing new guards, as the American founding fathers advocated, was repellent to Burke.

> Such a claim is as ill-suited to our temper and wishes as it is unsupported by any appearance of authority. The very idea of the fabrication of a new government is enough to fill us with disgust and horror. We wished at the period of the Revolution, and do now wish, to derive all we possess as *an inheritance from our forefathers*.
>
> (26–7)

Indeed, because humans are naturally neither entirely free nor entirely rational, perfect freedom is not possible, and "rational" political change can often have undesirable, even fatal, consequences. Moreover, humans are not naturally equal. "Some individuals are more capable of ruling than others; some individuals are better suited for political decision making than are others. Thus, society is best arranged when individuals who are natural rulers do the ruling" (Grigsby 2009: 109). All of this ultimately depends on a respect for "tradition, authority, and moral values" (108).

Burke's political philosophy can be described as *classical conservatism*, summarized in three points:

- because of the profound human tendency toward irrational behavior, humans need guidance and direction from traditional authorities for society to enjoy peace and stability
- traditional authorities should pass on long-standing moral teachings through the family, religious institutions, and governmental law
- compliance with traditional morality is more important than individual liberty; in other words, people should not have the freedom to violate moral precepts.

(109)

Karl Marx and Classical Communism or "Scientific Socialism"

The nineteenth century was a time of considerable political unrest and economic injustice. New social systems, like the factory city, were materializing; new social classes and class relations were forming; and governments were being challenged throughout the Western world (often by the "philosophy of the bomb" discussed in Chapter 2), including a set of uprisings in 1848.

Many thinkers and activists appeared on the scene to criticize existing society and to advocate more just and moral alternatives. Among these idealists were Robert Owen (1771–1859), who founded the utopian community of New Harmony, Indiana in 1826, and Charles Fourier (1772–1837), whose ideas contributed to projects like Utopia, Ohio; Brook Farm in West Roxbury, Massachusetts; and Community Place, New York. Owen, Fourier, and others like them believed that competition and inequality were destructive of humanity and that cooperation, sharing, and even the abolition of private property (and sometimes of traditional institutions like marriage or the family) were the surest path to human happiness.

It is phenomenally important to see the socialist movements of the nineteenth century (and beyond) as more than economic programs but as political and seriously moral ones too. As introduced in the previous chapter, though, it was Karl Marx who claimed to have found the scientific key to economics, politics, and history itself. This key was the material conditions of life, including resources and tools and above all labor, which formed members of society into unequal classes (see Chapter 4). Politically, throughout history these classes "stood in constant opposition to one another, carried on an uninterrupted, now hidden, now open fight, a fight that each time ended, either in a revolutionary reconstitution of society at large, or in the common ruin of the contending classes," (Marx 1977: 246) he wrote in *The Communist Manifesto* of 1848. In his own time, the lower/working class was not only oppressed but beginning to organize, literally to establish a political party and movement—or a variety of parties and movements, both socialist and communist. Marx's own communist party, he wrote in its manifesto, supports "every revolutionary movement against the existing social and political order of things," all of which "bring to the front, as the leading question in each, the property question." He concluded the party statement with these energized words:

> The Communists . . . openly declare that their ends can be attained only by the forcible overthrow of all existing social conditions. Let the ruling classes tremble at the Communistic revolution. The proletarians have nothing to lose but their chains. They have a world to win.

Central to Marx's more thorough analysis of politics is that the dominant class in any society erects institutions to legitimate and perpetuate its dominance. One of these institutions in the modern era is government or the "state." Even democratic states pretend to rule in the interests of the people, but (as Plato and Aristotle feared) they really rule in the interests of the ruling class. But since the state is an *effect* of modern society, not a *cause*, it too will disappear when the revolution rights the wrongs of capitalism. Like religion, Marx predicted, the state will "wither" when people (i.e. workers) are free to make their own decisions collectively, that is, communally.

From Political Philosophy To Political Science

Since the late 1800s political thinking has substantially moved away from political "philosophy" and toward political "science," even as "politics" has differentiated from "political economy" (see Chapter 4) to become an independent topic of research and planning. This means that the kinds of questions that scholars ask, and the methods they employ, have substantially changed. Interestingly too, as "politics" has become a "thing" to study, it has also become less the monopolistic domain of "political scientists" and more a domain trod by social scientists of many if not all disciplines. As evidence, an internet search of twentieth-century political thinkers calls up a long line of intellectuals, not all or even most of them political scientists formally, such as Martin Buber, Walter Benjamin, Herbert Marcuse, Friedrich Hayek, Erich Fromm, Karl Popper, Jean-Paul Sartre, Louis Althusser, John Rawls, Michel Foucault, Jürgen Habermas, and scores more. It might be fair to say that while "politics" has become *a* thing to think about, it has become *the* thing to think about, the central issue of almost all social thought.

The institutionalization of political science begins in the late 1800s, as does the crystallization of all the social sciences. Herbert Baxter Adams (1850–1901) is widely recognized as the first modern Westerner to use the term "political science," and John William Burgess (1844–1931) is credited with founding the first American academic department of political science, at Columbia University in 1880. The American Political Science Association was formed in 1903.

It might be fair to say that the twentieth century was the "century of politics," as assorted parties and movements vied for the reins of societies and imposed their political visions on those societies, from fascism on the far right to communism on the far left. In much of this thinking—and acting—the assumption and the practice have been to equate "politics" with the "state": political control equals control of the state or government, and revolutionary political change equals change to forms of the state or government. Contemporary thinkers by and large reject this simple equation.

Carl Schmitt: The Concept of the Political

Looking back over the history of political thought, it seems that no one may have paused to contemplate what "political" means. Most writers apparently either conceived it narrowly as the ruler or sovereign or widely as all of social organization and the "good society." Carl Schmitt (1888–1985) in 1927 published his thoughts on *The Concept of the Political*, maintaining that "the political" must

> rest on its own ultimate distinctions, to which all action with a specifically political meaning can be traced. Let us assume that in the realm of morality the final distinctions are between good and evil, in aesthetics beautiful and ugly, in economics profitable and unprofitable. The question then is whether there is also a special distinction which can serve as a simple criterion of the political and of what it consists.
>
> (2007: 26)

His conclusion was that the "specific distinction to which political actions and motives can be reduced is that *between friend and enemy*" (26, emphasis added). Not entirely rational and certainly not symbolic, Schmitt argued that the political "is the most intense and extreme antagonism, and every concrete antagonism becomes that much more political the closer it approaches the most extreme point, that of the friend-enemy grouping" (29). This is perhaps why Schmitt's countryman, Carl von Clausewitz, described war as politics by other means and as violence intended to force one people or state to bend to the will of another.

The Concept of Power

If Schmitt and Clausewitz are correct, then opposition and compulsion are central to politics, which raises the crucial issue of "power." Political thinkers have always stressed the matter of power—of the sovereign's power, of the citizens' power, and so on—and contemporary political scientists have moved power to the center of their discipline. Again interestingly, one of the most fertile discussions of power was given by a sociologist, Max Weber (see Chapter 6), who defined power as "the probability that one actor in a social relationship will be in a position to carry out his will despite resistance, regardless of the basis on which this probability rests" (1997: 152).

Weber further analyzed the bases upon which this capacity rests. He identified three:

1. Authority, or legitimate power that followers believe the holder has a right to hold. Authority itself fell into three types:
    a. traditional, derived from past practice
    b. rational–legal, derived from written laws, formal office, explicit rules and regulations, etc.
    c. charismatic, emanating from the personal qualities of the power-holder.
2. Persuasion, or the ability to influence or manipulate people, for example through the control of resources or the skillful use of language.
3. Coercion, or the threat or use of force.

Thinking on the question of power has evolved considerably since Weber's contribution almost a century ago. In the first chapter, we mentioned Antonio Gramsci's concept of hegemony, the taken-for-granted power present in the "'spontaneous' consent given by the great masses of the population to the general direction imposed on social life by the dominant fundamental group; this consent is 'historically' caused by the prestige (and consequent confidence) which the dominant group enjoys because of its position and function in the world of production" (1971: 12). In this Marxist view, hegemony is the pervasive power of the upper class.

Political scientist Steven Lukes (1974) also stressed the need to expose the invisible or inaccessible aspects of power. He regarded the familiar, conspicuous kind of power as merely the first dimension or layer of power. The second and more subtle dimension relates to control over the political agenda, what questions are asked in the first place and how political issues are defined. The third and most covert dimension of power pertains to the influence over people's very thoughts and wishes, their values and preferences, leading them to misunderstand their own interests—to want what is not in their interest and to oppose what is.

The next practical question is "where" power is located in a society, that is, who holds and exercises power. Obviously the government has power, but that is not the full answer; besides, power is never the property of only one individual or institution. The two competing schools of thought on the question are the "pluralism" and "power elite" perspectives. Pluralism contends that power is (frequently if not always) distributed among many different participants—individuals, groups, institutions, political parties—such that decision-making ultimately requires negotiation and compromise. No one gets everything they want, but no one is utterly powerless. The power elite approach, most associated with sociologist C. Wright Mills, responds that a small clique of individuals dominates the power of a society. In his 1956 book *The Power Elite*, Mills described the power elite as

> composed of men whose positions enable them to transcend the ordinary environments of ordinary men and women; they are in positions to make decisions having major consequences. . . . For they are in command of the major hierarchies and organizations of modern society. They rule the big corporations. They run the machinery of the state and claim its prerogatives. They direct the military establishment. They occupy the strategic command posts of the social structure, in which are now centered the effective means of the power and the wealth and the celebrity which they enjoy.
>
> (1956: 3–4)

To his troika of government/corporation/military, we might today add those individuals who control media (like Rupert Murdock) and entertainment, like music and movie stars. Mills further noted that these various constituencies are interlocked, coming from the same families, attending the same colleges, even intermarrying, and moving from one elite position to another (e.g. from government to corporation or vice versa).

The Concept of State

As we have noted a few times already, another key concept of modern political science is the "state," by which we mean more or less "central government." "The equation state = politics becomes erroneous and deceptive," Schmitt (2007: 22) warned us, though, and we began this chapter by acknowledging that pre-state societies had politics of their own. Even more, as we will shortly see, politics is not contained solely within the state or government.

Weber once again figures prominently in the conceptualization of the state. In his *Politics as a Vocation*, he defined the state as "a human community that (successfully) claims the *monopoly of the legitimate use of physical force within a given territory*" (1919: 1). Imagining the state in terms of force alone is quite limiting, and the definition also raises the difficult problem of the "successful" monopolization of force: in any given state, there may be entities (gangs, militias, armed ethnic or political groups) that contest the state's monopoly or its legitimacy, and of course other states or entities (like terrorist organizations) can threaten a state's monopoly, sovereignty, or very existence.

Sociologist Anthony Giddens more recently and usefully characterized the state as "a political apparatus, recognized to have sovereign rights within the borders of a demarcated territorial area, able to back its claims to sovereignty by control of military power, many of whose citizens have positive feelings of commitment to its national identity" (1989: 303). In this more extensive analysis, a state consists of four essential elements:

1. the political apparatus, including governmental institutions
2. the territory
3. sovereignty
4. national identity, including shared culture (e.g. "collective memory") and loyalty or patriotism.

An important lesson of contemporary political science is that states are not as objective or stable as we like to think. It goes without saying that states

---

Governmentality: Power Beyond the State

States never have, never will, and could not possibly hold a complete monopoly on power; this is crucially true in the modern world. A very persuasive way of thinking about this question is Michel Foucault's concept of *governmentality*. For Foucault, a state or government is only one familiar manifestation or institutionalization of governmentality or all of the forms of power that individuals and groups can exercise on each other. Governmentality refers to both obvious "political" tools like laws, police, courts, and armies and to more subtle—and much more widely-diffused—instruments and tactics of power including "methods of examination and evaluation; techniques of notation, numeration, and calculation; accounting procedures; routines for the timing and spacing of activities in specific locations [e.g. time and motion studies]; presentational forms such as tables and graphs; formulas for the organization of work; standardized tactics for the training and implantation of habits; pedagogic, therapeutic, and punitive techniques of reformulation and cure; architectural forms in which interventions take place (i.e. classrooms and prisons); and professional vocabularies" (Lemke 2007: 50). All of these practices constitute what Foucault regarded as the means to control the conduct of a population, whether that population is a classroom, a corporation, or a country. These "technologies of power" can operate at a level *below* the state as well at a level *above* the state, the latter in the form of international organizations like the United Nations or NATO or "nongovernmental organizations" (NGOs) like the Red Cross or Doctors Without Borders.

are social and historical constructions (states do not occur in nature, and their boundaries are often quite arbitrary). States come and go throughout history; indeed, much of conventional history is the history of the rise and fall of states (see Chapter 2). More, individuals and groups can contest states—their boundaries, their population composition, not to mention their governmental forms and their very existence. The state status of some entities is in dispute, like Tibet or Taiwan by China or Palestine by Israel; which particular state a territory belongs to is also up for grabs, as developments in the Crimea have recently shown.

Research Methods and Goals in Political Science

Political science has matured into an academic discipline dedicated to "the study of governments, public policies, political processes, and political behavior," according to the 15,000-member American Political Science Association. In their guide to political science, Simon Hix and Matthew Whiting teach that their field examines "political behavior or why individuals and groups behave as they do," "political institutions, the formal and informal rules that tell political actors what they can and cannot do," and "political outcomes, such as why some countries redistribute more wealth than others or why some states have better environmental policies than others" (2012: 2). Political behavior includes practices like voting, volunteering, running for office, participating in violence, and such. Political institutions refer to the formal and informal systems of power-sharing and power-using, like America's three-part government structure (executive, legislative, and judicial), as well as the multiple levels of politics (federal, state, county, municipal, etc.). Political outcomes "covers a broad range of issues, from specific policy outcomes such as economic growth or higher public spending or better protection of the environment, to broader political phenomena, such as political and economic equality, social and ethnic harmony, or satisfaction with democracy and government" (15).

According to Grigsby, like other disciplines and professions, political science consists of multiple subdisciplines, the chief of which are

1. comparative politics, "focusing on examining how different political systems operate"
2. American politics
3. international relations, "focusing on relationships between and among states [such as] war, regional integration, international organizations, military alliances, economic pacts, and so on"
4. public policy, "studying how laws, regulations, and other policies are formulated, implemented, and evaluated"
5. political research methods, "focusing on a study of the many details of empirical social science. Data collection, measurement, and analysis are key areas of inquiry in this subfield"

6. political theory, "the study of the history of political philosophy, philosophies of explanation or science, and philosophical inquiries into the ethical dimensions of politics."

(2009: 14)

A still clearer sense of the interests of political scientists can be perceived in the forty-four "sections" or official professional subgroups of the APSA, some of which are federalism and intergovernmental relations, law and courts, public administration, conflict processes, presidents and executive politics, religion and politics, urban politics, women and politics, information technology and politics, European politics and society, political psychology, political science education, race/ethnicity and politics, human rights, experimental research, and African politics. Political scientists typically belong to and work within one or more of these professional areas.

The eclectic topics studied by political scientists support the claim made by Peter Burnham, Karin Gilland Lutz, Wyn Grant, and Zig Layton-Henry in their *Research Methods in Politics* that the discipline "is the junction subject of the social sciences," arising out of history, philosophy, and political economy and incorporating perspectives and methods from most if not all its sister disciplines (2008: 9). In a different textbook on political science methods, Phillips Shively (2009: 4) asserts that there are four discrete types of research, distinguished by whether they are empirical or nonempirical and whether they are applied or pure (political scientists sometimes say "recreational").

1. Normative philosophy (nonempirical and applied) refers to work that is less about what *is* in politics and more about *what should be* and characterizes most of pre-modern political writing from Plato and Aristotle to Hobbes and Marx.
2. Engineering research (empirical and applied) is oriented to solving social and political problems and collects political facts to craft those solutions.
3. Formal theory (nonempirical and pure), which Shively associates with the second half of the twentieth century, seeks "to develop reasonably broad and general theories based on a small number of agreed-upon assumptions." (5)
4. Theory-oriented research (empirical and pure) aims to discover new political knowledge not for guiding social change but for testing political theories or devising new theories.

Burnham et al. further note that contemporary political science has passed through several modes of thought (they actually call these modes "paradigms" in the Kuhnian sense of Chapter 1) since abandoning the classic normative focus of Plato, Hobbes, and Marx that has sometimes been called "the old institutionalism." In the 1950s and 1960s political science adopted

Research Topics in Political Science

There is an annual review journal in political science, and the articles in the 2015 volume of *Annual Review of Political Science* are as follows:

"Income Inequality and Policy Responsiveness"
"How Do Campaigns Matter?"
"Electoral Rules, Mobilization, and Turnout"
"The Rise and Spread of Suicide Bombing"
"The Dysfunctional Congress"
"Political Islam: Theory"
"Borders, Conflict, and Trade"
"From Mass Preferences to Policy"
"Constitutional Courts in Comparative Perspective: A Theoretical Assessment"
"Epistemic Democracy and its Challenges"
"The New Look in Political Ideology Research"
"The Politics of Central Bank Independence"
"What Have We Learned about the Resource Curse?"
"How Party Polarization Affects Governance"
"Migration, Labor, and the International Political Economy"
"Law and Politics in Transitional Justice"
"Campaign Finance and American Democracy"
"Female Candidates and Legislators"
"Power Tool or Dull Blade? Selectorate Theory for Autocracies"
"Realism about Political Corruption"
"Experiments in International Relations: Lab, Survey, and Field"
"Political Theory as Both Philosophy and History: A Defense against Methodological Militancy"
"The Empiricists' Insurgency"
"The Scope of Comparative Political Theory"
"Should We Leave Behind the Subfield of International Relations?"

behavioralism, holding that the discipline "should be concerned with observable behavior that could be rigorously recorded" (2008: 20); this meant paying more attention to the political actions of individuals. In reaction, a "new institutionalism" responded that politics cannot be understood merely as individual behavior and re-introduced institutions, power, and inequality. Influenced by economics, the third paradigm was "rational choice," which returned to the individual who was viewed as a rational actor whose chief motivation was to maximize his/her own interest or "utility" (see Chapter 4). By the 1990s, the perspective of "constructionism" had seized many political scientists (and other social scientists too), emphasizing how political institutions are constructed by human action and understanding (thus highlighting ideas and symbols) even as institutions and culture construct people as political actors. Anne Schneider and Helen Ingram offered a revealing example of this process in what they called the "social construction of target populations" or social/political groups or categories that presumably demand public policy responses.

> The social construction of a target population refers to (1) the recognition of the shared characteristics that distinguish a target population as socially meaningful, and (2) the attribution of specific, valence-oriented values, symbols, and images of the characteristics. Social constructions are stereotypes about particular groups of people that have been created by politics, culture, socialization, history, the media, literature, religion, and the like.
>
> (1993: 335)

Some illustrations of politically-salient "target populations" would be the much maligned "welfare queens" of 1990s American politics or today's "immigrants," or, on the positive side, "veterans."

The kinds of questions and paradigms that characterize contemporary political science call for a battery of research methods, many shared broadly across the social sciences. Among these methods are:

- Case studies of particular countries, institutions, or political events.
- Historical analyses of the changes in a country or its institutions over time.
- Comparison between two or more countries, institutions, or policies. Comparisons may involve a small number of cases (dubbed "small-N" studies) or a large number (called "large-N"). Burnham et al. explain that two different approaches to comparative research are "most similar research designs" and "most different research designs" (2008: 73). In the former, the logic is to choose cases that closely resemble each other, to isolate the effects of small minor political differences; in the latter, the intention is to test the effects of major political differences.

- Surveys, polls, and focus groups. Political scientists may design their own surveys and questionnaires or take advantage of other sources of survey data, such as Gallup polls or Pew Research Center data (see the box on U.S. party affiliation). Distinguishing between a survey and a poll, Burnham et al. write:

> A survey, or more precisely a sample survey, attempts to obtain accurate information about a population by obtaining a representative sample of that population and using the information from the sample to make generalizations about the whole population. ... Opinion polls are snapshot surveys concerned to measure the opinions of the population and in particular the political opinions of the electorate. They are less concerned with probing the social characteristics of supporters of a particular party or their motivations for voting than with forecasting the result.
>
> (97)

- Focus groups, a method pioneered by market researchers, allow political scientists to have a controlled conversation with a number of people and/or to gauge their attitudes toward certain ideas or experiences.
- Documentary and archival analysis, for instance studying records or writings.
- Interviews, especially "elite interviews" posing questions to prominent political figures like heads of state or law-makers.
- Field observation or observing people as they engage in their political behavior.
- Experiments.

Naturally, any particular political science study may incorporate more than one method. Janoski's work on Chinese citizenship discussed at the top of this chapter, for instance, includes historical research on Chinese political concepts, statistical analysis of political data, and comparison between China and a variety of other modern countries.

We might wonder how political scientists conduct experiments, and some political scientists themselves have wondered how experiments might fit into their discipline. Indeed, James Druckman and Arthur Lupia remind us that the president of the American Political Science Association in 1909, A. Lawrence Lowell, urged his colleagues to avoid the experimental method of natural science (2012: 1177). Not surprisingly, in her 2002 review article, Rose McDermott conceded that "experiments have not been as widely employed in political science as in either psychology or behavioral economics" (2002: 41). She first asked why the dearth of political science experiments, finding that "methodology in political science has moved toward large-scale multiple regression work" as well as toward "cultural

Statistical Research in Political Science: U.S. Party Affiliation

Political scientists have many sources of quantitative and statistical data at their disposal, including on such vital topics as the political party affiliations of the population. These affiliations, while not perfect predictors of voting behavior, provide important information on the likely voting behavior of the populace and also reveal the relationship between party identification (and thus presumably political ideology) and a number of other basic social variables, such as gender, race, and class. For the year 2012, a Pew Research Center survey collected the following information on American voters.

Social Variable	Republican/ Lean Republican (%)	Democrat/ Lean Democrat (%)	No Leaning (%)
Male	43	44	13
Female	36	52	12
White non-Hispanic	49	40	1
Black non-Hispanic	11	80	9
Hispanic	26	56	12
Asian	23	65	12
Generation: Millennial	35	51	14
Generation: Baby Boomer (50–68)	41	47	11
Generation: Silent (69–86)	47	43	10
Education: Postgraduate	35	57	8
Education: College graduate	42	49	9
Education: High school or less	37	47	16
Income: $150,000 or more	47	45	9
Income: $50,000–74,999	45	45	9
Income: less than $30,000	31	54	15
Married	48	41	12
Living with partner	31	55	14
Single/never married	30	56	14

Source: Pew Research Center 2014.

and social aspects of particular phenomena" (42), neither of which avail themselves of experiments. Additionally, political scientists, she con-tended, are not trained in experimental research and believe that their subject is too complicated with too many variables to be amenable to experimentation.

Yet, she discovered 105 articles describing political science experiments published between 1926 and 2000, including a now-defunct journal called *Experimental Study of Politics*; of these articles, almost half (forty-five) were published in the 1990s, indicating that political science experimentation is becoming more popular, not less. Of the political topics subjected to experi-mentation, voting behavior was the leader, followed by bargaining, games, and international relations. Also mentioned were committee work, race, media, and leadership. For example, a number of experiments investigated how factors affect voter turnout, party affiliation, or candidate preference. Specific questions studied included the effects of media on voting behavior or the perception of candidates relative to their gender. Other experiments have explored jury and committee decision-making. Finally, a body of experimental research has shed light on how people cooperate or coordinate their behavior in diverse social settings, sometimes testing models of behavior against real laboratory observation.

Finally, it is worth noting that political science as an academic discipline has practical applications to everyday political life and government. Two prominent allied fields, with their own academic departments and even their own educational institutions, are criminal justice and law, and political scientists may also be active as consultants in political campaigns.

Disciplinary Study #2: Politics of Terrorism

Political scientists have been at the forefront of the academic study of terrorism, because virtually all scholars and other observers agree that terrorism is a fundamentally political phenomenon. In other words, terrorists cause fear and harm, but the question is what distinguishes "terrorism" from other frightening and harmful behavior like crime.

In the bluntest possible language, the eminent scholar of terrorism, Walter Laqueur, defined terrorism as "the use of covert violence by a group for political ends" (1987: 72). More recently and informatively, C. L. Ruby described it as "politically motivated violence perpetrated against noncom-batant targets by subnational groups or clandestine agents, usually intended to influence an audience" (2002: 10). There is no authoritative definition of terrorism, but two more quick definitions make a vital point. Albert J. Bergesen and Omar Lizardo regarded it as "the premeditated use of violence by a nonstate group to obtain a political, religious, or social objective through fear or intimidation directed at a large audience" (2004: 38). Finally, the United States Department of Defense identifies it as the "calculated use of unlawful violence or threat of unlawful violence to inculcate fear; intended to coerce or to intimidate governments or societies in the pursuit of goals that are generally political, religious, or ideological" (US Army TRADOC 2007: 6).

From these perspectives, it can be concluded that terrorism is political in a variety of senses:

- it is a chosen tactic in pursuit of a specific goal
- it is an exercise of power
- it typically targets and seeks changes by or in governments
- it is an act against a perceived "enemy" (evoking Schmitt's concept of "the political").

As the comments of many terrorists convey, terrorists tend to see themselves as at war, and since Clausewitz reminded us that war is politics by other means, then it is incumbent upon us to understand terrorism as politics by other means.

But two crucially important and interconnected elements of terrorism in most evaluations are that it is "unlawful" and that it is generally committed by "nonstates." To grasp the significance of this statement, we return to Weber's definition of the state, which in his judgment possesses a monopoly on legitimate violence. The political problem, then, is that the perpetrators of terrorism are typically not states or governments but other sub-state or trans-state kinds of agents. When nonstates act in such violent ways, the action is deemed politically illegitimate; the US Army opines that terrorist actions "may have political and other motives" but that ultimately and almost logically "terrorism is a criminal act" (2007: 6).

The political illegitimacy of terrorism also flows from its tactics and targets. As Ruby emphasized above, terrorism normally seeks noncombatant victims, who are off limits by the widely-accepted "rules of war." There are two problems with these supposed rules of war, though. First, not all individuals or groups may abide by them; they are basically Western inventions (that not even all Western governments obey in practice, such as banning torture or avoiding civilian death). Second, the definition of "combatants" is relative: al Qaeda, for example, has insisted that it is at war with the United States and that all Americans, not just American soldiers, are enemy combatants. Third, terrorists often feel that not they but their enemy is illegitimate—either that its government and political policies are illegitimate or that its boundaries and territories (or in the case of Israel its very existence) are illegitimate.

Still more problematically, Bergesen and Lizardo rightly contended that while terrorism "is certainly a form of political violence, coordinated destruction, and heavy violence," these features are also true of "other collective events, such as race riots, some protest events, or violent encounters between management and labor" (2004: 40). Worst of all, political scientists have acknowledged that states themselves also periodically engage in terrorism; so-called "state terrorism," as in the campaigns of Cambodian leader Pol Pot against the Cambodian people in the 1970s (immortalized as "the killing fields") or in Nazi Germany's official program of extermination of Jews, is hardly distinguishable in attitude or tactics from other terrorism and is actually much grander in scale and institutionalization.

Political scientists can also study terrorism from a number of other angles. They can examine the "issues, grievances, tactics, recruitment, and training practices" of terrorist groups, as well as performing "organizational analyses of network and other forms of terrorist organization," including command structure and decision-making (Bergeson and Lizardo 2004: 39). Or they can try to expose "state policies and financial support that go to terrorist groups" and "the policies of states that might make them targets of terrorism" (40). For example, some groups have aimed their terrorism at specific local state targets, such as the Basque organization Euskadi Ta AsKaTasuna (ETA) against the Spanish state, or the Irish Republican Army (IRA) against the authorities of Northern Ireland and the United Kingdom. Other terrorist organizations and networks have more international ambitions, like al Qaeda or Islamic State (ISIS/ISIL), which in their various decentralized national incarnations have attacked the United States, France, the United Kingdom, Yemen, Bali, Kenya, Morocco, Turkey, and many other countries.

Political scientists certainly can and do research specific acts of terrorism or specific terrorist organizations, but as the above comments suggest, they also do and must consider the wider, even global, political context. Political scientist David Laitin, in collaboration with sociologist Rogers Brubaker, made two salient points about the international political scene that contribute to the incidence of terrorism in the new century. First, they noted the "eclipse of the left-right ideological axis that has defined the grand lines of much political conflict—and many civil wars—since the French Revolution" (1998: 424–5). Most recently, the Cold War between communism and the West preoccupied almost all players on the world stage, but with the end of that confrontation, many small and/or previously unresolved political and social disagreements and hostilities came to the fore, ones that cannot easily be classified in the old "left versus right" categories.

Second, and equally if not more serious, has been what they called the "decay of the Weberian state," that is, the decline of "states' capacities to maintain order by monopolizing the legitimate use of violence in their territories and the emergence in some regions . . . of so-called quasi-states, organizations formally acknowledged and recognized as states yet lacking (or possessing only in small degree) the empirical attributes of stateness" (424). Challenges to the state as the exclusive legitimate actor in world politics have come from "below" and "above" the state. From below, racial, ethnic, class, religious, linguistic, and other sorts of identities and political organizations have asserted their right to use force for their cause. From above or outside the state, Brubaker and Laitin mentioned that "a thickening web of international and nongovernmental organizations has provided greater international legitimacy, visibility, and support for" trans-state ethnic, religious, and other groups that want to contest particular states or the entire state-oriented global system (425).

Indeed, in the eyes of many terrorist individuals and organizations, states are the problem and the adversary. Analyzing suicide terrorism specifically, Robert Pape and James Feldman find that certain types or actions of states are the irritant that spark terrorism. At least in current times, a singularly prominent motivation of terrorism is to end a military occupation: violent attacks in multiple settings, from Iraq and Afghanistan to Pakistan, Uzbekistan, and Somalia, "occurred as part of coherent and organized campaigns designed to compel democratic societies to abandon the occupation or political control of territory the terrorists view as their national homeland" (2010: 22). Additionally, terrorists are often incensed by their own allegedly (and often enough actually) corrupt and unjust governments, frequently propped up by the same rich, powerful states that occupy terrorist-claimed territory.

Finally, criminologist Mark Hamm has discovered one other way that governments and political institutions contribute to the making of terrorists —through their prisons. Hamm's research indicates that prisons can be incubators of terrorism, producing men who "were not terrorists when they went into prison but became terrorists as a result of their prison experience," especially when that experience includes violence coupled with "prison conditions that were chaotic and violent" (2013: 80), allowing charismatic inmate figures to implant extremist ideas and agendas in their conveniently-provided new recruits.

4 Economic Outlook

Key organizations

American Economic Association (www.aeaweb.org), founded 1885
Royal Economic Society (www.res.org.uk), founded 1890
History of Economics Society (www.historyofeconomics.org), founded
1974
World Economics Association (www.worldeconomicsassociation.org),
founded 2011

Key journals

American Economic Review
Journal of Economic Literature
Cambridge Journal of Economics
The Economic Journal

It has been widely observed—and by many, intensely felt—that economic inequality is on the rise in the twenty-first century. In his surprise bestseller *Capital in the Twenty-First Century*, French economist Thomas Piketty examines the history of the distribution of income and wealth, not only constructing a description of inequality but deriving a theory and even economic laws, and offering predictions and policy recommendations. He notes first and foremost that the "history of the distribution of wealth has always been deeply political, and it cannot be reduced to purely economic mechanisms" (2014: 2), that is, how a society organizes its laws, for instance concerning taxes and finance, shapes the outcome of wealth and poverty. Analyzing more than a century of data from the countries around the world, he formulates the "first fundamental law of capitalism," which is $\alpha = r \times \beta$, meaning that the "capital/income ratio β is related in a simple way to the share of income from capital in national income, denoted α . . . where r is *the rate of return on capital*" (52). The rate of return on capital, r, refers to "the yield on capital over the course of a year regardless of its legal form (profits, rents, dividends, interest, royalties, capital gains, etc.), expressed as a percentage of the value of capital invested" (52). His central claim, then, is that, while there are economic and social forces operating both to equalize and unequalize wealth, in the long run, "the private rate of return on capital, r, can be significantly higher for long periods of time than the rate of growth of income and output, g" (571); more simply, the people who already have wealth earn more on their wealth than those who depend on paid labor. Therefore, "Once constituted, capital reproduces itself faster than output increases. The past devours the future" (571)—or as the saying goes, the rich get richer. But since such results are not inevitable or natural but depend on policies and institutions, Piketty explains and advises that the "potentially terrifying" level of inequality can be avoided through steps like higher tax rates for the rich and for "unearned income" like dividends, capital gains, and inheritances.

Humans in all times and places have had needs and wants, and they have always arranged to fulfill these needs and wants in some way. However, they have not always had formal economic institutions like money, banks, markets, and corporations, and they have certainly not always studied and predicted their own economic behavior. In this way, "the economy" as a human social practice and "economics" as a professional social science are parallel to "the past" versus "history" or to "politics" versus "political science."

Most simply, then, economics can be defined as "*a study of how people organize the use of resources to satisfy their wants. In other words, economics is a study of economic organization*" (Van Sickle and Rogge 1954: 6, emphasis in the original). This is generally understood as a three-part process of *production*, *distribution*, and *consumption*, in which humans act on the physical world and transform its resources into "goods" and "services" that humans can use.

Economic processes avail themselves to more "scientific" analysis than most aspects of human behavior, so economists are prone to generating and studying massive data sets, using technical terminology, constructing models (often represented mathematically or graphically), making predictions, and formulating laws. According to one of the pioneers of modern economics, Alfred Marshall (1842–1924), "Economic laws or statements of economic tendencies are those social laws which relate to branches of conduct in which the strength of motives chiefly concerned can be measured by a money price" (quoted in Jain and Khanna 2007: 69). This means, of course, that economic laws "are human laws . . . concerned with human behavior" (69), so economics has a clearer and more specific notion of human nature and, even more essentially, of human *decision making*, since the "problem of choice is, in fact, [the] problem of economics" (8).

Van Sickle and Rogge also argued that, despite its claims to scientificity, economics is many other things besides science. It is also history, they asserted, "to the extent of how economic systems have developed (and declined) and of how they have worked in practice"; further, it is sociology "to the extent that the economist must examine the social conditions necessary to permit each type of economic system to operate efficiently" (1954: 8). It is assuredly political science "to the extent that every economic system must operate in a political environment and will influence and be influenced by that environment" (8–9). And as we will see shortly, it is most definitely psychology too, in that "it must be based on the behavior of human beings" (8) and on the thought-processes we use to make our choices.

Finally, like political science, economics was originally, and substantially continues to be, a form of "statecraft," providing guidance for political leaders to manage the economy, both nationally and internationally. Economics has thus always been both a theoretical and a highly practical endeavor, predicting economic trends and suggesting and analyzing economic policies. Like political science again, academic economists share interests and concepts with other, more purely practical fields and careers such as business, finance, banking, marketing, and accounting.

The Origins of Economic Thought

It is remarkable to realize that the very first things that humans ever wrote down, once they developed writing systems, were economic records. The earliest-known pieces of writing, from Mesopotamia some five thousand years ago, were essentially business transactions and trading accounts. The first historical use of writing was bookkeeping.

Perhaps more remarkable, while ancient Egypt "had a kind of planned economy that turned upon her irrigation system," and the Mesopotamians "developed monetary institutions to a high degree of perfection, and knew credit and banking," yet "there is no trace of analytic effort" in these magnificent civilizations (Schumpeter 2006: 49). Even in ancient China, with its "highly developed public administration that dealt currently with agrarian, commercial and financial problems," it is extraordinary to find that "no piece of reasoning on strictly economic topics has come down to us that can be called 'scientific' within our meaning of the term" (49–50).

As with history and political science, the earliest roots of the modern disciplines can be traced to the Greeks, but there too, the great economist Joseph Schumpeter judged, "rudimentary economic analysis is a minor element—a very minor one—in the inheritance that has been left to us by our cultural ancestors" (50). The word "economics" or *oeconomicus* was known to the Greeks, but like *historein* and *politeiai*, it did not have the modern meaning. Rather, *oeconomicus*, literally derived from *oikos* for "house" and *nomos* for rule or law, "meant only the practical wisdom of household management" (50). The closest equivalent to contemporary economics, Schumpeter contended, was *chrematistics*, Aristotle's term for wealth or possessions, which "refers mainly to the pecuniary aspects of business activity" (50).

Practical Advice for the Successful Greek Man: Hesiod's *Works and Days*

Works and Days, attributed to Hesiod and composed around 700 BCE, is often considered the oldest example of economic thinking. However, it is far from modern, social-scientific analysis of the economy. First, it opens more like an epic poem than a scientific treatise, with the words, "Muses of Pieria who give glory through song, come hither, tell of Zeus your father and chant his praise. Through him mortal men are famed or unfamed, sung or unsung alike, as great Zeus wills. For easily he makes strong, and easily he brings the strong man low" (Hesiod 1914: section 1–10). The book then consists primarily of mythical comments about how the gods make or unmake human fortune, along with an assortment of practical—and impractical—suggestions for how best to conduct one's affairs. For instance:

"Do not get base gain: base gain is as bad as ruin. . . . Give to one who gives, but do not give to one who does not give" (352–69).

"Let the wage promised to a friend be fixed; even with your brother smile—and get a witness; for trust and mistrust, alike ruin men" (370–2).

"Do not let a flaunting woman coax and cozen and deceive you: she is after your barn. The man who trusts womankind trusts deceivers" (373–5).

"First of all, get a house, and a woman and an ox for the plough—a slave woman and not a wife, to follow the oxen as well—and make everything ready at home, so that you may not have to ask another, and he refuses you, and so, because you are in lack, the season pass by and your work come to nothing" (405–13).

"Never put the ladle upon the mixing-bowl at a wine party, for malignant ill-luck is attached to that" (744–5).

"When you are building a house, do not leave it rough-hewn, or a cawing crow may settle on it and croak" (746–7).

"Take nothing to eat or to wash with from uncharmed pots, for in them there is mischief" (748–9).

Plato on the "Division of Labor" in Society

Émile Durkheim is famous for launching sociology with his late-nineteenth century study of the division of labor (see Chapter 6). However, Durkheim was hardly the first to ponder the proper place of various citizens in a well-ordered society. Xenophon (430–355 BCE), a follower of Socrates, opined on the distribution of work and rewards in society, but it was Plato who provided the clearest model of economic specialization, not only as an economic but as a political and moral matter.

Plato's *Republic* does not so much analyze Greek society as plan it, describing a stable and beautiful system in which population and wealth are both constant and in which every element of "economic and non-economic activity was strictly regulated—warriors, farmers, artisans, and so on being organized in permanent castes, men and women being treated exactly alike" (Schumpeter 2006: 52). To the class or caste of Guardians was given the right to rule, and each lower stratum knew its place and was prepared through education for its place. The result was a socio-moral order where specialization is imposed not only for "the efficiency that results from division of labor per se" but for "the increase in efficiency that results from allowing everyone to specialize in what he is by nature best fitted for" (53). In a word, the ideal republic should have a fixed division of labor because such a plan is *perfect*, whether or not it is profitable.

Aristotle on Work and Wealth

Anything resembling an economic analysis, though hardly shorn of its moral critique, must wait for Aristotle, who, as previously mentioned, distinguished between *oikonomiks* and *chrematistiks*. The former refers to real productive activity, labor that generates goods and services, while the latter concerns moneymaking as such, trade and exchange for the simple purpose of acquiring wealth.

Aristotle did not write a work called *Economics*, rather his economic thinking is distributed across his writings called *Politics* and *Ethics*. The fundamental building-block of the economy, in good Greek fashion, was for him still the household, which ideally satisfied its own basic needs (for food, clothing, etc.). From there, Aristotle "introduced division of labor, barter, and, as a means of overcoming the difficulties of direct barter, money" (Schumpeter 2006: 57).

More importantly, Aristotle discussed a number of other significant concepts that would come to figure in modern economic thought. Among these was the notion of "value," which he differentiated into "use value" and "exchange value," also realizing "that the latter phenomenon derives somehow from the former" (57). In modern parlance, "use value" is the worth of something in terms of what you can do with it (say, a car can be used to drive to work or to run a taxi service) while "exchange value" is what the good or service can be traded for (that is, how much money one can get from selling a car). A basic concern, then, both in regard to use and exchange was a "just price" for labor and commodities. Monopoly, for instance, was unjust, since it allowed one person or group to set prices.

Aristotle also attempted to make some sense out of the concept of "money," which we take very much for granted but which is a thoroughly social concept and practice. As most professional economists agree, "whatever other purposes money may come to serve, its fundamental function, which defines it and accounts for its existence, is to serve as a medium of exchange" (60). Second, though, "in order to serve as a medium of exchange in the markets of commodities, money itself must be one of these commodities" (60), that is, money too must have a price, reflected today in international currency exchange rates, interest rates, and inflation rates. In short, money, like other commodities, can be bought and sold. And money itself must be socially and politically created: "money exists not by 'nature' but by convention or legislation" (60).

Since interest (or the cost of buying or borrowing money) is an inevitable consequence of the social construction and trade of money, Aristotle also commented on interest. He, like other classical thinkers, "condemned interest—which he equated to 'usury' in all cases—on the ground that there was no justification for money, a mere medium of exchange, to increase in going from hand to hand (which of course it does not do)" (62). Curiously, though, "he never asked the question why interest was being paid all the same" (62). Perhaps influenced by Aristotelian thinking, or perhaps arriving at the essential immorality of making money off of money (rather than productive labor), Islam also condemns interest or *riba*, which the Islamic website inter-islam.org defines as "excess or increase," "effortless profit or that profit which comes free from compensation or that extra earning obtained that is free of exchange."

Pre-Modern Economic Thought and Practice

"The rest of Aristotle's 'pure' economics, *considered from our standpoint*, is hardly worth mentioning. Many, if not most, of the things that were to become problems for the economist of later times he took for granted in the spirit of prescientific common sense" (Schumpter 2006: 61, emphasis in the original). Nevertheless, Aristotelian thinking on the economy (and most other subjects) was the standard of knowledge for more than a thousand years, as both Arabic and European scholars perpetuated and interpreted his teachings. In Europe, as with the case of historical and political thinking, economic thinking became entangled with Christianity, in which economics was a worldly pursuit of no great spiritual concern—or even of spiritual alarm. Remember, for example, the Gospel admonitions *against* wealth, from Jesus upsetting the money-changers' tables to his sermon on the spiritual benefits of poverty: a rich man can hardly expect to get to heaven, a good man sells all of his property and gives to the poor, and a tax collector is inherently a sinful person.

Early Church fathers like Tertullian and Cyprian in the third century CE accordingly "preached against wanton luxury and irresponsible wealth, they enjoined charity and restraint in the use of worldly good, but they did not analyze at all" (Schumpeter 2006: 68). A thousand years later, as Aristotle's thoughts were rediscovered in Christian Europe, things were not much different. For instance, Aquinas taught that

> there is "something base" about commerce itself, though commercial gain might be justified (a) by the necessity of making one's living' or (b) by a wish to acquire means for charitable purposes; or (c) by a wish to serve *publicam utilitatem* [public usefulness], provided that the lucre be moderate and can be considered as a reward of work (*stipendium laboris*), or (d) by an improvement of the thing traded; or (e) by intertemporal or interlocal differences in its value, or (f) by risk.
>
> (Schumpeter 2006: 87)

In other words, in this Christian and pre-capitalist worldview, "economic" matters boiled down to ethical and religious questions like the "socially useful activity" from which payment arose and the individual's "(moral) right to the produce of one's labor" (87–8).

More consequential than the economic theorizing of the Middle Ages, of which there was little or none, were the practical changes to technology and society that occurred during those centuries. While the system of feudalism that formed in Europe aimed at self-sufficient production on feudal estates or manors through extraction of the labor of peasants or "serfs" who were attached to the land (and therefore free neither to sell their labor nor to leave their "employer" or lord) led to a rigid economic and social order in which growth was only possible via conquest or increased exploitation and taxation, other changes boded a new era in the economy and society.

Among these changes were new agricultural techniques and technologies, including crop rotation, windmills, and the heavy plow, not to mention small but significant advancements like the horseshoe and horse collar, which increased yields and reduced labor costs. By the eleventh or twelfth century, trade and literacy began to revive. In the meantime, a revolution in mathematics was taking place, with scholars in India first introducing the concept of "zero" around 500 CE; then in the 700s in the Muslim world, fractions were invented. Roman numerals lacked both the zero and the use of fractions, which made them painfully inadequate for business transactions or any complicated mathematical calculations. It was only around 1200 CE that so-called "Arabic numerals," with their long non-Western history, reached Europe by way of Italy, where a man named Leonardo Pisano Bigollo, but more famously known as Fibonacci, studied them and helped promote them in Europe with his book *Liber Abaci*. Suddenly banking, finance, and theoretical mathematics were much easier to conduct.

One last practical/economic modification to the European landscape, literally, was the new and increasing practice of "enclosure." As land became more productive and valuable, landowners began to fence their property, sometimes kicking peasants/serfs off the land and sometimes claiming formerly "common" land (open for use by all) as private property. Land was transforming socially, from an inherited privilege of the nobility to a resource and commodity—what we call today "real estate." Landless peasants were further compelled to search for new work, either as wage-earning farm laborers or as artisans and craftsmen (and sometimes beggars and thieves) in the newly-emerging cities. When the "Black Death" of the bubonic plague hit in the mid-1300s, the annihilation of one-third of the population shifted forever the relations between lords and employers on the one hand and workers on the other.

Colonialism and Mercantilism

As early as 1350, Nicholas Oresme offered what is widely recognized as "the first treatise ever on inflation and, in fact, the very first treatise on an economic problem" (Hülsmann 2008: ix). Titled *A Treatise on the Origin, Nature, Law, and Alterations of Money*, it still expressed a moralistic attitude toward the economy, castigating inflation and the erosion of the value of money as evil, but more importantly for our discussion, it insisted that the ruler does not own money and cannot alter or debase it at will. Instead, money is the property of those who make and possess wealth; in a word, money belongs to the individual, to the community, and to the country or commonwealth.

Interestingly, inflation and the national management of currency and wealth were about to become pressing problems in Europe as the colonial era arrived. By the 1400s Europeans were engaged in long-distance trade, mainly for Asian rarities such as spices, silk, and porcelain. However, this trade required trekking slowly over land as well as dealing with hostile third parties, like Muslim merchants. Seeking their own trade routes to the East (to cut out the middle man and speed transport), Europeans sailed south around the cape of Africa and west across the Atlantic. They planted trading posts and supply stations on the coast of Africa or islands along the way, aiming ultimately for China, India, and what would later be called Indonesia.

In the "East Indies" Europeans traded profitably with local princes and kings, gradually penetrating deeper into those lands and eventually seizing the sources of production. To the west, in the Americas, Europeans encountered rich sophisticated civilizations like the Aztecs and Incas and robbed their gold. The Spanish and Portuguese transferred their feudal economies to the New World, establishing landed estates (the *encomienda* and *hacienda*) that were ideally self-sufficient and that depended on the forced labor of native peoples now converted to peasants and serfs—and soon on imported African slaves.

As a result of these economic and political successes, wealth began to pour into Europe. South American gold and silver arrived in such abundance that high inflation resulted, and governments were required to manage their new global imperial systems. The political-economic theory and practice of *mercantilism* emerged, with a strong alliance between government and business, quickly represented by the "corporation" or group of investors who pooled money in order to launch a trading venture. The most famous and powerful of these corporations were the Dutch East Indies Company and the British East India Company, both founded around 1600; for two centuries, the British East India Company acted basically as a government in India and parts of Asia, building its own forts, conducting its own diplomacy, and fighting its own battles. Other noteworthy corporations were the Hudson's Bay Company (Canada) and the Plymouth Company (Massachusetts).

The great goal of mercantilism, and the measure of national wealth, was precious metals, particularly gold and silver. Thus, each country and its government struggled to maximize its supply of gold. Moreover, "the government should manage the economy for the purpose of increasing national wealth and state power," which involved four actions: "the government should (1) stimulate the output of domestic goods, (2) limit domestic consumption, (3) put tariffs on imports, and (4) try to create a favorable balance of trade (more exports than imports)" (Canterbury 2001: 33).

Mercantilism naturally strengthened national governments (and national identities) and created competitive colonial systems, each European country attempting to monopolize trade with its colonies. Other epochal social changes were also wrought by this new political economy. As mentioned, the influx of gold and silver "caused product prices to triple in Europe between 1500 and 1650, and because the prices of simple manufactured goods rose much more than either wages or rents, the merchant class ascended along with prices" (34). This ascent fundamentally restructured European societies, in which land had previously been the measure of wealth and status and in which the landed aristocracy had been the dominant group. In fact, merchants had occupied a comparatively low status in feudal (and ancient) society. But this rising "middle class" between the nobles and the peasants, this *nouveaux riches* or "new rich" class, would change society radically—and redesign society in its own image. With it would come new and more modern ideas about how to understand—and how to manage—an economy.

Early Modern Economic Thought

As we have already illustrated, early modern scholars were polymaths, pontificating on many different subjects under the general heading of philosophy. In fact, one of the main points of this book is that the modern social sciences had not yet differentiated, so thinkers tended to combine analysis of the economy with remarks about politics, human nature, and of course morality and religion.

For example, in his *Leviathan*, which deals predominantly with politics, Thomas Hobbes stressed the nation as a "commonwealth," which is held together by contracts. More valuably, John Locke, known mostly for his political (see Chapter 3) and psychological (see Chapter 5) ideas, also gave lectures on economic questions. In the second of his two treatises on government in 1689, he argued for a natural and rational basis for property. He insisted that the most basic and inalienable property of the free person is his/her own body; then, the "labor of his body, and the work of his hands, we may say, are properly his. Whatsoever then he removes out of the state that nature hath provided, and left it in, he hath mixed his labor with, and joined to it something that is his own, and thereby makes it his property" (Chapter V "Of Property," section 27). That is, we can represent the essence of property in a simple equation:

Nature + Labor = Property

This emphasis on labor, which would reach a crescendo with Karl Marx (see later), informed one of the first schools of economic thought, the Physiocrats of the eighteenth century. The Physiocrats dominated in France, where figures like François Quesnay (1694–1774) and Anne-Robert-Jacques Turgot (1727–81) taught that wealth originated in productive labor, contradicting the mercantilist view that wealth equaled accumulating gold. However, their view was still rather traditionalist, praising land as the ultimate source of wealth. In his 1759 *Tableau économique* Quesnay maintained that the "productive class" was agricultural laborers, while merchants were consigned to the "sterile class" that moves things around but does not actually produce anything. Then there was of course the "proprietary class" that owned the land.

Another key ancestor of modern economic thought is Richard Cantillon, an Irishman who published his 1755 *Essai sur la nature du commerce en general* in French. Although he was conventional in insisting that the price and value of a commodity were determined by the inputs of land and labor, he was much more original in identifying the flow of money and the relationships between components of the economy as vital factors. He attempted to make economic analysis more scientific by adopting a causal approach and differentiating economics from politics and morality, and he introduced basic concepts such as "equilibrium" and "entrepreneur" to the economic vocabulary.

Adam Smith and the Market

Of all the early economic theorists, none is more important than Adam Smith, whose *An Inquiry into the Nature and Causes of the Wealth of*

Nations, often called simply *The Wealth of Nations*, was published in the fateful year of 1776. Smith (1723–90) was not only one of the first scholars to propose a model of the economy in terms of "the market" and individual economic/market behavior, but he also showed how strongly economic issues are related to both psychology and morality, that is, to how people reason and make choices and how they should live or what the good way of life is. Indeed, before he penned his great economic opus, Smith was a moral philosopher, composing *The Theory of Moral Sentiments* in 1759, in which he considered society to be a moral system, relying on certain shared sentiments like compassion and justice and simple "fellow-feeling."

In *The Wealth of Nations*, Smith painted a very different picture of the nature of the economy and of the glue that holds it and the society together. In one of the most famous passages in the history of economic writing, he asserted:

> It is not from the benevolence of the butcher, the brewer, or the baker that we expect our dinner, but from their regard to their own interest. We address ourselves, not to their humanity but to their self-love, and never talk to them of our own necessities but of their advantages.
>
> (Book I, "On the Principle which gives occasion to the Division of Labour": 13–14)

The starting point of an economy, then, is the division of labor, with different individuals engaged in different kinds of productive activities (the butcher, the brewer, the baker, etc.). In such a system, each individual decides what to produce and how much of it to produce. It is not rational to produce goods that no one wants, or more goods than buyers want, or more expensive goods than buyers will purchase. Thus, efficient and profitable production entails some careful calculation.

Economic calculation takes us, if you will, inside the mind of the producer, into his/her economic calculus. For Smith, the most basic fact of the psychology and morality of the individual market actor is *self-interest*: individuals do what they perceive to be in their own best interests. Additionally, Smith assumed that social actors are *rational*: given sufficient information and the freedom to choose, they will make the best decisions to reach their individual goal, which is generally to maximize their self-interest. This will result in the exploitation of opportunity and in competition.

Say that a person owns some land and grows corn. If the demand (and hence price) for corn increases, the farmer will act to take advantage of this opportunity—buy more land, hire more laborers, invent better techniques, and so on. And other people will also enter the corn-growing business, leading to competition, which will be won by the farmer who can grow the best or cheapest corn. Conversely, if the price of corn declines, he will switch to a different crop, or struggle to reduce his production costs, or leave farming altogether.

Thomas Malthus and the Tragedy of Growth

No discussion of early economic thinking would be complete without a mention of the moralistic perspective of Thomas Malthus (1766–1834). In his 1798 *An Essay on the Principle of Population, as It Affects the Future of Society*, Malthus concluded that human populations inevitably grow faster than their productive capacity. After all, there is an absolute limit to land, and there are, he believed, limits to technological innovation and thus to increases in the output of food and other goods. The consequences of this imbalance would be desperate, he predicted. When populations expanded beyond our ability to feed people, there would be conflict and war, as well as famine and disease, crime and vice. Fortunately Malthus, an Anglican priest, had a solution: Christian morality. If people would exercise moral self-control, marrying later, having fewer children, and practicing celibacy in general, the population disaster could be averted. He also discouraged public welfare programs, which he felt perpetuated poverty and sapped the personal responsibility of the poor. Ironically, Malthus' thinking influenced a young Charles Darwin to envision species competition, "natural selection," and evolution.

Smith is most remembered for his characterization of this "self-regulating" quality of the market and of the economy as a whole. He wrote that it was as if an *invisible hand* were guiding the economy always to produce the right goods at the right price. However, there is no hand; there is only the sum of all of the decisions and actions of individual market actors, acting in their own best interests.

Contrary to mercantilism, Smith's version of economic behavior supports a *laissez-faire* relationship between government and economic players (individuals, businesses, and corporations). French for "let them do it," in a self-regulating economy, markets work best when they are allowed to work without interference (or what modern economists call "distortion").

Advancing Economic Theory and Methods in the Early 1800s

By the first years of the nineteenth century, economic thought was beginning to assume some of its modern forms. For instance, to open the century, William Playfair in 1801 published his *The Statistical Breviary, Shewing, on a Principle Entirely New, the Resources of Every State and Kingdom in Europe*, in which he gave the world its first "pie chart"; he is also widely credited with inventing the line graph and bar graph, two indispensable economic tools.

Some pivotal books were also released in the first decades of the nineteenth century, such as the 1817 *Principles of Political Economy and Taxation* by David Ricardo (1772–1823). In fact, economics was known as "political economy" until the very late 1800s. In 1832 Charles Babbage applied operations research, including mathematical tables, to the new industrial

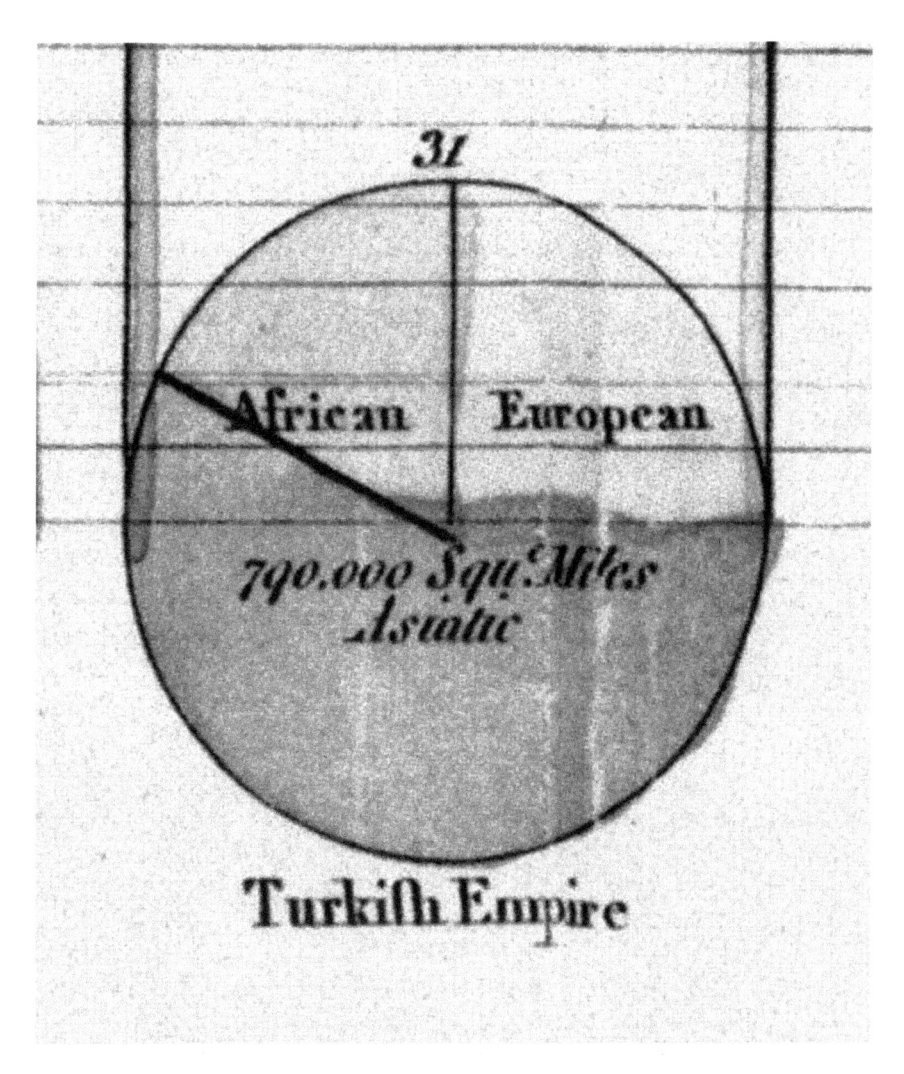

Figure 4.1 Pie Chart depicting the proportions of the Turkish Empire situated in Asia, Europe, and Africa after 1789, from William Playfair's *The Statistical Breviary*

Source: Wikicommons.

economy in his 1832 *On the Economy of Machinery and Manufactures*. Soon thereafter, Charles Mackay described the "economic bubble" and the exuberant irrationality that created it in his 1841 *Memoirs of Extraordinary Popular Delusions and the Madness of Crowds*. Meanwhile, one of the classic instruments of modern economics, the "demand curve," was first presented in 1838 by Antoine Augustin Cournot in his *Researches on the Mathematical Principles of the Theory of Wealth*. The demand curve depicts the relationship between supply and demand, indicating the "equilibrium point" at which supply and demand are in balance.

Another mid-century contribution worth acknowledging was the theory of "utilitarianism," originally promoted in the moral thinking of Jeremy Bentham (1748–1832). Bentham believed that human behavior could be explained and guided rationally as a calculated pursuit of happiness. He thought that decision-making could or should be based on the objective number of "hedons" or pleasure-units that a person can achieve, and in his 1823 *An Introduction to the Principle of Morals and Legislation* he reasoned that an action or decision "may be said to be conformable to the principle

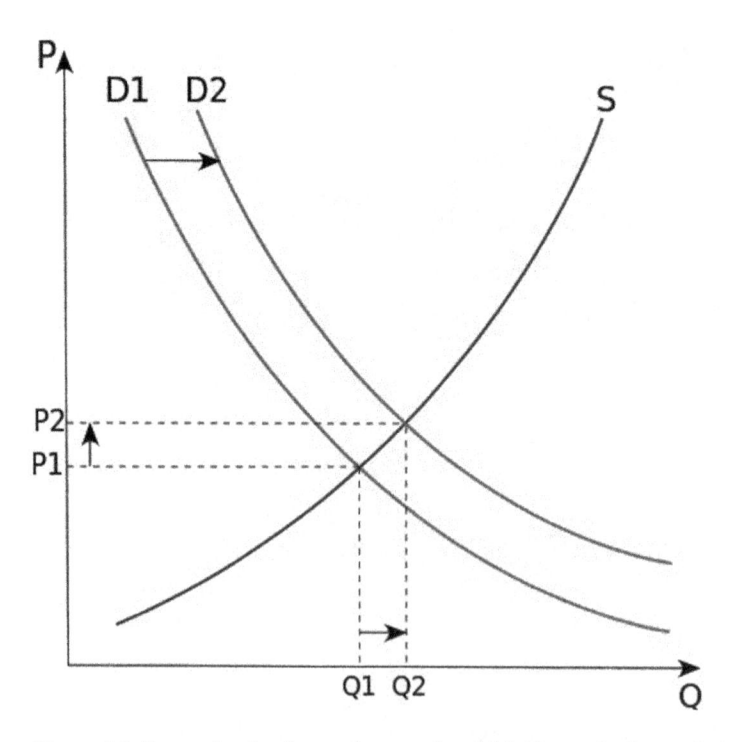

Figure 4.2 Example of a demand curve, in which D equals demand, S equals supply, P equals price, and Q equals quantity

Source: Wikicommons.

of utility ... when the tendency it has to augment the happiness of the community is greater than any it has to diminish it." John Stuart Mill applied this moral concept to economics in his 1848 *Principles of Political Economy*, which divided economic activity into "production," "distribution," and "exchange" and advocated a normative, ethical economic system founded on the principle of "the greatest good for the greatest number."

Karl Marx on Labor, Class, Value, and Alienation

While Smith, Mill, and many more were analyzing how the economy could and should provide satisfaction for most members of society, other thinkers were more suspicious of the realities of the new industrial capitalist economy. In the previous chapter we mentioned the utopian socialists who tried to ameliorate the worst abuses of their modern world, but the idealism of Owen and Fourier lacked a serious economic and social theory. Meanwhile, earlier in the century, disgruntled workers remembered as "Luddites" were breaking machinery that they thought was destroying their way of life.

Into the fray of the mid-1800s stepped Karl Marx, who had already established himself as an activist for the Communist party and movement. As we saw in previous chapters, by 1848 in his *The Communist Manifesto* Marx had developed the outline of a historical-economic theory of society, with each particular society (or "social formation") understood as a product or effect of basic economic, material forces and relations.

By 1867, Marx augmented his partisan work with one of the weightiest studies of political economy in Western history, *Das Kapital* ("Capital"). In this multi-volume set, Marx revolutionized the concept of "value," which had previously been understood as a rather primitive function of the cost of labor and resources. On the old model, a "fair"or "just" price could be determined for labor and for goods. However, in his "surplus value" theory of labor, he fundamentally challenged the notion that wages were fair or just.

Capitalism, he reasoned, operates on the basis of the *surplus value of labor*. Owners and employers (the bourgeois class) hire workers (the proletarian class) and pay them a wage. The price of goods produced by workers, however, is higher than the cost of labor; the difference between wages and prices—the surplus value of the labor—is skimmed off by the bourgeoisie. Thus, the owning class lives off of the surplus generated by the working class, and the working class earns less than its fair share of the value that its labor generates.

This situation was inherently unethical in Marx's view, and he reasoned that if the workers eliminated the bourgeoisie, they could not only make their own decisions but could retain the full value of their productive activity. Communism ideally would abolish private property, the bedrock of economic exploitation, along with phenomena such as rent, and place the

---

The Historical Forms of Society, according to Marx

Marx eventually offered a typology of historical social forms, based on their production systems, including:

primitive communism, such as prehistoric tribal societies, which were (allegedly) essentially classless

Asiatic mode of production, including ancient civilizations such as Mesopotamia and Egypt, which exploited labor to create great works such as the pyramids

antique modes of production, such as ancient Greece and Rome, where private property existed and was the basis for social stratification

feudalism, exemplified by the European Middle Ages during which workers were "serfs" tied to the land

early capitalism, before the rise of modern industry and the fully-formed institutions of "the state" and "the corporation"

late capitalism, the form of society characteristic of Marx's time as well as our own, with industrial capitalism firmly in control and society sharply divided into owners and workers

communism, the predicted, desired, and (for Marx) inevitable future society in which private property and class inequality would be abolished, along with institutions specific to the capitalist mode of production such as the state, religion, and the bourgeois family

---

"means of production" directly in the hands of the productive people (the workers).

Marx added another analysis, and to appreciate it we must realize that before Marx was a political economist he was a philosopher. In his early writings, he described humanity as a "species being," a comprehensively social species that comes to know itself from its collective action; that is, humans make objects and thus "objectify" themselves, literally depositing some of themselves in the objects they make. But under the conditions of industrial capitalism, Marx asserted that people were *alienated* from their labor. First, they did not control the processes or products of their activity. Second, they typically performed rote or unskilled labor rather than craftsmanship, with the production process broken down into many trivial steps; each individual performed one small step over and over. Third, their productive activity was driven by machines and the needs and schedules of those machines, instead of the natural and social rhythms of humanity.

Fourth, the finished products of their labor were seized from them and sold as commodities that had no social meaning other than their exchange value or *price*. Everything in the world was reduced to a commodity to be bought and sold, including the workers' time and very bodies.

In the end, then, Marx was an enemy of industrial capitalism not only because it engendered class inequality (all historical societies had done so), but because it threatened the very humanity of both workers and owners. It turned workers and their works into meaningless things, and it turned owners into soulless exploiters willing to throw anything—including society, morality, and humanity—into the maw of production.

Thorstein Veblen and the Leisure Class

A very different take on the question of class came in Thorstein Veblen's work, oriented not around production but around consumption. Veblen (1857–1929) investigated the behavior of the upper class and its impact on society in his celebrated 1899 book *The Theory of the Leisure Class: An Economic Study of Institutions*. As the title indicates, he considered the upper or ruling class to be a relatively idle group, doing little work (and hardly any productive work); of course, this has been true throughout history.

Beyond their direct domination of the economy and society through ownership, Veblen concentrated on what and how the upper class consumes. Clearly they can and do consume more and better goods and services than the lower classes, but their consumption is not determined by utility alone: they do not really need another car or home or even a more expensive care or home. Rather, he argued that the upper class engages in *conspicuous consumption*, extravagant and unnecessary consumption for the purpose of displaying status, not fulfilling needs. Veblen realized that goods and services, including food and clothing, are not just necessities but *status symbols*, observable signs of one's place in society. This is why it is crucial not only to consume but *to be seen consuming*, to consume publicly. And one of the things that the upper class consumes conspicuously is *free time*, what he called *conspicuous leisure*. The upper class can play golf during the day, spend time strolling museums and art galleries or attending parties, and take long vacations with travel to remote—and conspicuously elite—locations.

Equally important to Veblen's analysis was the relationship of the upper class to the other classes of society. He claimed that the leisure class was also the trend-setting class, defining "style" for the entire population. The clothes they wore, the food they ate, the cars they drove, the neighborhoods they inhabited, even the vocabulary and grammar they used became the standard of "class," sophistication, and taste. The lower classes would imitate them and strive to be like them, shopping in certain stores, buying certain brands, and, if they were able, moving into certain neighborhoods.

All of this meant for Veblen that humans are not the exclusively rational creatures that economists tend to portray them (see later). Rather, people are often driven to make basically irrational decisions and to construct entire irrational institutions, which fundamentally shape society. Among the consequences of these tendencies, he asserted, were the oppression of women, the popularity of sports (consider, for example, who actually gets to attend the Super Bowl), "refined" practices like etiquette, and the whole realm of religion, which for him was a waste of money and resources supporting an unproductive class of priests.

Modern Economic Thought and Research

The era of modern (sometimes called neoclassical) economics is often marked by the arrival of Alfred Marshall's *Principles of Economics*, published in 1890, which was a popular textbook in the subject for many years. Interestingly, like many other social scientists, he began his career in philosophy and never abandoned his concern for ethics. Among his contributions to economics, Marshall championed the use of mathematics in studying economic questions. According to the Library of Economics and Liberty (www.econlib.org/library/Enc/bios/Marshall.html), Marshall also advanced the understanding of the relationship between supply and demand and introduced important economic concepts such as "price elasticity of demand" (how much changes in price affect buyers' behavior), "consumer surplus" (the difference between the amount paid for a unit of goods and the consumer's value for all of the units purchased), and "producer surplus" (the difference between what a producer receives in payment and what s/he would accept in payment).

With Marshall, the old "political economy" became the contemporary "economics." More specifically, he is heralded as foundational to the subfield of *microeconomics*, which focuses on the small scale of economic behavior, by individuals, households, groups, and corporations (commonly called "firms" by economists). Microeconomics usually studies taxation, corporate behavior, and the structure of markets (e.g. competition, monopoly, oligopoly, etc.). The other subfield of economics is *macroeconomics*, which examines national and international economic systems. Subjects covered in macroeconomics include employment, inflation, economic policy, money, banking, economic cycles (such as recession and depression), and the role of government in the economy. The two levels of economics are sufficiently distinct that they typically have separate textbooks and university courses.

James Cochrane (1970) further divided contemporary economics into three areas of thought and investigation—descriptive, analytical, and applied. Descriptive economics consists of reports, often in narrative form, of particular industries, countries, or economic systems. Analytical (or theoretical) economics strives to explain the operation of economic systems and to identify relationships and laws. Applied economics seeks to use economic understanding to solve problems and control economic variables like the money supply, employment, or interest rates.

Economists have at their disposal all of the familiar methods of the social sciences, including surveys and questionnaires, case studies, comparisons, experiments, and secondary data generated by governments and various research institutions. However, what is really unique about economics is not how professionals collect data but how they think about and analyze data. The important aspects of economic thought and analysis are its terminology,

---

Research Topics in Economics

The titles of articles in the 2015 issue of *Annual Review of Economics* include:

"Knowledge-Based Hierarchies: Using Organizations to Understand the Economy"

"Beyond Ricardo: Assignment Models in International Trade"

"The Roots of Gender Inequality in Developing Countries"

"Reconciling Micro and Macro Labor Supply Elasticities: A Structural Perspective"

"International Trade, Multinational Activity, and Corporate Finance"

"Policy Implications of Dynamic Public Finance"

"Media and Politics"

"Forecasting in Nonstationary Environments: What Works and What Doesn't in Reduced-Form and Structural Models"

"Political Decentralization"

"Household Debt: Facts, Puzzles, Theories, and Policies"

"Making Progress on Foreign Aid"

"Credit, Financial Stability, and the Macroeconomy"

"Job Creation, Job Destruction, and Productivity Growth: The Role of Young Businesses"

"The Evolution of Social Norms"

"Crime and Economic Incentives"

"Entrepreneurship and Financial Frictions: A Macrodevelopment Perspective"

"The US Electricity Industry After 20 Years of Restructuring"

"Is College a Worthwhile Investment?"

"The Schumpeterian Growth Paradigm"

"Climate and Conflict"

"The Gains from Market Integration"

its assumptions, its laws and models, and, as we will see later, its policy implications.

First, more than other social sciences, economics speaks a special disciplinary language full of technical terms including but hardly limited to:

- *scarcity*, a central concept in modern economics. A basic premise of economics is that resources are scarce while human needs and wants are virtually limitless. Indeed, in 1935 Lionel Robbins defined economics as "the science which studies human behavior as a relationship between ends and scarce means which have alternative uses" (1935: 16).
- *opportunity cost* (or "trade-off"), what an individual, group, corporation, or institution must give up in order to gain something else. Under conditions of scarcity, every economic choice involves a trade-off.
- *marginal utility*, the change in gain that results from increasing consumption, or the change in loss that results from decreasing consumption, of a good or service. This is often associated with *diminishing return*, that is, that each additional unit consumed provides less satisfaction than previous units consumed (i.e., the first gallon of ice cream is very satisfying but the second gallon less so).
- *marginal cost*, the change in the total cost of a good or service as it is affected by the production of additional units (it is almost always cheaper to produce the second, third, and further units than the first, which is the premise behind mass production).
- *price elasticity*, how much changes in price affect demand for a commodity. Some commodities are much more price-elastic than others, depending for example on whether they are essential to life or not.
- *equilibrium*, the condition (particularly, the price) at which supply and demand are balanced, that is, firms produce as much of a commodity as consumers demand.

Second, economics begins with a number of more or less explicit assumptions. As we have seen, the most pervasive and fundamental assumptions in economics are psychological, concerning human wants and decision-making. Humans are generally seen as rational (that is, sensibly applying their knowledge and preferences in making choices) and self-interested, acting to maximize those interests (primarily, to buy at the lowest price or to sell at the highest price). Another assumption that economists make is expressed in the Latin phrase *ceteris paribus*, which they frequently invoke to mean "other things being equal." In a complex and dynamic world, economists often, for the purpose of studying certain variables and their economic effects, assume that other variables are constant or absent. As Harvard economics professor Gregory Mankiw (2000) explained in one of his many textbooks, such assumptions simplify the world and make modeling possible.

According to Mark Blaug in a scathing critique of economics, one common and troubling assumption in the discipline has been that economic knowledge is "derived from introspection or the casual observation of one's neighbors and in that sense constituted *a priori* [before experience, independent of empirical investigation] truths" (1992: 51). He accused economics before the twentieth century, but even in that century, of assuming that "the right procedure is the *a priori* method of starting from 'a few and indispensable facts of human nature' " (73) and that "the verification of economic predictions" with actual data "was at best a hazardous enterprise" (51). As late as 2000, David Gordon, describing "economic reasoning" from the perspective of the so-called "Austrian school," reasserted that economics is a deductive science—proceeding from generalities and "self-evident" premises—and overtly rejected the insistence that economic claims should "be subject to test" by the facts (2000: 22).

Most economists are not so averse to facts and empirical research, and indeed economics is rich in facts, gleaned from a range of sources. Again, economists can collect original data, but less of their information comes from experiments, surveys, and focus groups than from figures published by sources such as the United States Bureau of Labor Statistics, Department of Commerce, and Federal Reserve Board or, in the case of international data, the World Bank. Further, for the U.S., huge amounts of data are available through Resources for Economists on the Internet (www.rfe.org), the National Bureau of Economic Research, the Real-Time Data Research Center, and Quandl (www.quandl.com).

The fact that so much of economics deals with numbers leads to the third characteristic of the discipline—its mathematical nature and its attempt to derive laws and to formulate models. Economics is, unsurprisingly, the most quantitative of the social sciences, thereby resembling natural sciences. Economists process reams of numerical data and generate numerical analyses of that data. In fact, a special subdiscipline of *econometrics* concerns

> the development of statistical methods for estimating economic relationships, testing economic theories, and evaluating and implementing government and business policy. The most common application of econometrics is the forecasting of such important macroeconomic variables as interest rates, inflation rates, and gross domestic product.
> (Woolridge 2013: 1)

Francis Diebold adds that econometrics "must confront"—and is designed to confront—"the fact that economic data is not generated from well-designed experiments" (2015: 2) but from the messy real world.

Economists regularly perform sophisticated mathematical analyses of their data (indeed, "economics methods" books are largely constituted of statistical methods), and economics knowledge is commonly represented

Behavioral Economics: The Study of Real-World (Irrational?) Decision-Making

As we have seen, economics has an implicit—and often quite explicit—psychological model, in which human beings are rational, self-interested actors. Yet we cannot help but notice that human choices are not always self-interested (one of the greatest conundrums of economics, biology, and philosophy is "altruism," the willingness to risk or sacrifice oneself for another person) or rational. Dan Ariely is an advocate of another approach, called behavioral economics, which "does not assume that people are rational. Instead, behavioral economists start by figuring out how people actually behave, often in a controlled lab environment in which we can understand behavior better, and use this as a starting point for building our understanding of human nature" (danariely.com/tag/behavioral-economics-2). Whether the issue is consumer behavior, stock market investment, or national economic policy, people often make choices that mark the influence of other factors besides rationality or violate rationality completely. As an example, some citizens of Scotland are currently pushing for independence from the United Kingdom, even though evidence suggests that they would be economically worse off. Ariely's research shows, indeed, that people are frequently quite irrational in their decision-making, as in his aptly titled book *Predictably Irrational* (2008). The reasons for this not only irrational but *predictably* irrational behavior are many—conflicting values, intuitions, past experience, lack of information, inadequate processing of available information, weak mathematical or statistical skills, emotional appeals, and so on. In fact, Ariely claims that one basic problem with thinking about economic behavior in terms of the satisfaction of wants is that "most people don't know what they want unless they see it in context" (2008: 3), which means that our desires can be engineered in all sorts of subtle and unsubtle ways. Truly, isn't that what advertising is all about? Interestingly, there are now graduate schools that offer programs in behavioral economics (or even neuro-economics), including University of California-San Diego, New York University, Wharton School, and Harvard University.

as mathematical equations, like this statement of elasticity (ε), where P equals price, Q equals quantity, and x equals demand:

$$\varepsilon = \%\Delta Q / \%\Delta P \quad \text{or} \quad \frac{dx/x}{dp/p} = \frac{px'/(p)}{x(p)}$$

To be sure, economics equations can be much more elaborate than this. Many of these equations specify supposed economic "laws," such as the "law of demand" or the "law of supply," which are held as universally valid.

The highest form of economics knowledge is theories and models. Models especially represent or depict the workings of the economy, sometimes expressed in words, numbers, or graphic form (charts, tables, graphs, etc.). Two basic economic models, according to Mankiw, are the "circular-flow diagram" or "a visual model of the economy that shows how dollars flow through markets among households and firms" and the "production possibilities frontier" or "a graph that shows the combinations of output that the economy can possibly produce given the available factors of production and the available production technology" (2000: 25).

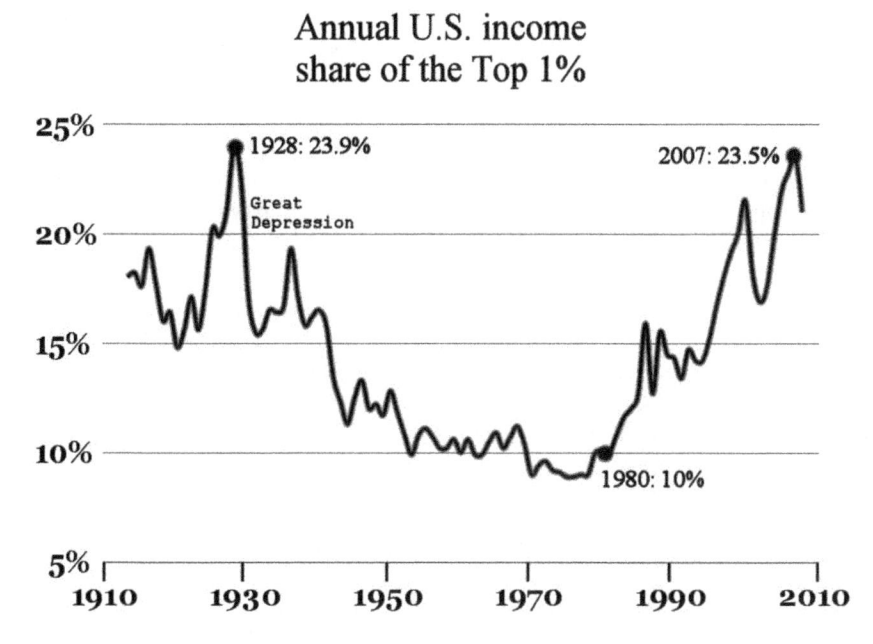

Figure 4.3 A chart demonstrating increases in American income inequality over the past decades

Source: Wikipedia.

Economics as a Policy Science

In addition to the division into micro and macro, economics has long been a dual theoretical and practical—even *descriptive and normative*—discipline. Like political science, economics was applied to practical matters of governance long before it evolved into a modern quantitative and statistical profession. Today, economic theories and econometric modeling are widely and consistently used not only by government agencies but corporations, financial institutions, consulting firms, and many other entities. An entire allied field of business research uses economic methods to plan, monitor, and evaluate production and sales as well as the internal operation of companies.

Economic knowledge holds out the possibility of prediction, as theories and models should yield forecasts of economic conditions, *ceteris paribus*. Curiously, economics shares this ambition with a non-social science, meteorology, which likewise applies models and current data to make forecasts. Both also share the problem of the complexity of many variables dynamically changing at the same time, as well as the limitation of using past trends to predict future events—when, whether from global climate change or historical/institutional factors, all things *are not* the same as in past circumstances, which explains why the forecasts of both fields are notoriously unreliable. The greatest contrast with meteorology is that economic theories, models, and predictions augur the potential for management of the economy, particularly because, as Thomas Piketty argues, economic outcomes are the product of social factors such as policies and regulations as much as of purely "economic" forces.

Nowhere is economics more present, or more important, than in government, where leaders look for guidance on economic policies and where economics can "suggest how distinct changes in laws, rules and other governmental interventions in markets will affect people, and in some cases, one can draw a conclusion that a rule change is, on balance socially beneficial" (McAfee 2006: 1). Some economists have gone so far as to assert that "economics is basically a normative policy science adorning itself with the fig leaf of hard-headed positivism" (Blaug 1992: 238). In the twentieth century, economics became a primary tool of state, and economic theories—although shifting and contradictory ones—have shaped economic policy and economic performance in the United States and globally.

John Maynard Keynes and the Role of Government in the Economy

New and traumatic experiences force people to rethink their definitions and assumptions, and the Great Depression of the 1930s was such a trauma. The cycle of boom and bust appears to be endemic to capitalism, as individuals and businesses chase opportunities and flee threats. However, in the

---

Economists Prevent a Depression?

During the Great Recession beginning in 2008, economists like U.S. Secretary of the Treasury Henry Paulson (MBA, Harvard Business School) and Chairman of the Federal Reserve Ben Bernanke (Ph.D., economics, Massachusetts Institute of Technology) stepped in to stabilize the American economy through such policies as "quantitative easing" (printing money to buy troubled assets) and historically low interest rates (effectively zero). Many analysts applaud such people and institutions for preventing a complete collapse of the housing and general credit markets that could have eventuated in another Great Depression (although others blame previous policies and practices, like risky home loans and complex "derivatives," for contributing to the crisis in the first place). In December 2015, for the first time in almost a decade, the Federal Reserve raised interest rates and then only by a modest 0.25 percent, and the Federal Reserve carefully weighs predictions of interest rates, inflation, and unemployment in its decisions. Overall, Gregory Mankiw says that governments face five debates about macroeconomic policy: (a) Should monetary and fiscal policymakers try to stabilize the economy? (b) Should monetary policy be made by rule rather than by discretion? (c) Should the central bank aim for zero inflation? (d) Should the government balance its budget? (e) Should the tax laws be reformed to encourage saving? (2009: 414–25).

---

bust that began in 1929, unemployment hit extreme levels and stubbornly persisted for years. Policymakers had neither the theories nor the institutions to respond to the problem.

In 1936, John Maynard Keynes published *The General Theory of Employment, Interest, and Money*, which became the guiding model of the American economy for a couple of generations. In it, he directly attacked the neoclassical theory of wages and employment, which claimed, in Keynes' view, that wages were equal to the value of labor and that employment was tied to the marginal utility of wages. In simpler terms, neoclassical economics held that unemployment was either voluntary (because wages were not high enough to induce people to work) or "frictional" (because people were changing jobs or searching for work). What they failed to account for, Keynes insisted, was "involuntary unemployment."

Reducing unemployment was understandably a crucial matter to societies in the 1930s. However, according to an old (and recently revived) principle called Say's Law, attributed to Jean-Baptiste Say (1767–1832), the supply of a commodity creates a demand for that commodity. Keynes and others saw this as unlikely, since people without incomes cannot demand goods, no matter how much is in supply. Keynes introduced the concept of "aggregate demand" to explain and remedy the lingering economic depression. Aggregate demand is simply the total demand for goods and services in a society, at their current price. Keynes argued that increasing the aggregate demand was the key to ending the Depression and to regulating the economy more generally. But increasing aggregate demand meant putting more money in the hands of potential consumers, or turning the government itself into a consumer, or both. Enabling more consumers to demand required steps like creating jobs, raising wages (or setting a minimum wage), providing direct aid to the unemployed, and/or educating and training the work force for employment. Or the government could literally buy goods and services (for example, food) and distribute them to citizens, or even hire those citizens itself. Either way, the government would be more deeply involved in the economy, and government spending would carry society through periods of high unemployment or other economic crises. In a word, government would be the consumer of last resort.

Supply-Side Economics and the Return of Economic Conservatism

While Keynesian economics, calling for an active, spending government, won the day in the 1930s and dominated American economic policy for decades, it was not without opponents at the time or since. In the 1930s one of the main rivals of Keynesian thinking was Friedrich Hayek (1899–1992), associated with the so-called "Austrian school." Winner of the 1974 Nobel Prize in economics (along with Gunnar Myrdal), Hayek disbelieved in big government and especially in socialist or centrally-planned economies. In books like his 1944 *The Road to Serfdom*, his 1945 *The Use of Knowledge in Society*, and his 1988 *The Fatal Conceit*, he recommended a more classical, Adam Smith-style approach to economics, in which the market, through prices or "price signals," organizes efficient economic decision-making. Prices were the "information" that an economy generated, and human beings were well-advised to pay attention to and use this knowledge and not to interfere with it. Indeed, from his perspective the market or "free price system" was virtually a force of nature, "the result of human action but not of human design."

Just as the market was self-organizing, so attempts to impose ethical or moral principles on it were ill-conceived. The goal of an economy was not, he contended, justice (or injustice), and in his revealingly-named *The Mirage of Social Justice* he defended the position that "social justice is an empty phrase with no determinable content" (1976: 133). Surprisingly, he was not averse to all forms of social welfare and is known to have supported universal health care and unemployment insurance; at the same time, he recommended abolishing national currencies and allowing corporations to print their own money. (One wonders how he would have felt about a non-state currency like Bitcoin.)

Hayek taught at the University of Chicago from 1950 to 1962, where a group of economists known as the "Chicago school" (or less formally, the "Chicago boys") congregated. Among its leading figures was Milton Friedman (1912–2006), who published his own book *Capitalism and Freedom* in the year that his mentor left the university. In that volume, he overtly jousted with John F. Kennedy's famous line, "Ask not what your country can do for you, ask what you can do for your country," endorsing alternatively that a "free man" should ask neither but instead "'What can I and my compatriots do through government' to help us discharge our individual responsibilities, to achieve our several goals and purposes, and above all, to protect our freedom?" (1962: 10). In order to secure this freedom, Friedman asserted first that "the scope of government must be limited" (10) and second "that government power must be dispersed. If government is to exercise power, better in the county than in the state, better in the state than in Washington" (11).

In 1976, like his predecessor, he won the Nobel Prize, by which time he had transformed from an academic to a policymaker, advising Richard Nixon's presidency. But the United States was not yet ready for an experiment in Hayek/Friedman-style economic policy, so the "Chicago school" first got an opportunity to implement its ideas in Latin America, as in Chile in 1973. Naomi Klein characterized Friedman's plan as "shock therapy" to the Chilean economy and society: "Chile's economy contracted by 15 percent and unemployment—only 3 percent under [previous leader Salvador] Allende—reached 20 percent, a rate unheard of in Chile at the time" (2007: 101). This was necessary pain, in the economists' opinion, to wring out the "distortion" to the market and economy caused by socialist and statist policies.

When political conservatives like Margaret Thatcher and Ronald Reagan were elected to office in the United Kingdom and the United States, respectively, Chicago school or "supply-side" economics were introduced to those countries. On the argument that big government, redistributive taxation, and the welfare state distorted the economy and threatened individuals' freedom and self-responsibility, a battery of initiatives was undertaken that continues to inform American and global politics and economics, including tax reduction, deregulation, privatization, and the dismantling of social programs (with the vivid but much-resisted exception of Barack Obama's Affordable Care Act).

One product of the early supply-side era ("supply-side" economics claiming that freeing up the productive capacity of businesses would create jobs and wealth, rather than worrying about Keynes' demand-side or the poor workers themselves) was the so-called Laffer curve. Attributed to Arthur Laffer, a member of Reagan's Economic Policy Advisory Board

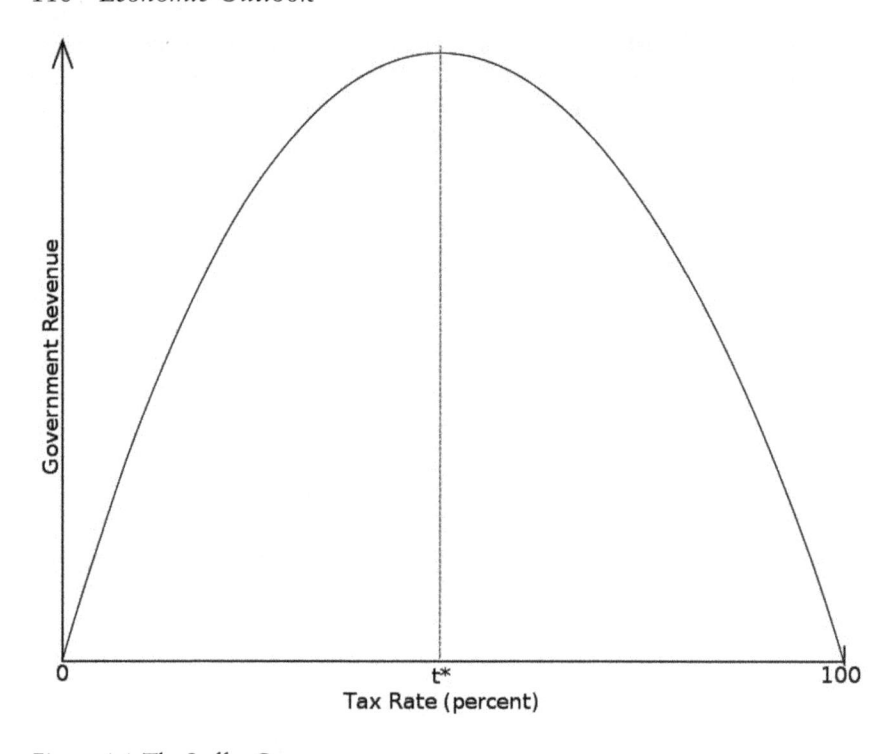

Figure 4.4 The Laffer Curve
Source: Vanessaezekowitz at en.wikipedia.

(although Laffer did not personally take credit for inventing the diagram), the curve allegedly depicted the relationship between tax rates and government revenues. Parabolic in shape, the idea was that if tax rates were too low, the government of course collected little or no revenue; however, if tax rates were too high, they would discourage business and entrepreneurship and also negatively impact revenues. There was then a sweet spot for taxes, although Laffer and others never determined precisely where that spot lies. But as a quantitative statement of the principle, Christina Romer and David Romer (2007) calculated that for every 1 percent increase in taxes there would be a 3 percent decrease in gross domestic product (GDP), suggesting that the ideal tax rate is 33 percent or less.

Disciplinary Study #3: Economics of Terrorism

At first glance, many people might doubt that there can be a meaningful economic analysis of terrorism. At best, terrorism is a psychological (see Chapter 5) or social (see Chapter 6) phenomenon, and at worst it is pure pathology or irrationality, driven by fanatical religious commitments but not rational economic calculation. If there is a conventional economic association with terrorism, it is that terrorists (and other revolutionaries) are motivated by poverty and misery. However, as research has strongly suggested, "terrorism seems unrelated to economic deprivation" (Gold 2004: 7), and indeed it is seldom the poorest individuals who engage in terrorist acts but rather middle-class and educated people.

As David Gold reasoned, we can inquire into the "direct role of economic factors" related to terrorism, but we can and must also "look at how terrorism affects behavior, how economic concepts can help us understand the behavior of individuals and organizations that employ the tools of violent terrorism, and how economic concepts can help fashion measures to combat terrorism" (1). After all, whatever else it is, terrorism is a decision.

Accordingly, there are a number of economic angles from which to approach terrorism. These include:

- economic causes or preconditions
- economic organization
- economic costs
- economic responses (counter-terrorism).

The first step is to imagine the "two main actors, terrorists and antiterrorists, as *economic agents*, each maximizing their objective function (or utility) subject to constraints" (Intriligator 2010: 1, emphasis in the original). We can then conceive of terrorism in terms of supply and demand; from this perspective, "the supply of terrorists acts as a perverse type of 'good' from the vantage point of the terrorists" (2). The variables that increase the supply of terrorists are thus essential to understand, and among these variables Michael Intriligator, like the political scientists in the previous chapter, emphasizes "humiliation and retribution for past actions" (3). In short, according to Louise Richardson (2006), terrorists are motivated by three R's: revenge, renown, and reaction (that is, the desire to provoke a reaction, either to resolve their complaints or to stimulate more terrorist acts).

The economic organization of terrorism covers a variety of issues. Most obviously, terrorist acts must be planned and financed. Terrorist organizations need cash for training, weapons, and operations, and economists can treat such organizations as "firms" engaged in the "business" of terrorism. Terrorists often receive financial support from the surrounding population, from citizens overseas, or from governments. Surprisingly to many observers, terrorist organizations also sometimes *provide* economic support and social services to the surrounding population. Groups like Hamas in Palestine, the Irish Republican Army in Northern Ireland, or the Tamil Tigers (Liberation Tigers of Tamil Eelam) in Sri Lanka actually carried or carry out education, health care, and welfare work, serving "as an unofficial charity and social work system" and "helping the poor, taking care of widows, and providing a safety net for the disadvantaged" (Moghaddam 2006: 3), especially when the state is too weak or corrupt to do so.

Another organizational issue is decision-making, which raises the question of the "rationality" of terrorism. Unfortunately, for aggrieved groups without the capacity to confront domestic or foreign states directly, terrorism is often a sadly rational course, especially because terrorism can have an impact far greater than the material or human cost of perpetrating it. To be sure, the decision to conduct terrorism, especially in the case of suicide terrorism, involves some "extreme tradeoffs" (Llussa and Tavares 2006: 191) that appear to reflect "a 'non-rational' evaluation of risk" (193). Certainly we can think of terrorism in terms of "opportunity cost," that is, all of the things that the terrorist gives up in exchange for participating in such acts (including his/her very life), but on the other hand many economic choices seem irrational to the outsider and are influenced by non-economic considerations such as nationalism, pride, or sacrifice for the group or cause. When religion is in the mix, terrorists may believe that the ultimate rewards (including eternal life and praise as a martyr) are far greater than the personal cost.

Of course, the costs of terrorism (and of counterterrorism; see later) can become too great to bear, and groups may lose the taste for terrorism, leading to what Intriligator calls the "business cycle" of terrorism.

> When enforcement is low, terrorists have lesser costs associated with terrorist activities, so terrorist attacks increase. In response, governments increase the level of their enforcement, increasing the costs to terrorists and effectively decreasing the level of terrorist activities. After the frequency of terrorist attacks declines, governments have less incentive to invest in enforcement and the cycle repeats itself. . . . The subsequent "lull" in terrorist attacks is then a period when terrorist organizations replenish their resources.
>
> (4)

Finally, in regard to organization, while economic deprivation does not seem to cause terrorism, it can increase the attractiveness of such action and improve the "quality" of the pool of potential terrorists. Efraim Benmelech and Claude Berrebi have published a series of articles on the relationship between economic conditions and the skills of terrorists. Writing with Esteban Klor, for example, they conclude that "Poor economic conditions may lead more able and better-educated individuals to participate in terror attacks, allowing terror organizations to send better-qualified terrorists to more complex, higher-impact terror missions" (Benmelech, Berrebi and Klor 2012: 113). Obviously, poverty and deprivation "dampen individuals' opportunities in the labor force and, as a consequence, lower the opportunity cost of their participation in terror activities" (118). Consequently, terrorist recruits bring more "human capital"—education, skill, and maturity—to the task than if only young and uneducated individuals joined the ranks. The really dangerous fact, as they discover in another article, is that high-quality terrorists are much more effective: examining attacks against Israel, Benmelech and Berrebi find that older and more educated terrorists are more "productive": "An educated suicide bomber kills roughly four to six more people when he attacks a large city target compared to an uneducated suicide bomber" (2007: 234)—and has a better chance of carrying out his mission without getting caught.

We have said some things about the cost to terrorists, but victims also pay a cost, which is the whole point of terrorism. Most immediately, there is the cost of lost lives and physical resources such as buildings. There is also the cost of rebuilding. Further, there is an effect, often quite intended by the terrorists, on the wider economy of the targeted society: after an attack, common reactions are a drop in the stock market and decreases in consumption, investment, and economic growth. Llussa and Tavares calculate that terrorist acts "do reduce economic growth," although the "direct cost to output seems to be relatively low and short-term" (2006: 194). Much more lasting, and costly, are typical responses to terrorism, such as war or the intensification of security measures including guarding sensitive facilities and screening people as they pass through airports or across borders. Tightening of travel and visa restrictions can have a negative impact on the economy.

Lastly, counterterrorism measures can themselves take economic form, such as sanctions, boycotts, and the freezing of terrorist assets. Indeed, Intriligator reasons that "the most valuable approach to defeating terrorism is that of *denying resources to the terrorists*" (2010: 5, emphasis in the original). Likewise, multiple analyses have determined that large military responses and heightened security in the homeland are not effective or efficient reactions to terrorism. Intriligator insists that "it is almost impossible to raise the cost of these acts by protecting assets at risk given their numbers and the technical difficulty of providing such protection" (5), and such actions do nothing to address the supply side of terrorism. Further, war abroad and security at home impose opportunity costs on the victims. David Gold has added that one worthwhile strategy could be foreign aid spending, to assist the economic development in the countries where terrorists originate, so that terrorists have fewer grievances and more opportunity to pursue life-courses other than terrorism.

5 Psychological Careers

What is a person, and what or where is an individual's "personality"? According to Joseph LeDoux, a psychologist and member of the Center for Neural Science at New York University, the personality or self, "the essence of who you are, reflects patterns of interconnectivity between neurons in your brain" (2002: 2). In fact, his book is titled *Synaptic Self: How Our Brains Become Who We Are*. The brain is more than the storage place of memory and learning; it is a product of memory and learning, due to the remarkable "plasticity" of the brain or "the ability of neurons to be altered by experience" (137). Brains literally change—grow and rewire—as a result of experience, which bridges the gap in the old nature-and-nurture debate: inheritance and experience "are simply two different ways of making deposits in the brain's synaptic ledger" (5). All of our psychological capacities are, in one way or another, embrained—with profound consequences for knowledge and action. Memory, for instance, is "a reconstruction of facts and experiences on the basis of the way they were stored, not as they actually occurred. And it's a reconstruction by a brain that is different from the one that formed the memory" (97). Motivation or what drives us to act is "neural activity that guides us toward goals, outcomes that we desire and for which we will exert effort, or ones that we dread and will exert effort to prevent, escape from, or avoid" (236). But because the brain is a physical organ, and experience comes through our bodily senses (and interaction with other people), the resultant self or personality is "the totality" of a person, "physically, biologically, psychologically, socially, and culturally. . . . It includes things that we know and things that we do not know, things that others know about us that we do not realize" (31).

Psychology, defined as "the scientific study of behavior and mental processes" (Gleitman, Gross, and Reisberg 2011: 1), shares many of the same questions with other social sciences; even economics (see Chapter 4) and anthropology (see Chapter 7) have manifest interests in mental processes. However, as LeDoux's work illustrates, psychology has the deepest ties with—sometimes overlapping with—natural science, from biology to chemistry (e.g. psychopharmacology) and physics. Many psychologists or subfields of psychology are intimately involved in medical/physiological subjects and research, and in at least some universities psychology is not even housed among the social sciences, classified instead as a behavioral science or in some cases a natural science.

Psychology is also probably the most diverse of the social sciences, and we introduce the concept of "careers" to capture the multiplicity of psychology (which we will also find in anthropology). We can think of psychology as a collection of careers generally oriented around the "brain" and/or the "mind"—or what is sometimes called the mind/brain—although these subdisciplines are often so different in theory, method, and terminology that they result in separate jobs, journals, and professional organizations. Also, as with political science and economics, only more so, psychology is not only studied but applied and practiced: "psychologists don't merely seek to *understand* . . .; they are also interested in *change*: how to help people become happier or better adjusted, how to help children learn more effectively, or how to help them get along better with their peers"(1). This therapeutic motive psychology also derives from its medical origins.

The Ancient Roots of Psychology

"It is common these days to begin a history of psychology at the point where psychology became a separate science," wrote B. R. Hergenhahn in his voluminous historical study of the discipline; but as we have come to appreciate, this perspective "is unsatisfactory for two reasons":

(1) It ignores the vast philosophical heritage that molded psychology into the type of science that it eventually became, and (2) it omits important aspects of psychology that are outside the realm of science. Although it is true that since the mid-19th century psychology has, to a large extent, embraced the scientific method, many highly influential psychologists did not feel compelled to follow the dictates of the scientific method.

(2000: 2)

Indeed, glancing back at the previous chapters of this book (and ahead at the upcoming chapters) shows that all of the social sciences—and not only the social sciences—have had a profound and fundamental interest in what we might more generally call "human nature." Economics especially operates with an implicit, if rudimentary, notion of how humans think and choose.

The word "psychology" can be defined today as the study of the mind or the personality, but its Greek origin suggests something quite different and significantly less scientific: *psyche* most immediately meant "breath" and *psychein* meant "to breathe or blow," *breath associated (as in many cultures and languages) with life*. Worse, breath or life was personified by the Greek goddess Psyche, the goddess of "soul" and wife of Eros, the god of love.

Psyche then has always been (and continues to be) a complex word and concept. It refers to something interior to the individual and something that animates the individual, and as the goddess implies, this something has been conceived as either "mind" or "soul" or both. In the epic poetry of Homer (see Chapter 2), a term that often appears is *nous*, referring to mental processes of humans (and gods), that is, their interior thoughts and feelings in contrast to their public words and actions.

In early philosophical speculation, *nous* tended to convey the notion of "thought" or "reason" as opposed either to sense-perception or divine revelation. Anaxagoras, writing a century before Plato, opined that *nous* was "intelligence," but also an almost supernatural force that created order out of chaos. Heraclitus distinguished between the things that we think we know, or that we are taught, and genuine *nous*, asserting that "much learning does not teach *nous*."

As we have seen, Plato was ultimately interested in what humans could know, in "truth" which was assumed to be beautiful, virtuous (the "good"), and eternal. His famous Parable of the Cave contrasted popular or conventional knowledge, which was mere shadow and illusion for him, to real knowledge, which could not be perceived with the senses but only grasped with the mind. Lower knowledge consisted of the things that we could sense, as well as the things that we imagine or believe; this was the world of appearances. But the higher and truer world, the world of *ideas*, was not available to the senses. From the position of *idealism*, only ideas were real, and in Plato's extreme idealism the physical world is a poor pale copy of perfect Ideas or Forms, which Ideas or Forms exist independent from matter in a separate realm or dimension approachable by the (philosophically trained) mind or intellect. This mind/body or idea/body dualism has serious repercussions throughout Western history.

According to Hergenhahn, Aristotle "was the first philosopher to extensively treat many topics that were later to become part of psychology. In his vast writings he covered memory, sensation, sleep, dreams, geriatrics, and learning" (2000: 41). In fact, his treatise *De Anima* (On the Soul) has been recognized as the first work of psychology, although he still uses semi-religious terminology to name his subject. Aristotle was also more "scientific" or empirical than Plato, insisting that knowledge does not originate in disembodied mental or intellectual activity but in studying nature with our senses as well as our mind. (Even so, he proposed that the heart was the mental organ, whereas Plato knew—or correctly guessed—that the brain was where mentation occurred.)

As his book title shows, Aristotle did not distinguish "mind" from "soul," but he did allow for different kinds of souls, including a "vegetative" soul for plants, a "sensitive" soul for animals (which could feel pleasure or pain and could remember), and a "rational" soul for humans. Here, "soul" seems to mean something more like "life," and the complicated word *anima* itself does not so much translate to "soul" as to "movement" or that which animates a body and makes it alive.

Although Aristotle emphasized sense perception as the basis of knowledge (in a way that Plato rejected), it was merely the first step or raw material in knowing. "Common sense" then processed and synthesized these isolated sense-perceptions, and "passive reason" applied this synthesized knowledge to the world. But it was "active reason" that provided abstract and general knowledge—knowledge of laws, principles, and "essences"—from the lower forms or sources of information.

If Joseph Schumpeter (see Chapter 4) had written a history of psychology instead of or in addition to economics, no doubt he would have dismissed the medieval era as a millennium of no progress, or even of regress, in psychological speculation. To be sure, those centuries mostly consisted of rehearsals of and commentaries on Aristotle, blended with Christian theology. Central to medieval European/Christian psychology were the mind/body dualism already present in Greek thought and the association of the concept of *nous* with Christian divinity.

The results were often quite unusual. For instance, an early Christian scholar named Valentius (c. 100–160 CE) offered the unorthodox and heretical notion that *Nous*, now a proper name, was actually a being or spirit formed as an emanation from God (and a male one at that, with his female counterpart *Aletheia* or Truth). The great Augustine posited the more orthodox doctrine that *nous* (along with Plato's "Good") was God or one of God's qualities or aspects.

The Evolution of "Mind"

Is it possible that the ancients did not have "mind" or consciousness in the modern sense of the term—that "mind" is indeed a modern phenomenon? This was the radical thesis of psychologist Julian Jaynes (1976), who claimed that "mind" is a metaphor for some interior space (understood by contemporary Western culture as "inside the head") where the self, the ego, the "I" resides. Sometimes this "I" is conceived as a passive spectator, almost a person within a person, that records events outside the head, in the "real world." Sometimes this "I" is conceived as an active participant in creating experience (see the discussion of Kant later). More profoundly, Jaynes argued that until fairly recently in human history, the brain was not a fully integrated organ. Its functions were disconnected in two relatively independent systems, which he called the "bicameral" mind, such that one part of the brain experienced the activities of the other part almost as if they were a separate person. Hence, he asserted that what people experienced as the voice or guidance of gods was actually their own brain talking to itself. He presented a deep psychohistory of humanity to propose that Mesopotamian citizens four or five thousand years ago heard the god-in-their-head speaking through statues, with which they interacted ritually to make the idols speak—literally rituals to "open their mouths." As recently as the early Greek era, Jaynes contended that humans did not yet have a distinct and completely "mental" idea of mind. For instance, in Homer's *Iliad*, he believed that there "is in general no consciousness" and "no words for consciousness or mental acts" (1976: 69). Instead, words that we today see as mental were quite physical for the early Greeks: "The word *psyche*, which later means soul or conscious mind, is in most instances life-substances, such as blood or breath: a dying warrior bleeds out his *psyche* onto the ground or breathes it out in his last gasp. The *thumos*, which later comes to mean something like emotional soul, is simply motion or agitation. When a man stops moving, the *thumos* leaves his limbs. But it is also somehow like an organ itself" (69). Likewise, *phrenes*, which gives us the latter-day practice of phrenology (see later) "objectively referred to the lungs" and was "associated with *phrasis* or speech" (263), and *kradie* meant "heart" (265), which is still a common metaphor for courage or emotion. *Nous* simply indicated vision (from *noeo* for "to see/perceive"). Jaynes' conclusions are controversial, but if he is even a little correct, we must be very careful not to assume that humans in all times and places have thought about or experienced "mental" activity in the same way.

Eastern Christianity, which evolved separately from the Roman Catholic version, also picked up the Greek term *nous*, understanding the *nous* of humans as the "eye of the heart or soul" or "the mind of the heart"; it was the part of humanity that was created in God's image. Thus, *noesis* or this sort of "soul-knowing" was often equated to faith (*pistis*). The angels too had *nous*, but humans combined sense perception and reason (including logical and mathematical reasoning) with *nous*.

Early Modern Thought on Knowledge and Human Nature

It should be apparent that one of the enduring questions in the history of human thought has been precisely the nature of human thought: what can we know and how can we know it? This is the philosophical problem of *epistemology*, the study of the nature and possibility of knowledge.

During most of the pre-modern era, two perspectives of human knowledge and human nature vied for supremacy. On the one side, most closely aligned with Plato, was idealism, also known as rationalism, which held that knowledge is independent of, even distorted by, sense experience; knowledge is pure disembodied mentation, the mind's piercing through the veil of material reality. In the most radical interpretation (sometimes advocated by Plato), knowledge is already present in the mind, only requiring a skilled teacher (like himself) to pull it out; this position is called *innatism*, because knowledge is supposedly innate, not learned. On the other side, more consistent with Aristotle (although beyond even his claims), was *empiricism*, which claimed that sense perception is the ultimate if not the only source of knowledge. To know is to perceive.

René Descartes: Humanity as a Thinking Thing

Early modern speculation on mind and knowledge commences with René Descartes (1596–1650), whose 1637 *Discourse on Method* and 1647 *Meditations on First Philosophy* (*Méditations metaphysiques* in the original French) were stirred by his anguish over what humans could know with certainty. He began with the observation that much traditional knowledge has proven to be false and that our senses are easily fooled. So the first step was a radical skepticism about knowledge: his maxim was to accept as true only that of which we can be absolutely certain. But what if anything is that?

His epic answer came in the second of his meditations, titled "The Nature of the Human Mind, and How It is Better Known than the Body." Here he discovered that, even if he thinks of himself as wrong or deluded, he nevertheless *thinks*. In the most famous of all philosophical statements, he declared *Cogito, ergo sum*, or "I think, therefore I am." It is impossible to think of oneself or one's knowledge without thinking; we can even imagine ourselves without a body but never without a mind. Therefore, thinking is the essence of being human. Taken still further, he argued (consistent with Platonic and Christian philosophy) that the body was nothing more than inert matter, a *res extensa* or "extended thing" (early-modern terminology for an object that occupies space), a mere machine. As such, the body is irrelevant for knowledge or humanity itself. A human is a *res cogitans*, a "thinking thing," and the only subject of which we can have knowledge is our own ideas or mental world.

In good Platonic style, in other words, Descartes took the process of thinking and turned it into a "substance" or thing. This left him with two major problems. First, how does "thinking stuff" interact with "physical stuff," for instance, how does my mind make my arm move? Second, how do we know that our thought—indeed, our very self—is real and not just an illusion or, worse, a deception perpetrated by an Evil Deceiver? The equivalent would be a cartoon or computer-generated character who thinks that s/he is alive and thinking. To solve this latter problem, Descartes snuck back in the Christian God, who can be trusted not to be an Evil Deceiver, and thus our thinking is safe.

Thomas Hobbes and the Nature of Man

It will be remembered from Chapter 3 that Thomas Hobbes opened his political thesis *Leviathan* with an analysis of human nature, in which Part One, Section One was "Of Sense" or the role of sense perception in knowledge. The "thoughts of man," he asserted, "are every one a representation or appearance of some quality, or other accident of a body without us, which is commonly called an object." In other words, our senses are the source of knowledge, and the human body is the locus of the senses. Further, all of the sense experiences we have are "but so many several motions of the matter, by which it presses our organs diversely." Further, human imagination is nothing more than "those things which have been formerly perceived by sense," and memory is the residue of these experiences. Imagination during sleep is dreaming. Finally, our sense perceptions can be connected together to create a "train of thought" or, by combining or compounding different perceptions we can create complex or fanciful ideas like a centaur, which is nothing but the idea of a man joined to the idea of a horse. But in the end "we have no imagination, whereof we have not formerly had sense."

John Locke and the Tabula Rasa

If Hobbes' philosophy represents basic empiricism, John Locke's is the zenith of the empirical standpoint. In his 1690 *An Essay Concerning Human Understanding*, which launches with a Bible quote, he inquired "into the original [sic], certainty, and extent of human knowledge, together with the grounds and degrees of belief, opinion, and assent" (1796: 1), illustrating that a theory of human knowledge is essential to an analysis of human social or political organization. Chapter One of Book One states flatly that there is no such thing as innate knowledge, the bedrock of idealism/rationalism. Worse still for theologians and moralists of his time (and ours), he denied the existence of innate moral principles.

Where then do human ideas originate? The answer is experience, either from sensation or reflection. Sensation, or sense perception, is the absolute ground of knowledge, from which we get ideas of "yellow, white, heat, cold, soft, hard, bitter, sweet, and all those which we call sensible qualities" (78). But the mind also reflects on these primitive, simple ideas, knowing its own contents and processes. Therefore, when we contemplate our immediate sense perceptions and their various "modes, combinations, and relations" in the mind, "we shall find to contain all our whole stock of ideas; and that we have nothing in our minds which did not come in one of these two ways" (79).

Locke's theory of mind has been famously symbolized by the metaphor of the *tabula rasa* or "blank slate." The mind at birth is blank or empty, and it is filled as experience writes on this board. Our ideas or knowledge are just the mental images of sense experiences, and the only way to construct more complex knowledge is through combining simple ideas into composite ones. In other words, as in his 1693 *Some Thoughts on Education*, Locke came down solidly on the "nurture" side of the nature/nature debate.

David Hume and the Limits of Empiricism

David Hume (1711–76) marks the apex and the endpoint of classical empiricism, because he explicitly reached its limits. In his 1739 *Treatise of Human Nature, Being an Attempt to Introduce the Experimental Method of Reasoning into Moral Subjects*, abbreviated in 1748 as *An Enquiry Concerning Human Understanding*, Hume first divided "moral philosophy, or the science of human nature," into two parts, one dealing with man-acting and the other with man-thinking. (Karl Marx more than any other pre-twentieth century scholar would emphasize the dimension of man-acting.) However, in the realm of man-thinking or human knowledge and ideas, Hume made a distinction between primary sense experience, or "impressions," and "ideas," which "never reach the *force and vivacity* of the original sentiment" (Section II, paragraph 11, emphasis added). In short, to reverse Plato completely, not only are ideas dependent on sense experience but they are *weaker* than that original experience. Perhaps the best example of Hume's point is to distinguish the *experience* of pain from the *idea* of pain.

For Hume as for Locke, what the mind initially knows, based on bodily sensations, are "simple ideas" like redness or coldness, but the mind can assemble these building blocks into "complex ideas" through the faculty of *imagination*. More powerfully, though, the mind can also process ideas to extract other, greater knowledge via three "principles of association," namely "Resemblance, Contiguity in time or place, and Cause or Effect."

But here Hume reached an impasse. If all knowledge derives from sense experience, and every sense experience is particular, how can we with confidence, let alone certainty, "know" things like cause and effect? That is, we might see one ball move across a billiard table, then collide with another ball, then the second ball begin to move. But we do not experience "cause." Even if we see the same demonstration again and again, all we perceive is "ball 1 moves," "balls collide," "ball 2 moves." We cannot perceive "ball 1 *caused* ball 2 to move," so we cannot "know" causation. At best, causation is a habit of thought—an extremely important one, indeed critical to science—but if we cannot "know" it, then our knowledge is seriously limited, if not completely dubious.

Immanuel Kant and the Categories of Mind

The work of Immanuel Kant (1724–1804) was a turning point in philosophy, as well as in psychology, anthropology, and geography. He himself claimed that Hume's dilemma shook him from his "dogmatic slumber" and spurred him to solve the problem of human knowledge. Kant's contribution can perhaps be summed up in these words: the mind is not a passive receptor of knowledge but an active constructor.

In his 1781 *Critique of Pure Reason* he unveiled his theory of "transcendental idealism," in which the senses and thus human thinking or reasoning only have access to perceivable phenomena, or what he called the "phenomenal." But, as Hume warned us, experience of the phenomenal does not include ideas like "cause." Kant intervened to insist that we know "cause" not from experience but from the mind itself. The mind, he answered, brings its own concepts or "categories" to experience; humans experience the world *through* these innate and universal mental categories. Among the innate "categories of understanding" were space and time, unity (oneness) and plurality (the many), necessity, existence, and of course causality. Knowledge in his model was ultimately *synthetic*: we do not and cannot know the world directly but only as a product of sense experience and mental functions. In short, no knowledge is innately stored in the mind, but knowledge is made possible in the first place because of the structure of the mind.

An important consequence of Kant's thinking is that some things are beyond the scope of human knowledge or reasoning. For instance, in his famous discussion of the "antinomies" or oppositions of thought, he showed that we could not reason our way to answers for questions such as whether the universe had a beginning or not, or whether humans have free will or not. Both sides of the debate could be equally well defended by reason. Further, since human knowledge was limited to the perceivable or phenomenal, we could not have knowledge of things beyond perception, including what he called "things-in-themselves." That is, we can see and touch a chair but only from some particular angle and only with our specific human senses and mental powers. We cannot transcend our senses to experience the chair-in-itself, the chair as it really is, the chair's inherent "chair-ness." Such things (if they exist) and the ideas of them were beyond phenomenal knowledge and belonged to the "noumenal" realm (the word derived, once again, from *nous*).

The upshot of Kant's revolutionary analysis was that knowledge is a construction, an interaction between the world and the human *mind and body*. But as such, human knowledge would always bump up against the limitations of our senses and the inherited mental and physical traits. So Kant would inspire his successors to explore the capabilities of the senses and the features of this synthesizing mind.

The Birth of Scientific Psychology from Nineteenth Century Medicine and Physiology

As the 1700s gave way to the 1800s, the philosophy of mind began to spawn a science of mind, linking mental activity to brain—and even more specifically, neural—activity. A key to this new direction was the discovery and initial study of electricity in the late 1700s. Then in 1801 two pioneers of scientific psychology were born—Gustav Fechner (1801–87) and Johannes Müller (1801–58).

Already before these men and others did their crucial work, Charles Bell and François Magendie had independently explained some of the functioning of nerves, particularly that some nerves controlled motor functions or movement while other nerves carried sensory information. In 1811 Bell published his *Idea of a New Anatomy of the Brain* and in 1830 his *The Nervous System of the Human Body*. Between those two books Magendie published his own research on nerve activity in animals.

Johannes Müller became the first professor of physiology at the University of Berlin in 1833, which, as Hergenhahn stressed, "marked the acceptance of physiology as a science" (2000: 207). Müller's investigations revealed that each kind of nerve fiber responded to stimulation in its own particular way, putting to rest once and for all the pre-modern notion that "tiny copies of physical objects go through the sensory receptors, along the nerves, and to the brain, causing an image of the object. According to this old view, any sensory nerve could convey any sensory information to the brain" (207). Instead, in a dramatic breakthrough in understanding, he and his students pronounced that "if we could cut and cross the visual and auditory nerves, we would hear with our eyes and see with our ears" (207).

Even more profoundly, and illustrating once again the prestige of natural science (especially physics), Gustav Fechner proposed a "psychophysics" as in his 1860 *Elements of Psychophysics*. Trained as a physicist and chemist, he had the earlier insight that "mind and body are but two aspects of a fundamental unity" (Watson 1978: 241). Researching vision, hearing, and touch, he went so far as to propose a mathematical relationship between the intensity of a stimulus and the intensity of a sensation; known as the Weber-Fechner law, it states that perception or sensation (the feeling of a stimulation) increases as the natural logarithm of the strength of the stimulation.

> While Fechner's scientific work would inspire many successors, he was still inspired himself by older philosophical and theological questions, namely "the nature of the relationship between the spiritual and material worlds" (Watson 1978: 242), and he wrote on spiritual and aesthetic subjects as well as scientific psychology.

Many other scientists contributed to the nineteenth-century formulation of physiological psychology. Hermann von Helmholtz (1821–94) was significant not only for refining the understanding of how nerves operate—for instance, that there is a measurable speed at which nerve signals travel—but also for discovering the adaptable and plastic nature of perception. In one clever experiment,

> Helmholtz had subjects wear lenses that displace the visual field several inches to the right or left. At first, the subjects would make mistakes in reaching for objects; but after several minutes *perceptual adaptation* occurred, and even while wearing the glasses, the subjects could again interact accurately with the environment. When the glasses were removed, the subjects again made mistakes for a short time but soon recovered.
>
> (Hergenhahn 2000: 209)

More importantly still, he subjected Kant's philosophy to a scientific revision. "One by one, Helmholtz took the supposed innate categories of thought Kant had proposed and showed how they were derived from experience" (Hergenhahn 2000: 209). That is, Kant's categories *seemed* innate and universal because (virtually) all humans acquired and possessed them in the same way. But this alleged universalism was an achieved capability, not an inherited one.

Also vital for classic physiological psychology was the work of Paul Broca (1824–80), whose intellectual breakthrough was to associate a behavior disorder with a specific location in the brain. He observed that individuals with injuries to a certain part of the brain exhibited a characteristic speech pathology, later labelled "Broca's aphasia," which was caused by damage

---

The Value of Phineas Gage's Brain

If one man's brain is more valuable to psychological science than any other, it might be that of Phineas Gage, who suffered frightening brain trauma during a railroad accident in 1848, when an iron rod penetrated his face and exited through the top of his head. Miraculously, he was not killed, but he was changed. Friends and physicians, like Dr. John Harlow, reported that he became "fitful, irreverent," obscene, "obstinate, yet capricious and vacillating." In other words, very specific personality alterations were attributed to very specific brain injuries. While subsequent research has called into question some of the grander claims, insisting that Gage's symptoms were subject to exaggeration and distortion, his case was crucial for the emerging notion that psychological functions—even personality traits—were localized to the specific regions of the brain.

---

to the section of the frontal lobe (usually on the left side near the parietal lobe) named "Broca's area" in his honor.

Localization of function, along with brain plasticity or the ability of the brain to grow and change in response to experience, has become an accepted aspect of neuro-psychology today, but this does not mean that the idea has been exempt from excesses and pseudo-scientific uses. One example is phrenology, a concept that goes back at least to Franz Gall's 1808 assertion that brain physiology—literally manifested as tangible shapes on the skull—can be interpreted to reveal personality traits. As depicted in Figure 5.1, phrenologists thought that they could actually map the skull, and the underlying brain, ascribing such amorphous features as cautiousness or self-esteem to local spots on/in the head. Such simple one-to-one associations between personality and macro-physiology are generally dismissed today—along with notions that beady eyes or receding chins indicate criminality.

Wilhelm Wundt and Laboratory Psychology

Given the advances in scientific thinking on mental/psychological questions, it was only a matter of time until a psychologist would adopt the classic scientific method of laboratory experimentation. This honor usually goes to Wilhelm Wundt (1832–1920), who began conceiving an experimental psychology as early as 1862. With his so-called "thought-meter," he claimed to be able to determine "that humans could attend to only one thought at a time and that it takes about 1/10 of a second to shift from one thought

Phre-nol'o-gy (-nŏl'ȯ-jў̆), *n.* [Gr. φρήν, φρενός + *-logy.*] **1.** Science of the special functions of the several parts of the brain, or of the supposed connection between the faculties of the mind and organs in the brain. **2.** Physiological hypothesis that mental faculties, and traits of character, are shown on the surface of the head or skull; craniology. — **Phre-nol'o-gist,** *n.* — **Phren'o-log'ic** (frĕn'ȯ-lŏj'ĭk), **Phren'o-log'ic-al,** *a.*

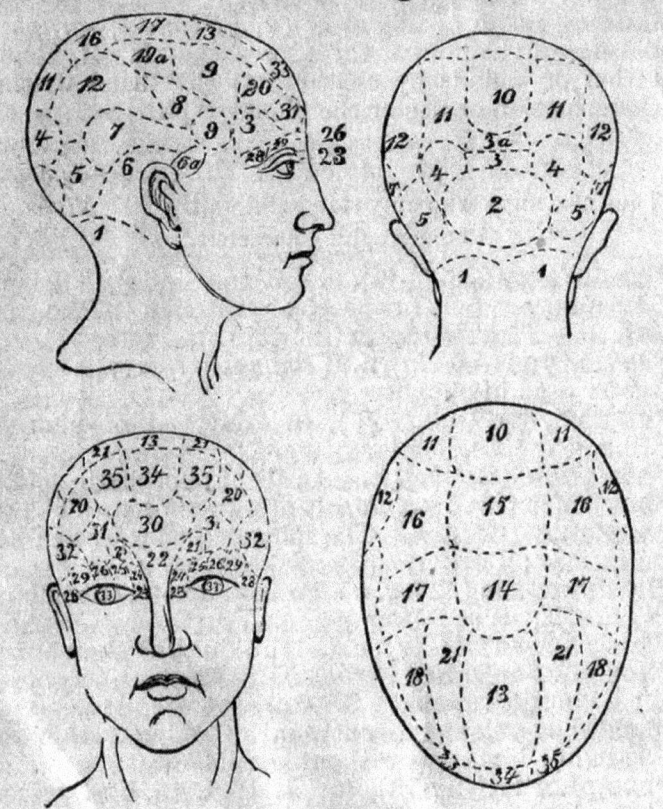

A Chart of Phrenology.

1 Amativeness : 2 Philoprogenitiveness ; 3 Concentrativeness ; 3 *a* Inhabitiveness ; 4 Adhesiveness ; 5 Combativeness ; 6 Destructiveness ; 6 *a* Alimentiveness ; 7 Secretiveness ; 8 Acquisitiveness ; 9 Constructiveness ; 10 Self-esteem ; 11 Love of Approbation ; 12 Cautiousness ; 13 Benevolence ; 14 Veneration ; 15 Firmness ; 16 Conscientiousness ; 17 Hope ; 18 Wonder ; 19 Ideality ; 19 *a* (Not determined) ; 20 Wit ; 21 Imitation ; 22 Individuality ; 23 Form ; 24 Size ; 25 Weight ; 26 Coloring ; 27 Locality ; 28 Number ; 29 Order ; 30 Eventuality ; 31 Time ; 32 Tune ; 33 Language ; 34 Comparison ; 35 Causality. [Some raise the number of organs to forty-three.]

Figure 5.1 Phrenological Chart, 1895

Source: Webster's Dictionary, public domain, Wikicommons.

to another" (Hergenhahn 2000: 230). In such writings as his 1862 *Contributions to the Theory of Sense Perception*, Wundt

> enunciated the need for a new field of experimental psychology that would uncover the facts of human consciousness; in his epoch-making book *Principles of Physiological Psychology* (1874/1904), he clearly stated that his goal was to create such a field. It should be noted that in Wundt's time the term *physiological* meant more or less the same as *experimental*. Thus, reading "physiological psychology" in the title of Wundt's book as "experimental psychology" is more accurate than viewing it as emphasizing a search for the biological correlates of thought and behavior, as is the case with much physiological psychology today.
>
> (231)

In his aforementioned *Principles of Physiological Psychology*, he explicitly addressed Kant, who had declared that psychology would never qualify as a science and that mental experiences and processes were beyond the reach of experimental knowledge. Instead, Wundt placed psychology on a scientific footing and demonstrated its relationship to the natural science of physiology. So seminal was the model of Wundt that some historians of social sciences regard his laboratory—and specifically the year 1879, when the first research of his lab students was published—as the founding place and moment of modern psychology.

Significantly, Wundt's lab did not do animal experiments, but this may be precisely because he was concerned with questions of "consciousness" for which he did not find animals useful. Rather, a legendary method in his research was "introspection," in which he would have subjects examine and describe their own mental experiences and processes. The key process or concept for Wundt was "will," as he held "that much behavior and selective attention are undertaken for a purpose; that is, such activities are motivated" (231).

From Mental Illness to Clinical Psychology

As suggested at the outset, modern academic psychology has two natural-scientific sources, the first being physiology and advances in the knowledge of brain and nerve function. The second was medicine, namely, the study and treatment of "mental illness," along with the investigation into abnormalities of thought and consciousness. Humans had of course always been aware of mental illness—without necessarily calling it such—from epilepsy (seen in ancient times as being touched by the gods) to hysteria (derived from *hyster* or "uterus," inflictions in women long presumed to stem from deformities or misbehavior of their reproductive organs). People had also always noticed, and sometimes valued while other times castigating, alternative states of mind, like trance and "possession" states.

Wundt on "National Psychology"

Wundt stood at the confluence of psychology and anthropology, at a moment (only a century ago) when the various social sciences had not yet fully differentiated. In this formative era of nation-states and national identities, Wundt, like Herder before him (see Chapter 2), appreciated social influences on thought-processes and personality and therefore the possibility and significance of *Völkerpsychologie*, "folk psychology" or "psychology of a people" in addition to an "individual psychology" (Diriwachter 2004: 87–8). "That is, the study of psychology was also to include the products of collective mental processes of peoples identified as a unified body (e.g. the Germans), distinctly separate from others (e.g. the French). Individual psychology was limited to the focus of the capabilities of one person" (88–9). Other contemporaneous scholars like Moritz Lazarus and Heymann Steinthal subscribed to the national psychology view, and in an 1887 book, Steinthal advanced a three-part research agenda, including general psychology, individual psychology, and *Völkerpsychologie*, which would address "the general requirements of collective mental life" as well as the functions and outcomes of these requirements in the form of "ethnology, prehistory, and history" (91). Consequently, the collection and analysis of cultural materials became critical for the development of this new science. Much of the initial research centered on texts, but soon an interest in *Völkskunde* (folklore) emerged, conceived as the examination of a *Volk* "in all its life expressions" (93). Wundt, so central to modern psychology, also advocated folk/national psychology, writing in an 1888 article: "Just like it's the objective of psychology to describe the actuality of individual consciousness, thereby putting its elements and developmental stages in an explicatory relationship, so too is there a need to make as the object of psychological investigation the analogous genetical and causal investigations of those actualities which pertain to the products of higher developmental relationships of human society, namely the folk-communities (*Völkergemeinschaft*)" (quoted 96). However, for *Völkerpsychologie*, familiar (especially experimental) methods would not suffice; rather, it was necessary to employ an ethnographic method, to do "historical comparisons," to examine the products of these collectivities and collective minds. For Wundt, then, *Völkerpsychologie* was not a strictly psychological enterprise but "in essence a social-developmental discipline: social because it predominantly moves within societal dimensions; and developmental because it also needs to examine the different steps of mental development in humans (true psychogenesis), from underdeveloped to higher cultures" (97). Wundt even attempted to offer an outline of this historical-developmental progression from "primitive man" to "the totemic era" to "the ages of heroes and gods" to "the development of humanity."

The modern study of non-normal mental processes and conditions begins with the explorations of Franz Anton Mesmer (1734–1815), who thought that "animal magnetism" or "mesmerism"—which we know today as hypnosis—could be used to cure various mental ailments. Hypnosis would figure prominently in the therapy and theory of Sigmund Freud (see later).

By the early 1800s, major changes were also occurring in the handling of the mentally ill. A key contributor to modern medical psychology was Jean-Martin Charcot (1825–93), who directed the influential French hospital called La Salpêtrière for thirty-three years. From his post he researched hypnosis and hysteria on his patients, as well as making signal contributions to knowledge about spinal cord injuries, multiple sclerosis, Parkinson's disease, and general neurology. His influence spread through the teaching and clinical demonstrations that he conducted at the hospital.

Lightner Witmer is credited with introducing the term "clinical psychology" through his journal *The Psychological Clinic*, founded in 1907.

The Rise of Modern Psychologies

By 1900, psychology was poised not only to become a modern social science but to become multiple, quite disparate "psychologies" or psychological *careers*. While some of these psychologies have faded into obscurity and some have matured into theoretical schools under the umbrella of academic psychology, others have maintained an intellectual and institutional exclusivity, even as new psychologies have entered the family.

In its very self-understanding and its ambitions, psychology is plural. For instance, most twenty-first century introductory textbooks state that psychology is the study of mind and of behavior, in other words of both internal unobservable mental processes and of external observable action, on the not-unreasonable presupposition that public action can be understood in terms of private cognition. We should add that psychology is also the study of the brain and nervous system, including neurochemistry, the biological basis of mind and behavior.

Another way to look at the scope of psychology is to consider what textbook writer Eric Shiraev (2011: 5) calls the discipline's three "recurrent themes":

1. The mind-body problem
2. The interaction of biological and social factors in human behavior and experience, and
3. The balance between theoretical knowledge and its practical applications.

Another textbook author, Karen Huffman (2012), adds that modern psychology has four goals—description, explanation, prediction, and change. These goals are consistent with all sciences, but psychology has arguably gone further than other social sciences in becoming a practical therapeutic profession as well as an academic or theoretical one.

> One of the very first summaries or textbooks of psychology was William James' massive 1890 *The Principles of Psychology*.

Sigmund Freud and Psychoanalysis

Psychoanalysis, one of the first complete psychological schools of thought, demonstrates all three recurrent themes and all four modern goals. Sigmund Freud (1856–1939), the founder of the approach, originally trained as a medical doctor, his early research focusing on brain anatomy and nerve function. In 1886 he entered into private practice to treat patients complaining of "nervous disorders" or neurosis, after meeting Charcot in 1885 and learning about the therapeutic uses of hypnosis. Many of Freud's initial patients (mostly upper-class women from Vienna) became the subjects of his first psychological publications, as in his papers on "Anna O.," "Frau Emmy von N.," and "Elisabeth von R."

These patients suffered from strange physical behaviors like tics and stammers, or even pain and paralysis, which Freud treated with hypnosis as well as physical manipulations. However, he soon abandoned hypnosis in favor of what became known as the "talking cure," asking his patients to simply start talking about whatever they had on their minds (so-called "free association") and to share their dreams for interpretation. By 1896 he introduced the term "psychoanalysis" for his method, and just as the century turned he produced his paradigm-shifting *The Interpretation of Dreams*.

Over the next thirty-plus years and more than two dozen books, Freud's thinking evolved extensively, as he formed a circle of followers around him and exerted influence not only on his own discipline but on anthropology (see Chapter 7) and even on humanities such as art, literature, and religious studies. Among the ideas in psychoanalysis with the most enduring impact are:

- the concept of the unconscious, that is, that there are aspects of mind of which we are not aware and which are not rational
- a dynamic model of the mind as an energy system, with drives and instincts seeking outlets and with a force of "repression" holding these drives and instincts back
- an architecture of mind, with its three renowned parts of "id" (the unconscious and irrational part, the stranger inside us), the "ego" (the "I" or sense of self), and the "superego" (the conscience or internalized disciplinarian)
- the centrality of the body, especially sexuality, and therefore the integration of body and mind
- the critical importance of childhood
- a system of developmental stages, related to bodily experiences and body parts (therefore "psychosexual stages"), from the "oral" to the "anal" to the "phallic" and "latency" and ultimately and ideally "genital" phase, which basically ended with successful adulthood
- the impact of traumatic or painful experience on mental health—that neurosis is basically caused by "reminiscences" or negative memories
- an understanding of all human behavior as psychological "symptom," not only mental illness but small everyday actions like slips of the tongue (dubbed "Freudian slips") as described in his 1901 *Psychopathology of Everyday Life*, as well as major intellectual and social systems such as art and religion.

Again, Freud's ideas reached far beyond his own clinical and theoretical work. He influenced a generation of scholars like Carl G. Jung and Erik Erikson, who developed "depth psychology" in new and important ways—Jung, for instance, into religion and spirituality and Erikson into adulthood and life-span psychology.

Behaviorism

We might see behaviorism as a backlash against highly speculative mentalist psychology such as Freud's work, although its roots are in more modest biological experiments. Behaviorism, as the name suggests, focuses on observable behavior with less concern, even disdain, for internal unobservable mind.

Ivan Pavlov (1849–1936) is the forefather of behaviorism, whose research with dogs indicated that supposedly reflexive behavior like salivation could be trained and conditioned. When dogs learned spontaneously to associate a sound with feeding time, Pavlov realized that they had acquired a "conditioned reflex," and he came to conclude "that all behavior is reflexive, that is, caused by antecedent stimulation. If not modified by inhibition, unconditioned stimuli and conditioned stimuli will elicit unconditioned and conditioned reflexes, respectively" (Hergenhahn 2000: 343).

Behaviorism is essentially a learning theory, and Edward Lee Thorndike (1874–1949), better known as E. L. Thorndike, investigated a form of more active learning in animals in which they had to discover the solution to a problem like how to escape from a box. His insight, labeled the "Law of Effect," was that if a behavior is successful or rewarding—that is, if it is *associated* with a "satisfying state of affairs"—then it is likely to be repeated and to become part of the individual's behavioral repertoire. This led him to a number of other scientific pronouncements, such as the "law of use" (the more we use an association, the stronger it gets) and the "law of disuse" (the less we use it, the weaker it gets). Also, a new skill acquired in one context could be "shifted" to and applied in a different context.

The two key figures in modern behaviorism, however, are John Broadus Watson (1878–1958), also known as J. B. Watson, and Burrhus Frederic Skinner (1904–90), or B. F. Skinner. Watson laid out the perspective of behaviorism in his 1913 manifesto "Psychology as the Behaviorist Views It," saying:

> Psychology as the behaviorist views it is a purely objective experimental branch of natural science. Its theoretical goal is the prediction and control of behavior. Introspection forms no essential part of its methods, nor is the scientific value of its data dependent upon the readiness with which they lend themselves to interpretation in terms of consciousness. The behaviorist, in his efforts to get a unitary scheme of animal response, recognizes no dividing line between man and brute. The behavior of man, with all of its refinement and complexity, forms only a part of the behaviorist's total scheme of investigation.
>
> (1913: 158)

The power of the behaviorist model rested, he claimed in his work, on the ability not only to predict what behavior will follow from what stimulus or situation but *to control behavior by providing the appropriate stimulus or situation to elicit the desired behavior.*

For behaviorists like Watson and Skinner, two of the three fundamental subjects of psychology (namely, the mind and the brain) were of little consequence. Because we cannot see "mind" and because brain activity does not equal overt behavior, Watson considered the mind/brain to be a "mystery box" or, as it has been called, a "black box." Understanding the mind or brain was simply irrelevant, if we can explain, predict, and control behavior. Skinner is particularly infamous for this position, insisting that personality is learned as an effect of "operant conditioning," in which the individual acts or "operates" on the world and monitors the results. Skinner made significant contributions to the study of "reinforcement" or the factors that strengthen or weaken the acquisition of a response, and he claimed most grandly that a psychologist with absolute control over the learning environment of a human individual could shape that individual's knowledge and personality—and thus behavior—completely.

Jean Piaget and Cognitive Psychology

More than most social sciences, psychology has been a struggle between contending models of human nature and human learning. Psychoanalysis and behaviorism constitute virtually polar opposites, behaviorism arising to challenge the excesses of mentalist theories. However, behaviorism suffered from its own excesses, and linguist Noam Chomsky smashed the behaviorist approach to language learning in his 1959 review of Skinner's *Verbal Behavior*. Chomsky persuasively argued that actual verbal behavior had properties—including systematic errors—that could only be explained with reference to some mental or cognitive processes.

By 1959, Jean Piaget (1896–1980) had been studying and writing on children's learning for thirty years, in such classic works as *The Language and Thought of the Child, The Child's Conception of the World, The Origins of Intelligence in Children*, and *The Construction of Reality in the Child*. As these titles suggest, Piaget was deeply interested in the most fundamental question of philosophy and psychology, that is, the nature and origin of knowledge. He noticed that at certain ages children did not seem to "know" particular things, such as that an object that rolls out of sight still exists, or that liquid poured from one container into another retains the same volume. This prompted him to reason that knowledge—including knowledge of the basic facts of physical reality—was not innate but that it was not simply gleaned from experience either.

Piaget proposed a stage-model of the child's developing knowledge of the world, related to his/her age and mental maturity:

1. Sensorimotor stage (birth to two years), during which knowledge comes from the interaction of the child's body and the outside world.
2. Preoperational stage (age two to seven), during which the child lacks logical thought and the ability to perform complex mental operations; s/he is also egocentric and unable to grasp the perspective of others.
3. Concrete operational stage (age seven to eleven), during which children demonstrate the capability to perform mental operations like reversibility and to appreciate the perspective of others.

4. Formal operational stage (age eleven and beyond), during which individuals can think abstractly and logically.

In a way, Piaget tackled some of the same questions as Kant, but his discoveries refuted the basic Kantian approach. Rather than supporting Kant's claim that the mind comes fully furnished with *a priori* (pre-experience) categories of understanding, Piaget revealed that humans are not born with concepts such as quantity or substance or necessity or causality but that humans gradually, over a matter of years, build these concepts out of embodied interactions with the physical world. This is why Piaget characterized his own model as *genetic epistemology*, because knowledge slowly grows or develops ("genetic" derives from the Greek for "to become" or "to be born"); it is not innate, it is not mere sense perception, and it is not constructed by categories of mind that exist prior to experience.

As powerful as it is, one complaint about Piaget's view is that it is rather asocial: it posits an individual learning about the world alone. Psychologists like Albert Bandura (born 1925) offered a social-cognitive alternative, in which individuals also learn from each other. Of course, social learning is not a matter of mere imitation, but Bandura argued that peers and elders provide "models" for potential behavior, which we can observe and copy. Bandura did a famous series of experiments with children and violent cartoons, testing whether animated models would affect human behavior, in the form of punching an inflatable clown. Bandura subsequently stressed the significance of role models to suggest courses of behavior to others, as well as "rehearsal" or practice for strengthening the tendency toward a behavior.

Later in the twentieth century, with the advent of computers, some psychologists proposed a "computational model" of thought, with the mind/

The so-called Gestalt (from the German for "whole" or "global form") school of psychology, founded on the early twentieth-century work of Max Wertheimer, emphasized how the mind combines and processes raw sense-perception into meaningful wholes or experience. Based on the notion that the mind actively reaches out to the world with "intentionality," Gestalt psychologists took much inspiration from optical illusions, which evinced efforts by the mind to impose order and meaning on ambiguous sensory data. From such data, scholars like Kurt Koffka and Wolfgang Köhler aimed to identify innate mental processes that shaped how humans make sense of the jumble of sense stimuli— what American psychologist William James called the "blooming, buzzing confusion."

brain functioning like a computer. Even Hobbes likened reasoning to computation, and key modern proponents like Hilary Putnam, Jerry Fodor, and John Searle popularized the idea. Fodor went so far as to posit that the mind operates in terms of its own "language of thought" much as a computer operates in machine language. Research and development in "artificial intelligence" has shown that machines can perform many of the tasks formerly believed to be exclusive to human minds, which has raised the ultimate question of whether the human mind is unique and whether we could always tell if we are interacting with a human or a very talented machine—or whether, if Descartes and Hobbes are correct, we *are* very talented machines.

The Methods and Practice of Modern Psychology

All of the history, discoveries, theories, and controversies discussed previously (and more not mentioned due to lack of space) highlight the multiplicity of modern psychology. The field today covers a breath-taking array of topics and questions: for instance, typical introductory textbooks feature chapters on brain physiology and function, sensation and perception, consciousness, learning, memory, thinking and intelligence, childhood and life span development, gender and sexuality, motivation and emotion, personality, mental illness, therapy, and social psychology.

Beyond its content, the realm of psychology is inhabited by a wide variety of academic, experimental, clinical, medical, and applied professions, many of whom "practice" psychology in the same way that physicians practice medicine; in fact, many psychological practitioners *are* medical doctors, like psychiatrists and psychoanalysts. Further, practicing psychologists may combine two or more psychological paths or professions in their individual careers, for instance teaching along with counseling or forensic psychology (i.e. assisting the police or the courts). Among the discrete career choices in psychology are:

- *clinical psychology*, treating patients with any number of complaints from addiction to depression to eating disorders to sexual abuse to suicidal tendencies.
- *counseling psychology*, defined by the Society of Counseling Psychology as "a focus on facilitating personal and interpersonal functioning across the life span. The specialty pays particular attention to emotional, social, vocational, educational, health-related, developmental, and organizational concerns." One example is the school psychologist.
- *psychiatry*, a medical profession specializing in psychological disorders. A psychiatrist follows a very different career path than a psychologist, first attending medical school and earning a M.D. degree before doing several more years of residency in psychiatry. As medical doctors, psychiatrists are qualified to prescribe medication.

Research Topics in Psychology

The articles in the 2015 issue of *Annual Review of Psychology* include:

"Consolidating Memories"
"The Nucleus Accumbens: An Interface Between Cognition, Emotion, and Action"
"Adult Neurogenesis: Beyond Learning and Memory"
"Motivation and Cognitive Control: From Behavior to Neural Mechanism"
"The Cognitive Neuroscience of Working Memory"
"Why Sleep is Important for Health: A Psychoneuroimmunology Perspective"
"Critical Periods in Speech Perception: New Directions"
"Perceptual Learning: Toward a Comprehensive Theory"
"Causality in Thought"
"Perspectives on Culture and Concepts"
"Information Processing as a Paradigm for Decision Making"
"Beyond Simple Models of Self-Control to Circuit-Based Accounts of Adolescent Behavior"
"The Evolutionary Roots of Human Decision Making"
"Hemodynamic Correlates of Cognition in Human Infants"
"Developmental Flexibility in the Age of Globalization: Autonomy and Identity Development among Immigrant Adolescents"
"Global Health and Development in Early Childhood"
"Childhood Antecedents and Risk for Adult Mental Disorders"
"The Science of Mind Wandering: Empirically Navigating the Stream of Consciousness"
"Multiple Identities in Social Perception and Interaction: Challenges and Opportunities"
"The Evolution of Altruism in Humans"
"Social Pain and the Brain: Controversies, Questions, and Where to Go From Here"
"Polycultural Psychology"
"Action Errors, Error Management, and Learning in Organizations"
"School Readiness and Self-Regulation: A Developmental Psychobiological Approach"
"The Neuroendocrinology of Social Isolation"
"Physical Activity and Cognitive Vitality"
"Emotion and Decision Making"
"Diffusion Tensor Imaging for Understanding Brain Development in Early Life"

- *psychoanalysis*, also a medical specialty offering treatment based on the theories and methods of Freud.
- *experimental psychology*, conducting research in laboratories and/or in natural settings. Psychologists are the only social scientists who routinely use scientific labs, as well as deal with chemical compounds like psychoactive drugs. Experimental psychology may study behavior, learning, memory, and other psychological processes, or brain and neurological function and damage, in humans and in non-human animals such as mice and monkeys. A subspecialty of experimental psychology is *neuropsychology*, which may involve implanting electrodes in brains, using MRIs to observe brain function, or intentionally causing damage to brains to detect the behavioral and cognitive effects.
- *ethology*, the study of animal behavior, with implications for human behavior.

Each of these careers, and their sub-careers, has its own training programs, professional standards and credentialing agencies, organizations, journals, conferences, and such.

Not all psychologists are researchers, but the diversity of psychological careers calls for appropriate diversity in research methods. Psychologists may employ all of the standard tools of social science, such as questionnaires and surveys, interviews, focus groups, case studies, and naturalistic observation. However, as just mentioned, classic experimentation and the scientific laboratory are more common in psychology than in any of its sister disciplines. The lab may be as simple as a controlled environment where subjects are brought for questioning or for exposure to some particular stimulus, equipment, or experience; a famous example of such experimentation is Stanley Milgram's seminal research on authority and obedience, in which people were asked, as part of an alleged learning study, to administer electric shocks to other participants (happily, there were no actual shocks). Psychological laboratories and the experiments conducted there may include mazes for rats and machinery to teach and test language skills in apes, and they may go so far as to involve medical operations (like placing electrodes in animals' brains) and dissection.

Psychological research generates an abundance of quantitative data, which are commonly analyzed statistically and represented graphically. Psychology's findings have been interpreted to identify mechanisms (for example, "procedural memory" for skills, "episodic memory" for experiences, and "semantic memory" for facts), to construct models (like Freud's model of the mind), and to suggest laws (like Hebb's law, that neurons that fire together wire together). Highly significantly, psychology can expose how humans produce knowledge and the "heuristics" or short-cuts that we use to think—not to mention the mental errors and cognitive biases that plague us and lead to systematic and predictable mistakes (see Tversky and Kahneman 1974).

Another noteworthy feature of psychology is its invention of various tests, scales, inventories, and other such instruments for measuring psychological qualities or even diagnosing psychological pathologies. Among the first and most important variables to measure was intelligence, particularly for purposes of assessing (and treating) children or immigrants or workers or soldiers. A pioneer in the measurement of intelligence was Alfred Binet (1857–1911), who published *The Experimental Study of Intelligence* in 1903. In 1905 he and a colleague named Simon devised the Binet-Simon scale of intelligence, which

> consisted of thirty tests ranging in difficulty from simple eye movements to abstract definitions. Three of the tests measured motor development, and the other twenty-seven were designed to measure cognitive abilities. The tests were arranged in order of difficulty, so that the more tests a child passed the more fully developed his or her intelligence was assumed to be. The scale was given to normal children and to children thought to have retardation, all of them between the ages of two and twelve.
>
> (Hergenhahn 2000: 274)

In 1916 Binet's device was modified to the better-known and widely-used Stanford-Binet test. Meanwhile, in 1911 William Stern introduced the concept of "intelligence quotient," a simple arithmetic calculation of test-determined "mental age" divided by chronological age; a quotient of 100 (or essentially 100 percent or one-to-one) meant that a person performed at the appropriate mental age or average.

Another classic psychological device also debuted in 1921. After the experimentation of many psychologists including Binet with amorphous shapes to test personality, Hermann Rorschach published *Psycho-diagnostics* (*Psychodiagnostik* in the original German), introducing ten inkblots that would come to be known as the Rorschach test (see Figure 5.2). Only intended to diagnose schizophrenia, the inkblots were widely adopted to measure all manner of personality traits and became closely associated with psychoanalysis (and were even used by some anthropologists in their fieldwork).

Since those early days of psychological testing, an explosion of more or less reliable devices has given us hundreds of potential instruments and masses of quantitative psychological data. The website "A Guide to Psychology and its Practice" (www.guidetopsychology.com/testing.htm) organizes psychological tests into several categories including achievement and aptitude tests, intelligence tests, neuropsychological tests, occupational tests, personality tests, and clinical tests. Among the vast battery of tests and instruments available to psychologists today are:

- Minnesota Multiphasic Personality Inventory
- Draw-a-Person test

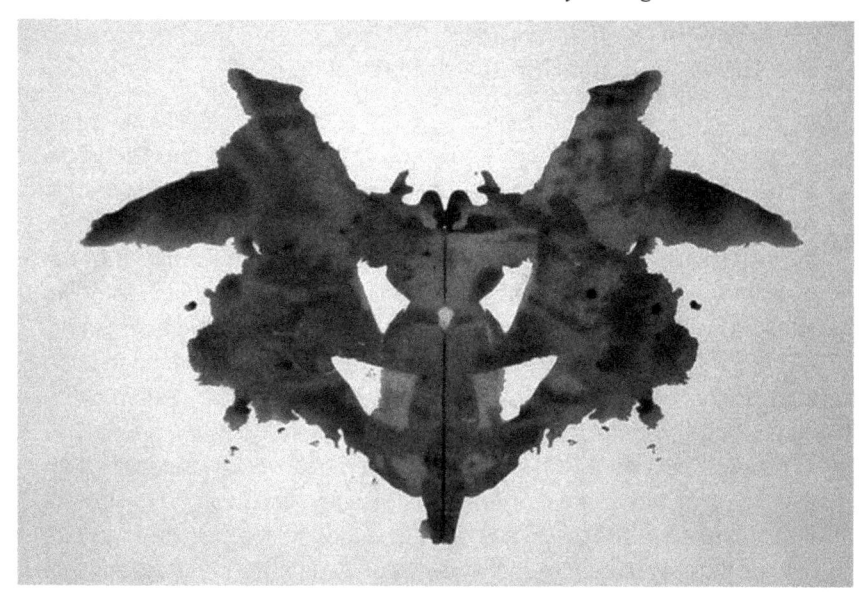

Figure 5.2 A Rorschach ink blot
Source: Rorschach Ink Blot Test, U.S. public domain, Wikicommons.

- House Tree Person (drawing test)
- Adolescent Anger Rating Scale
- Psychopathy Checklist
- Beck Hopelessness Scale
- Suicidal Ideation Questionnaire
- Porteus Maze
- Wechsler Adult Intelligence Scale
- Marital Satisfaction Inventory
- Posttraumatic Stress Diagnostic Scale

and many, many more, assessing everything from perception to pain to reading to depression to brain function.

Finally, psychology stands out among the social sciences for its popularity among non-professionals and the general public, as in such magazines as *Psychology Today* and *Scientific American Mind*, as well as televised psychological celebrities as Dr. Phil (McGraw) and, in earlier years, Dr. Joyce Brothers and Dr. Ruth Westheimer, the small woman who specialized in sex advice. Predictably, then, psychology has found many applications outside of the academy and the clinic, particularly in studying (and manipulating) consumer behavior by testing aspects of marketing, packaging, and display as they affect buying habits, and in the more general question of "persuasion" or "influence," whether this concerns leadership

The Diagnostic and Statistical Manual

Psychology is the only social science with a standard guidebook, a sort of "bible" of the profession. Known as the Diagnostic and Statistical Manual (or DSM for short) and published by the American Psychiatric Association, its first edition was released in 1952, and according to the Association's website, "contained a glossary of descriptions of the diagnostic categories and was the first official manual of mental disorders to focus on clinical utility." The DSM has been through several revisions, with the third edition published in 1980; the Association admits that the third edition "revealed a number of inconsistencies in the system and a number of instances in which the criteria were not entirely clear." One of the most noteworthy changes was the removal of homosexuality from the list of mental disorders in the 1974 second edition. The DSM-IV was published in 1994, with numerous changes "to the classification (e.g. disorders were added, deleted, and reorganized), to the diagnostic criteria sets, and to the descriptive text based on a careful consideration of the available research about the various mental disorders." The current version is the DSM-V, made public in 2013, which like previous editions consists of classifications of psychological disorders, sets of "diagnostic criteria" with which practitioners can determine the presence of a disorder, and a written description of each disorder, with such headings as "Diagnostic Features," "Associated Features Supporting Diagnosis," "Subtypes and/or Specifiers," "Prevalence," "Development and Course," "Risk and Prognostic Factors," "Diagnostic Measures," "Functional Consequences," "Culture-Related Diagnostic Issues," "Gender-Related Diagnostic Issues," "Differential Diagnosis," and "Recording Procedures."

and management or changing people's attitudes and beliefs on any particular topic (see e.g. Robert Cialdini's [2001] *Influence: Science and Practice*).

Disciplinary Case #4: Psychology of Terrorism

Ask most people for an explanation of terrorist behavior and they will give you a psychological explanation, typically that terrorists are irrational or crazy or at least angry and hateful. And no doubt this profile fits some individual terrorists. However, as in the previous chapter, if a mature and educated person makes a better terrorist, then presumably so does a sane person.

There has been a great deal of research on the psychology of terrorism—or of terrorists—some of it supporting the popular pathological view. Richard Pearlstein, for instance, in his *The Mind of the Political Terrorist*, concluded that "the individual who becomes and remains a political terrorist generally appears to be psychologically molded by certain narcissistic personality disturbances" (1991: ix). However, terrorism expert Martha Crenshaw, writing in the journal *Political Psychology*, countered that

> most analysts of terrorism do not think that personality factors account for terrorist behavior, nor do they see significant gender differences. One of the basic research findings of the field is that terrorism is primarily a group activity. It is typically not the result of psychopathology or a single personality type. Shared ideological commitment and group solidarity are much more important determinants of terrorist behavior than individual characteristics.
>
> (2000: 409)

This perspective suggests a social and cultural perspective, which we will explore in the next two chapters.

However, psychological concepts and methods can yield valuable insights into terrorist behavior. For instance, some decades ago Frederick Hacker (1976) proposed a three-part typology, including "crazies" who really are mentally troubled, along with "crusaders" who are ideologically motivated and "criminals" who are merely violent people (sadists or just thugs) who channel their violence into terrorism.

Insofar as there is a "terrorist personality," Laurence Miller makes two salient points. First, "insular organizations," that is, groups that segregate their members from the outside world and promulgate a doctrine, "seem to contain many of these same characters, whether they explicitly espouse violent terrorism or not" (2006: 260). Second, the personality traits of terrorists vary according to their role in the terrorist organization. So *leaders* of terrorist groups often manifest narcissism or paranoia; in the former case, they exhibit "a pattern of grandiosity, sense of entitlement, arrogance, need for admiration, and lack of empathy for others' feelings or opinions" (262). But these same traits are common in all extreme group leaders. Paranoia, on the other hand, presents as "a pattern of pervasive distrust and suspiciousness so that others' actions and motives are almost invariably interpreted as deceptive, persecutory, or malevolent" (262).

Non-leaders but *true believers* show a different personality type, characterized by borderline and antisocial personalities, with "erratic and intense relationships, alternating between overidealization and devaluation of others; self-damaging impulsiveness; emotional instability, including inappropriate intense anger and/or depressive mood swings and suicidality" (263); antisocial personality is associated further with "impulsivity, criminal behavior, sexual promiscuity, substance abuse, and an exploitive, parasitic, and/or predatory lifestyle" (264). Then there are the *good soldiers*, whose personalities are more characteristically avoidant or dependent—hypersensitive, submissive, clingy, and "hungry for validation" (265). Finally, there are what Miller calls the *limelight seekers and loose cannons* who tend to be histrionic and schizoid or schizotypal, either displaying "a pattern of excessive emotionality, attention seeking, need for excitement, flamboyant theatricality in speech and behavior, an impressionistic and impulsive cognitive style, and the use of exaggeration" or "aloof detachment . . . with a restricted range of emotional expression" and "severe distortions of thought, perception, and action, including delusions and hallucinations. In fact, schizoid and schizotypal personality disorders may episodically deteriorate into psychotic states" (266). Again, these conditions are not unique to terrorists.

Beyond the simple question of terrorist personality, a psychological perspective leads us to ask other questions. One such question is the motivation of terrorists. Social psychologist Albert Bandura advised that we think of terrorist violence as a "principled resort to destructiveness" (1990: 191), which forces us to consider the principle and the cause for which they commit terrorist acts. Three psychological tactics that Bandura identified were justifying the acts in the terrorist's mind, minimizing or distorting the harm, and blaming or dehumanizing the victims.

The eminent psychologist Philip Zimbardo (2000), who conducted the classic simulation of prisoner and guard behavior at Stanford University, added that a number of psychosocial factors contribute to the perpetration of violence such as terrorism. He emphasized:

1. indoctrination into a thought-system that rationalizes or legitimizes violence
2. obedience to authority, with no opportunity for dissent
3. anonymity and deindividuation (e.g. getting lost in a crowd or having your individual decision-making powers taken or suppressed)
4. diffusion of responsibility (e.g. "just following orders" or dividing the violent behavior among a group of people)
5. gradual escalation of violence
6. dehumanization of the enemy or the victim.

Likewise, Roy Baumeister (2001) stressed diffusion of responsibility, deindividuation, "division of violent labor" (that is, separating the violence into small tasks and distributing them among an organization of violence), dehumanization or demonization of the victim, separation of decision-makers from those who actually carry out the violence, egotism, and idealism.

Another facet of motivation or how people understand their own behavior is "attribution," that is, to what they attribute their actions. According to

Wagdy Loza, humans in general but especially those engaged in "deviant" behavior "have a tendency to attribute their own undesirable behavior to some external force such as blaming sociological factors or provocation by the victim" (2007: 149). This allows them to "rationalize killings and violence on moral ground as they believe that their actions are defensive, they are saving themselves from the great evil and they are compelled to commit their violence" (149).

Since individuals are not born subscribing to terrorist principles and causes, psychologists further examine processes of belief and of learning. How people acquire beliefs and principles, and what kinds of beliefs and principles contribute to terrorism, are prime psychological issues. Learning theories from behaviorism to Piagetian cognitivism offer explanations of terrorist behavior; for instance, Bandura would and has emphasized modeling and rehearsal.

Fathali Moghaddam (2005) offered a fascinating and useful analysis of the "staircase of terrorism" by which the pre-terrorist gradually escalates to become a perpetrator of terrorist acts. On the ground floor, individuals begin to interpret economic, political, and social conditions in a particular way, perceiving those conditions as injustices and deprivations. If they move up to the next level, that interpretation of reality leads to the consideration of violent options to combat injustice. A level up, the individual, usually influenced by a leader, identifies an "enemy" to blame for circumstances and begins to project aggression toward that enemy. One more level up, s/he starts to envision violence as a justified course of action; at this stage, potential terrorists "are persuaded to become committed to the morality of the terrorist organization through a number of tactics, the most important of which are isolation, affiliation, secrecy, and fear" (2005: 165). If recruits keep ascending the ladder, they enter the stage of "categorical thinking," in which they divide the world into "us-versus-them" and endow themselves with moral virtue. At the final stop, recruits must learn to overcome their natural inhibitions against harm; those who can make this mental shift are prepared to commit terrorism. A particularly important aspect of Moghaddam's model is that not every individual takes every step up the ladder; any person may hesitate at any level of terrorist preparation—or, given the same socio-economic conditions, not mount the ladder at all.

Two other related psychological dimensions are rationality and moral reasoning. Psychologists from Piaget to Lawrence Kohlberg have found that not all individuals attain the same levels of reasoning or of morality, so how people make decisions and how they legitimate those decisions morally are of profound consequence. Terrorists certainly do reason or think about their actions (just as they make decisions and choices in the economic sense), but they may reason differently from other people—which raises the crucial possibility that there may be more than one form or mode of reasoning. Based on many sources, Loza finds that the thought-process of terrorists (and other extremists) is "rigid, primitive, and unsophisticated. They oversimplify complex issues" and their decision-making "is limited to right or wrong or dividing the world into good and evil. . . . Their analytical thinking is not developed" (2007: 147). The unfortunate upshot of this psychological understanding of terrorist reasoning is that "terrorism has an autonomous logic that is comprehensible, however unconventional" (Crenshaw 2000: 410). Terrorists are not insane or irrational, but their reasoning is indisputably different.

Central to the motivation, the beliefs, the learning, and the morality of terrorism is emotion, and many observers have asserted that the driving emotion of terrorists is *humiliation*. Terrorists (and other extremists on the right or left) tend to be "filled with disappointment, frustration, fear, disgust, anger, and hatred" (Loza 2007: 147) as a result of real life experiences as well as of the teachings of influential opinion-makers. Terrorist violence, in the words of Arie Kruglanski and Shira Fishman, thus "affords the emotional satisfaction of watching the enemy suffer, which boosts one's sense of potency and prowess" (2006: 207).

Finally, because psychologists recognize that psychological processes operate not only at the individual level, Jerrold Post contends that it "is not individual psychology, but group, organizational, and social psychology, with a particular emphasis on 'collective identity,' that provides the most powerful lens for understanding terrorist psychology and behavior" (2005: 196). And he also advocates a potentially mediating or therapeutic role for the psychologist: "Given that terrorism is a vicious species of psychological warfare, waged through the media, one does not counter psychological warfare with smart bombs and missiles; one counters psychological warfare with psychological warfare. Each phase of the terrorist life cycle is a potential focus of intervention" (201).

6 Sociological Imagination

Key organizations

American Sociological Association (www.asanet.org), founded 1905
British Sociological Association (www.britsoc.co.uk), founded 1951
International Sociological Association (www.isa-sociology.org),
  founded 1949
European Sociological Association (www.europeansociology.org),
  founded 1992

Key journals

American Sociological Review
American Journal of Sociology
Contemporary Sociology
Current Sociology
Social Currents
Social Forces
Sociology
European Societies

Family and marriage are undergoing great change in the United States, not only in terms of the greater acceptance and legalization of same-sex marriage. In fact, sociologists find the term "family" to be vague—and clearly not equivalent to "household" since nonfamily members may share a household while family members may be distributed across multiple households. Sociologists thus distinguish between "nuclear" or "stem" family and "extended family," as well as between "family of orientation" (where the individual grows up) and "family of procreation" (where the individual raises his/her own children). Actually, in their classic study of the American family, Ernest Burgess and Harvey Locke (1945) identified five types of family structures and family dynamics, from the broken family, the relatively unorganized family, the habit-bound family, and the highly solidified family to the (preferred) dynamically unified family. Even more, they noticed that the central institution of the family—marriage—was transforming. Data showed that marriage increased steadily from 1900 to 1940, with only 54.6 percent of men and 57 percent of women married in 1900 and 61.2 percent and 61 percent, respectively, married in 1940. Interestingly, they could not know that the high point of marriage would be 1970, after which marriage levels dropped to near-1900 levels by 2009. At the same time, though, divorce was increasing, with only 0.3 percent of men and 0.5 percent of women divorced in 1900 and 1.3 percent and 1.7 percent, respectively, divorced in 1940 (and 9 percent and 11.4 percent, respectively, in 2009). More profoundly but related to these figures, they detected that the very nature of marriage was changing, from a rigid and patriarchal social obligation to a voluntary (and thus comparatively fragile) relationship based on "demonstration of affection, the sharing of experiences, mutual confiding, sharing in the making of decisions," and "companionship" (1945: 335). They called this new form the "companionate marriage"; others have called it (and condemned it as) the "deinstitutionalization" and maybe even the death of marriage.

As we said in the first chapter, although humans have always lived in social groups with defined rules, roles, and institutions, "society" was one of the last things to be discovered by scholars and scientists. This is particularly surprising because "society" would seem to be central to social thought. Some of the questions that would eventually fall within the domain of sociology were previously asked, to be sure, although they were posed by philosophy, theology, or other disciplines like political science or economics and therefore were not posed in a distinctly "sociological" way. And thoughts and speculations about society were not accompanied by empirical and statistical investigations into social organization and social behavior.

Sociology has self-consciously come to stress and prize the ability to see beyond and outside of the individual's immediate experience or "mind" to the forces that operate on, integrate, and construct individuals. Following C. Wright Mills, they are proud to call this the "sociological imagination." Writing originally in 1959, Mills insisted that most people are not "aware of the intricate connection between the patterns of their own lives and the course of world history" and the web of rules and institutions that form their own particular society (2000: 4). Thus, the sociological imagination begins with "the ideas that the individual can understand his own experience and gauge his own fate only by locating himself within his period, that he can know his own chances in life only by becoming aware of those of all individuals in his circumstances" (5). That is, there are many unseen—and in some cases unseeable—external and interpersonal factors that shape our individual thoughts, opinions, and behaviors, factors that we did not individually create but that we perpetuate through our social action. It requires imagination to "see" these factors and forces.

Accordingly, Mills explained that "those who have been imaginatively aware of the promise of their work [on society] have consistently asked three sorts of questions":

1. What is the structure of this particular society as a whole? What are its essential components, and how are they related to one another? How does it differ from other varieties of social order? Within it, what is the meaning of any particular feature for its continuance and for its change?
2. Where does this society stand in human history? What are the mechanics by which it is changing? What is its place within and its meaning for the development of humanity as a whole? How does any particular feature we are examining affect, and how is it affected by, the historical period in which it moves? And this period—what are its essential features? How does it differ from other periods? What are its characteristic ways of history-making?
3. What varieties of men and women now prevail in this society and in this period? And what varieties are coming to prevail? In what ways are they selected and formed, liberated and repressed, made sensitive and blunted? What kinds of "human nature" are revealed in the conduct and character we observe in this society in this period? And what is the meaning for "human nature" of each and every feature of the society we are examining? (6–7).

These questions, along with its terminology and methods, make sociology a unique social science.

The Ancient Study (or Lack Thereof) of Society

Compared to the modern social sciences previously described, sociology seems to lack ancient roots. Indeed, most introductory sociology textbooks ignore ancient scholarship completely, picking up the trail of the discipline in the nineteenth century (or occasionally in the eighteenth century) as if it were invented out of thin air.

It is true enough that, unlike "history" or "politics" or "economics" (and "geography" see Chapter 8), there was no ancient term equivalent to "sociology"; the word was only invented in the 1800s. Yet, as we have observed repeatedly, pondering and planning society is not an exclusively modern practice. But pre-modern and ancient ruminations about organized human life did not isolate "society" as a "thing" apart from its various institutional expressions. For example, the ancient Greeks used the term "politics" much more inclusively—as the system of all (good) social order and collective existence—with roughly the same meaning as "society" for us today. In Aristotle's thinking, to be social was to be political, to participate in the affairs of the city and the state.

Another reason why "society" was not an early subject of analysis and critique is that, for most people throughout most of history, "society" was utterly taken for granted. Insofar as people speculated on the origins and forms of their own societies, they tended to understand those origins and forms as either *natural* or *supernatural*. In the natural view of social life, the ways that humans live collectively—their leadership, their language, their families, their clothing, etc.—are simply how things are; they are the only ways humans *can* live, because they are a product of human nature (or even of non-human nature, like Darwin's idea of natural competition). Aristotle provides an instance of naturalistic thinking about social relations in his analysis of slavery. Slavery is most assuredly a social institution, as it does not occur in nature or in all human societies. But Aristotle reasoned that slavery exists because there are, among humans, inherent differences that make some individuals "natural slaves." In his *Politics* he wrote:

> But is there any one thus intended by nature to be a slave, and for whom such a condition is expedient and right, or rather is not all slavery a violation of nature? There is no difficulty in answering this question, on grounds both of reason and of fact. For that some should rule and others be ruled is a thing not only necessary, but expedient; from the hour of their birth, some are marked out for subjection, others for rule.

Exactly what this "mark" of slavery is, Aristotle does not elucidate.

On the other hand, from the supernatural view of social life, human rules and institutions are established or ordained by non-human and super-human ("divine" or "spiritual") beings and/or forces over which humans have little or no control. From language (consider the "Tower of Babel") to economic and technical practices and knowledge (farming, metallurgy, even fire itself) to politics (e.g. the divine origin and "right" of kings), shared ways of life are given to and imposed upon humans. The place of humans is to submit to these commands (Islam, a more complete social plan than many religions, takes its name from the Arabic word for "submission," which also implies "peace"), to accept the obligation to live in a specific way and to perpetuate (and in some cases spread) their decreed social/moral order.

Insofar, then, as the ancients contemplated social order, they were contemplating either nature or the supernatural, neither of which path leads to sociology. The only place where "social" analysis might arise was in those areas where humans clearly created their own institutions—and created them differently—as in the various constitutions of the Greek cities. Such political comparisons can be construed as early sociological thinking.

Further, what humans create they can manage and modify, which is the crucial social lesson in Plato's *Republic*. All of Plato's writings grapple with "social" questions, although once again these questions tend to have a political or moral character (about, for instance, justice or piety). *Republic* was a

---

The Domesday Book: An Early Sociological Document

Social science or any science cannot flourish in a vacuum of information, and one reason why nothing quite like sociology appeared in ancient times was the lack of any systematic collection of social data. While the Greeks were conducting observations on physics and geography, they were not doing similar information-gathering on society. One of the first efforts to organize knowledge about society was the compilation of the *Domesday Book* in England in the late eleventh century. Prepared for the new king William I to inform him of his kingdom, the document surveyed the country, listing aristocratic land holdings, towns, markets and products, and even the number of livestock. Obviously, the book had a very practical motivation: it made administration—and especially taxation—more thorough and efficient.

---

product of Plato's "sociological imagination," describing not an actual but an ideal social system with its government, its class structure, and its division of labor. All of these would become central concerns of modern sociology.

Other civilizations contemporary to the Greeks evinced the same lack of sociological imagination, offering at most normative statements on how humans *ought* to live. The Hebrews did not do sociology: their writings were a combination of national and supernatural history and moral law, with hundreds of injunctions on how to eat, dress, and otherwise organize society. In China, Confucius (551–479 BCE) also codified social and moral ideals, specifically endorsing social hierarchy (the authority of emperor over subjects, husband over wife, and elder over younger) and admonishing people to observe *li* or ritual respect. He even offered a version of what Westerners would call the Golden Rule: "Do not do to others what you do not want done to yourself."

Pre-Modern Precursors of Sociology

Although the pre-modern world was notoriously lacking social information and social imagination, the academic discipline of sociology did not appear miraculously overnight in the nineteenth century. Philosophy and theology reflected on many of the same issues, as previous chapters of this book have amply illustrated, and bits of social data (tax records, contracts, birth and death records, and historical writing) were produced and preserved. Then, in the late medieval and Enlightenment eras, two figures emerged who would establish the very earliest lines of sociological thinking—Ibn Khaldun and Giambattista Vico.

Ibn Khaldun, the Father of Sociology?

Ibn Khaldun, mentioned in Chapter 2, was a fourteenth-century Islamic scholar born in Tunisia. He anticipated many of the ideas of Western sociology, although according to Doyle Johnson he "had no influence on the development of sociology in Europe" (2008: 49). Since the founders of European sociology were apparently unaware of his work, he is mentioned, usually only in passing, in some but by no means all modern sociology textbooks. George Ritzer, for example, says merely that Ibn Khaldun "developed sociological theories that dealt with such issues as the scientific study of society, the interrelationship between politics and the economy, and the relationship between primitive societies and the medieval societies of his time" (2013: 39). Others such as Faridah Hj Hassan attach much more importance to him, deeming him the "real father of sociology" and a scholar who "more than meet[s] the definition of a contemporary sociologist" (2006: 15). Arnold Toynbee lauded Ibn Khaldun's ideas in books like *Muqadimmah* as "the greatest work of its kind that has ever been created by any mind in any time or place" (1962: 322).

Johnson is more explicit about Ibn Khaldun's originality. The Arab intellectual's ultimate goal

> was to explain the historical process of the rise and fall of civilizations in terms of a pattern of recurring conflicts between tough nomadic desert tribes and sedentary-type societies with their love of luxuries and pleasure. He believed that the advanced civilizations that develop in densely settled communities are accompanied by a more centralized political authority system and by the gradual erosion of social cohesion within the population. As a result such societies become vulnerable to conquest by tough and highly disciplined nomadic peoples from the unsettled desert. Eventually, however, the hardy conquerors succumb to the temptations of the soft and refined life-style of the people they had conquered, and so the cycle is eventually repeated. Although this cyclical theory was based on Khaldun's observations of social trends in the Arabian desert, his goal was to develop a **general** model of the dynamics of society and the process of large-scale social change.
>
> (2008: 24, bold in the original)

Fundamental to Ibn Khaldun's understanding of society and of historical processes was the concept of *asabiyyah* (tribalism or communitarianism), that is, the phenomenon or identity that integrated individuals into cohesive social units or communities. Modern Western sociologists would propose similar concepts.

Giambattista Vico: The "New Science" of Society

Giambattista Vico (1668–1744) was born in Italy almost three hundred years after Ibn Khaldun and lived in that fertile time between Hobbes' *Leviathan* and Smith's *Wealth of Nations*. In 1725 he offered his own *New Science*, which straddled traditional and modern ways of thinking.

According to Werner Stark, writing in defense of Vico's "theoretical and practical relevance" for today's sociology, Vico's seminal notion was "the creativity of man" (1976: 820).

> But by man we must mean, in the context of Vico's sociology, not the individual but the collectivity.... Vico asserted that the cooperation of men, the anonymous forces of society, were the fund of life which could and did bring forth social and cultural institutions without number, and the most essential ones to boot.
>
> (820)

Thus, it "is not an exaggeration to say that Vico revealed the secret of social life—the fact that there are hidden yet real forces which create society (human and not physical or physiological forces), and that society is in this way a self-created entity" (821). If so, then Vico can truly be credited with introducing a sociological imagination.

In his much more robust study of Vico's work, Isaiah Berlin expressed some of the key principles of the great man's thinking:

- "That the nature of man is not, as has long been supposed, static and unalterable or even unaltered; ... that men's own efforts to understand the world in which they find themselves and to adapt it to their needs, physical and spiritual, continuously transform their worlds and themselves"
- That "men's knowledge of the external world which we can observe, describe, classify, reflect upon, and of which we can record the regularities in time and space, differs in principle from their knowledge of the world that they themselves create, and which obeys rules that they themselves imposed on their creations"
- "That there is a pervasive pattern which characterizes all the activities of any given society: a common style reflected in the thought, the arts, the social institutions, the language, the ways of life and action, of an entire society. This idea is tantamount to the concept of a culture"
- "That the creations of man—laws, institutions, religions, rituals, works of art, language, song, rules of conduct and the like—are not artificial products created to please, or to exalt, or teach wisdom, nor weapons deliberately invented to manipulate or dominate men, or promote social stability or security, but are natural forms of self-expression"

- "From which it follows (in effect a new type of aesthetics) that works of art must be understood, interpreted, evaluated, not in terms of timeless principles and standards valid for all men everywhere, but by correct grasp of the purpose and therefore of the peculiar use of symbols, especially language, which belong uniquely to their own time and place, their own stage of social growth"
- "That, therefore, in addition to the traditional categories of knowledge—*a priori*-deductive, *a posteriori*-empirical, that provided by sense perception and that vouchsafed by revelation—there must be added a new variety, the reconstructive imagination. This type of knowledge is yielded by 'entering' into the mental life of other cultures, into a variety of outlooks and ways of life which only the activity of *fantasia*—imagination—makes possible."

(1976: xvi–xix)

In this impressive catalogue of ideas, Vico can be judged to have prophesied many of the bedrock assumptions and concepts of twenty-first century sociology and anthropology.

The Nineteenth Century Ancestors of Sociology

When present-day sociologists tell the story of their own profession, the tale usually begins in the early 1800s. The context, which we have already seen, was rapid and often traumatic social change, including urbanization, industrialization, and political revolution. In fact, the experiences of the American Revolution (1776–83) and even more so the French Revolution (1789–99) disturbed some and inspired others, but they forced all to rethink the nature and the knowability of society.

Sociology was also the heir of the Enlightenment thinkers who tried to make sense of social order through the examination of perception, the formation of ideas, and political and economic organization specifically, as well as the processes of history. One scholar not mentioned in previous chapters was Baron de Montesquieu (1689–1755), who according to John Drysdale and Susan Hoecker-Drysdale "pioneered a sociological approach to the classification and study of societies focusing on their social laws and institutional organization" (2007: 29), particularly in his 1748 *The Spirit of the Laws*.

However, the first step toward sociology proper is typically attributed to Claude-Henri de Rouvroy, Comte de Saint-Simon (1760–1825), better known simply as Saint-Simon. Living through the French Revolution, he was excited by the changes in society and the economy and judged social change as social *progress*, in which science and industry would finally improve the conditions of life for all people. The newly-emerging social order would solve society's problems through great collective efforts like the construction of railroads but also through the emergence and dominance of new kinds of people—the "productive" classes among whom he counted scientists, engineers, manufacturers, and bankers but also artists and poets. The old parasitic classes such as the nobility and the priesthood would be overthrown at no great loss to society, ushering in an era of peace and prosperity.

Saint-Simon was something of an idealist, but his secretary, Auguste Comte (1798–1857), would elaborate on many of his predecessor's ideas and put them into action. Comte is credited with introducing the word "sociology" (although it was apparently first used by Emmanuel Joseph Sieyès) and for conceiving of the new discipline as a science or a form of "positive knowledge" or "positivism"—that is, as we described in the first chapter, a body of knowledge built on factual observations and measurements. Indeed, Comte like many others was impressed with the successes of natural science in his time and envisioned a "social physics" that would

> comprise both rational and empirical methods in the study of both structural (*social statics*) and processual (*social dynamics*) aspects of culture. Above all, this new science was to contribute to the knowledge of human social evolution and to the improvement of human societies by the application of sociological knowledge to social life.
>
> (Drysdale and Hoecker-Drysdale 2007: 30, emphasis in the original)

Over a span of a dozen years, Comte incorporated his thoughts into a six-volume study known as *Course in Positive Philosophy*.

Comte is chiefly remembered for his theory, first propounded in 1822, of the three stages of social history. As indicated by C. Wright Mills' explanation of the sociological imagination, early sociology (and anthropology—see Chapter 7) was intensely interested in history, in "big" history including the history of institutions like government or the family or religion and in the grand processes of universal human history. Comte's model was, thus, a hybrid of modern-day history and sociology, offering a periodization of society on the largest scale.Comte's three stages, representing the social and intellectual progress of mankind, consisted of:

Stage 1: Theological (primitive era)

The basic unit of society—the family
The basic unifying sentiment of society—attachment or affection (shared kin identity and feeling)
The basic material or organizational form of society—militarism

Stage 2: Metaphysical (ancient/classical era)

The basic unit of society—the state

The basic unifying sentiment of society—veneration or respect (what we might call patriotism or nationalism)

The basic material or organizational form of society—law (especially the contract)

Stage 3: Positive (modern/scientific era)

The basic unit of society—humanity, the entire human species
The unifying sentiment of society—benevolence or human goodwill
The basic material or organizational form of society—industry

(based on Collins and Makowsky 1993: 28)

If this early sociology felt a comradeship with history, it wrestled against psychology and the philosophical precursors of psychology. According to Randall Collins and Michael Makowsky, for Comte "the individual psyche or soul was merely a religious and philosophical superstition; a truly scientific psychology would treat humans as the activity of body and brain, and hence psychology was part of physiology, a division of biology" (28).

The key to Comte's new science of society was the assertion that every specific form or level of reality demands its own appropriate science. Society, "although composed of individuals, is not identical with those individuals, but is structured according to its own principles"; like a language, society "is not just the behavior of individuals, but something that accumulates across many generations. . . . [Since it] develops a vocabulary and a grammar that no one person ever does much to modify, society remains and unfolds by laws of its own, while individuals come and go" (26). Unfortunately, later in his life Comte abandoned his scientific perspective and turned his beliefs into a cult—a Religion of Humanity—with society as the god or supreme being.

The last of the proximate ancestors of academic sociology worth was Herbert Spencer (1820–1903), who applied the new Darwinian thinking of the day to society and social history. It was Spencer who coined the term "survival of the fittest" in his 1864 *Principles of Biology*, an idea that was subsequently expanded into "social Darwinism" or the notion that societies fall on various levels of a social scale and that more "advanced" societies are apt to defeat and dominate less advanced or more "primitive" ones— thus providing a justification, indeed a natural basis, for colonial conquest and war. At any rate, as a scientist as well as a social theorist, Spencer sought the "laws" of society that shape it just as surely as the laws of physics or biology determine the behavior of matter and life. He posited that individual humans are subjected to non-individual (that is, social) forces that are not of their invention and may actually be outside of their control or even knowledge. A social science, a sociology, is necessary to discover and apply these social laws.

Harriet Martineau: The Mother of Sociology

Attentive readers may have noticed that we have mentioned hardly any women in this book so far. This is an unhappy consequence of the patriarchy in the Western tradition, which did not allow women access to education and publication. One prominent although relatively un-heralded exception is Harriet Martineau (1802–76), an Englishwoman and contemporary and supporter of Comte who translated his work into English in 1853. She was an accomplished political economist in her own right, offered the editorship of a journal of sociology in 1838. Drysdale and Hoecker-Drysdale consider her 1838 *How to Observe Morals and Manners* to be "the first treatise on methodology in sociology" (2007: 30), but her most memorable contribution was probably her 1837 study *Society in America*. With passion uncharacteristic of scholarly writers then or now, she criticized the status of women in American society:

> If a test of civilization be sought, none can be so sure as the condition of that half of society over which the other half has power, from the exercise of the right of the strongest. Tried by this test, the American civilization appears to be of a lower order than might have been expected from some other symptoms of its social state. The Americans have, in the treatment of women, fallen below, not only their own democratic principles, but the practice of some parts of the Old World. . . . While woman's intellect is confined, her morals crushed, her health ruined, her weaknesses encouraged, and her strength punished, she is told that her lot is cast in the paradise of women: and there is no country in the world where there is so much boasting of the 'chivalrous' treatment she enjoys.
>
> (1837: 105)

Spencer was the first scholar to use the term "sociology" in the title of a book, his three-volume *Principles of Sociology*, the first volume of which was published in 1874–5. The earliest sociology course by that name was taught in 1875 by William Graham Sumner, and the first academic department of sociology was founded in 1892 at the University of Chicago, which would become the center of American sociology (see later discussion).

The Three Founders of Contemporary Sociology

While the figures in the previous section were significant for initiating the process of social thinking and for launching a new social science, they are not generally recognized as founders of sociology as we know and practice it today. That honor belongs to three men whom we have met before and whose influence extends beyond the discipline of sociology itself. These men, in chronological order, are Karl Marx, Émile Durkheim, and Max Weber.

Karl Marx: The Materialist Theory of Society

Marx is important to almost all of the modern social sciences; indeed, only psychology and geography do not bear his direct stamp, and many of his followers have explored his relevance to psychological (or sometimes anti-psychological) theory.

We are well acquainted with Marx's general theory by now. His fundamental contention was that every particular historical society was a "social formation" built upon the base of its practical, material, economic activity. Marx's philosophy of history, then, was exactly and explicitly the opposite of Hegel's, who believed that "spirit" or "ideas" drove the physical/material world. For Marx, physical/material action—namely, work or labor—drove ideas.

Marx further analyzed that every social formation, like a geological formation, was layered. These layers were the "classes" of society, which were distinguished by their unequal wealth but, more profoundly, by their different *interests* and their unequal *power*. Each class or type/group in society had its specific interests; in the nineteenth century, the interests of the working class were shorter working hours, better working conditions, more dependable employment, and of course higher wages, while the interests of the owning class were precisely the opposite. Classes therefore necessarily clashed over their conflicting interests, and it was this clash that drove the historical evolution of societies.

However, within any particular social formation, the economically-dominant class also enjoyed greater power, in two senses of the term. First, the upper or ruling class controlled the resources, the weapons, and the political institutions; they could compel the labor of the lower classes, use force against the lower classes, and create laws in their own favor. But, as discussed in Chapter 2, they also exercised more subtle social power (what Gramsci called *hegemony*), controlling the discourse of the culture and literally the institutions by which society was perpetuated and legitimated. The upper classes set the agenda for society, establishing the issues that society would talk about and even the terms in which they would talk. They further controlled institutions like the education system, the media, and the religion. All of these institutions they designed and deployed to inculcate certain ideas and values in members, such as the notions of "hard work" or "responsibility" or "competition"—or worse yet, "sin" or "spiritual cleanness." Such ideas served to justify the existing social system by purporting to explain social differences (that is, that the rich worked harder or were more responsible or were spiritually superior) in such a way that each class seemed (naturally or supernaturally) to belong in its station.

An illustrative analysis of a social institution other than politics or the economy is found in the study by Friedrich Engels, Marx's friend and collaborator, on the origin of the family. Published in 1884 after Marx's death, and drawing on the cross-cultural descriptions of early ethnographer Lewis Henry Morgan (see Chapter 7), *The Origin of the Family, Private Property, and the State* maintained that family as we know it did not exist in the earliest societies. Rather, men and women alike participated freely and equally in wider kinship and tribal life. However, it was the concept of *private property* that generated the enclosed and patriarchal monogamous family—and transformed the status of women—as men treated their households, including their wives, as productive resources. The husband became the owner and ruler of the household, wives and children became laborers in the husband's pursuit of wealth, and paternity became crucially important, since the wife now had the task of providing legitimate heirs to inherit the man's property.

Finally, it is worth understanding that practical material conditions did not only shape institutions and relations in Marx's theory but literally shaped minds. Just as each society was historically contingent, so human personality and thought-processes were likewise historically contingent; human nature was not fixed and universal in this view but constructed by activity—activity that was always and necessarily social. As Marx wrote, "It is not the consciousness of men that determines their being, but, on the contrary, their social being that determines their consciousness" (1977: 389).

Émile Durkheim: Social Facts and Collective Conscience

If any individual deserves the title of inventor of modern sociology, it is Durkheim (1858–1917), whose writing and organizational achievements established the channels in which sociology (and much of anthropology) runs to this day. Born into a French Jewish family during a period of great social upheaval, his life's work shows his deep concern with "the instability, violence, and decadence of modern society, at least as it displayed itself in France" (Collins and Makowksy 1993: 102). He studied philosophy and intellectual history under the famous scholar Fustel de Coulanges and had Henri Bergson as one of his classmates; after graduation he taught philosophy for a time and in 1885 moved to Germany, where he became acquainted with the research of Wilhelm Wundt (see Chapter 5). He returned to France in 1887 to teach the first social science course ever offered at the University of Bordeaux.

Durkheim began his sociological career by publishing three foundational texts. In 1893 he released *The Division of Labor in Society*, arguing that it was the very complexity of modern society that gave it cohesion. Following the prior work of Ferdinand Tönnies on two distinct kinds of societies— *gemeinschaft* or "community" and *gesellschaft* or "society"—Durkheim suggested that older, rural, or primitive societies functioned as "mechanical societies" in which

- all members performed the same tasks and were thus more or less interchangeable
- members shared social knowledge and values, and
- society was held together by common sentiments of kinship and affection.

However, modern societies, he judged, functioned as "organic societies," like complex organisms with specialized internal systems, in which

- members performed quite different tasks or jobs, like Adam Smith's butcher, brewer, and baker (see Chapter 4)
- members could not be assumed to share social knowledge and values and often in fact held quite different ideas and beliefs
- society was held together by mutual dependence and by formal mechanisms like law and contracts.

His second book, the 1895 *The Rules of Sociological Method*, was one of his most important because it announced and described "a sociology that is objective, specific, and methodical" (Durkheim 1982: 35). Pivotal for Durkheim's case was the concept of *social fact*, which was a distinct and irreducible kind of fact that only a science of society could understand. Indeed, the first chapter of the book is "What is a Social Fact?" and he explained this unfamiliar idea in the following terms:

> When I perform my duties as a brother, a husband, or a citizen and carry out the commitments I have entered into, I fulfill obligations which are defined in law and custom and which are external to myself and my actions. Even when they conform to my own sentiments and when I feel their reality within me, that reality does not cease to be objective, for it is not I who have prescribed these duties; I have received them through education. Moreover, how often does it happen that we are ignorant of the details of the obligations that we must assume, and that, to know them, we must consult the legal code and its authorized interpreters! Similarly the believer has discovered from birth, ready fashioned, the beliefs and practices of his religious life; if they existed before he did, it follows that they exist outside him. The system of signs that I employ to express my thoughts, the monetary system I use to pay my debts, the

credit instruments I utilize in my commercial relationships, the practices I follow in my profession, etc. all function independently of the use I make of them.

(50–1)

> Novelist and poet Oscar Wilde famously quipped, "Most people are other people. Their thoughts are someone else's opinions, their lives a mimicry, their passions a quotation."

Durkheim acknowledged that this was such an odd way to think in his day that the new field of sociology met with strong opposition. Yet he concluded the chapter with a succinct definition: "A social fact is any way of acting, whether fixed or not, capable of exerting over the individual an external constraint; or: which is general over the whole of a given society whilst having an existence of its own, independent of its individual manifestations" (59).

His third book in a four-year span aimed to demonstrate how a putatively private behavior could be understood best in sociological terms. His 1897 *Suicide: A Study in Sociology*, employed the method he outlined two years before, arguing first that statistical information, like the "social suicide rate," was crucial to explaining suicide, and second that there were a number of identifiable and consistent social causes and social types of suicide. For example, suicide was more common in some societies than others and more common at certain times of year than others. Further, suicide could be correlated to too little attachment to society (being more prevalent among men, unmarried people, and the upper class), too tight a control by society (as among soldiers or samurai), or individual or social crises (divorce, death in the family, or economic downturns, for instance). As he concluded, psychology could not account for these trends; "the social suicide rate can be explained only sociologically" (1951: 299).

Finally, at a time when sociology and anthropology were not completely differentiated, Durkheim and his associates studied cross-cultural issues in society as well. For instance, Marcel Mauss employed Bronislaw Malinowski's fieldwork on exchange practices among the Trobriand Islanders in his celebrated essay *The Gift*. The most famous result was Durkheim's 1912 *The Elementary Forms of Religious Life*, which sought to identify the origin and essence of religion and society via ethnographic reports from Australia of what seemed to be the most basic or minimal form of religion in the world—Australian Aboriginal "totemism." This afforded Durkheim an opportunity to reconsider the fundamental questions of human thought, the same ones previously explored by writers from Aristotle to Locke, Hume, and Kant.

Durkheim referred to the ideas in people's heads as "representations" and asserted that many if not most of these ideas were actually *collective representations*, ideas that they have received from society and by social means. Still more importantly, such collective representations were socially and historically specific: they differed between "human groups" and were "laboriously forged over the centuries" (1995: 25). Sharing and transmitting—and internalizing—particular collective representations produced a uniquely socialized mind or personality or thought-process, a *collective consciousness/conscience* (the French word he used can be translated either way). The ultimate reality for Durkheim was not mind, and certainly not "religious truth," but society, and it was society that provided the ideas and classifications that furnished thought. This perspective relates (and Durkheim overtly related it) to the perennial question of the

---

Durkheim and the Institutionalization of Sociology

Sociology, like any new discipline, did not just happen, and it could not be achieved simply by one person or a few people writing books. Establishing and promoting sociology required energetic leaders and entrepreneurs, group organization, and formal and intentional institutionalization. Durkheim was the man for the job. Not only was Durkheim, according to Alexander Tristan Riley (2010), an indefatigable advocate of sociology, but he also gathered a group around him and established various elements of a sociological institution. The key members of Durkheim's group were Marcel Mauss, Henri Hubert, and Robert Hertz. Activating pre-existing social networks, Mauss was Durkheim's nephew (son of his sister), while Hubert was best friends with Mauss, and Hertz was a student of the older triumvirate. Naturally, a main transmission point for early sociology—and another institutional resource exploited by Durkheim and his circle—was the university system, in which Durkheim taught first at the University of Bordeaux and then in Paris at the Sorbonne. From these platforms he was able to secure a place for sociology in the academy (over objections from the philosophers) and to influence a great many students. Even more, he served as what Riley calls a "master of ceremonies" for the fledgling science, defining many of its terms and problems. He also obviously wrote extensively, including on the very method of sociology, and even produced his own sociological journal (with his inner circle of followers), *L'Année Sociologique* or "Sociological Year" through which he and his collaborators could develop and steer sociology.

"categories" of thought. Some philosophers had believed that the categories were innate; others claimed that they were entirely gleaned from experience. According to Durkheim, though, ideas and mental categories were clearly not innate or entirely derived from individual cognition; rather, they were an external, transpersonal phenomenon, a "concrete reality which alone historical and ethnographic observation can reveal" (3). Thus, as Susan Stedman Jones opines, his goal was "to solve the philosophical problem of the categories with sociological methods" (2013: 159).

Max Weber: Social Science as Understanding

If there was one man who epitomized the turn-of-the-century state of the pre-differentiated social sciences, it was Max Weber (1864–1920). A contemporary of Durkheim, he originally studied law before acquiring expertise in history, economics, politics, religion, linguistics, and almost every field of knowledge in his day. Collins and Makowsky claimed that he "was a one-man crucible for the intellectual currents of the nineteenth century," a man whose knowledge of history and society "probably exceeded that of any other person who had ever lived," and that "from his central position he forged a viewpoint for sociology as both a science and a study of meaningful human creations" (1993: 118). Having encountered him in previous chapters, we know that he made lasting contributions not only to sociology but to political science (e.g. his analysis of the state and of power) and economics (e.g. his analysis of class).

Much of Weber's early work was directed against Marx, who insisted that material forces drive ideas. In his classic 1904 *The Protestant Ethic and the Spirit of Capitalism*, Weber combined social, historical, religious, and economic perspectives to argue that ideas—in this case, a new religious idea called Protestantism—could be a force for social and even economic change in their own right. The beliefs and values taught by Protestant (especially Calvinist) Christianity encouraged, he claimed, economic behaviors like hard work and frugality that contributed to the formation of modern capitalism.

Weber wrote on most of the weighty social topics of his (and our) day, including religion, economics, politics, and ethnicity and nationalism. However, crucial to his approach, as manifested in his essays from 1903 to 1917 assembled in the volume *On the Methodology of the Social Sciences*, was the notion that human behavior cannot be explained apart from the *meaning* that this behavior has for the humans engaging in the behavior. Doing a science of human behavior then required *Verstehen*, the German word for "understanding." Thus, sociology for him was "a science concerning itself with the interpretive understanding of social action and thereby with a causal explanation of its course and consequences. We shall speak of 'action' insofar as the acting individual attaches a subjective meaning to his behavior" (1968: 4). In fact, we faced this issue in the first chapter, in the discussion of whether social sciences were and could be identical to natural sciences, given that humans unlike atoms or rocks have their own knowledge, their own meanings, and their own subjectivity.

Weber, like other social thinkers of his era, was also interested in the grand sweeping questions of social history. His studies in the sociology of religion, for example, embraced not only Protestantism but Hinduism, ancient Judaism, and Chinese religions. Like Durkheim he was particularly curious about—and troubled by—modern society and therefore the historical changes in society that brought us to modern society. Two subjects investigated by Weber, then, were organizations and bureaucracies, since these seemed to be among the critical social forces of modernity.

More generally, he characterized modernity as a specific social formation with distinctive traits. In another classic analysis, he described modern society as characteristically if not essentially urban, bureaucratic, "rational" (that is, not necessarily "logical" or clear-headed but driven by the search for quantification, efficiency and "what works"), and secular or non-religious. If Marx was correct that each economic or material base grew its own religious system, then Weber reckoned that modern society was infertile ground for any religion. He perceived and grieved a "disenchantment" of the world as religion was pushed aside by practical, quantifiable, and effective concerns.

Like Durkheim, Weber left his institutional mark as well. In 1919 he founded the sociology department of the Ludwig Maximilian University in Munich. His intellectual footprint is found throughout the social sciences.

Contemporary Sociological Thought and Method

The triumvirate of Marx, Durkheim, and Weber did more than inaugurate modern sociology. They continue to stalk the discipline, as every introductory textbook recounts their contributions and, often enough, refracts each sociological topic through their three lenses. More than any other social science, the three founding fathers of sociology shape the discipline's identity, each associated (somewhat loosely) with the three major theoretical schools in the field.

The Schools of Sociological Theory

Every sociology textbook also introduces (and usually runs through every topic) the three predominant theoretical perspectives of the discipline. These are not "careers" as in psychology; they are not distinct professions or languages or applications of sociology, and in fact most practicing sociologists combine them in their research.

In no particular order, the first theoretical approach is *functionalism*, which sees society as a (more or less) stable system with parts working in harmony to satisfy the basic needs of its members. Most associated with Durkheim, functionalism accepts that societies are internally complex—that there are different "parts" such as classes, genders, and of course institutions like government and religion—but that this complexity operates like a machine or an organism. Each internal part, group, or institution makes a contribution to the whole, that is, it has a function; further, the parts/groups/institutions interact to maintain "equilibrium": changes to one element of society will spark related changes in other elements.

This does not mean that society always functions well or that all of its functions are obvious. For example, Durkheim commented that society's rules, values, and institutions can break down or fail, resulting in a condition of "anomie" or unruliness. In such a condition, individuals are likely to be unhappy or even to commit suicide; crime and deviance may spike. However, in a sense, these responses are like "symptoms" of a sick society, calling attention to its pathologies and crying out for a solution. Further, sociologists like Robert Merton (1957) have refined functionalism, observing for instance that some functions are "manifest" or obvious or anticipated, while others are "latent" or unexpected or unseen. For example, the manifest functions of education are to provide students with information, to prepare them for a job, and to shape them into good citizens; the latent functions include perpetuation of the class system, phenomena like "gate-keeping" that set standards for admitting some individuals and excluding others, and the entrenchment of the interests and power of teachers.

These last comments take us to the second major school of sociological thought, *conflict theory*, which views society as a system of difference if not inequality and exploitation. Most associated with Marx, conflict theory emphasizes social distinctions and competition; consensus and harmony in society are unlikely from this perspective, as individuals and groups occupy different places in society, and while society certainly functions, it does not function equally satisfactorily for everyone.

Conflict theory is much more likely than functionalism to focus on *stratification* or the division of society into unequal layers or groups, as well as on the specific dimensions of this stratification, such as race, class, and gender. It casts a critical eye on the optimistic assumptions of functionalism, often being conspicuously critical of society's organization and operation. Hence, it is often called "critical theory." Central to its viewpoint is the notion of power, which is unevenly distributed and advantageously exercised. According to George Ritzer's (2013) introductory textbook, some elaborations of conflict/critical theory include feminist theory (which particularly examines and critiques the power differences between men and women), "queer theory" (which explores how gender categories are created and perpetuated in the first place), and critical race theory.

Conflict theory does not stipulate that groups are necessarily or always in open conflict but rather that there are fundamental fractures in society. Nor does it inevitably see conflict as a bad thing. For Marx and Marxists, conflict was and is the motor of social change, and for sociologists like Lewis

Coser and Georg Simmel, conflict or the friction between groups could provide the very structure of a society.

It will be noted that functionalism and conflict theory are both large-scale theories of society or what has been called *macro-social* theories. The third theoretical school, taking a *micro-social* perspective, is called *symbolic interactionism* and is often associated with Weber, although he never used the term. Instead, "symbolic interactionism" was coined by Herbert Blumer, who extended Weber's attention to meaning and understanding to include three key premises:

- "that human beings act toward things on the basis of the meaning that the things have for them"
- "that the meaning of such things is derived from, or arises out of, the social interaction that one has with one's fellow"
- "that these meanings are handled in, and modified through, an interpretative process used by the person in dealing with the things he encounters."

(1969: 2–3)

The theory has roots in the social psychology of Charles Cooley (1864–1929), John Dewey (1859–1952), and George Herbert Mead (1863–1931) —all born within five years of each other—who emphasized the role of action and social interaction in learning and even in the formation of the "self." Cooley offered the phrase "looking-glass self" to describe how we learn about ourselves by observing how others react to us. Mead added that "significant others" are particularly important for feeding back information about ourselves, while Dewey in such works as the 1909 *Moral Principles in Education*, the 1916 *Democracy and Education: An Introduction to the Philosophy of Education*, and the 1938 *Experience and Education* improved on Piaget's (and all pre-modern) theories of learning by stressing the practical/active and social origin of knowledge.

The other key concept of symbolic interactionism besides meaning is "situation." Behavior always occurs in a specific social situation (the classroom, the court room, a date, etc.), and people must recognize the situation they are in and know the proper actions for that situation. In that sense, social activity can be likened to a play, in which each person is "on stage" and knows his/her "role." This is precisely the metaphor that Erving Goffman developed in his famed 1959 *The Presentation of Self in Everyday Life*. He gave a "theatrical" or "dramaturgical" interpretation of social interaction, in which people are "actors" playing a "scene." Each of us knows (because we have learned it through previous interaction) the "script" for the scene, and we play as best we can. Social action is subsequently, as social scientists have come to say, a "performance," and individuals actively participate to establish and maintain the meaning of the scene and to bring it to successful completion.

This concentration on the small mundane knowledge and skills of social actors asks for a new method, and Harold Garfinkel proposed one in his 1967 *Studies in Ethnomethodology*. Ethnomethodology, the study of the strategies and tactics that people utilize to conduct social action, examines things like conversation skills, turn-taking, and all manner of minute social knowledge (most famously, how to stand properly in an elevator). The methodology exposed and continues to expose the incredible amount of social knowledge that an individual needs to master to function in a society.

The Development of American Sociology

The United States was one of the first countries to embrace sociology, if only because that country experienced such radical social transformations at exactly the moment when the discipline arose. American sociology was especially sensitized by the "problems" of immigration and race in the late nineteenth century. Indeed, one of the unsung heroes of American sociology, writing at the same time as Durkheim's early work, was the African American scholar W. E. B. Du Bois (1868–1963). Realizing that race relations in the United States could not be understood or advanced without empirical data, he published his *The Philadelphia Negro: A Social Study* in 1899, based on door-to-door surveys and interviews and featuring statistical charts and graphs. In 1909–10 he followed up with *The Negro American Family*, describing marriage, household structures, and family finances.

Sociology was seen immediately in the U.S. as a way to study, and then solve, "social problems," so most early sociological research fixated on the lower classes, urban populations, and minority races and ethnicities. The center of American sociology became the University of Chicago, where the "Chicago school" of sociology investigated modern social (dis)order. Much attention naturally fell on cities, where social problems were believed to be concentrated. One of the leaders of the Chicago sociologists was Robert Park (1864–1944), who applied biological thinking to the urban physical and social environment, suggesting what he called "human ecology." He observed, for instance, that, like non-human species in their ecosystems, humans competed for space, constructed their lived spaces for specialized uses (e.g. residential, commercial, or industrial), and transformed the use of spaces over time by pushing old groups out and moving new groups in (e.g. a neighborhood that was formerly lower class or non-white might become upper class or white).

Many American sociologists (and other Americans) shared a jaundiced view of the city. It is difficult to appreciate today, but the city was still a relatively new and unfamiliar scape in the early 1900s, as portrayed in Robert and Helen Lynd's ground-breaking 1929 book *Middletown: A Study in Modern American Culture*. Marx, Durkheim, and Weber each in their own way decried the disorganization, the poverty, the pollution, the alienation, and the sheer diversity of the city, and Louis Wirth (see later

---

Louis Wirth on Life in the Big City

As early as 1903 Georg Simmel, in his *The Metropolis and Mental Life*, condemned urban society for speeding up and overstimulating people, producing a modern personality that was overly "intellectualistic" (similar to what Weber called rationalized), self-conscious, blasé, and "homogeneous, flat, and grey." More than three decades later, Louis Wirth analyzed the modern city as more than just a physical place but "a set of attitudes and ideas, and a constellation of personalities engaging in typical forms of collective behavior and subject to characteristics mechanisms of social control" (1938: 18–19). The large and diverse populations of twentieth-century cities were responsible for "the relative absence of intimate personal acquaintanceship, the segmentalization of human relations which are largely anonymous, superficial, and transitory," which "tends to break down rigid social structures and to produce increased mobility, instability, and insecurity" (1). In short, the quality of urban society bred "superficiality," "anonymity," and a "transitory character" (12), producing a person with "no sentimental and emotional ties" (16). Consequently, "Personal disorganization, mental breakdown, suicide, delinquency, crime, corruption, and disorder might be expected under these circumstances to be more prevalent in the urban than in the rural community" (23).

---

discussion) summed up this discontent in his short but memorable essay "Urbanism as a Way of Life."

This sociological emphasis on the marginalized and "troubled" classes and categories in society, and the location of those groups predominantly in cities, led researchers not only to comb through data and statistics for patterns and trends but to venture into urban neighborhoods themselves to observe and document the lives of modern urban dwellers. The result was a stream of field studies of communities (often African American or ethnic communities) such as Herbert Gans' 1962 *The Urban Villagers: Group and Class in the Life of Italian-Americans*, Elliott Lebow's 1968 *Tally's Corner*, Gerald Suttle's 1968 *The Social Order of the Slum*, Ulf Hannerz's 1969 *Soulside: Inquiries into Ghetto Culture and Community*, Carol Stack's 1974 *All Our Kin: Strategies for Survival in a Black Community*, and Elijah Anderson's 1978 *A Place on the Corner* and 1990 *Street Wise: Rae, Class, and Change in an Urban Community*. As all of these investigations discovered, and as Suttle's title particularly suggests, the lives of the poor and the marginal were not utterly disorganized and anomic but rather evidenced their own, if different, social order.

Sociological Research Methods

Thanks to the efforts of the founding generation and of generations of descendants, sociology has amassed considerable knowledge about modern societies and, in the process, has developed a distinct way of thinking about society. Sociologists use all of the standard methods for collecting data on human behavior—questionnaires, surveys, interviews, direct observation and fieldwork, even experiments, and of course the analysis of secondary and statistical data—but what is particularly characteristic of sociologists is the

---

Research Topics in Sociology

The articles in the 2015 issue of *Annual Review of Sociology* include:

"What Sociologists Should Know about Complexity"
"Beyond Altruism: Sociological Foundations of Cooperation and Prosocial Behavior"
"The Emergence of Global Systemic Risk"
"The Stigma Complex"
"The Sociology of Consumption: Its Recent Development"
"Punishment Regimes and the Multilevel Effects of Parental Incarceration"
"Sociology and School Choice: What We Know After Two Decades of Charter Schools"
"Effects of the Great Recession: Health and Well-Being"
"Financialization of the Economy"
"Human Trafficking and Contemporary Slavery"
"New Directions in the Sociology of Development"
"Empire, Health, and Health Care: Perspectives at the End of Empire as We Have Known It"
"Incarceration and Health"
"Is Racism a Fundamental Cause of Inequalities in Health?"
"STEM Education"
"The Far-Reaching Impact of Job Loss and Unemployment"
"Environmental Dimensions of Migration"
"Intraregional Migration in South America: Trends and a Research Agenda"
"Reproduction"
"Does Schooling Increase or Reduce Social Inequality?"
"Marriage and Family in East Asia: Continuity and Change"

kind of information they seek and the correlations and conclusions they draw from it. Sociological research also can be, and often is, recruited in policy debates and decisions, and the sociological approach is key in two practical applied fields—criminology and social work.

Since sociology had to wrestle for space in the academy at the turn of the twentieth century, it has been especially aware of the burden to establish a unique subject-matter and method. In Durkheim's1895 *The Rules of Sociological Method*, he stipulated that social facts must be and are separable from other kinds of facts, primarily psychological or individual ones: "Social phenomena must therefore be considered in themselves, detached from the conscious beings who form their own mental representations of them. They must be studied from the outside, as external things because it is in this guise that they present themselves to us" (1982: 70). Precisely because they are public, collective, and observable—laws "enshrined in legal codes" (71), educational principles in the concrete form of schools and curricula and textbooks, religious attitudes visible in churches and rituals—social facts had a better claim to facticity than psychological facts.

Like economics (see Chapter 4), modern sociological thought and method begins with its lexicon, which strives to make visible the positions, forces, and systems within which persons live and act. The overarching concept is *social structure*, which is the enduring "shape" of a society produced and perpetuated by learning (what sociologists call *socialization*), socialized behavior, and the complex interconnection between the parts of society. Social structure establishes the "field" of social action or the rules and circumstances within which we formulate our behavior. The most basic unit of social structure is not the individual but the *status* or a "location" or "kind of person to be" in social system, for instance teacher or student, boss or employee, or priest or layperson. A particular status carries with it a *role* or the expected "part to play" in society; a status also gives the individual a distinctive perspective on society, including specific knowledge and specific "moves" that s/he can legitimately make.

For sociologists, the most significant statuses include race and ethnicity, class and income, gender, age, and education. Each of these categories obviously shapes the individual's experience of society, as well as collective social outcomes. But sociologists also understand that statuses do not operate in isolation; rather, each individual can be described as a bundle of statuses or a *status set*. I, David Eller, can be sociologically located as a white, middle-age, middle-income, highly educated, suburban, married, male college professor; armed with that knowledge, sociology can predict the probability of the behaviors and attitudes of people like me. More, individual members of society are organized into *groups* based on shared characteristics, and groups are largely where we get our identities, our interests, and our social knowledge. Groups are further integrated into *institutions*, the most long-lasting of the elements in the "skeleton" of social structure. Sociologists typically identify five major institutions—economy, politics, family, religion, education—each of which consists of many lower-level institutions (e.g. education involves elementary schools, high schools, college, professional schools, textbook publishers, teacher organizations, testing companies, even food-service and janitorial businesses).

As mentioned, to study and analyze such phenomena, sociologists may and do conduct original research, but there is also a wealth of social information already collected and processed for sociologists to exploit. In the United States, one valuable source of data is the General Social Survey, which, according to its website (gss.norc.org), "contains a standard core of demographic, behavioral, and attitudinal questions, plus topics of special interest. Among the topics covered are civil liberties, crime and violence, intergroup tolerance, morality, national spending priorities, psychological well-being, social mobility, and stress and traumatic events." Depending on the subject under investigation, sociologists can turn to the Census Bureau, Bureau of Labor Statistics, National Center for Health Statistics, National Survey of Families and Households, FBI Uniform Crime Report, Bureau of Justice Statistics, Association of Religion Data Archives, or American Religious Identification Survey, not to mention hospitals, schools, and other agencies. Polling agencies like Gallup or Pew provide a variety of data, and specialized organizations collect even more statistics on their topics of interest.

A hallmark of sociological research is linking major statuses like race, class, and gender to social behaviors and attitudes. This commonly involves combing through large amounts of data and performing statistical analyzes to discover trends and relations. Some representative findings of sociology for the United States include:

- women are more likely to be religious than men
- women (38.2 percent), African Americans (6.4 percent), and Hispanics (7.6 percent) are less likely to hold management positions than white men
- in 2000, the most common household arrangement was one person living alone (25.8 percent), followed by spouses living with children (22.4 percent) and spouses living without children (21.2 percent)
- there is a persistent "achievement gap" in education, with a high school dropout rate of 4.8 percent for whites, 9.9 percent for blacks, 14.6 percent for Native Americans, and 18.3 percent for Hispanics
- troubling health disparities exist between races, with white Americans living on average considerably longer than non-whites and with African Americans dying more often from accidents, diabetes, homicide, and AIDS than other races.

Because much of their data is quantitative, sociologists are likely to grace their research with numbers and statistics and to state and test hypotheses.

However, not all sociological work is quantitative or statistical; sociologists also collect and report qualitative data from interviews, observation, or participation. The range of sociological activities can be appreciated in regard to the sociological approach to religion.

1. Sociologists name and define variables like "religiosity" to make it possible to measure and compare levels of religious belief and behavior relative to other social statuses and variables such as race, class, gender, age, region, marital status, and such. They can then quantify such specific behavior as prayer, Bible reading, church membership, and church attendance. They can ask who changes religious affiliation over time and who disaffiliates from or leaves religion.
2. Sociologists classify and describe different kinds of religious institutions. Since Weber, sociologists for instance have distinguished the "church" from the "sect," adding other categories such as the denomination and the cult.
3. Sociologists describe the beliefs, attitudes, and organization of particular religious groups or organizations. Nancy Ammerman (1987), for example, reported on an evangelical church that not only believed that the outside world was wicked and sinful and so maintained strict boundaries between itself and nonbelievers but went so far as to create its own institutions, from schools to social activities.
4. Sociologists propose theories for how religion functions. One of the most influential recent theories is Rodney Stark's "religious market" model (e.g. Stark and Iannaccone 1994), in which he envisioned churches as "religious firms" that offer a product to religious consumers; because demand for religion, he argued, is constant, churches create supply and craft their product to the tastes of consumers, competing with each other for members and thus ultimately offering the product that people want or losing customers.

Disciplinary Study #5: Sociology of Terrorism

Just as stereotypes portray the terrorist as a disturbed or deranged individual, they often portray him or her as an *individual*, a lone wolf and antisocial character. But all of the previous examinations of terrorism in this book have emphasized that terrorism is almost always highly organized, usually collective, and inevitably related to shared perceptions and beliefs as well as social institutions. Thus, turning the sociological imagination on terrorism is very welcome. In a review of research on terrorism, Austin Turk identified several angles from which sociology has analyzed the behavior, including "(a) the social construction of terrorism, (b) terrorism as political violence, (c) terrorism as communication, (d) organizing terrorism, (e) socializing terrorists, (f) social control of terrorism, and (g) theorizing terrorism" (2004: 271).

To start, the social construction of terrorism means that terrorism is not a phenomenon of nature—indeed, is not a "thing" at all—but is created, practiced, and perpetuated by specific persons in specific places and situations. As Turk writes,

> terrorism is not a given in the real world but is instead an interpretation of events and their presumed causes. *And these interpretations are not unbiased attempts to depict truth but rather conscious efforts to manipulate perceptions to promote certain interests at the expense of others.*
>
> (271–2, emphasis added)

In other words, as we will also argue in the next chapter, terrorism is not only constructed by the acts of individual terrorists and of terrorist organizations *but it is also constructed by those who label some acts "terrorism" and not others.*

We have previously discussed terrorism as political violence (see Chapter 2), so let us move on to terrorism as communication. Remembering the concept of "propaganda of the deed," it is important to consider what terrorists are trying to communicate and to whom. Most obviously, they are communicating dissatisfaction to their targets, ordinarily governments/states. However, terrorism is not a dyadic but a *triadic* relationship between terrorists, victims, and *an audience*. That audience includes the citizens of the target-society, the citizens of the society the terrorists claim to represent, and the world at large. Part of their motivation is to bring attention and sympathy to their cause. At the same time, labeling an act as "terrorism" is communication too: it communicates the perceived illegitimacy of the act and seeks to mobilize people *against* the terrorists and their cause.

Terrorism, other than individual acts of random violence, would not exist without organization, and elsewhere we have surveyed the political and economic organization of terrorist groups. Sociologists encouraged us additionally to regard terrorism as a form of "collective behavior" and even more generally as a "social movement." Just as early sociologists were typically leery of urban society, they were also leery of collective behavior and social movements, seeing them as destabilizing and disorderly. In his classic statement on collective behavior, Herbert Blumer echoed some of this sentiment, calling it "unorganized, unregulated, fluid, and active" in circumstances in which "routines have broken down" (1939: 228). At the same time, he recognized collective behavior as "the ways in which social order comes into existence, in the sense of the emergence and solidification of new forms" of social organization (223). That is, collective behavior is creative destruction; it seeks to overthrow an old order to usher in a new one.

For Blumer and others, the "crowd" was the primary actor in collective behavior, and its forms included the fad, the craze, the mania, and the panic.

In these agitated crowds, all of the processes of social psychology and crowd behavior were activated, including group-think, idealism, irrationality, suggestibility, and violence. A few years later, Neil Smelser advanced the sociological thinking on collective behavior by adding the notions of *belief* and *strain*. He wrote that collective behavior is "mobilization on the basis of a belief which redefines social action" (1962: 8), whether this is a specific religious belief or a general belief that things need to change. More precisely, Smelser contended that collective behavior arises from conditions of "strain" when there is "an impairment of the relations among and consequently inadequate functioning of the components of action" (47). In other words, when society is not functioning well, and its statuses and groups and institutions are dys-integrated, collective behavior is likely to erupt. But this means ultimately that collective behavior, even violent group behavior, "is analyzable by the same categories as conventional behavior" (17). Both normal and extremist behavior "must be legitimized by values; both involve an assessment of the situation in which they occur, and so on" (23).

One of the pioneers of collective action theory in sociology, Anthony Oberschall, accordingly noted firstly that "terrorism is only one of several modes of confrontation ranging from peaceful and conventional political actions to extremes of group violence" and therefore that terrorism "is explained in the same way as other forms of collective behavior" (2004: 27). Among the key variables in collective behavior theory are discontent and grievances, opportunity, and "capacity to organize" (27). Oberschall and other theorists described the capacity to organize in terms of the *resources* that a group can mobilize such as money, members, leaders, media, supporters, and cultural/symbolic resources, such as the discourse of "freedom," "justice," or "self-determination."

The organization of terrorism is clearly a question for sociology. As Turk posited, the

> classic model of the terrorist organization is a tightly organized hierarchy comprised of small, isolated cells whose members have little if any knowledge of planning and organization above and outside their cell. They are disciplined by a blend of social isolation from all outsiders (especially family and former friends), blackmail after crimes demonstrating their commitment, physical threat, and indoctrination without access to other sources of ideas and information.
>
> (2004: 276–7)

Of course, different terrorist organizations are organized differently, which calls for empirical research on specific cases. Even so, some general group/organizational processes are identifiable in terrorist groups. Leadership and hierarchy—especially the phenomenon of charisma (see Chapter 2)—are critical. Equally essential are identification with the group and erection of boundaries against other groups. Experiments by social psychologist Henri Tajfel (1978; 1981) illustrated just how rapidly individuals form attachments to their group and begin to exaggerate the goodness of their own kind as well as the badness of others. Gordon Allport (1979) recognized the powerful integrating effect of negative behaviors like prejudice and stereotyping, which create a psychological and social (and sometimes literally physical) "fence" between different kinds of people and allow them to maintain biased and even false impressions of each other, facilitating hate and harm.

These considerations lead us finally to the socialization of terrorists, since, as is patently clear, terrorists are not born but made. Individuals learn to be terrorists, and they accept the status and learn the role from the ambient culture and from role models and leaders. If the culture values warriors or "martyrs," if it celebrates individuals who have perpetrated violence or engaged in acts of extraordinary self-sacrifice, if it dehumanizes non-members and enemies, then it effectively socializes people to play the terrorist role. Then, if social circumstances provide the grievances and discontent, as well as the resources and mobilization, terrorism is much more likely.

Turk admitted that not all individuals who live in the fertile circumstances for terrorism actually become terrorists. We can and must thus ask which social positions and experiences precipitate terrorism. As acknowledged before, it is not from the ranks of the poorest and least educated that terrorists are recruited. If terrorists hail from relatively educated and middle-class backgrounds, still those who make the move into the terrorist status and organization "appear to have undergone something of a conversion experience in making the transition from a willingness to 'trash' public property and fight riot police, to a readiness to murder specific politically significant persons. . .and then to the random targeting of populations including noncombatants as well as combatants" (279).

"The key to explaining the socialization of terrorists," Turk concluded, "is understanding how specific individuals are brought to the point where they see themselves as bearers of the responsibility for violent actions. Education, training, socialization—deliberate or not—may encourage the development of a self-concept as one who must fight against the threat to 'us'" (280). And after individuals are mobilized, group processes take over: "Once underway, campaigns of terrorism and related political violence tend to gain momentum. Inspired by the ideological messages, the charisma of leaders, the potential for material or status gains, or whatever else attracts them, others are likely to join" (280).

7 Anthropological Perspective

Joseph LeDoux's neuropsychology (see Chapter 5) firmly reunified brain, body, and mind in the study of knowledge and personhood. In other societies, the Greek, Christian, and Cartesian rift between body and mind never occurred. For the Cashinahua, a tribal people of Brazil and Peru, the body is where knowledge resides. Indeed, "a healthy body is one that constantly learns through the senses and expresses the accumulated knowledge in social action and speech," and a sick body "is one that no longer knows. Curing, therefore, acts to restore a person's capacity to know" (McCallum 1996: 347). Cecilia McCallum explained that for the Cashinahua the body is a nexus and product of a person's spirits (in the plural) and "physical, mental, and emotional capacities" including speech (348). Spirit and body are not opposed; they are hardly distinguished. Nor is mind separate from body: the Cashinahua do not even assign knowledge to the brain, and they have no word that means "mind" in contrast to body. They attribute no special role to the brain, rather conceiving knowledge to be distributed throughout the body. Each organ—"skin, hands, ears, genitals, liver, and eyes"—is "linked to a specific process of acquiring knowledge and of putting it to use in physical action" (355–6). "Thus the body integrates different kinds of knowledge acquired in a varied manner, in different body parts" (356). Not surprisingly, changes in spirit are experienced in the body, as "medical" symptoms like fainting and dizziness. Illness and ultimately death are understood as loss of knowledge, specifically of closing off connections with other people, and illness is treated with various kinds of *dau* or medicine, which is any substance "used to transform the body's capacity to know" (363). This case shows that societies may understand body, mind, and knowledge in ways completely foreign to the Western tradition and that grasping another society's worldview requires "a thorough examination of [its] epistemology" or how a society knows the body (347).

As social scientists and other casual observers have pondered and described human social institutions and behavior, they could not help but notice the tremendous diversity in these institutions and behaviors. Whatever the issues—marriage, family, language, clothing, food, religion—humans do it differently in different places and times. Humans also *look* different; we have different skin tones, hair color, facial features, and physiques.

The encounter with all of this human diversity led some people—but surprisingly rarely and surprisingly recently—to ask new questions about humanity. The result was *anthropology*, literally the science of man/humanity (from the Greek *anthropos* for man/humanity). Of course, all of the social sciences study humanity, so "the study of man" is hardly an adequate definition for anthropology. Instead, as a first attempt, let us regard anthropology as the study of human *diversity*.

More, the encounter with all of this human diversity called for and produced a new perspective on mankind, a new way of contemplating ourselves. Contemporary anthropologists call this the *anthropological perspective*, which they proudly promote as sociologists laud their sociological imagination. The anthropological perspective is usually identified by three components:

1. comparative or cross-cultural study, examining humans in all their diversity

2. holism, or investigating each aspect of human society in connection with all other aspects (say, exploring the connections between marriage, economics, and religion)
3. relativism, or understanding each human society in terms of or "relative to" its own ideas, beliefs, and values, rather than imposing our own assumptions on them.

Because humans are diverse in multiple ways, anthropology is itself a diverse and plural social science. It studies both physical and behavioral/social diversity, as well as diversity both in the present and in the past. To perform this ambitious task, anthropology has organized itself as a "four-field" discipline, with careers that are every bit as distinct as the careers in psychology. The premier professional organization for anthropologists in the United States, the American Anthropological Association, (www.aaanet.org/about/whatisanthropology.cfm) describes these four anthropologies as:

- cultural (or social) anthropology, which studies "social patterns and practices across cultures, with a special interest in how people live in particular places and how they organize, govern, and create meaning"
- physical (or biological) anthropology, studying "how humans adapt to diverse environments, how biological and cultural processes work together to shape growth, development and behavior, and what causes disease and early death. In addition, they are interested in human biological origins, evolution, and variation"
- archaeology, the study of "past peoples and cultures, from the deepest prehistory to the recent past, through the analysis of material remains, ranging from artifacts and evidence of past environments to architecture and landscapes"
- linguistic anthropology, or "the comparative study of ways in which language reflects and influences social life."

Significantly, archaeologist Paul Bahn (1996) informed us that the four-field organization of anthropology is predominantly an American version of the discipline, whereas in Europe archaeology tends to be an independent field. Further, British "social anthropology" has historically had a different view of society than American "cultural anthropology" (see below).

	Past	Present
Diversity in Body	Physical/Biological Anthropology	
Diversity in Behavior	Archaeology	Cultural Anthropology Linguistic Anthropology

Figure 7.1 The Four Fields of Anthropology

These varied interests also divide anthropology roughly into two camps, one focusing on social behavior (cultural anthropology and linguistic anthropology) and the other concentrating on physical objects (physical anthropology and archaeology); of course, the social anthropologists also may and do analyze material objects (for instance, how humans make and use artifacts), and the material anthropologists are also ultimately interested in how past humans and pre-humans behaved. So anthropology is at least as split in its careers as psychology, the material subdisciplines being much closer to natural science and the behavioral subdisciplines being much closer to classic social science. This is perhaps why Alfred Kroeber, one of the first generation of anthropologists trained in the United States, called the profession "the most humanistic of the sciences and the most scientific of the humanities" (quoted in Wolf 1964: 88). More recently, acknowledging anthropology's roots in the Western intellectual tradition, Tim Ingold called it "philosophy with the people in" (1992: 696), or what we might call *field philosophy*—getting out into the field to explore and test ideas about human nature and knowledge. Or, hearkening back to the central theme of this book, Kirsten Hastrup declared that the aim of anthropology is "to recover disappearing epistemologies" (1995: 44)—that is, to find and report other ways of human knowing and being.

It is interesting to note, finally, that anthropology as a modern academic discipline arose in the eighteenth and nineteenth centuries from the natural-scientific project to describe and categorize the various types of humans. Further, anthropology has a common origin and close connection with sociology, yet while sociology mostly wrestled to separate itself from psychology, anthropology has generally warmly embraced psychology but early on struggled to distance itself from history.

Ancient Views on Human Diversity

Humans have always known that there were other peoples out there who looked and behaved differently from themselves. No society has ever been so isolated that it did not have neighbors with different languages or customs. Oddly though, this obvious diversity seldom sparked much curiosity. Instead, most people through most of history have either ignored other societies or actively avoided them, even fearing and condemning them. For most humans who ever lived, their way of life and their kind of human was the right one. Indeed, in many languages the word that the group uses for itself simply means "the people" or "the real people." As anthropologist Napoleon Chagnon (The Coast Community College District 1994) told in a video about his research, the Yanomamo of Venezuela thought that he was not quite human.

No one in the ancient (or even the medieval or early modern) world did anthropology as we know it today. Yet there were glimmerings and promises of it, as in Herodotus' researches. In fact, from our previous introduction to Herodotus (see Chapter 2), it is apparent that he could as easily wear the title "father of anthropology" as "father of history." His writings were not simply chronologies but accounts of all the things he had seen, and he stated the basic premise of anthropology when, after visiting and meeting many different peoples, he concluded:

> if anyone, no matter who, were given the opportunity of choosing from amongst all the nations in the world the set of beliefs which he thought best, he would inevitably, after careful consideration of their relative merits, choose that of his own country. Everyone without exception believes his own native customs, and the religion he was brought up in, to be the best; and that being so, it is unlikely that anyone but a madman would mock at such things. . . . One can see by this what custom can do, and Pindar, in my opinion, was right when he called it "king of all."
>
> (1972: 219–20)

Custom, or what we today call "culture," is the prime source of our beliefs, values, and knowledge.

Illustrating the point that travel is good for feeding an anthropological perspective, Xenophanes (fifth century BCE) like Herodotus sojourned through the known world and came to an even more astonishing conclusion—that different peoples' religions vary *and that each society constructs its religion in its own image*: "Ethiopians [i.e., African] have gods with snub noses and black hair, Thracians have gods with gray eyes and red hair. . . . If oxen or lions had hands which enabled them to draw and paint pictures as men do, they would portray their gods as having bodies like their own, horses would portray them as horses, and oxen as oxen" (quoted in Wheelwright 1966: 33).

By and large, the philosophers before Socrates and Plato were more engaged in contemplation of nature and physics than of society, but as mentioned in prior chapters they did tend to compare the politics and constitutions of the various city-states. As for non-Greeks, especially the tribal peoples who lived outside of cities, the philosophical Greeks tended to dismiss them as "barbarians," derived from *barbaroi* for people who speak a foreign or unintelligible language or simply make stammering noises.

If travel was one inspiration for curiosity about others, war was a second inspiration (and often a cause itself for travel). Julius Caesar, as indicated already (see Chapter 2) wrote down his observations about the Gauls and the Germans as he journeyed and campaigned in their territories.

The Early Modern Origins of Anthropology

As in other intellectual domains, the Dark Ages were particularly dark for cross-cultural curiosity and knowledge. Travel was much less free and much more dangerous. More significant was the triumph of Christianity in the old Greco-Roman world, which promoted its own "anthropology" in the sense of its theory or model of humanity. Humans were created in the image of the Christian god, and all humans were descendants of the primal couple, Adam and Eve. Augustine championed the standard dogma of medieval Christianity when he opined that God created humans as a "rational animal consisting of soul and body" and that therefore human nature "was to be a mean between the angelic and bestial" (quoted in Slotkin 1965: 3). Humans were also contradictory in that we were distinct from other animals in our spiritual nature but also inherently "fallen" and sinful. As for non-Christians, they hardly merited attention except as allies of the devil or as potential converts. In the words of Michael Landmann in his study of philosophical anthropology, "For the Middle Ages only the 'Christian man'—an expression still familiar from Luther—was really a man in the full sense of the word" (1974: 31). Such an attitude is not conducive to a modern anthropological perspective.

Nor was the "knowledge," written into medieval books and taught in medieval universities, that there were monstrous races of humans inhabiting the remote corners of the world. Some, like the Antipodes, allegedly walked upside down, while the Astomi had no mouths and were covered with fur, the Blemmyae had no heads but faces in their chests, and the Cynocephali had the heads of dogs. Contemporary maps actually pointed to the homelands of these marvelous, terrifying creatures who, as monsters, would not be the subject of an anthropological science.

The humanistic turn in the Renaissance of the 1400s and 1500s brought humanity back to the center of literate thought, emphasizing not only the similarities between different human groups but between humans and non-human animals. Leonardo da Vinci, for example, noticed that the bones, muscles, and organs of humans and apes were much alike. Further, he argued that there was something inherited and transmitted between people of the same group or race: "The black races of Ethiopia are not the product of the sun; for if black gets black with child in Scythia [an area far from Africa], the offspring is black; but if a black gets a white woman with child the offspring is grey. And this shows that the seed of the mother has power in the embryo equally with that of the father" (quoted in Slotkin: 39).

With this kind of thinking, a new, naturalistic approach to humans and human diversity is opened, and the most obvious mission of such a naturalistic or "scientific" approach to mankind was to classify and describe the different types. Giordano Bruno (1548–1600) identified several "species" of humans, such as "the black race of the Ethiopians, and the yellow offspring of America," not to mention "the Pygmies always shut up in the hills" (quoted in Slotkin: 43). More controversially, he contested the *monogenetic* view of Christianity, insisting that all this diversity "cannot be traced to the same descent, nor are they sprung from the generative force of a single progenitor" (43). For his *polygenetic* (many origins or ancestors) theory and other heretical thoughts, Bruno was burned at the stake in 1600. Meanwhile, his contemporary Jean Bodin (1530–96), without speculating on origins, also categorized human physical and personality traits:

> The people of the South are of a contrary humor and disposition to them of the North: these are great and strong, they are little and weak; they of the north hot and moist, the others cold and dry; the one has a big voice and green eyes, the other has a weak voice and black eyes; the one has flaxen hair and a fair skin, the other has both hair and skin black; the one fears cold, and the other heat.
>
> (43)

The most important step toward a naturalistic science of human diversity, though, was taken by Carl von Linné (1707–78), better known as Linnaeus. In his *Systema naturae*, first published in 1735, he was the first to organize all living species into a single classification scheme, placing humans confidently within that scheme as animals, mammals, and primates. He then presented the four classes or races of humans (technical category *Homo*), as well as *Homo ferus* or "wild man" whose hairy bodies walked on four legs and *Homo monstrosus*.

Not long after Linnaeus' foundational contribution, Johann Friedrich Blumenbach (1752–1840) offered his five-race system of humanity. First described in 1779, on the basis of skull measurements it distinguished between the Caucasian/white, Mongolian/yellow, Ethiopian/brown, American/red, and Malayan/brown races (see Figure 7.2). With the work of men like Bruno, Bodin, Linnaeus, and Blumenbach, the study of human variation became established as a legitimate natural and scientific project.

The Colonial Encounter and the First "Reports from the Field"

These budding classifications of mankind manifestly demonstrate the importance of the early explorations and colonizations by Western travelers. The Crusades into the Middle East (1095 through 1204, with ongoing skirmishes for years after) and pilgrimages to holy lands brought many tales of fabulous sites and adventures. Itinerant missionaries wrote accounts of their activities and observations, like Friar John of Pian de Carpine during his time in the court of Mongol leader Kuyuk Khan from 1245 to 1247. More famously, Marco Polo (1254–1324) trekked across Asia and back, publishing his journals of the trip. One of the most popular examples of this genre of travel writing was *The Travels of Sir John Mandeville*, appearing in the mid-1300s.

The systematic explorations in the late 1400s provided additional knowledge about the peoples of the world, as the research of Linnaeus and Blumenbach indicates. Even more, the idea of "mankind" was being stretched, although not immediately or easily. For example, soon after the

Linnaeus' Classification of Humanity

Linnaeus divided the single human species into four branches, attributing physical, psychological, and behavioral traits to each:

Homo Americanus: "reddish, choleric, erect. Hair black, straight, thick; nostrils, wide; face harsh, beard scanty. Obstinate, merry, free. Paints himself with fine red lines. Regulated by customs"

Homo Europaeus: "white, sanguine, muscular. Hair flowing, long. Eyes blue. Gentle, acute, inventive. Covered with close vestments. Governed by laws"

Homo Asiaticus: "sallow, melancholy, stiff. Hair black. Eyes dark. Severe, haughty, avaricious. Covered with loose garments. Ruled by opinions"

Homo Afer: "black, phlegmatic, relaxed. Hair black, frizzled. Skin silky. Nose flat. Lips tumid. Women without shame. Mammae lactate profusely. Crafty, indolent, negligent. Anoints himself with grease. Governed with caprice" (quoted in Slotkin 1965: 177–8).

Of course, many of his characterizations conflate inherited and learned features, and some are absurd and offensive. Here we have, then, one of the first statements of Western race thinking and racism.

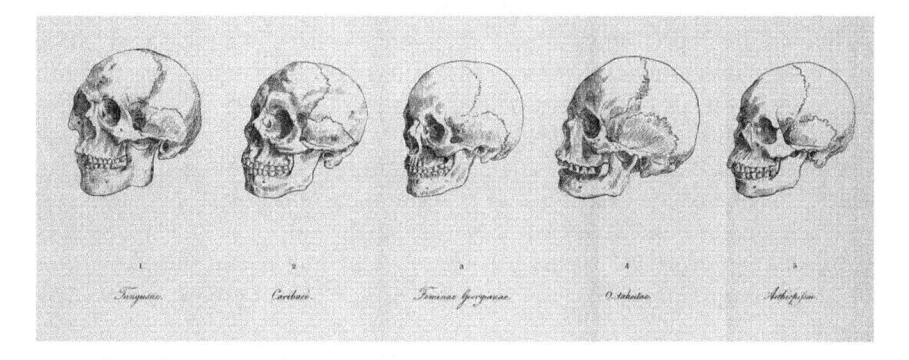

Figure 7.2 Blumenbach's Five Races
Source: Wikicommons. Published in the US before 1923 and public domain in the US.

Spanish conquest of Mexico, there was an actual debate within the Catholic Church on the humanity of the American natives. Bartolomé de las Casas famously defended the pro-human position, arguing (from Christian anthropology) that the indigenous people were humans because they possessed souls; as such, they required "saving" by the Church and instruction in the true religion. In 1537 the Church adopted this position, sending missionaries to civilize the natives while hopefully protecting them from the worst abuses of colonialism.

Many explorers, soldiers, settlers, and priests wrote eyewitness reports of their encounters outside of Europe, one of the first of which was Bernal Diaz del Castillo's *The True History of the Conquest of New Spain*. Castillo was a soldier in Hernán Cortés' invading army and preserved some of the earliest impressions of Mexican culture. In North America, the Jesuits penetrating Canada kept records that were published from 1610 as *The Jesuit Relations*; these documents provide some of the oldest details about northern Native Americans including aspects of their languages and religions. One last but quite important example was Joseph Lafitau's *Customs of American Savages Compared with Those of Earliest Times*, published in 1724.

Enlightenment Philosophy and Kant's Pragmatic Anthropology

Some scholars have traced the word "anthropology" back as far as 1501, but most historians of anthropology begin their story no earlier than the 1700s. Indeed, acclaimed twentieth-century theorist Marvin Harris (1968) declared that anthropological thinking was born in the century between John Locke's 1690 *An Essay Concerning Human Understanding* and the French Revolution of 1789, the era known as the Enlightenment. To be sure, there were inklings of anthropology even before Locke; Thomas Hobbes' *Leviathan* not only discussed human nature but speculated on the conditions of human life in prehistoric times, when humans lived in a pre-social "state of nature." Like Hobbes, Rousseau was influenced by incoming reports from the colonies on native or "savage" peoples for constructing his image of pre-social life and the "noble savage."

None of these scholars considered themselves anthropologists. If not the first, then one of the first thinkers to write on anthropology by name and to teach a course on the subject was Immanuel Kant. In 1798 he published *Anthropology from a Pragmatic Point of View*, and documents show that he lectured on anthropology at the University of Koenigsburg for twenty-five years.

Kant's anthropology is entirely consistent with, and crucially important to, his general philosophy and psychology of human nature, knowledge, and—above all else—morality. He famously wrote that philosophy asked four fundamental questions: What can I know? What should I do? What may I hope for? What is a human being? He explained that the first question is answered in *metaphysics*, the second in *morals*, the third in *religion*, and the fourth in *anthropology*. If so, then anthropology is raised to the center of human knowledge, along with metaphysics, morality, and religion.

Coming very close to a modern anthropological perspective, Kant insisted that "the most important object in the world" to which we can apply our human reasoning skills "is the human being. . . . Therefore to know the human being according to his species as an earthly being endowed with reason especially deserves to be called *knowledge of the world*, even though he constitutes only one part of the creatures on earth" (2006: 3). He added:

> A doctrine of knowledge of the human being, systematically formulated (anthropology), can exist either in a physiological or in a pragmatic point of view. Physiological knowledge of the human being concerns the investigation of what *nature* makes of the human being; pragmatic, the investigation of what *he* as a free-acting being makes of himself, or can and should make of himself.
>
> (3)

This last phrase is crucially important, as Kant recognized that humans make their own "pragmatic" (practical, in-practice, lived) ways of life, which will differ for different groups. Indeed, he stressed that "circumstances of place and time, when they are constant, produce *habits* which, as is said, are second nature" (5)—this "second nature" being what we call today "culture." Finally, like Herder before him (see Chapter 2) and Wundt after him (see Chapter 5), he emphasized that mental and political/economic features were neither purely individual nor universal but historically and socially specific. One of the later sections of his book is on "The Character of the Peoples," defining a people as "a *multitude* of human beings united in a region, in so far as they constitute a *whole*. This multitude, or even the part of it that recognizes itself as united into a civil whole through common ancestry, is called a *nation*" (213). The pivotal discoveries here are, first, that humans make their own lifeways and, second, that they make them not individually but collectively, as members of "peoples" or nations.

The Emergence of Anthropology in the Nineteenth Century

Out of the ideas and observations of previous centuries and allied disciplines, a field of anthropology began to coalesce in the early 1800s. In fact, at the very turn of the century, the *Société des Observateurs de l'Homme* was founded in Paris, and very soon "ethnological" organizations—*ethnology* being the description of particular peoples and ways of life (cultures)—were formed in the United States and the United Kingdom (the American Ethnological Society in 1842 and the Ethnological Society of London in 1843). At this early stage, anthropology represented an intersection of various intellectual interests (including biology, history, and psychology), and it was practiced in many sites other than "the field" as we think of it today.

History and Comparative Study of Institutions

One perennial question in philosophy and the nascent social sciences was the origin and development of institutions like government, family, or religion. This is plainly a question of history, and many scholars pontificated on it, from Plato and Aristotle to Hobbes and Rousseau. Particularly with the advent of evolutionary theory in the mid-1800s, it became possible and imperative to consider the evolution of major social institutions.

The rise and development of legal systems attracted a number of thinkers, including Fustel de Coulange, who was one of Durkheim's teachers (see Chapter 6). Historical research showed that laws and governments had grown and changed from "primitive" to ancient to medieval to modern times, and Marx suggested his materialistic explanation for this series of legal-social systems. Much effort subsequently went into describing the laws and governments of the Greeks and Romans, the ancient Hebrews, and other civilizations. In 1861, for instance, Henry James Sumner Maine (1822–88) published *Ancient Law*, which he soon followed with his 1875 *Early History of Institutions* and his 1883 *On Early Law and Custom*.

Meanwhile, researchers were discovering that the family was not a natural and universal institution but also had a social history. One of the most important of these thinkers was Johann Jakob Bachofen (1815–87), who reckoned that marriage and family had evolved through a series of stages from promiscuity or polyamory (no marriage or family) to patriarchy and monogamy by way of *matriarchy*. His influential 1861 book was thus titled *Das Mutterrecht*, translated as *Mother Right*. Shortly thereafter, John Ferguson McLennan (1827–81) wrote his 1865 *Primitive Marriage*, subtitled "An Inquiry into the Origin of the Form of Capture in Marriage Ceremonies," and a few years later, in 1871, Lewis Henry Morgan (see later discussion) published *Systems of Consanguinity and Affinity of the Human Family*, which is widely regarded as a founding document for the anthropology of kinship.

Finally, even religion was subjected to a comparative/historical treatment. William Robertson Smith (1846–94) wrote his important but controversial *Religion of the Semites: Fundamental Institutions* in 1889 (as well as a study of *Kinship and Marriage in Early Arabia* in 1885). Even more epoch-making was James George Frazer's *The Golden Bough*, first published in 1890 but expanded subsequently into many volumes, which traced and compared—and discovered great consistencies between—beliefs and myths from "primitive" to ancient to modern/Christian religions. As we noted elsewhere, Durkheim contributed a seminal study of the origin of religion in his 1912 *The Elementary Forms of Religious Life*.

Perhaps the crowning figure in the historical/evolutionary approach to social institutions and to society as a whole was Lewis Henry Morgan (1818–81). A lawyer, politician, and enthusiast of all things Native American, Morgan was one of the first to leave the office and the armchair and spend

---

Morgan's Seven Stages of Society

Lewis Henry Morgan categorized the path of social history through a set of phases based on economic/technological criteria. These stages included:

Lower Savagery: "From the infancy of the Human Race to the commencement of the next period"

Middle Savagery: "From the acquisition of a fish subsistence and a knowledge of the use of fire"

Upper Savagery: "From the invention of the bow and arrow"

Lower Barbarism: "From the invention of the art of pottery"

Middle Barbarism: "From the domestication of animals on the Eastern hemisphere, and in the Western from the cultivation of maize and plants by irrigation, with the use of adobe-brick and stone"

Upper Barbarism: "From the invention of the process of smelting iron ore, with the use of iron tools"

Civilization: "From the invention of a phonetic alphabet, with the use of writing, to the present time."

(1877: 12–13)

---

time among indigenous peoples, first the Iroquois of New York and then, from 1859 to 1862, tribes across the American West. By 1851 he had already published *League of the Iroquois*, and we just mentioned his 1871 *Systems of Consanguinity and Affinity of the Human Family*. However, by far his most influential work was the 1877 *Ancient Society*, where he combined the study of the Iroquois with chapters on the Aztecs, the Greeks, and the Romans. But what most anthropologists remember from the book is his scheme of seven stages of cultural evolution, bundled into three major periods— "savagery," "barbarism," and "civilization." Marx and Engels took note of Morgan's work, and Engels explicitly employed it in his speculation on the family and the economy.

Psychology and the Question of "Primitive Mind"

Very early and very securely, anthropology forged a bond with the emerging discipline of psychology. The problem was, of course, to explain the diversity of human ideas and actions. Why, in a word, did "those people" engage in the odd (and to the Western witness, patently false and irrational) thoughts and behaviors that we observed? Did all humans share a single universal mental process—was there a "psychic unity of mankind"—or did pre-modern and tribal peoples operate with a "primitive mentality"?

Scholars lined up on both sides of the debate. Adolph Bastian (1826–1905) argued that the similarities between human thought and behavior in all times and places suggested an underlying commonality beneath the diversity. He posited that all people shared basic *element-argedanken* or "elementary thoughts" which could be shaped and expressed variously as local *volkergedanken* or folk/national thoughts. (We have seen that early psychologists like Wilhelm Wundt were also on the hunt for *Völkerpsychologie* at the same time as they investigated universal individual psychological processes.) Franz Boas (1858–1942), one of the founders of modern cultural anthropology, also defended the psychic-unity position, stating in 1901 that the "functions of the human mind are common to the whole of humanity" (1901: 5).

Psychologist Sigmund Freud asserted to the contrary that two different and unequal mental processes worked in the human mind—a "primary" irrational and unconscious one and a "secondary" rational and conscious one; worse, "primitive" people as well as children, dreamers, and neurotics languished in the irrational process. (His former follower Carl Jung did counter that all humans share fundamental "archetypes" of the mind and a "collective unconscious.") However, the strongest proponent of primitive mentality was Lucien Lévy-Bruhl (1857–1939), who maintained that the minds of tribal or traditional peoples functioned in a pre-logical and mystical way. They failed to grasp cause and effect (believing, for instance, that a dance can make it rain) or the inherent difference of distinct beings or objects (believing, for instance, that an animal or rock could be a person or that a wafer could be a human body).

Having settled the question to their satisfaction in favor of psychic unity, anthropology preserved an intimate connection with psychology. Indeed, in his early article, Boas pronounced that among "the chief aims of anthropology is the study of the mind of man under the varying conditions of race and of environment" (1901: 1). Anthropology was long influenced particularly intensely by psychoanalysis, since that theory made universal psychological claims and offered practical methods and testable predictions. The founding father of British social anthropology, Bronislaw Malinowski (1884–1942), searched for Freud's purportedly universal (in males anyhow) Oedipus complex among the Trobriand Islanders, ultimately concluding that it was a product of specific Western social relationships (patriarchy and patrilineal nuclear households). In matrilineal Trobriand society, fathers were not prominent figures in their sons' lives and therefore not a source of Oedipal threat.

Other anthropologists took psychological theories and methods into the field. Géza Róheim applied psychoanalytical concepts to Australian Aboriginals, and Irving Hallowell used the Rorschach inkblot test on Ojibwa Indians, insisting that "personality structure is a psychological dimension of human societies that is directly relevant to the functioning of a human social order" (1967: 33). Two of the most celebrated of all anthropological books were Margaret Mead's 1928 *Coming of Age in Samoa: A Psychological Study of Primitive Youth for Western Civilization* and Ruth Benedict's 1934 *Patterns of Culture*. In the latter, Benedict described a culture as a particular pattern or configuration of psychological traits and

Figure 7.3 Franz Boas, c. 1915

Source: Wikicommons. Published in the US before 1923 and public domain in the US.

proceeded to analyze various cultures in terms of personality qualities, such as the fearful and paranoid Dobuans or the egocentric and individualistic Kwakiutl. Other important anthropologists like Ralph Linton collaborated with psychologists such as Abram Kardiner in cross-cultural studies like Kardiner's 1939 *The Individual and His Society: The Psychodynamics of Primitive Social Organization* and his 1945 *The Psychological Frontiers of Society*. Among the anthropological results of this approach were "national character" studies including Ruth Benedict's heralded 1946 *The Chrysanthemum and the Sword: Patterns of Japan Culture* and Geoffrey Gorer's 1950 *The People of Great Russia: A Psychological Study*.

Human Biology: Anthropometry and Scientific Racism

Interestingly but perhaps not surprisingly, just as psychology was emerging from nineteenth-century physiology and medicine, anthropology was simultaneously developing from the biological concerns and theories (and prejudices) of the day. As we have already seen, central to these concerns and theories was the concept of "race," especially in the United States where slavery was abolished in the 1860s. The confluence of scientific thinking and race thinking offered a natural subject for investigation, namely, the physical (and psychological and moral) comparison of the races and the documentation—literally, the physical measurement—of racial differences.

One of the first projects of the budding anthropological science was *anthropometry*, that is, the measurement of human bodies, not necessarily but frequently as representatives of racial categories. John Haller went so far as to assert that the "hallmark of anthropology in the nineteenth century was anthropometry" (1971: 7), and obviously here is an area where cultural anthropology, physical anthropology, and medical science overlap.

Measurements of various kinds were performed on races inside the United States and other Western countries, as well as on "primitive peoples" around the world. For the latter purpose, bodies were often taken from their society upon death for "scientific examination" or even exhumed from graves; many of these human remains are still held in museums or universities. All manner of physical traits were measured, from arm length to "facial angle" (on the premise that long arms and protruding faces were signs of primitiveness), but the most important marker was brain volume or "cephalic index," a concept introduced by neurologist Paul Broca (see Chapter 5). Brain volume was associated quite crudely with intelligence, and scientists—practicing what has been called "scientific racism"—reported the very racial differences in brain volume that racism would suggest, with Caucasians allegedly having the largest brains and Africans or Australian Aboriginals having the smallest. Subsequent modern retesting would refute these alleged facts.

Anthropometry was used not only to demonstrate the distinctness of the races but to justify social and political relations and policies. Scientific racists defended segregation and laws against "miscegenation" or the genetic mixing of the races on the basis of these spurious claims. Internationally, colonialism was also legitimated on the grounds that a superior race (Europeans) was conquering inferior races.

It is essential to understand that biological thinking and anthropometry were by no means limited to the question of race. Ideas about the "degeneration" of humans and about improving the human stock were rampant in the late 1800s and early 1900s. Everything from criminality and mental illness to poverty and immorality was attributed to physiological causes, and in the United States and elsewhere *eugenics* was the word of the day, intended to apply scientific knowledge to the physical and psychological betterment of the species.

It is also essential to understand that modern anthropology disowns such biological and racial thinking. Proudly, Franz Boas was one of the most tireless critics of racial/biological approaches to human difference. In popular works like his 1928 *Anthropology and Modern Life* and his 1945 *Race and Democratic Society*, he argued first that no existing race was "pure" but each had a complex history of interaction and interbreeding; second, he insisted that behavior could not be explained in exclusively physical terms, and most destructively to racism, he contended that physical traits are shaped by social experience as much as vice versa. Already by 1912, Boas claimed to have documented the plasticity of bodies among immigrants to the U.S., whose "racial" features changed due to their new social environment. If any anthropologist was more hostile to racial thinking than Boas, it was Ashley Montague who published *Man's Most Dangerous Myth: The Fallacy of Race* in 1945.

The Sites of Early Anthropology: Museums, Zoos, and the "Man on the Spot"

While anthropology today is associated (not entirely accurately) with the intrepid researcher alone among some remote tribe in a distant island or jungle, few scholars made such voyages before 1900. Instead, the fledgling discipline depended on two other strategies—bringing the natives to us for observation and relying on well-located amateurs to send data to us for scholarly analysis.

One of the first and most important sites where anthropology was practiced was the museum; indeed, the significance of museums for all of its subdisciplines cannot be overestimated. Boas himself began his anthropological career working in a museum. Museums were not only places where the objects and knowledge of other peoples could be collected and displayed, but they were also places where "knowledge" was created and transmitted. By collecting certain objects, labeling them, organizing them in various ways, and making them available to scholars and to the general public, other cultures could be "known." Another kind of knowledge was also at stake, namely the knowledge of the greatness of Western colonial empires: museums and other venues were opportunities for Western societies to show off their imperial holdings—their conquered territories in Africa, Asia, Australia, etc.—and to proudly distance their own modern civilization from the "primitives" on parade.

Among the oldest ethnological museums in the world were those in Haarlem, Netherlands (1784), St. Petersburg, Russia (1836), Leiden, Netherlands (1837), and Copenhagen, Denmark (1839); in the United States, the Peabody Museum of Harvard University was the first anthropological and archaeological museum, founded in 1866. Anthropological materials were and are also housed in "national museums," museums of natural history, and art museums. And an untold number of objects, including human remains, are held in private collections. Of course, how these objects got into the hands of individual and institutional collectors is a varied and often sordid story.

Even more sordid was the nineteenth-century practice of displaying living "primitive" people in world fairs, circuses, traveling shows, and literally in "human zoos." Individuals or entire families or villages were transported from the colonies to European or American sites for exhibition; sometimes they were provided with props like huts and tools, becoming living tableaux for viewers who would never make the long voyages to their places of origin. Sometimes they were displayed nude, so as better to study their "primitive anatomy" (and no doubt titillate their audiences), their bodies exposed to the Western gaze as in the case of the South African women Saartje Baartman, nicknamed the "Hottentot Venus."

The United States was both a source and destination for the exhibition of native peoples. Buffalo Bill's traveling "Wild West" show featuring Native Americans was a sensation in Europe, while academic and eugenicist Madison Grant put African pygmy Ota Benga on display in a cage in the Bronx Zoo in 1906. The so-called Great Exhibition of 1851 in London and the 1893 World Columbian Exposition in Chicago were occasions for assembling and displaying the peoples of the world, as was the 1931 Colonial Exhibition in Paris. And while gawkers were able to see exotic peoples for the price of a few pennies, serious scholars seized these chances to do their science. In her major study on the subject, Sadiah Qureshi finds that by mid-century "commercial exhibitions began to be routinely advertised as educational opportunities for budding ethnologists" (2011: 187). Leading scientists in fields from anthropology to anatomy attended such events, recognizing that the humans on display were "usable experimental material," and "the opportunities they provided for research were . . . taken up with enthusiasm" (221).

If scholars could not bring the people to them, they could at least take advantage of the Westerners who went to the native peoples. This included a steady stream of explorers, traders, administrators, missionaries, and ordinary settlers, many of whom—like Lewis Henry Morgan (mentioned

Figure 7.4 Illustration from an advertisement for Saartje Baartman, the "Hottentot Venus," c. 1810

Source: Wikicommons. Published in the US before 1923 and public domain in the US.

Notes and Queries: Formalizing Amateur Anthropology

Recognizing another occasion for gathering ethnological data, academics back in their home base prepared a handbook for the "man on the spot" to ensure high-quality, useable information. First issued in 1874 by the Anthropological Institute of London, it was called *Notes and Queries on Anthropology, or A Guide to Anthropological Research for the Use of Travelers and Others*. The preface to the first edition explained that the guidelines were intended "to promote accurate anthropological observation on the part of travelers, and to enable those who are not anthropologists themselves to supply the information which is wanted for the scientific study of anthropology at home" (Garson and Read 1899: vii). The book then listed topics and questions for the observer to consider while recording his observations. As the handbook instructed, anthropology was understood to consist of two projects, *anthropography* or the physical aspects of humanity and *ethnography* or the social and intellectual aspects. The first part of the text, then, occupying one-third of the pages, covered anthropography, including the instruments and devices of physical measurement and specific physiological variables from odor, senses, and movement to development, diet, pathology, surgery, and disease. The second part, filling two-thirds of the text, focused on ethnography with a litany of specific topics from clothing and tools to writing, religion, crime, morals, law, music, language, war, agriculture, games, money, and "tribal marks" and "memorial structures." Armed with this advice from scholars, and encouraged to use drawing and the new technology of photography, the experts were confident that the ordinary traveler could provide "facts about which there can be no question" (87).

---

earlier)—were eager amateur anthropologists. But then, there were few if any professional anthropologists yet.

Many valuable observations had already been made by what were often dubbed "men on the spot," including the conquistador Bernal and the French Jesuits. Adventurers kept Western audiences well entertained with their travel writings, constituting the first ethnological literature. A few of the very many examples include Mungo Park's 1799 *Travels in the Interior of Africa*, Charles Sturt's 1848 *Narrative of an Expedition into Central Australia*, Richard Burton's 1856 *First Footsteps in East Africa*, James Johnston's 1896 *My Experiences in Manipur and the Naga Hills*, and Henry Stanley's 1898 *Through South Africa*.

Thought and Method in Contemporary Anthropology

Despite some common roots and interests, the four anthropologies or anthropological careers call for quite different concepts and methodologies. They have also each pursued their own theoretical problems and intellectual histories, and each has grappled with its facts and its ways of knowing. The depth of their subdisciplinary specialization is evident in the fact that the *Annual Review of Anthropology* is the only edition of the *Annual Review* series that has formal sections for each of its discipline's subfields. The four subfields approximate "paradigms" in Kuhn's sense or "epistemic cultures" in Knorr-Cetina's sense (see Chapter 1), which means that there have often been communicative and institutional barriers between them. For the purposes of describing their theories and methods, we can conceive of them as two pairs of related anthropologies—the "behavioral" anthropologies and the "material" anthropologies.

The Modern Behavioral Anthropologies

While the domain of anthropology is conceptually divided into four subfields, the vast majority of practicing anthropologists are cultural or social anthropologists, who are similar enough to linguistic anthropologists to be discussed together. The behavioral anthropologies are similar enough to the other social sciences that all of the previously-outlined questions and methods are serviceable for them, although these anthropologies have some unique terminology and a paradigmatic method; more, these anthropologies stand out for their degree of self-reflection on their own knowledge and ways of knowing.

For cultural anthropologists, the key concept is understandably *culture*. In its simplest form, culture is the learned and shared ways of thinking, feeling, and behaving in a society. One of the first and most enduring technical definitions was given by Edward Burnett (E. B.) Tylor (1832–1917) in his seminal 1871 *Primitive Culture*: "Culture or Civilization, taken in its wide ethnographic sense, is that complex whole which includes knowledge, belief, art, morals, law, custom, and any other capabilities and habits acquired by man as a member of a society" (1958: 1). Culture includes ideas, actions, institutions, and the material objects that result from them.

The concept of culture has proven to be interesting and controversial in three ways. First, culture is an even more recent notion than anthropology itself. We have discussed, and Christopher Pinney in his analysis of early anthropology and photography stresses, "how uninterested many nineteenth-century anthropologists were in 'culture'" (2011: 15). Ethnologists of the 1800s were worried that "verbal data" and "personal observation" lacked "the methodological rigor" of science, which is why they favored physical measurement and photographic evidence as "the best, in fact the only tests" of anthropological knowledge (14). Second, culture has been a particularly popular concept in American anthropology, but British *social anthropology*

Research Topics in Anthropology

The articles in the 2015 issue of *Annual Review of Anthropology* include:

Part 1 Archaeology
"Pleistocene Overkill and North American Mammalian Extinctions"
"The Archaeology of Ritual"
"Recent Developments in High-Density Survey and Measurement (HSSM) for Archaeology: Implications for Practice and Theory"
Part 2 Biological Anthropology
"The Evolution of Difficult Childbirth and Helpless Hominin Infants"
"Health of Indigenous Peoples"
"Energy Expenditure in Humans and Other Primates"
"An Evolutionary and Life-History Perspective on Osteoporosis"
"Disturbance, Complexity, Scale: New Approaches to the Study of Human-Environment Interactions"
"Fallback Foods, Optimal Diets, and Nutritional Targets: Primate Responses to Varying Food Availability and Quality"
"Resource Transfers and Human Life-History Evolution"
"An Evolutionary Anthropological Perspective on Modern Human Origins"
Part 3 Linguistic Anthropology
"How Postindustrial Families Talk"
"Chronotypes, Scales, and Complexity in the Study of Language in Society"
"Linguistic Relativity from Reference to Agency"
"Politics of Translation"
"Breached Initiations: Sociopolitical Resources and Conflicts in Emergent Adulthood"
"Embodiment in Human Communication"
"The Pragmatics of Qualia in Practice"
Part 4 Social/Cultural Anthropology
"Virtuality"
"Anthropology and Heritage Remains"
"Urban Political Ecology"
"Environment, Anthropology, Systemic Perspectives"
"The Anthropology of Life After AIDS: Epistemological Continuities in the Age of Antiretroviral Treatment"
"Anthropology of Aging and Care"
"Anthropology of Ontologies"

"Oil and Anthropology"
"The Post-Cold War Anthropology of Central America"
"Risks of Citizenship and Fault Lines of Survival"
"Siberia"
"Of What Does Self-Knowing Consist? Perspectives from Bangladesh
    and Pakistan"
"Addiction in the Making"
"Waste and Waste Management"

has showed less interest in it and even disdained it. Cleaving more closely to the work of Durkheim in sociology (see Chapter 6), Alfred Reginald (A. R.) Radcliffe-Brown (1881–1955) for instance argued that culture is not the right focus at all, since investigators cannot see culture; culture is a mere abstraction from actual observable behavior, which should be the target of anthropological inquiry. He went so far as to doubt the very possibility of a "cultural" anthropology: "You cannot have a science of culture. You can study culture only as a characteristic of a social system ... If you study culture, you are always studying the acts of behavior of a specific set of persons who are linked in a social structure" (1957: 106). Third, lately even cultural anthropologists have questioned the utility of the concept, Lila Abu-Lughod (1991) for one urging anthropologists to "write against culture."

In conducting their research, social/cultural or linguistic anthropologists may use surveys, interviews, and secondary sources. It is extremely uncommon, verging on taboo, for them to do experiments. Instead, the distinguishing method of the behavioral anthropologies is *participant observation*, which entails learning about another society by actively participating in the life of that society—as much as possible, not only living with but living *like* people in that society. Understandably, this requires a substantial commitment of time, usually a year or more in the field, and commences with learning the local language while joining in the economic, kinship, and ritual activities of the group. For this reason too, social/cultural and linguistic anthropologists are much more likely to work alone, and to publish alone, than other social scientists, and their research tends to be much more qualitative and less statistical than the closest discipline, sociology.

Participant observation sets modern anthropology apart from the "armchair" and indirect anthropology of the nineteenth century, although there were early examples like the Torres Straits Expedition of 1898 and the voyage of Baldwin Spencer and Francis Gillen through the Australian desert, resulting in their 1899 *The Native Tribes of Central Australia* (which heavily influenced Durkheim's thinking on religion).

These turn-of-the-century travels, nevertheless, tended to be of very short duration and to be undertaken by scholars who were not formally trained in anthropology—partly because there was no formal training yet. Under the guidance of Boas in the United States and Malinowski in the United Kingdom, a generation of professional anthropologists were trained in the methodology of long-term fieldwork, based on what social/cultural anthropologists sometimes call *presence* or *co-presence* with the people they study. A stint of participant observation became a virtual rite of passage into the profession, and many researchers return for multiple field visits throughout their careers. Lately, though, some anthropologists have recommended short-term fieldwork or "rapid assessment," especially in matters of public health.

Like archaeology (see later discussion), the behavioral anthropologies experienced a crisis in the 1960s, as their subject-peoples underwent profound processes of decolonization and culture change. Neither social/cultural nor linguistic anthropology could claim to be sciences of "traditional" societies, since no societies were any longer purely traditional. Both subdisciplines painfully but successfully reoriented themselves as sciences of human social diversity, including modern urban societies, where the "field" might be the city, the corporation, the lab, or the internet.

Among all of the social sciences, the behavioral anthropologies have arguably been the most circumspect about their own knowledge. The problems of anthropological knowledge cluster around two issues— authority and representation. The problem of anthropological authority relates first to whether anthropologists, based on their limited time in the field, have sufficient knowledge to declare themselves experts on a society. This is aggravated by the problem of their right to speak *about* and *for* those societies, who increasingly claim the right to speak about and for themselves and sometimes express resentment at the academics who swoop in, "study" them, and then disappear. Native American scholar Vine Deloria, Jr., was one of the most vociferous, complaining that "Indians have been cursed above all other people in history. Indians have anthropologists" (1969: 83). He further abjured anthropologists "to get down from their thrones of authority and PURE research and begin helping Indian tribes instead of preying on them" (104). Admittedly, anthropology's relationship with colonialism has been an embarrassment to the discipline.

Representation refers to two issues—how anthropologists convert their experience into knowledge and how they transmit that knowledge to each other, to the peoples they study, and to the wider world. During their stint in the field, anthropologists ordinarily take notes (so-called field notes). After returning from the field, they "write up" those notes into an essay or book, which anthropologists call *ethnography* ("culture-writing"). How exactly that process occurs is a bit of a mystery, which is why Malinowski referred to "the ethnographer's magic." In the 1980s, anthropologists became especially sensitive to the literary qualities and practices of their discipline— that ethnography is not a simple matter of collecting social facts and publishing them but is a creative (though not thereby entirely fictional) process.

In early twentieth-century France, anthropologists had not only to struggle to win a place in the academy for their discipline but to contend with the objections of scholars of the humanities that their way of knowing was superior to the upstart social sciences. These scholars insisted that philosophy and literature described the human condition more accurately and fully than science ever could, and the obsession with social facts threatened to wring all of the "atmosphere" or lived quality of human existence out of social science accounts (Debaene 2014). In response, French anthropologists developed a fascinating habit of writing *two* books based on their field experiences—one technical and scientific, the other literary and humanistic. The most celebrated of these literary anthropology works is Claude Lévi-Strauss' *Tristes Tropique*, but other examples include Marcel Griaule's *Les Flambeurs d'hommes* and Michel Leiris' *L'Afrique fantome*.

Social/cultural anthropologists agree that ethnography, however, is not the goal of anthropology but a means to an end (the venerable Edmund Leach likened ethnographic description to butterfly collecting). More profoundly and consistent with this book, social/cultural anthropology is *comparative epistemology*, the discovery of the many and various ways that human groups think and experience the world. For that reason, it devotes itself more seriously to non-Western societies and ways of knowing (see Chapter 9) than any other social science—always aware that humans construct their own cultural realities.

Essential to any way of knowing is language—the words and concepts that we speak and think in—which makes linguistic anthropology especially valuable. Linguistic anthropologists, using many of the tools of social/cultural anthropology plus some of their own (recording devices, speech notation, etc.), not only investigate the differences between languages, and the differences *within* languages or language communities (such as dialects, specialized speech genres, and bilingualism) but the relationship between language and social action and organization. Linguistic anthropologists understand language *as* social action, which affects social relations and institutions; language is "effective" and has social effects. More, some linguistic and social/cultural anthropologists assert that language has psychological or cognitive effects. According to the linguistic relativity hypothesis (or Sapir-Whorf hypothesis, named after two of its proponents, Edward Sapir and Benjamin Lee Whorf), language does not only convey experience but *constructs* experience, societies speaking radically different languages experiencing and "knowing" the world in radically different ways.

Finally, since its inception, the behavioral anthropologies have gone through a series of stages or what have been called "turns." From the positivistic early stage, a "symbolic" or "interpretive" turn occurred in the 1950s, emphasizing symbols, meaning, and "reading" culture like a text. This was followed in the 1970s by a shift away from culture (as ideas, symbols, and meanings) and social structure (as rules and institutions) to *practice* or what people actually do and how those actions produce and reproduce culture and structure. In the 1980s, there was a "literary" turn, exploring the nature of anthropological writing. Since then, there has been a "material" turn, emphasizing the social significance—even the social life—of objects (including the human body as a cultural object or "embodiment"), re-opening a link between the behavioral anthropologies and the material ones.

The Modern Material Anthropologies

The subject matter and questions of physical anthropology and archaeology make culture less relevant and participant observation almost entirely irrelevant. Because they handle material objects—especially fossils in the first case and artifacts in the second—physical anthropology and archaeology have much more in common with each other methodologically than either has with the behavioral anthropologies. Both are also more quantitative and statistical, more likely to involve teams of investigators, and necessarily call in the assistance of the natural sciences to complete their analyses.

As recounted above, anthropology was physical before it was cultural, preoccupied with questions of human biological "types" and races. This project involved the collection and measurement of human body parts. When social/cultural anthropology diverged in the first decades of the 1900s, physical anthropology was left to continue its exploration of human physical diversity and evolution. And the origins and accomplishments of physical anthropology owe as much or more to natural scientists such as Charles Darwin (1809–82) and Gregor Mendel (1822–84), not to mention geologists such as Georges Cuvier (1769–1832) and Charles Lyell (1797–1875), as to the behavior anthropologies. Indeed, introductory textbooks customarily present these ancestors before turning to modern genetics, cellular biology, and paleontology.

This pedigree of physical anthropology suggests a much closer connection to natural science than any other social science, including psychology. And physical anthropology's natural-science connections go further. The first issue is the methodology of physical anthropology, which begins with *excavation*—in short, digging—or unearthing objects from under the ground. This requires material tools like shovels and picks, in order to exhume the key facts of paleoanthropology (the anthropology of early human life), namely *fossils*. Finding fossils in the first place is a daunting task, given their rarity and the uncertainty of where to begin searching. Much of the time in the field is spent conducting "pedestrian surveys," also called "fieldwalking," with experienced fieldworkers simply pacing the landscape looking for signs of objects. Louis Leakey (1903–72), perhaps the most famous of all physical anthropologists, literally traversed East Africa for two decades before making his epochal finds. Such discoveries when they happen—and they may not happen for seasons, years, or ever—are never the work of one person but require teams of professional anthropologists, graduate students, and often local laborers (the professional anthropologist seldom if ever does the main digging).

Figure 7.5 One example of a Phylogeny or Phylogenetic Tree

Source: Wikicommons, https://commons.wikimedia.org/wiki/File:Ihmisten_sukupuu3_vuosi 2004.jpg.

The work of physical anthropology does not end in the field. Back in the laboratory, physical anthropologists must reassemble bone fragments and reconstruct bodies. They must designate the species and finally place it within the historical relations between human-like species. The grand prize of physical anthropology is a *phylogeny*, an evolutionary tree, depicting each species in chronological order and in relation to its ancestors and descendants. The published writings of physical anthropologists not surprisingly very much resemble the papers of natural scientists, replete with photographs of teeth and skulls and other bones with elaborate, meticulous measurements and statistical analyses of these objects.

Further, physical anthropology could not achieve its results without the collaboration of many kinds of natural scientists. Once the fossils are recovered, physical anthropologists depend on an army of scientific specialists to date and interpret those materials—chemists and physicists, geologists, biologists and anatomists, botanists and palynologists (scientists who study pollen), and taphonomists (who study how objects decay and move). Physical anthropologists are also greatly interested in the research of primatologists, who study the behavior and social organization of monkeys and apes for clues to the nature of early humans. The best-known living primatologist is Jane Goodall, who began fieldwork with African chimpanzees in the 1960s and revolutionized our knowledge of those primate cousins. Finally, physical anthropologists may even hire artists to sculpt the features onto the bones and recreate in drawings what the beings looked like.

It is worth noting that not all physical anthropologists are paleoanthropologists, studying ancestral human species. Some explore more recent and even contemporary physical variation, and some apply their skills to present-day problems like *forensics*, for instance helping the police solve crimes or assisting in the identification of the remains of victims of war or genocide.

Man Makes Himself was the title of V. Gordon Childe's classic study of prehistory, echoing the fundamental theme of social/cultural anthropology and illustrating that archaeologists stand in the intersection of behavioral and material anthropologies. Their methods are akin to those of physical anthropologists, but their questions are, today more than ever, close to those of a social/cultural anthropologist: how did people live in the past? Curiously then, some introductory textbooks and courses combine physical anthropology and archaeology, but almost never are cultural anthropology and archaeology treated in the same textbooks and courses.

Where the facts of physical anthropology are human remains, the facts of archaeology are primarily *artifacts* and *features*. Both are material traces of past human lifeways, but artifacts include portable objects like tools, pots, jewelry, and such, while features are large permanent structures like buildings, roads, farms, and canals. Further strengthening their bond, physical anthropologists and archaeologists often work together on the same sites, since where there are human bodies there are usually artifacts too. Even in

---

Great Moments in Physical Anthropology

In its less than a century and a half of professional existence, physical anthropology has made some remarkable finds and has immensely changed our knowledge of our own species. Among the greatest discoveries in the history of physical anthropology are:

1856 — Neanderthal, first discovered in the Neander Valley of Germany and dated to between 140,000 and 35,000 years ago

1891 — Homo erectus, first discovered in Indonesia by Eugene Dubois and popularly known as "Java man," dated as far back as 1.8 million years ago

1925 — Australopithecus africanus, first discovered by Raymond Dart in southern Africa (his original discovery was the face of the "Taung child"), dated to 2.5 million years ago

1960 — Homo habilis, first discovered by Louis Leakey, perhaps the most famous physical anthropologist and the sire of a dynasty of anthropologists including his wife Mary and his son Richard; found in East Africa and dated to over two million years ago

1974 — Australopithecus afarensis, discovered by Donald Johanson in East Africa, nicknamed "Lucy" and one of the most complete and probably the best-known of all pre-human fossils, dated to more than three million years ago

---

very old sites, pre-human bones may be accompanied by stone tools, fire pits, or habitations of various sorts.

Because both subdisciplines collect and analyze material objects, archaeology shares much of physical anthropology's methodology, starting with the identification of a site for excavation. Sometimes the location of a site is obvious—as with an Egyptian pyramid or Mayan ruin—but sometimes it is difficult to find. Archaeologists may begin with fieldwalking, but they have many other tools at their disposal including "space imagery and aerial photography, and numerous geophysical methods (such as ground-penetrating and side-scanning radar, resistivity surveys, magnetometer surveys, etc.)" (Cherry 2005: 186). A great boon to archaeology has been geographical positioning systems (GPS) and geographical information systems (GIS) technology for plotting and recording locations. Like physical anthropologists, archaeologists must carefully extract objects, usually in fragments, noting their location and their context (the other objects in their vicinity). Because sites are often vast, archaeologists cannot hope to excavate

Figure 7.6 An archaeological excavation in Egypt

Source: Wikicommons, https://commons.wikimedia.org/wiki/File:Valle_de_los_Reyes,_Egipto, _trabajadores,_abril_de_2009.JPG.

them completely in one expedition, if ever. Back in the lab, they must date, reassemble, name, and otherwise analyze the objects, relying on the same battery of scientific specialists and typically resulting in equally technical publications with extensive quantitative data, maps, and drawings. To interpret their evidence, archaeologists may engage in *ethnographic analogy*, considering contemporary societies that live as the past society may have lived, and to determine how past peoples manufactured objects or features, they may conduct *archaeological experiments*, attempting to reconstruct a stone tool or to move huge blocks like the makers of the pyramids did.

Archaeology was born from the same impulse to travel, observe, and collect that motivated early social/cultural anthropology. Prior to the twentieth century, archaeology was largely unsystematic and unprofessional, often the activity of curious or greedy amateurs. One of the predecessors of modern archaeology was Heinrich Schliemann (1822–90), who, on the basis of the epics of Homer and latter-day accounts of local inhabitants, discovered and excavated the city of Troy from 1871, adding immeasurably to our knowledge of pre-classical or "bronze age" Greek civilization. William Flinders Petrie (1853–1942) extended early archaeology's reach to Egypt, where he conducted his first survey of Giza in 1880. Unlike many amateurs who damaged sites and absconded with artifacts, Petrie excavated sites carefully and kept detailed records, setting standards for professional archaeology that earned him the honor of the title of the father of archaeology from some later professionals. Sir Arthur Evans unearthed the extraordinary city of Knossos on the island of Crete around 1900, and Howard Carter opened the tomb of King Tutankhamun (King Tut) in 1922.

The first decades of professional archaeology emphasized grand sites and beautiful objects, mainly to describe past societies and to establish chronologies or timelines. However, by the 1960s archaeology experienced its own epistemological crisis, critiquing the project of mere description and sequencing. Led by scholars like Lewis Binford, a new approach often called *processual archaeology* emerged, since it was interested in general cultural processes and even laws. Past cultures, Binford insisted, should not be studied in isolation but as outcomes of adaptive processes combining the physical environment and technology. Influenced by cultural anthropologists, Binford demanded in an article meaningfully titled "Archaeology as Anthropology" that "change in the total cultural system must be viewed in an adaptive context both social and environmental" (1962: 217). "Until the tremendous quantities of data which the archaeologist controls are used in the solution of problems dealing with cultural evolution or systemic change," he warned, "we are not only failing to contribute to the furtherance of the aims of anthropology but retarding the accomplishment of these aims" (224). The goal was "systems" that operate today just as much as in the past.

This so-called "New Archaeology" was itself eventually criticized for being too positivistic or functionalist, leading to *post-processual* archaeology. The previous focus on systems was replaced among the post-processualists by "meaning or symbolism, history, agency, and critical approaches" (Hodder 2005: 155). This emphasis reconnected archaeology to many of the terms and questions of social/cultural anthropology, such as social organization, politics, religion, and even ethnicity and memory. Most fascinatingly, a specialty of "cognitive archaeology" appeared (see e.g. Renfrew and Zubrow 1994), aspiring to describe the mental processes that underlie material culture—the "mind in the cave," to quote the title of David Lewis-Williams' (2002) book, or better yet the mind that makes and inscribes itself in objects. One key contribution to this effort was André Leroi-Gourhan's (1964) notion of *chaîne opératoire* (operational chain/sequence) or the steps involved in producing an object. Analyzing the processes that result in a finished object

> makes it possible to document the steps and sequences of bygone material operations, and then reconstruct the dynamic links between these stages, their interlocking causes and effects, their attending equipment and settings, their temporal and spatial unfolding, and so on. This in turn

opens the way for addressing some of the complex social, ecological and cognitive dimensions surrounding ancient technical activities.

(Schlanger 2005: 19)

And this, in final turn, exemplifies the synthesis of mind, body, society, and object that marks contemporary anthropology and social science.

Disciplinary Case #6: Anthropology of Terrorism

Since most of us are not terrorists, and since terrorists by definition engage in illegitimate political violence, and since our first instinct is to dismiss terrorists as ill or evil, it is difficult to understand terrorism. More problematically, many people feel that to understand terrorism is in some way to condone it, as if grasping a terrorist's reasons entails accepting those reasons.

Anthropology's most important contribution to the science of humanity is the realization that humans differ and that each human way of life makes sense to itself. From the outside, a lifeway may seem bizarre, irrational, or reprehensible, but when we apply the anthropological perspective of comparison, holism, and relativism, we learn that each society or group within a society has *its own* perspective or view of the world, which we cannot completely understand if we insist in seeing it through the lens of our own worldview.

A leading anthropologist on the subject of terrorism, Jeffrey Sluka, has described what the discipline brings to the study of terrorism and "of human conflict in all its forms," namely

> a *cultural* perspective; extreme topical and theoretical eclecticism; a cross-culturally comparative and holistic perspective; an ethnographic approach based on long-term fieldwork and direct participant-observation in the community studied; a scientific commitment to both objectivity and getting as close as possible to the subject, participants', or *emic* point of view; an appreciation of the impact of ethnocentrism and cultural relativity; and a humanist concern for ethics, the potentially negative effects research may have on those studied.
>
> (2009: 138)

More precisely, he states that, first and most basic to the discipline, "anthropologists have written detailed critical ethnographies of popular armed resistance movements described as 'terrorists'" (140); Sluka himself has researched ethnic violence in Northern Ireland and anti-terrorism activities in New Zealand, for instance. Of course, it is difficult and dangerous to enter into a society gripped by terrorism, let alone into a terrorism organization, but that is the only way to discover what is happening "on the inside."

Second, he asserts that anthropology has maintained a historical and evolutionary angle on terrorism, recognizing that "terrorism, as a coercive strategy of political intimidation or fear, is as old as the state or civilization"; holistically, terrorism "is a dependent variable in the state equation of social inequality and stratification, rather than the independent variable most elites, governments, and orthodox terrorism studies experts treat it as" (139). In the modern context, "anthropologists are more aware than most of the fact that, historically, all the indigenous and other 'nation peoples' who have resisted state conquest and domination have been denounced and vilified by those states as inhuman 'savages'" (140).

This leads to Sluka's third point, that anthropologists "have applied our core concept—culture—to the debate, developing new conceptual models of state terrorism and 'cultures of terror' where fear becomes a 'normal' or everyday part of peoples' way of life" (140). But anthropologists go far beyond the description and analysis of the culture of terrorists; they have also examined and criticized how victimized cultures understand and apply the label 'terrorism' to certain acts, thus exposing "the *idea* of terrorism and how it is employed in society today" (140).

What Sluka and other anthropologists of terrorism generally advocate is a form of "critical terrorism studies," which, according to Richard Jackson of the National Center for Peace and Conflict Studies in New Zealand, entails appreciating that terrorism is culturally constructed (both by and for the perpetrators and victims), that "terrorism" is a concept and a label that is inherently *unstable* (that is, its meaning varies between groups and changes over time), and that scholars should be involved not only in analysis but in "emancipatory political praxis" (that is, trying to solve the problems that spark terrorism and other social violence in the first place) (2007: 244). Even scholars in other disciplines such as political science have adopted an essentially anthropological perspective in calling for a "completely constructivist critical terrorism studies" that comprehends terrorism as a discourse and "as a concept that is used in practice by various social actors," which practices "*constitute* identities, interests, and actors" (2012: 212).

This may be an extremely unfamiliar, perhaps even uncomfortable, way to think about terrorism, but a hallmark of the anthropological perspective is that it *destabilizes and corrodes conventional concepts and understandings*. Elsewhere, Sluka has asserted bluntly that the "empirical reality of the contemporary armed popular movements we have studied has simply not fitted with the 'terrorism' image presented by governments and the mainstream media" which is typically "unreliable, invalid, biased, and propagandistic" (2010: 51–2).

Another anthropologist who has even more strongly condemned the standard "mishandling of suicide terrorism" is Scott Atran. Atran wrote that a "common notion in the U.S. administration and media spin on the war on terrorism is that suicide attackers are evil, deluded, or homicidal misfits who thrive on poverty, ignorance, and anarchy," or worse that they "hate freedom"; on the contrary, "survey data reliably show that most Muslims who support suicide terrorism and trust bin Laden favor elected government, personal liberty, educational opportunity, and economic choice" (2004: 73). As we have seen in previous chapters, terrorists "exhibit no socially dysfunctional attributes" or major psychological pathologies" (76). Atran actually concludes that terrorists are "more ideologically driven than grievance-driven" (81), and ideologies are entirely cultural thought-systems. To learn more about these ideologies, Atran (2010) endorses doing something that politicians and victims seldom do but that anthropologists do for a living—actually *talking to* them, even if we regard them as enemies.

Beyond the ideologies and "cultures" of terrorist groups, anthropology can also investigate their social structure and institutional organization. Atran directs attention, for example, to the system of radical religious schools that prepare the next generation of terrorists; he also fully understands the positive social works that terrorist groups do in the absence of functioning governments and adequate social services. This suggests an approach for combatting terrorism: "democratic nations that fight terrorism therefore must discretely help others in these societies to compete with, rather than attempt to crush, such programs for the bodies, minds, and hearts of people" (2004: 84). In short, if terrorism is a culture and a social structure, then anti-terrorism must also be a culture and social structure.

Cultural anthropology probably has more immediate applications to terrorism than physical anthropology and archaeology, but these other anthropologies are not without their benefits. Physical anthropology can be a vital part of identifying victims and returning them to their families. Both physical anthropology and archaeology can shed light on past practices of violence and genocide and the cultural history of terrorism. Finally, lest we consider anthropology a tangential player in the social science of terrorism, it is worth noting that the U.S. Army has hired and deployed anthropologists in its "Human Terrain System" to collect ethnographic data on enemy combatants and their wider society in Iraq and Afghanistan and to supply that information in useable form for subsequent military action. Reasonably, anthropologists are concerned about the practical and ethical implications of such collaboration.

8 Geographical Worldview

Where is Zomia? You will not find it on any ordinary map, but Willem van Schendel thought that you should. Scholars tend to divide the Asian continent into several geographical and cultural areas, such as East Asia, South Asia, and Southeast Asia. There is nothing natural about such divisions, though, and they render a finite number of discrete "areas" that presume non-existent geographical and cultural similarities while erasing important differences. Scholars then gather around these presumed areas, forming professional groups of "area studies," like East Asian Studies, etc. Van Schendel proposed that Zomia (see Figure 8.1) qualified as an "area" because of its shared topographical features (largely a mountainous region) as well as its "language affinities," "religious commonalities" (tribal religions along with Buddhism and Christianity), "cultural traits" including kinship systems and ethnic distribution, "ancient trade networks, and ecological conditions" (2002: 653). Nevertheless, van Schendel accepted that Zomia has not been recognized as an "area" and further noticed that an "area" is more than a place; it is also "a site of knowledge production" and "a career machine" (649). Regional studies like Southeast Asian Studies, he argued, "use a geographical metaphor to legitimate the production of specific types of knowledge. This knowledge is structured geographically as well as according to academic disciplines" (650), manifested, for instance, in academic journals like *Journal of Southeast Asian Studies* or *South Asia: Journal of South Asian Studies*. More, like the main social sciences themselves, area studies perpetuate the current division of areas by recruiting individuals into careers like being a "Southeast Asianist" or "East Asianist." "As expressions of certain academic interests and disciplines," van Schendel wrote, areas and area studies are

> instruments in institutional strategies with regard to funds, students, jobs, and prestige. And they contributed to a certain ghettoization of critical insights as area studies tended toward the guild model. Area specialists were rewarded for "knowing their proper place": training in area studies centers, recognizing differences within the larger context of

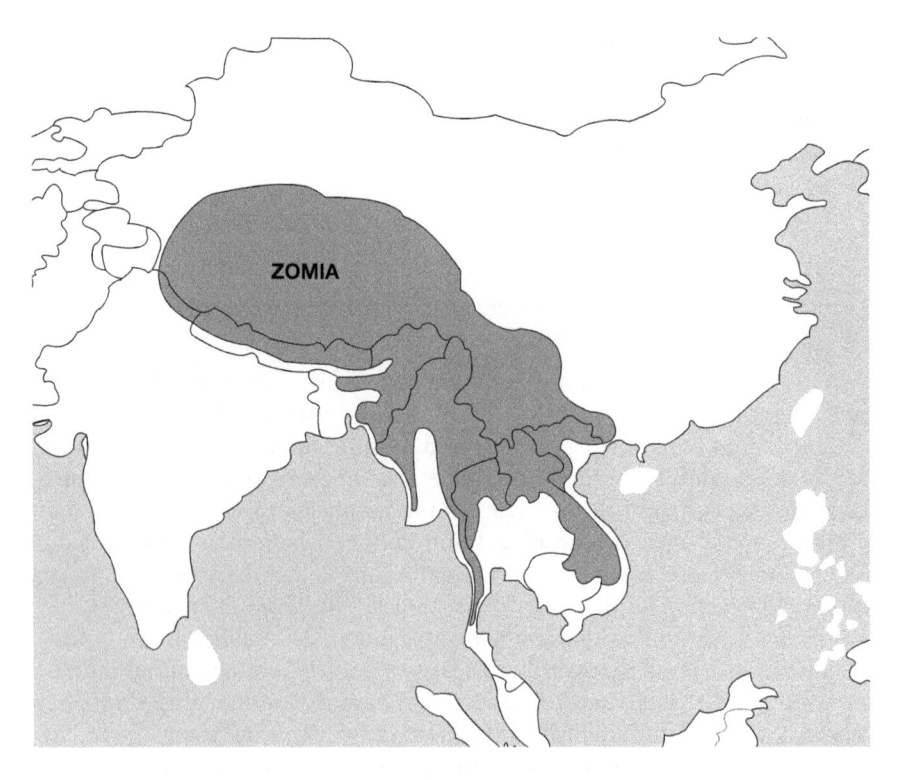

Figure 8.1 Zomia

Source: Wikicommons, https://commons.wikimedia.org/wiki/File:Zomia.jpg.

their area's unity, offering their findings to area-focused seminars and journals, and devoting their careers to the study of their area of training, without necessarily keeping abreast of intellectual developments next door.

(657)

One concrete and inescapable fact about the world is *place*: everything and everyone is located somewhere, and, despite the apparent contraction of space and time in the era of the internet, location still matters. Indeed, according to the credo of the American Geographical Society, "Geography is to space what history is to time. It is a spatial way of thinking, a science with distinctive methods and tools, a body of knowledge about places, and a set of information technologies old and new." Further, these professional geographers insist that geography "is essential to business" (recall the old adage that the three most important factors in real estate are "location, location, location"), to government, to science, and to education. In fact, you will recall that one of the ten key themes of social studies is "people, places, and environments," in which the National Curriculum Standards for Social Studies (www.socialstudies.org/standards/strands) specifies

- "the relationship between human populations and the physical world"
- "an understanding of spatial perspectives" including "changes in the relationship between peoples, places, and environments"
- "knowledge, skills, and understandings" to answer such questions as "Why do people decide to live where they do or move to other places? Why is location important? How do people interact with the environment and what are some of the consequences of those interactions? What physical and other characteristics lead to the creation of regions? How do maps, globes, geographic tools, and geospatial technologies contribute to the understanding of people, places, and environments?"

Like history, political science, and economics, geography has ancient origins. The Greeks used the term *geographia* (literally "earth-writing") in their descriptions of the world, very much in the modern sense of the term. Unlike history, political science, economics, or any of the social sciences we have examined in this book, though, geography is a hybrid or twin science, with one physical/natural and one social/cultural twin. The physical side of geography is aptly called *physical geography* and focuses on the description and analysis of the natural features and processes of the earth, like rivers and mountains and oceans. The other, more social branch of geography is *cultural geography* or *human geography*, paying attention to how humans relate to, interact with, and influence and are influenced by the physical environment. Surely, humans are part of the physical world, and human activity changes the physical, geographical world: humans cut down forests, move mountains, redirect or dam rivers, and build cities. Geographers and other social scientists also understand that humans inhabit not only a social environment but a "built environment" consisting of the material structures they make under and around themselves, such as houses and buildings, roads, canals, farms, parks, etc.

In this chapter, we will concentrate on human/cultural geography, but the social application of geography still depends on the scientific investigation of places and their physical qualities, as well as skills like map-drawing (cartography) and technologies like global positioning systems.

Geography in the Ancient World

Geography not only existed but was arguably one of the most advanced domains of knowledge in the ancient world. Related to the field of geometry (literally "earth-measure"), knowledge of local and distant places was essential for engineering (e.g. constructing pyramids, walls, and such monumental features), for trade and travel, and of course for war. Knowing and using terrain well was and is often the difference between victory and defeat in battle. It is no surprise, then, that all ancient civilizations—from the Chinese to the Egyptian to the Greek—drew maps and studied the landscape around them. A clay tablet dating back to nearly 1700 BCE depicts the area west of the Euphrates River with its system of irrigation canals (see www.alex-mitchellauthor.com/ancient-qanats). Mesopotamians even etched a map of the known world into a tablet, although their world and their mapping style look nothing like our own: it portrays the Middle East as a circle, ringed by an ocean, and suggests that mythical creatures dwelt in remote realms.

The Greeks practiced a form of geography easily recognizable to the modern eye and demonstrated sophisticated geographical knowledge. In his "historical" researches, Herodotus wrote prolifically on the physical and cultural geography of Greece and Persia, and Aristotle speculated that the earth must be a sphere. Most impressively, Eratosthenes (c. 276–194 BCE) very accurately calculated the circumference of the planet, using a clever method of comparing the length of shadows in different locations. He thereby arrived at a circumference at the equator of 40,233 kilometers, which is almost exactly the modern scientific measurement of 40,072 kilometers.

Two of the greatest ancient geographers were the Romans Strabo and Ptolemy. Strabo (c. 64 BCE–20 CE) published a seventeen-volume set titled *Geographia* based on his travels and observations. He began his series of books with a tribute to his discipline—"If the scientific investigation of any subject be the proper avocation of the philosopher, Geography, the science of which we propose to treat, is certainly entitled to a high place" (Hamilton and Falconer 1854: 1)—and acknowledged such illustrious predecessors as Homer, Democritus, and Eratosthenes. Before launching into his articulate accounts of places around the Mediterranean world, he added:

In addition to its vast importance in regard to social life, and the art of government, Geography unfolds to us the celestial phenomena, acquaints us with the occupants of the land and ocean, and the vegetation, fruits, and peculiarities of the various quarters of the earth, a knowledge of which marks him who cultivates it as a man earnest in the great problem of life and happiness.

(1–2)

Figure 8.2 A Mesopotamian Map of the World, circa 700–500 BCE
Source: © Trustees of the British Museum.

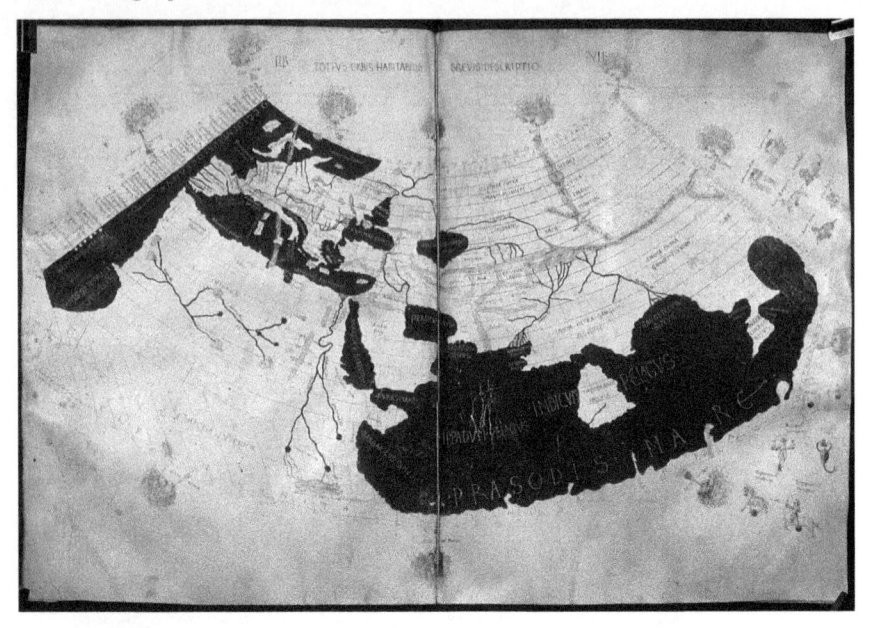

Figure 8.3 Ptolemy's Map of the World
Source: Wikicommons.

In short, Strabo's remarkably modern notion of geography treated both the differences between various parts of the world and the human occupation and use of those places.

Ptolemy (c. 100–178 CE) achieved greatness in both astronomy and geography, giving us a textbook on astronomy (the *Almagest*) and a seven-volume textbook or atlas *Geographia*, which, according to the Center for Spatially Integrated Social Science (www.csiss.org/classics/content/76) featured

> a world map, twenty-six regional maps, and sixty-seven maps of smaller areas. They illustrated three different methods for projecting the Earth's surface on a map (an equal area projection, a stereographic projection, and a conic projection), the calculation of coordinate locations for some eight thousand places on the Earth, and the development of concepts of geographical latitude and longitude.

Ptolemy's view of the world would dominate Western geographical knowledge for centuries.

Medieval Geography and the Era of World Exploration

The ancients knew the geography of the circum-Mediterranean world fairly well, but of course they had no awareness whatsoever of the lands beyond.

Indeed, they believed that the circum-Mediterranean world was *the* world, as the very name suggests: the Mediterranean Sea was the "middle of the earth" (*medi-terra*), encircled by the entire earth consisting of Europe, the Middle East, and northern Africa.

Even more problematically and inevitably—since maps specifically and geographic knowledge generally are human and social inventions—geography and cartography were saturated with cultural/political interests as well as current beliefs. Among these beliefs, as mentioned in previous chapters, were "knowledge" of monstrous human races that inhabited the remote parts of the earth and that were often depicted on maps.

Also among medieval and early modern European beliefs encoded into maps were Christian theology and sacred geography. For instance, many maps and geographical guidebooks were specifically designed for pilgrims to lead them to sacred sites, such as the *Bourdeaux Itinerary* and the *Epitome about Certain Holy Places*. Geographical knowledge was also filtered through scriptural doctrine and Church authority, as in the *Christian Topography* of Cosmas, which depicted the earth as flat with heaven covering the earth like a lid or bowl. Cosmas further dismissed the claim of a spherical earth in motion as pagan and blasphemous. Finally, Christian geography naturally privileged Christian places, often putting Jerusalem at the center of the world and indicating the locations of other such significant sites as the Garden of Eden. Sometimes God, Jesus, and/or various saints loomed over the earth, as they were believed to do in Christian doctrine.

Among the most famous of the medieval maps were

- the so-called "T-O" map of Isidore of Seville (c. 560–636), so dubbed because of its schematic portrayal of the world as a circle (the O) with Asia in the top half and the bottom half divided between Europe and Africa (the "T")
- the Mappa Mundi (world map) of Saint Beatus (c. 730–800), a more detailed and moderately more accurate image of the known world
- the Hereford Mappa Mundi, made in the late 1200s in the T-O style and including locations for the Tower of Babel, Noah's Ark, and Greek mythical references like Jason's golden fleece and the minotaur's labyrinth on Crete (see www.medievalists.net/2013/07/28/ten-beautiful-medieval-maps).

Clearly, perfect geographical accuracy was neither achieved nor actively sought; maps were intended to convey and strengthen cultural and theological knowledge.

Meanwhile, Islamic scholars were developing their own geographical and cartographic traditions. The most renowned of these was Muhammad al-Idrisi (1099–1165/6), who designed the Tabula Rogeriana map and published his book *Entertainment for Those Wanting to Discover the World* (also translated as *A Diversion for the Man Longing to Travel to Far-Off*

Places) in 1154. His map contains a lot of information but degenerates to obscurity and guesswork on the outskirts of the Mediterranean world. Other Muslim scholars like Ibn Khaldun and Ibn Battutah also contributed to geographic, historical, and cultural knowledge.

As told in prior chapters, European travels in the late Middle Ages began to revolutionize knowledge in many fields, including anthropology and geography; indeed, the two disciplines have long been intimately linked. Starting with the Crusades and the journeys of Marco Polo, better information of Asia became available, but it was the ocean voyages of the 1400s and beyond that really rewrote the geography (and other) books of Christendom. Portuguese navigators sailed along and mapped the west coast of Africa until they discovered the Cape of Good Hope and the southern tip of the continent. Shortly thereafter, Christopher Columbus led a small Spanish fleet west across the Atlantic Ocean—where many of his contemporaries feared falling off the edge of the flat earth, despite the fact that in the same year (1492) Martin Behaim had introduced a "globe" to depict the spherical shape of the planet—and touched the previously unexpected and unimagined American continents. Ironically, it was not Columbus' name that was forever attached to the continents he "discovered" but rather the name of Amerigo Vespucci, chief navigator of the Spanish fleet from 1508, who was immortalized in Martin Waldseemüller's 1507 map of the world.

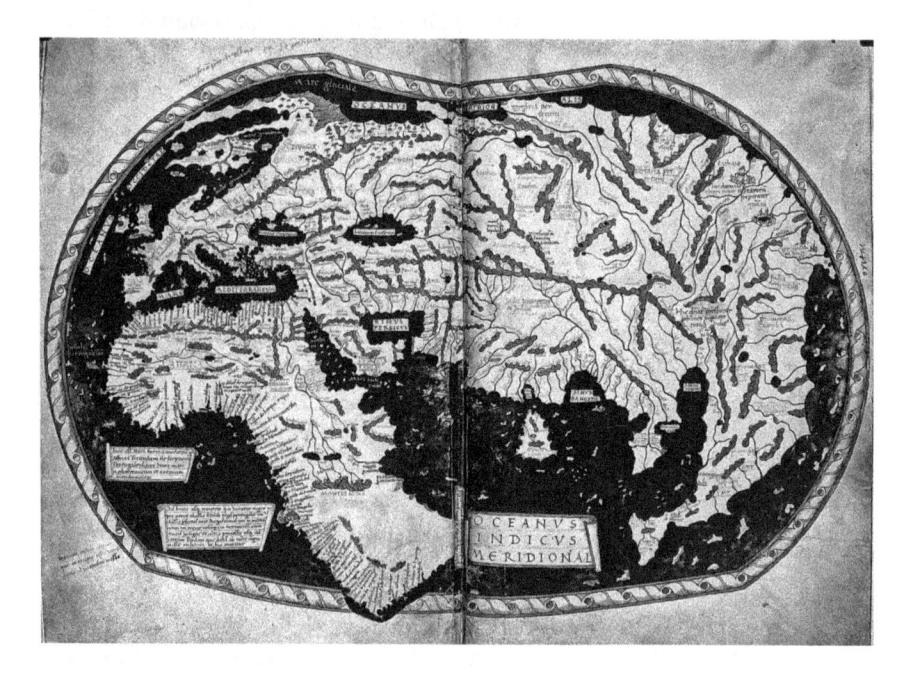

Figure 8.4 Henricus Martellus' World Map 1490

Source: Wikicommons. Published in the US before 1923 and public domain in the US.

These explorations and the data they brought back to Europe sparked a quantum leap in geographical knowledge and accuracy, not only of the Americas but of Eurasia and Africa too. In 1490 Henricus Martellus produced a much more complete map of the Old World, although the southern appendages of Africa and Asia were still distorted.

These advances enabled Bernhardus Varenius (1622–50) to prepare his *Geographia Generalis* in the final year of his life. This text became the standard of geographic knowledge for a century and first separated the branches of the new science, namely the physical size and shape of the earth and the processes and variations of climate (roughly physical geography) and the variations of culture and society across the earth's myriad regions and environments (roughly cultural geography).

The Formative Period of Modern Geography

Historians of geography have noted that geography was taught in European universities in the early-modern era before there were actually official departments of geography. Geography had an ancient pedigree, was practically useful, and was considered a domain of general philosophical inquiry. Thus, like other nascent social sciences, it was subsumed under the heading of philosophy and professed by experts of philosophy like Immanuel Kant.

It should be clear by now that Kant's influence on Western intellectual history cannot be overestimated; he was crucial to philosophy, psychology, anthropology, and to geography. From the mid-1770s he offered a course in geography at the University of Koenigsberg, typically doing geography in the summer term and anthropology in the winter. Records indicate that his geography course ran forty-nine times in the second half of the eighteenth century. His lectures were published as *Physische Geographie* in four volumes in 1805.

According to Stuart Elden's reassessment of Kant's geography, "Kant was an innovator in geography, if for no other reason that [sic] he was one of the very first to lecture on it as an explicit topic, before it was common to have chairs in geography in Germany" (2009: 12); indeed, he complained that no textbook on the subject was yet written. Kant's approach was also unique, reflecting his epistemological and moral orientation. Most basically, he was intent "to move geography—not always successfully—beyond mere 'earth description'" (12), conceiving it as having three different but equally important dimensions:

- physical geography, examining the "range of physical processes concerning earth and water: oceans; land and islands as examples of the earth and its terrain; earthquakes, volcanoes and electricity; springs and wells; rivers and water, wind currents; climate, the atmosphere and temperature; transformations of the earth; and seafaring"

- "the three realms of nature: fauna, flora, and minerals. Many of the aspects of this second part would not fall within the remit of modern day geography"
- an early form of cultural/human geography or "a regional geography of the world, with descriptions of particular regions and places in Asia, Africa, Europe, and America."

(13)

As can be appreciated from this summary, Kant's geography was both more and less than the twentieth-century version of the discipline. Above all,

> Kant's *Physical Geography* was also a moral and political account, and included human beings in it, usually just before the section on animals, discussing racial differences. In addition there are a range of comments in the third part concerning their geographical differentiation. Humans are thus seen as part of physical geography, both because they are one of the features of the *Erdboden*—the earth's surface—but also because they a [sic] causal mechanism for change to the earth itself, because they build dams, drain swamps, and fell forests, thus changing landscape and climate.

(13)

In short, Kant overtly promoted geography as "a physical, moral, and political" science, which would be "the essential foundation of all history" and presumably of a better human future. He envisioned the serious possibility of not only physical, moral, and political geographies but of "commercial geography" concerning trade and "theological geography" concerning the relation of religion to space and place (14).

Geography and Politics

Strabo is quoted as saying, "Geography subserves the needs of states," which urges us to consider the *uses* of geographic knowledge. As stressed previously, good geographic information can be indispensable for governing a country, conducting trade, and triumphing in war, and all of these activities were central to the rise of European states in the early-modern and modern eras. Indeed, it is possible to speak, and leaders and scholars did speak, of *geopolitics*, of place-power or the value of controlling strategic locations of the world. European regimes scrambled to seize islands and coastal ports, as well as to dominate trade with rich civilizations like India and China; by the late 1800s they were in a literal and open "scramble for Africa" that carved the continent between them. As a commercial and military resource, geographical information was often a corporate or state secret.

Kant's lifelong interest in geography, and the inclusion of the subject in university curricula, suggests the growing value of geographical knowledge

In his chronicle of a mutiny aboard a ship of the Dutch East Indies Company, Mike Dash (2002) reported that the overseas route to the Spice Islands was a well-guarded secret in the 1600s, so much so that accurate maps were not drawn for fear that the competition might learn the route. Unfortunately, one consequence was unnecessary ship-wrecks on rocks and reefs that could have been charted but were not.

for running states and empires. Another example during Kant's lifetime was William Playfair's 1785 *The Commercial and Political Atlas; Representing, by Means of Stained Copper-Plate Charts, the Exports, Imports, and General Trade of England, at a Single View*. Soon, the expanding United States began to explore and chart its hinterland: George Washington authorized a Geographers' Department even before the country won its independence, and President Thomas Jefferson dispatched the team of Lewis and Clark to cross the continent from 1804 to 1806, explicitly to collect geographical along with botanical, zoological, mineralogical, and even ethnological information. In 1818 a department of Geography, History, and Ethics was inaugurated at the U.S. Military Academy, and many famous and influential explorers and geographers served the army's purpose of mapping America's unknown western possessions, including Zebulon Pike and John Fremont. Not long after, trains of settlers in their covered wagons were trekking along the various "trails" to the Great Plains and the Pacific coast of North America.

As the discussion of eighteenth and nineteenth-century "race science" in the previous chapter illustrated, geography was also central to the developing Western concept of race. Races were assigned geographical locations or origins, and racial differences (and inequalities) were often explained in terms of geographic, environmental, and climatic influences. However, Alastair Bonnett argued for a stronger connection between geography and the politics of race, asserting in regard to British geographers during the colonial and imperial era that those professionals who were "interested in issues of 'race' saw their task as the elucidation of the hierarchy of the world's 'races' and the provision of informed speculation on the implications of White settlement and colonial government" (1997: 193). Among the practical problems was European penetration into the "wet tropics" where exotic diseases repelled white settlement. Indeed, as early as 1792 Leonhard Ludwig Finke published *Attempt at a General Medical-Practical Geography*, which featured a map of disease-distribution around the world. But Bonnett insisted that the collusion of race and geography went much deeper, positioning race as something "out there" in the remote, colonial, non-Western world. "Race" was equated with foreignness and largely with inferiority, and he claimed that even late twentieth-century studies like Peter Jackson's edited volume *Race & Racism: Essays in Social Geography* (1987) continued to endorse "a perversely intense focus upon the marginal subject-groups constituted within the Western and imperial imagination. The White center of that imagination is not discussed" (1997: 194). In short, in another act of geographical power, white Europeans erased themselves from the ideology of racism and advanced a "scientific" notion of race as real, objective, and spatially based—everywhere except in Europe.

The Clash of Civilizations: A Geography of Inevitable Global Conflict?

Originally in a 1993 article in the journal *Foreign Affairs* and then in a 1996 book, political scientist Samuel Huntington opined that geography would define the political relations and conflicts of future decades and centuries. Huntington contended that the world was divided into distinct cultural-geographic areas, which he called "civilizations." Each civilization has relatively clear spatial boundaries, and each had a culture—especially a religious tradition and identity—that sets it apart from the others. Among these civilizations are "the West" or "Christendom" (basically Western Europe, North America, and Australia and New Zealand), "Latin America" (with its unique Hispanic-Catholic culture), "Islam" or the lands of the Muslims (the Middle East and North Africa, but also Central Asia and Indonesia), "China," "Hindu India," "sub-Saharan Africa" (a region of extreme cultural and linguistic variation), and perhaps a few others (see Figure 8.5). More important than the mere existence of such geographical civilizational systems was the perennial tension between them: civilizations tend to compete with each other, misunderstand each other, and ultimately oppose each other. The result was a "clash of civilizations," and he especially prophesied friction and conflict on the frontiers where civilizations abutted and, like geological tectonic plates, grated against each other; key candidates were where Islam meets its most Western-like neighbor Israel, or where Hindu India meets Islam along the India-Pakistan border, or where "the West" meets Latin America on the U.S.-Mexico border, or where "the West" meets Eastern-Orthodox civilization in the Balkans and Ukraine. In the twenty-first century, Islam-versus-the-West has become the paradigm of civilizational clashes.

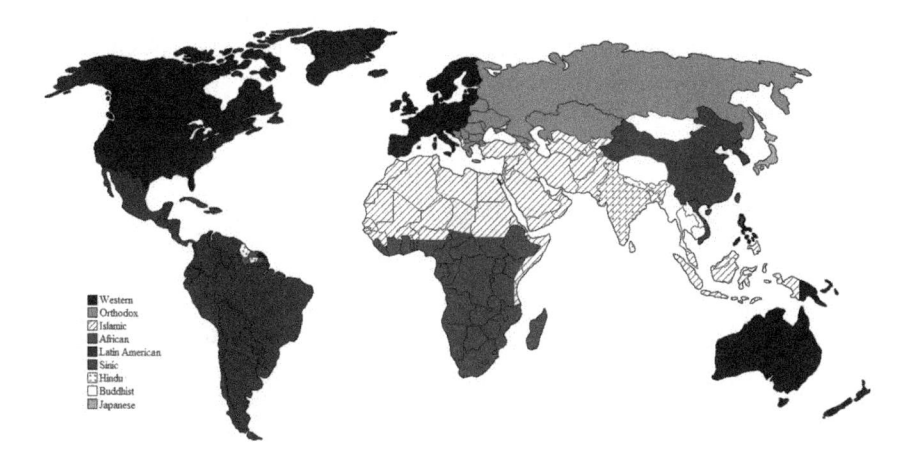

Figure 8.5 Huntington's Geographical "Civilizations"

Source: Kyle Cronan at the English Language Wikipedia, permission granted under the terms of the GNU Free Documentation License, version 1.2.

The Founders of Modern Geography

It is perfectly evident that geography had an intellectual identity and a place of practical prominence by the early 1800s. Even so, it was established as a distinct academic discipline largely through the contributions of two men, the Marx/Durkheim/Weber or Boas/Malinowski of geography, namely Alexander von Humboldt (1769–1859) and Karl Ritter (1779–1859). Working at precisely the same moment in history, they helped give contemporary geography its shape.

Based on his journeys through Central and South America as well as Asia, and years of teaching and lecturing, between 1845 and his death von Humboldt wrote five volumes of a work called *Cosmos: A Sketch of a Physical Description of the Universe*. Intended as an "assemblage of all things in heaven and earth, the universality of created things constituting the perceptible world" (1864: 53), he explained that

> the object at which we aim ought to be an inward one—an ennoblement of the intellect—so ought we likewise, in our pursuit of science, to strive after a knowledge of the laws and the principles of unity that pervade the vital forces of the universe; and it is by such a course that physical studies may be made subservient to the progress of industry, which is a conquest of mind over matter.
>
> (34)

Over the course of the volumes von Humboldt moved from the farthest reaches of the galaxy to the earth and its physical geography and plant and animal life to a history of science and the intellectual achievements of mankind. Most importantly for our purposes, he recognized and emphasized the interactions between the physical environment and humanity, comparing places and the people who inhabited them.

Simultaneously, Karl Ritter was championing, in his words, "the new scientific geography." In his magisterial nineteen-volume *Geography in Relation to Nature and the History of Mankind*, published over forty years from 1816 until his death, Ritter developed a vision of geography as "a kind of physiology and comparative anatomy of the earth" with humanity occupying the planet's body and being determined by it. Thus, the physical features of the environment were seen as "a leading element in the historic progress of the nation." A website dedicated to the great man (karlritter. weebly.com/ritters-contributions-to-geography.html) holds that for Ritter

> the object of geography is to learn about relationships between different forms of matter on the earth's surface and to study individual geographic areas. Using the comparative method, Ritter attempted to classify and explain many natural phenomena and came very close to the concept of landscape, which he considered as an indivisible unit.

More, he "attempted to prove that nature was a determining influence on the fortunes of man, which promoted the development of geopolitics." Particularly significant was his move away from the study of specific countries or states and toward the study and description of "regions" defined and unified by common geography, such as "river basins, plateaus, or terraced areas." For example, the United States consists of multiple geographical regions, and those regions also straddle national boundaries, like the arid Southwest that the U.S. shares with Mexico or the Great Plains or Rocky Mountains that cross the U.S.-Canadian border.

Many others contributed to the formation of the modern discipline of geography, not all of whom were exclusively or professionally geographers themselves. George Perkins Marsh's 1864 *Man and Nature, or Physical Geography as Modified by Human Action* took a deep historical view of human-environment interactions, ranging as widely as the "natural advantages of the territory of the Roman Empire" to the introduction of new species to the Americas, the reclamation of land from the ocean in northern Europe, and the digging of the Suez Canal through the sands of Egypt. Friedrich Ratzel, often claimed as an ancestor of anthropology, was also a geographer, and his ambitious ten-year project (1882–91) *Anthropogeographie* set out to document all of the earth's geographic regions and their impact on human culture and history. Even Franz Boas himself (see Chapter 7) was a geographer and argued in his 1887 essay "The Study of Geography" for the independent scientific status of geography. Acknowledging that "Humboldt's admirable works and Karl Ritter's comparative geography arose out of the rapidly extending knowledge of the earth" (1887: 137),

Boas' article is an early and rather old-fashioned and positivistic defense of geography as a descriptive and explanatory science equal to the theoretical and experimental natural sciences.

But by the end of the 1800s, geography hardly needed a defender like Boas, because it was well ensconced in the academy and in the popular mind. For instance, the Wharton School of Business, part of the University of Pennsylvania, offered an "economic geography" course in 1893, and the University of California created the first higher-education geography department in the country in 1898, with the University of Chicago introducing a doctoral degree in geography in 1903. Meanwhile, millions of Americans and others began enjoying the experience of *National Geographic* magazine in 1888, which brought remote and exotic places and peoples vividly into their homes. At the same time, historians and political leaders continued to appreciate the value of geographic knowledge for the exercise of military and political power, as in American Navy captain Alfred Thayer Mahan's 1890 *The Influence of Sea Power on History*.

One figure who re-imagined geography, and stirred considerable criticism in the process, was Carl Sauer (1889–1975), who judged geography to be in a fairly sorry state in the 1910s and particularly rejected the simplistic "geographical determinism" of the age—that is, that experts could find direct cause-and-effect relations between geography and human activity and culture (and thus, presumably, "geographical laws"). His seminal essay "The Morphology of Landscape" (1925) rejected the determinism of the discipline and argued that the real subject-matter or rationale for geography as a science was "the existence of places and areas as landscapes" (Solot 1986: 509).

In 1923 Sauer relocated to Berkeley, California, where, through anthropologists Alfred Kroeber and Robert Lowie, both trained by Franz Boas (see Chapter 7), he was exposed to the culture concept and especially the reigning interests in "culture areas" (that is, large regions that were home to closely-related cultures) and the diffusion of cultural traits across such regions. Under this influence, Sauer's Berkeley School of cultural geography centered on the notion of *landscape*, which consisted of two elements—the physical place or site and its natural characteristics to be sure, but also the *cultural expression* of the place. That is, humans could not be understood apart from their places, and places could not be understood apart from human habitation and activity. "The natural landscape," he wrote, "is being subjected to transformation at the hands of man, the last and for us the most important morphologic factor. By his cultures he makes use of the natural forms, in many cases alters them, in some destroys them" (1925: 45).

Twenty-five years into the twentieth century, he insisted that the "study of the cultural landscape is, as yet, largely an untilled field" (45), but he proposed a rather simple model for the approach, which we can summarize as:

culture + time + natural landscape = cultural landscape

In a word, "The cultural landscape is fashioned out of a natural landscape by a culture group. Culture is the agent, the natural area is the medium, the cultural landscape is the result" (46). The precise forms that this cultural landscape take include population density and mobility, housing arrangements, production and communication systems, and similar.

Contemporary Human/Cultural Geography Thought and Method

Geographical knowledge has always been primarily for practical use, motivated by human interests in the land and its resources and features. Human/cultural geography, however, brings society and culture to the center of geographical thought, as defined by Pamela Shurmer-Smith:

> Cultural geography, then, becomes the field of study which concentrates upon the ways in which space, place and the environment participate in an unfolding dialogue of meaning. This includes thinking about how geographical phenomena are shaped, worked and apportioned according to ideology; how they are used when people form and express their relationships and ideas, including their sense of who they are. It also includes the ways in which place, space and environment are perceived and represented, how they are depicted in the arts, folklore and media and how these artistic uses feed back into the practical.
>
> (2002: 3)

Because, according to Kay Anderson, Mona Domosh, Steve Pile, and Nigel Thrift in their *Handbook of Cultural Geography*, it is "a living tradition of disagreements, passions, commitments, and enthusiasm" (2003: 2), it is hardly surprising that human/cultural geography is understood and practiced differently by different scholars and overlaps with other subdisciplines of geography as well as with other social sciences. Indeed, Anderson et al. go so far as to opine that "if there is one thing about cultural geography that we know for sure, it is that it is not a field" (xviii) but more "a series of intellectual—and, at core, politicized—engagements with the world" (2).

The Fives Themes of Human/Cultural Geography

One way that modern human/cultural geographers organize and express their own way of knowing is in terms of a set of guiding themes. Although they are sometimes stated slightly differently, a representative formulation of the five themes of the discipline is given by Mona Domosh, Roderick Neumann, Patricia Price, and Terry Jordan-Bychkov in their textbook *The Human Mosaic* (2012).

The first of the themes in their reckoning is *region*, which is the analytical unit of geography, just as "period" is the analytical unit of history, or

Research Topics in Human/Cultural Geography

There is no *Annual Review of Human/Cultural Geography*, but there are some journals dedicated specifically to the subfield within geography. Articles from the most recent issues of two representative journals include:

Human Geography (volume 8, issue 3, 2015)
"Concrete Jungle: The Planetary Urbanization of the Ecuadorian Amazon"
"Hope as a Critical Resource for Small Scale Farmers in Mpumalanga"
"Mutual Aid, Environmental Policy, and the Regulation of Faroese Pilot Whaling"
"Live Music, Intercity Competition, and Reputational Rents: Austin, Texas the 'Live Music Capital of the World'"
"What 'Drives' Capitalist Development?"
"Uneven Development: Lessons from the Ongoing Greek Tragedy"
"Reflections on the Illusory and Forgetful Geographies of Settler Colonialism"
"The New Urban Question"
"Worlding Citites: Asian Experiments and the Art of Being Global"
"Neoliberal Urbanism and Its Contestations: Crossing Theoretical Boundaries"
"Debtfare States and the Poverty Industry: Money, Discipline, and the Surplus Population"
"The Future of Development (A Radical Manifesto)"
"Everyday Utopias: The Conceptual Life of Promising Spaces"
Progress in Human Geography (volume 39, issue 6, 2015)
"Conceptualizing International Education: From International Student to International Study"
"The Boundaries of Urban Metabolism: Towards an Augmented World City Hypothesis"
"Geographies of Ageing: Progress and Possibilities after Two Decades of Change"
"Social Geography I: Food"
"Geographies of Race and Ethnicity 1: White Supremacy vs White Privilege in Environmental Racism Research"
"Cultural Geography III: Objects of Culture and Humanity, or Re-'thinging' the Anthropocene Landscape"
"History and Philosophy of Geography III: Charting the *Anabasis*?"

"society" is the analytical unit of sociology. Region might seem like a self-evident concept, but it is not. For instance, they differentiate between a "formal region" (an area inhabited by people who share one or more cultural traits, like "the Arabic-speaking region") and a "functional region" (an area that operates as a political, social, or economic unit, like the "Eurozone"). They also separate out "vernacular region," which is a place perceived by its inhabitants as a distinct coherent entity, often with its own name, like "the South" or "Dixie" in the United States. Finally, a region may have its "core" area (which is most closely and deeply associated with a place and people) and its "periphery" and its border zones. In other words, not all places within a region are equal.

W. R. Tobler is often credited with postulating the "first law of geography": "everything is related to everything else, but near things are more related than distant things" (1970: 236).

The second theme is *mobility* or "the relative ability of people, ideas, or things to move freely through space" (2012: 10). Places and people are not static, and the authors mention "relocation," "expansion," and "contagion" as some of the process of geographic mobility. It is also worth recognizing that people might stay in one place while geographically-defined entities change their boundaries, as when the United States acquired the Louisiana Purchase and Alaska or annexed Texas.

Their third theme is *globalization*, which is central to all social sciences today. They define globalization as "the binding together of all the lands and peoples of the world into an integrated system driven by capitalistic free markets, in which cultural diffusion is rapid, independent states are weakened, and cultural homogenization is encouraged" (13). From these words it is easy and imperative to see the interconnection of geography, economics, politics, society, and culture. A major factor in this global binding is communication technology like the telephone and the internet, which often seems to have compressed—if not eliminated altogether—differences in space and time. However, despite proclamations like Thomas Friedman's 2005 *The World is Flat*, which argued that technology and capitalism had "leveled" the world so that all peoples and places were equally connected and equally able to participate, there are still great regional and local variations in wealth, power, and access to cultural resources.

Nature-culture is the fourth theme of human geography, which is "the complex relationships between people and physical environment, including how culture, politics, and economies affect people's ecological situation and resource use" (16). Again, almost all geographers reject a simplistic environmental determinism, since individuals and societies can use the exact same environment in different ways (think, for instance, of the contrast between how Native American societies and modern U.S. society exploit the landscape). The authors recommend an approach called *possibilism* or the notion "that any environment offers a number of different possible ways for a culture to develop, and that the choices among these possibilities are guided by cultural heritage" (18). Thus, an environment places certain limits on its possible occupation and use and makes particular occupations or uses more likely. Much of the actual decision on how to live within a place depends on *environmental perception* or "the belief that culture depends more on what people perceive the environment to be than on the actual character of the environment; perception in turn is colored by the teachings of culture" (20).

The fifth and final theme is *cultural landscape*, sometimes also called "the built environment," defined as "all the built forms that cultural groups create in inhabiting the earth—roads, agricultural fields, cities, houses, parks, gardens, commercial buildings, and so on. . . . Landscape mirrors a culture's needs, values, and attitudes toward the earth" (23). In this sense, humans never live in "nature," and "nature" itself is a cultural concept: for example, even "natural spaces" such as national parks are actually highly managed spaces. The authors stress a subset of *symbolic landscapes* or places "that express the values, beliefs, and meanings of a particular culture" (24), that is, places filled with special cultural significance and importance. Some of these are "natural" but also symbolic, like Mount Fuji in Japan or Mount Olympus in Greece. Others are created or transformed by human action, such as Arlington National Cemetery, the Civil War battleground at Gettysburg, or the presidential faces on Mount Rushmore, where Americans have literally etched their history onto the stones. All of these are instances and sites of social or collective memory.

Place: A Key Geographical Concept

Human/cultural geography shares with physical geography the quality of being fundamentally a spatial science, curious about how phenomena are arrayed and organized across space. Benno Werlen insisted that human/cultural geographers "have analyzed societies in terms of their so-called spatial character or in spatial categories. They have explained the world in the context of spatial differentiation and tried to solve problems arising in this context (unequal opportunities in different regions, territorial conflicts, regional struggles, etc.)" (1993: 139). Even so, most human/cultural (and physical) geographers would concur with Werlen that "there is no such thing as 'space'" (3) or rather that "space" is an abstract concept that does not capture how humans inhabit the world. This is why Werlen called for a human/cultural geography that was not a science of space but of *action* and of how human thought and behavior constructs spaces.

Scholars therefore tend to emphasize the notion of *place* over space. In their *Dictionary of Human Geography*, Derek Gregory, Ron Johnston, Geraldine Pratt, Michael J. Watts, and Sarah Whatmore explain that place is generally seen "as a human-wrought transformation of the Earth's surface or of pre-existing, undifferentiated space. It is usually distinguished by the cultural or subjective meanings through which it is constructed and differentiated, and is understood by most human geographers to be in an incessant state of 'becoming'" (2009: 539). The crucial variable that separates place from space, or carves a place out of space, is meaning, including "perceptions of place, senses of place, and human dwelling in and memories of place" (539). Or, as R. D. Sack put it, "Place refers to something we humans make. A place is made when we take an area of space and intentionally bound it and attempt to control what happens within it through the use of (implicit and/or explicit) rules about what may or may not take place" (2004: 243).

Place does not automatically refer to any pre-determined level or size of location but can function at many different physical and social levels, often simultaneously. For instance, the living room or the kitchen can be considered a place (and, historically and culturally, such places can be associated with different people, like the old-fashioned belief that the kitchen is "a woman's place"); an entire house can be a place, as can be a neighborhood or block, a city, a state, a country, a continent, or a planet. Nor do places have absolute unchanging meanings or names; new places can be created and old places forgotten as humans occupy and reconceive space; a good example is a Chinese or Indian city built from scratch (see later discussion) or a country like Yugoslavia fragmenting into multiple independent states. As groups arrive in or depart from areas, like upper-middle class people "gentrifying" formerly depressed urban neighborhoods, places are constructed anew.

Thus, Jon Anderson submits that human/cultural geographers envision a place as "constituted by imbroglios [i.e. tangled, complex, even painful masses] of *traces*," which are "most commonly considered as material in nature (material traces may include 'things' such as buildings, signs, statues, graffiti, i.e. physical additions to our surroundings), but they can also be non-material (non-material traces might include, for example, activities, events, performances, or emotions)" (2015: 5). This perspective in turn suggests a number of questions:

> What cultural traces dominate a particular place? Who and what do these traces stand for? In other words, whose place is this anyway?
>
> Are the traces in this place challenged and resisted? If so how?
>
> What do these alternative traces stand for? Whose places do they seek to make, and what would these places be like?
>
> What are the consequences of this ongoing composition? What trace-chains are set in motion, and what cultural orders and geographical borders are being established, new or otherwise?

As cultural geography (CG) also positions us within our world, two further questions are raised:

Do these changes have any effect on how we should think about place?

Do these changes have any effect on how we should act in place?

(11)

Human/cultural geographers also recognize that the social world contains exceptional places that perhaps do not seem like places at all, although they occupy physical space, and for two examples they embrace the ideas of non-geographers Michel Foucault and Marc Augé (Gregory et al.'s *Dictionary of Human Geography* contains entries for both ideas). Foucault coined the term *heterotopia* (literally "other-place") for real physical sites (not fantasy locations like "utopias") "which are something like counter-sites ... [where] all the other real sites that can be found within the culture are simultaneously represented, contested, and inverted" (Foucault and Miskowiec 1986: 24). To be clearer, he proposed that heterotopias function "to create a space of illusion that exposes every real space" (that is, exposes real places as either real *or unreal*, or both) and "to create a space that is other, another real space, as perfect, as meticulous, as well arranged as ours is messy, ill constructed, and jumbled" (27). Some observers regard Las Vegas as a heterotopia, a real-enough place but one where the normal rules do not apply and where "what happens there, stays there." More than a few scholars (and critics) have dubbed Disneyland a heterotopia, especially in Foucault's second sense, as a place that is unnaturally orderly and happy. Indeed, many heterotopias may exist in modern society, from cruise ships and resort hotels to bars and brothels.

Anthropologist Marc Augé went a step further in positing the existence of *non-places*. Especially in the contemporary world of what he called *supermodernity*, the quality of life creates non-spatial "places" such as online communities, Facebook and Twitter, and web-based shopping "sites." But non-places need not be "virtual places"; they can be quite physical and geographical. Because people and objects are in constant and rapid motion, mobility and travel have become common, perhaps formative, experiences. Augé considered the transit-points on the earth—airports, train and bus stations, etc.—to be non-places since they surely occupy space but are home to no one. We literally pass through them as if they are not there. He formulated his concept of non-place, then, in this way: "If a *place* can be defined as relational, historical, and concerned with identity, then a space which cannot be defined as relational, or historical, or concerned with identity will be a *non-place*" (1995: 77–8). For early sociologists, the classic non-place was the city (recall Louis Wirth's critique of the urban lifestyle in Chapter 6), and many commentators have expressed alarm at "the consequences of placelessness, inauthenticity, sameness and the standardization of landscapes" (Arefi 1999: 184) in today's world, using negative terms like "plastic" or "sterile" or "unliveable" or "soulless" to describe these empty places (187).

Research Methods in Human/Cultural Geography

As the social-scientific twin of physical geography, human/cultural geography has access to both social-scientific and natural-scientific methods. Among the natural-scientific methods distinctive of geography are *geographic information systems* and *geo-informatics*. Geographic information systems (GIS) does not refer to any single tool or procedure but rather "to a collection of practices, software and hardware with the ability to collect, story, display, analyze, and print information about the Earth's surface (or any other scale of geographical data" (Gregory et al. 2009: 279). This suite of tools

> allows the combination of geographical data sets (or layers) and the creation of new geospatial data to which one can apply standard spatial analysis tools. Comprehensive GIS require a means of: (i) data input, from maps, aerial photos, satellites, surveys and other sources (cf. remote sensing); (ii) data storage, retrieval, and query; (iii) data transformation, analysis and modelling, including spatial statistics; and finally (iv) data reporting, such as maps, reports and plans.
>
> (279–80)

Geo-informatics further links geography with computer science to use geo-coded data to better model, visualize, and understand the Earth's complexity" and encompasses "discovery, integration, management and visualization of geoscience data; internet-enabled geographic information systems (GIS); location-based services, including global positioning systems; spatial data modelling in hyperspaces; remote sensing; and interoperability" (299). All of this information can then be processed with geostatistics, akin to econometrics or specialized statistical methods in other sciences, the basic tool of which is the *variogram* to model the correlation of variables across space.

Because the questions they ask are ultimately social rather than physical, these admittedly important methods may be embedded in human/cultural geographers' research but do not usually rise to the surface. Indeed, Shurmer-Smith maintains that human/cultural geographers seldom collect such data themselves (2002b: 97), relying instead on the data assembled and shared by governments, universities, institutions, and the media. Among the many sources to which they may turn are America's fedstats.gov, Canada's statcan.gc.ca, and England's statistics.gov.uk, as well as research by the United Nations and Eurostats. There are also numerous sources of maps such as the Perry-Castañeda Library Map Collection of University of Texas (www.lib.utexas.edu/maps), the British Geological Survey (www.bgs.ac.uk), and the United Nations Cartographic Section (www.un.org/Depts/Cartographic), to name but a few.

Some sense of the topics investigated by human/cultural geographers reveals how the standard methods of the social sciences are perfectly appropriate for its purposes. At the most general level, as evinced by textbook chapters and course descriptions, the discipline is interested in population and migration, politics (state boundaries, ethnic groups, and conflicts), agriculture and rural land use, industrialization and development, and urbanization and urban land use. At a finer level of precision, human/cultural geography may include any of the following:

> migration, transnationality and diaspora; geographies of "social nature"; work inspired by the "new mobilities paradigm"; studies of the cultural economy of food, fashion and other commodities; geographies of architecture and the built environment; geographies of waste and related matter; geographies of "race" and racism; physical and mental health; religious identity; childhood and youth; media and visual culture. There have also been important new studies of the intersectional geographies involved in "living with difference" and exciting new work on sexuality and queer theory.
>
> (Jackson 2012: 4)

Such subjects avail themselves of all the standard methods of social science, such as perusing historical archives, analyzing texts, reading diaries, conducting interviews and focus groups, collecting oral histories, and performing participant observation. Visual geographers Antje Schlottmann and Judith Miggelbrink (2009) also recommend the use of photographs, film, and of course maps.

Of Maps and Men: Creating and Representing Geographical Knowledge

If people have a single association with geography, it is maps. *Cartography* or the drawing of maps has been a fundamental corollary of geography since its ancient origins, and most former students probably remember geography as map-drawing and map-coloring, learning the locations of the mountains or rivers. But geography is not merely mapping, and mapping is not merely the graphic representation of physical features. There are also political maps (showing the borders of countries and the placement of cities), ethnographic maps (showing the distribution of different cultures or ethnic groups), and many other types. Truly, a map can convey any information that is spatially distributed, which is virtually any information.

The International Cartographic Association defined a map as "a symbolized image of geographic reality resulting from the creative efforts of cartographers and designed for use when spatial relationships are of special relevance" (quoted in Perkins 2010: 352). A map is "an efficient way of storing large amounts of spatial information" and thus a crucial tool in

Why Did Europe Conquer the World: Guns, Germs, and Steel?

One of the most momentous questions for geography and all social science is why Europe colonized the world instead of some other civilization. This is especially interesting to ponder given Gavin Menzies' (2003) controversial claim that China reached the shores of the Americas in 1421 but failed to take colonial possession of the continent. Jared Diamond, whose work combines cultural geography and evolutionary biology, rejected the comfortable assumption of Western cultural (let alone racial) superiority in favor of a historical-environmental explanation. In his famous *Guns, Germs, and Steel: The Fates of Human Societies* (1999) he noticed first that societies occupy different geographic spaces with different environmental properties and potentials. Some peoples, through migration or whatever process, found themselves in harsh climates (arctic tundra, desert, rainforest) that hampered their population growth as well as their technological development. Other lucky peoples inhabited temperate zones that could support larger populations, particularly after the discovery of agriculture. Some environments were rich in resources such as iron, others impoverished. Equally if not more history-making, some areas contained herd-animals suitable for domestication; the resultant close contact between humans and animals—and the crowded conditions of large dense human settlements—led to the transmission of germs between humans and between animals and humans. Many people died as a consequence of this contact (think of the Black Death of the bubonic plague), but those who survived acquired immunity, strengthening their bodies against such diseases. Europeans, hanging off their little peninsula of Eurasia, enjoyed all of these conditions. Thus, when Europeans first struck out from their continental homes—and notice that those who first ventured across the seas were those who inhabited coastal places, such as Portugal, Holland, and England—they carried with them germs absorbed over millennia, steel developed from their mines of iron and coal, and guns forged from this steel plus the gunpowder obtained through their long-distance trade with China. The historical outcome speaks for itself: armed with a few guns and horses (also obtained from Central Asia), small squads of Europeans could lay low entire civilizations such as the Aztec or the Inca. In fact, it is well known that advancing soldiers or settlers often found entire villages and towns of native Americans already dead and deserted, as the contagious germs arrived even before the leading edge of the invaders did. Once the first natives were infected, they quickly infected each other, decimating the indigenous populations and leaving the land relatively vacant. On the other hand, European penetration into Africa was much slower, and never fully complete, partly because the morphology of the land (its rivers, mountains, and forests) was more forbidding to Europeans and partly because of its deadly local diseases (which spawned, as mentioned earlier, a field of tropical medicine and medical geography).

geography (and most other social and natural sciences), but it accomplishes more than storage; "Mapping above all else is a practical form of knowledge creation and representation" (353). Therefore, as Maria Villanueva and Carmen Gonzalo reminded us, maps "are social constructions and the concepts and images they transmit are also the knowledge of the world from which they emerge" (2000: 61). That is, what we put on maps or how we draw maps—or that we make maps at all—is an exercise in and a source of geographical knowledge. This implies that "maps do not show only reality but bias because they are cultural constructions" (63). Maps are "cultural texts" that are written and read by humans: by making maps "cartographers manufacture power and this power intersects and is embedded in knowledge" (63), while for those who look at maps, those texts "can be read, rewritten and reinterpreted; different readers can find different meanings" (62). Because of their political nature, maps are especially functional for governments and the territories they rule—or would like to rule—and as persuasive devices, making national spaces and boundaries seem real.

J. B. Harley (1988) specified four kinds of decisions that go into the construction of a map and affect our experience of one. The first is "hierarchies of representation," determining what is more or less important to display on the map. The second is "geometries" or how the map is to be oriented, centered, and projected; consider, for instance, that world maps generally place Europe at the center, with regions measured from Europe like "Middle East" and "Far East" (see Figure 8.7). Third is the symbolism and decoration embedded in the map, such as color, lettering, emblems, and other information. Finally, of course, are the "silences," the information that is excluded and ignored.

Many kinds of information can and should be mapped, not only physical facts but social facts like, for instance, crime. Crime is also not randomly or evenly distributed: certain neighborhoods, cities, and regions have higher crime rates than others, having to do with other spatially-distributed variables such as income, race, jobs, and physical living conditions. Marilyn Brown discussed a not-too-surprising effect of space on crime, called the "friction of distance," which means that violent crimes tend to happen within

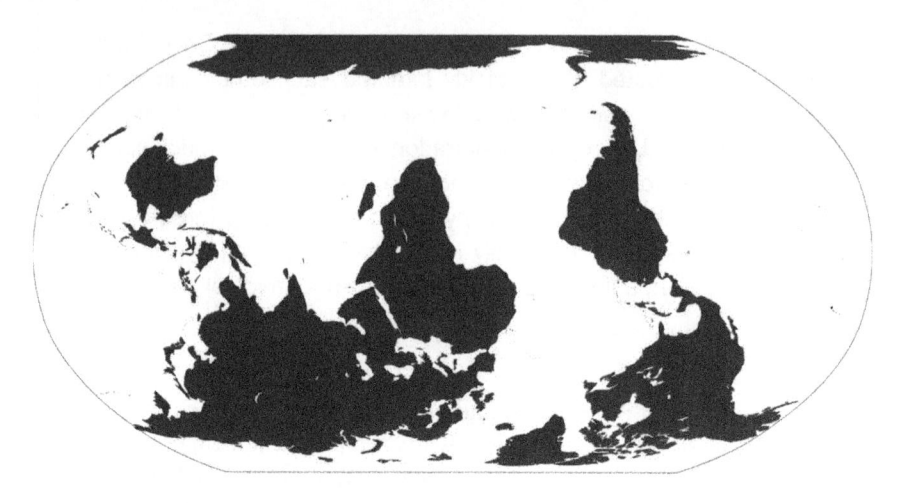

Figure 8.6 The World Displayed "Upside Down"
Source: Wikicommons, https://commons.wikimedia.org/wiki/File:World_map_upside_down.svg.

the perpetrator's community (people do not travel far to commit murder and assault), although perpetrators are willing to travel to other communities to commit theft or burglary; writing in the journal *Economic Geography*, she concluded that "the higher the value of the potential booty, the longer the journey is likely to be" (1982: 249).

Finally, if we think of the essence of geography as the relationship not necessarily between physical places but between "sites" or "locations," then it becomes clear that maps need not depict physical space at all. Rather, any type of relationship, between any variables or nodes, can be graphed and "mapped." One quite useful application of this principle is the *social map*, which is any visual representation of connections between persons, processes, or institutions. Basically a network chart, a social map can portray the links between people (say, a diagram of a person's friendships, business associates, family tree, or Facebook relations), between corporations (say, a model of the links between a company and its suppliers, customers, and competitors), or institutions and ideas (say, a chart of the historical and intellectual associations between the various social sciences). Obviously such visual depictions of often invisible affiliations can be very informative and very useful for decision-making or marketing.

The Evolution of Human/Cultural Geography in the Twentieth Century and Beyond

Since the days of Carl Sauer in the early twentieth century, human/cultural geography has evolved in a way reminiscent of the disciplinary history of archaeology (see Chapter 7). Within a few decades, Sauer and his Berkeley

School were accused of positivism and of operating with a simplistic and overly deterministic concept of culture, which functioned like an "agent" in producing cultural landscapes (the latter criticism was also aimed at anthropologists like Kroeber). By the 1960s there was a movement to make human/cultural geography less "cultural" and more "human" by putting human action and meaning back into the discipline. One example was *behavioral geography*. Conspicuously influenced by psychology and similar to behavioral economics (see Chapter 4), behavioral geography was intent on inserting human decision-making into geographical phenomena and applying psychological concepts such as cognition, learning, and perception. Carol Ekinsmyth and Pamela Shurmer-Smith also hold that from the beginning "behavioral geography was policy oriented":

> The outcome of effort in behavioral geography was a body of work that attempted to understand the reasons for the environmental behavior of people. Investigations into perceptions of flood hazard, for example, would help to explain why people change address, or experience stress in their homes. . . . Understanding people's misunderstandings of distance and direction might help explain why some do not use the facilities, such as shopping centers, which are closest to them in real distance.
>
> (2002: 22)

Still more qualitative and philosophical was *humanistic geography*, appearing in the 1970s. Humanistic geography gave a central place to issues of consciousness, creativity, and meaning.

Many observers note a "cultural turn" and a "new cultural geography" in the 1980s, which signaled the influence of Marxist theory and a further rejection of positivism, as is evident from the title of Denis Cosgrove's 1984 book *Social Formation and Symbolic Landscape*. This *critical human geography* was "committed to Leftist politics, social justice, and liberation through scholarly enquiry" and "drew from a number of theoretical wells, including political economy, queer theory, post-colonialism, and feminism" (Gregory et al. 2009: 123). Among the many social forces that critical human geography was critical of were racism and colonialism/imperialism, which are closely connected and with which geography was often seen as complicit (see earlier discussion). Critical human geographers, like anthropologists at the same moment, critiqued their own discipline for contributing to the colonial project of dominating and subordinating non-Western peoples through social-scientific ways of "knowing" or "reading" those peoples, including cartography and climate/adaptation theories of racial difference and inferiority.

Some human/cultural geographers, like Cosgrove (1983) himself, went further in calling for a *radical cultural geography* that transcends Marxist/critical geography in questioning Marxist concepts of class,

---

Inventing the Neocolonial City in India

Colonialism sought not only to rule but to reorganize non-Western societies socially, economically, demographically, and geographically. Urbanization was a common if not requisite part of colonial management. While the old colonialism is (mostly) over, many if not all social scientists see a new era of "neocolonialism" arising, implemented this time by corporations and non-Western governments themselves. One telling example is India's plan to create one hundred "smart cities" with all the benefits of modern technology. Dholera is one such planned city, which "will rely almost exclusively on a technocratic mode of urban governance shaped by corporate interests to control and monitor its population" (Datta 2015: 5). In fact, the Smart City Council, an organization based in the United States and partnered with IBM, Cisco, and Microsoft, moved into India in 2013 to advance the plans. Hardly the first time that Westerners have tried to urbanize another society, Dholera ideally sidesteps "the challenges of existing Indian cities struggling with pollution, traffic congestion, and slums. Dholera promises to be a new city without the 'annoyances' of everyday urban life" (4). In effect, such smart cities turn their back on the troubled urban spaces of India and start fresh. However, they introduce their own problems. For instance, at present Dholera is merely a village, "one of the 22 villages that will be pooled together to constitute 'Dholera smart city'" (11). Worse, the coastal land tends to be flooded for much of the year, and the current mostly low-caste and undereducated population resists the development. Working in concert with planners and corporations, the Indian government has "begun to issue notices to several farmers to either hand over the land and take whatever compensatory land is offered or prepare to be evicted by the state officials" (15).

---

structure/formation, and theory. Unlike Marxism, radical cultural geography "does not trace a line, or provide a model, but instead points to a strategy of breaking the bonds of coercion and the chains of exploitation by encompassing an infinite number of everyday acts of resistance and cooperation" (Springer 2014: 254). Radical cultural geography has its own professional presence, including a journal, *Antipode: A Radical Journal of Geography*.

Finally, also dismayed by the concentration on ideas, meanings, and systems, Nigel Thrift asserted that human/cultural geography and all of the social sciences "suffer from a certain kind of over-theoretization" (2007: 3), to the neglect of the actual lived experiences of people in places under power. He and others insist that there is too much attention to "representation" (ideas, meanings, and theories), which becomes reified and dehumanized. His antidote is *non-representational theory*, which in the words of Hayden Lorimer examines "how life takes shape and gains expression in shared experiences, everyday routines fleeting encounters, embodied movements, precognitive triggers, practical skills, affective intensities, enduring urges, unexceptional interactions and sensuous dispositions," offering "an escape from the established academic habit of striving to uncover meanings and values that apparently await our discovery, interpretation, judgment, and ultimate representation" (2005: 84). Demanding an even more profound revision of geographical and social-scientific thought than the Marxist/critical geographers, and echoing the discoveries of archaeologists (especially cognitive archaeologists), Thrift asserts that knowledge and thought itself is constituted by *practice* or culturally-informed and spatially-situated action, which implicates humans, places, and material objects. The product of action is a "world" that is "made up of all kinds of things brought in to relation with one another by many and various spaces through a continuous and largely involuntary [and substantially preconscious] process of encounter, and the violent training that such encounter forces" (2007: 8).

Disciplinary Case Study # 7: Geography of Terrorism

Geographers understand better than most that everything happens somewhere, that is, all social (and natural) events have a spatial location and are near to some things and far from others. This universal fact applies to terrorism in particular and violent conflict in general. In other chapters we have seen how social scientists have treated terrorism as a political or economic or psychological or social/organizational or cultural phenomenon, but John Rock (n.d.) insists that "it seems that we have never understood that terrorism is by nature about geography and not merely related to it. When we consider the geography of terrorism, we assume that the actual areas where it occurs are only incidental or contingent upon the presence of some specific groups with certain ideologies." However, if he is correct, terrorism does not just occur in places but is fundamentally *about* places.

The spatial distribution of terrorist attacks in the opening years of the twenty-first century certainly suggests that there is a geographic component to these behaviors (see Figure 8.8). The 2010 U.S. National Counterterrorism Center report on terrorism provides more detailed information on the geography of terrorism. According to the document, the highest number of attacks (5,537) occurred in South Asia (which usually refers to the Indian subcontinent), which resulted in the highest number of deaths (6,172) but not the most injuries (10,360). More injuries (12,781) happened in the Middle East but with fewer attacks (3,416) and fewer deaths (3,750). No other region on the planet suffered similar levels of violence, although

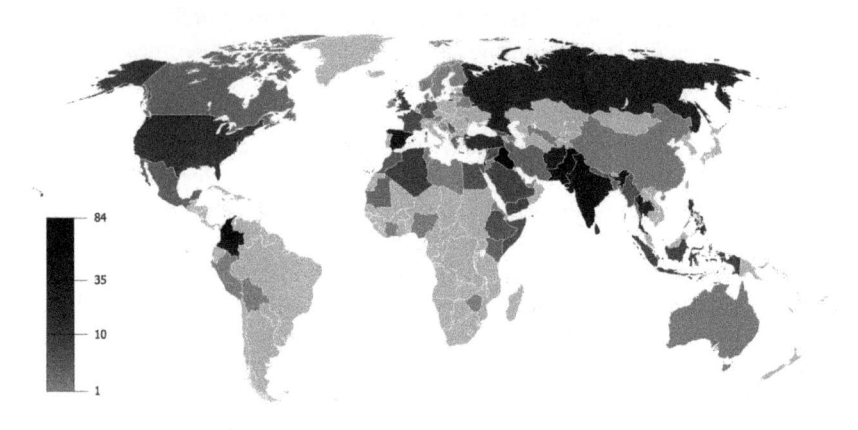

Figure 8.7 Number of Terrorist Incidents, by Country, 2000–2008
Source: Wikicommons. Released to public domain by its creator, Emilfaro.

Africa was next with 879 incidents, 2,137 deaths, and 4,539 injuries. Interestingly, though, Africa led the world in hostage-taking events with 2,651, compared to only 1,748 in South Asia and 1,206 in the Middle East. Europe and the Americas were relatively spared terrorist casualties, with the Western hemisphere experiencing a mere 340 attacks, 279 deaths, 480 injuries, and 190 kidnappings (2011: 11).

It is not surprising, then, that scholars like Craig Bennell and Shevaun Corey have investigated the possibility of "geographic profiling" for terrorism, not unlike the way that police and criminologists profile crime; in fact, their work has been published in a volume on criminal profiling. As they describe it, "geographic profiling involves using knowledge about the relative location of an offender's crime sites to predict the highest probable location of his or her residence" (2007: 190). Examining two case studies (*Actione Directe* in France and the Revolutionary People's Struggle in Greece), they find at least some value in approaching terrorism like crime and profiling it geographically like law-enforcement authorities do, taking into consideration such variables as victim activities and schedules (to identify when and where an attack may occur), physical and psychological barriers against attacks, zoning and land use, transportation routes, neighborhood demographics, media coverage, and the presence of police or soldiers in particular places (201).

John Rock makes a stronger and more controversial claim when he asserts that "terrorism is by nature intrinsically directed at dominating geographic space." That is, he contends that ideological motivations and goals alone do not account for terrorism but that territorial goals must also be factored in: "Terrorist A does action X for cause Y with the ultimate goal of acquiring territory Z."

If this is so, then it strengthens the relationship between terrorism and war (see Chapter 3), and many experts have explored the significance of geography for war and other such armed struggle. Likewise, geographers "have a long history of studying armed conflict and have by no means always been dedicated to peace" (Kobayashi 2009: 819). At least since the early 1800s and the campaigns of Napoleon, geographers have played a role not only in analyzing war but in making war. Audrey Kobayashi reminds us that the United States actually employed geographers in its World War II Office of Strategic Services. However one may feel about social scientists participating in war (see Chapter 7 for a mention of anthropologists participating in the Human Terrain System), Kobayashi is no doubt correct when she declares, "Warfare is certainly spatialized" (821).

The twentieth-century application of geography to war commenced with H. J. Mackinder's classic 1904 article "The Geographical Pivot of History." Interestingly, Americans have begun to use the term "pivot" in regard to their contemporary foreign policy and military deployment, contemplating a "pivot toward Asia" as the key geopolitical region of the future. More than a century ago, Mackinder opined that

> in the present decade we are for the first time in a position to attempt, with some degree of completeness, a correlation between the larger geographical and the larger historical generalizations. For the first time we can perceive something of the real proportion of features and events on the stage of the whole world, and may seek a formula which shall express certain aspects, at any rate, of geographical causation in universal history.
>
> (1904: 422)

Significantly, he warned that for too long Westerners had believed that "the only history which counts is that of the Mediterranean and European races" and places (422).

In 1969, at the height of the Cold War, geographer Robert McColl added an important statement about geography and revolutionary/insurgent movements. In light of struggles in Latin America and Southeast Asia, he concluded that for "contemporary national revolutions, the capture and control of territory has virtually become a territorial imperative. Control of a geographic part of the state is a manifesto proclaiming: 'We have arrived. We are ready to replace the existing government'" (1969: 613). He also introduced two new alternatives to conventional or regular war, namely "mobile war" and "guerrilla war." Or we might better think of these as phases in the war process. Initially an insurgent movement lacks a "geographic base" and its members are condemned as "rebels or bandits" (616). "Once the need for a territorial base becomes evident, the insurgents must choose a specific area for their activity. Naturally, the first choice, if possible, is the capture and control of some key city or region, preferably the capital"

(616). However, in its early days, such movements often locate in remote or rural areas, where government control is weak and where they may train and hone their military skills; particularly attractive are border regions and places with easy-to-defend and difficult-to-penetrate terrain like mountains.

"Once established in a fixed area," McColl wrote, a mobile insurgency becomes a guerrilla one. The guerrilla base "becomes the 'core area' of the insurgent movement. Not only must the base act as the headquarters for military operations of the movement, it must also provide the daily necessities and supplies for future military engagements. The base will also act as the genesis point for expansion of political ideas and influence" (621). It is probably no coincidence then that the term *al-Qaeda* translates roughly to "the base."

Not all twenty-first century terrorist individuals and organizations aim for territorial conquest and domination, but this might be because their progress is primitive and/or that they have not thought out their long-term objectives. Surely, though, they are not engaging in terrorism for terrorism's sake but for some ultimate political end, and politics is almost always and necessarily emplaced. And at least one prime example—IS or Islamic State—has taken the crucial leap from ideology and terrorist practice to territorial rule.

Currently, terrorism (like all politics) occurs within a system of territorial states, and many political scientists and geographers have linked terrorism— either as a source of terrorist recruits or a target for terrorist action—to "failed states" that cannot control their land, deliver social services, or both. Perhaps unexpectedly, Anna Simons and David Tucker, in their "socio- geography" of contemporary terrorism, argue that international terrorists do not overwhelming originate in failed states. "Nor do failed states house many organizations that support terrorism" (2007: 387). Rather, terrorist organizations and individual terrorists often hail from, and are financed by, successful states like Iran or Saudi Arabia.

"The same cannot be said," they add, "for the connection between failed states and terror*ism*": failed states are "where all sorts of low-cost tactics, techniques and procedures are not only practiced, but perfected" (389). Afghanistan under the Taliban, or contemporary Yemen, offer good examples; such "zones of insecurity" not only "serve as training grounds for youth attracted to and predisposed to violence" but also provide "test beds for innovation" in terrorist tactics (390).

Speaking of terrorist finance, Philippe Le Billon stresses that natural resources can both fund and motivate violence and terrorism. Most readers are familiar with the term "blood diamonds," which come from conflict zones, the money from which often goes back to conflict zones. Le Billon describes three processes by which resources can contribute to political violence.

> The first, *resource curse,* argues that resource dependence results in economic underperformance and a weakening of governing institutions

that makes a society more vulnerable to armed conflict. The second, *resource conflicts,* suggests that grievances, conflicts, and violence associated with resource control and exploitation increase the risk of onset of larger scale armed conflicts. The third, *conflict resources,* recognizes resources as providing financial opportunities motivating belligerents and financially sustaining armed conflicts.

(2008: 347)

One of the more enduring targets of terrorism over recent decades has been Israel, and Nurit Kliot and Igal Charney (2006) performed an analysis specifically on the geography of suicide terrorism in that country. They discovered a number of geographic regularities across 120 Palestinian attacks against Israel, the West Bank, and Gaza between 1994 and 2005. For instance, cities were the most common targets, with 65 percent of all suicide attacks occurring in urban settings. They noted the same distance-decay effect as noted above, that attacks tended to happen near the home areas of the perpetrators; additionally, transportation facilities were favored targets, and the attacks were synchronized to work days and business hours, to maximize the damage.

One last issue to consider here is the practice of building security walls to prevent terrorism. Walls—whether in Israel, Northern Ireland, Berlin, or the United States—understandably operate "as a technology of occupation, separation, or security," a geographical feature that establishes and defends other geographical features by "spatially regulating bodies and populations" (Alatout 2009: 958). Walls naturally also become the target of terrorism and sabotage, just as they are intended to curb such violence. Finally, walls are only one manifestation of the effort to physically and spatially separate hostile groups, other examples of which include segregated (sometimes locked and patrolled) neighborhoods, forced population relocation, concentration camps, and selective imprisonment (with prison serving to isolate and punish disobedient bodies). All of these techniques and mechanisms of control and governmentality add up to what Rock calls the "new geography of conflict."

9 Social Science and Other Ways of Knowing

The word itself, "research," is probably one of the dirtiest words in the indigenous world's vocabulary. When mentioned in many indigenous contexts, it stirs up silence, it conjures up bad memories, it raises a smile that is knowing and distrustful. It is so powerful that indigenous people even write poetry about research. The ways in which scientific research is implicated in the worst excesses of colonialism remains a powerful remembered history for many of the world's colonized peoples. It is a history that still offends the deepest sense of our humanity. Just knowing that someone measured our "faculties" by filling the skulls of our ancestors with millet seeds and compared the amount of millet seed to the capacity for mental thought offends our sense of who and what we are. It galls us that Western researchers and intellectuals can assume to know all that it is possible to know of us, on the basis of their brief encounters with some of us. It appals us that the West can desire, extract and claim ownership of our ways of knowing, our imagery, the things we create and produce, and then simultaneously reject the people who created and developed those ideas and seek to deny them further opportunities to be creators of their own culture and own nations. It angers us when practices linked to the last century, and the centuries before that, are still employed to deny the validity of indigenous peoples' claim to existence, to land and territories, to the right of self-determination, to the survival of our languages and forms of cultural knowledge, to our natural resources and systems for living within our environments.

(Smith 2012: 1)

In the late 1960s and early 1970s, as we have seen in various chapters, the social sciences went through a crisis—a crisis of epistemology, of method, and of morality. Perhaps no discipline felt the pain more exquisitely than anthropology, which produced volumes like Dell Hymes' (1972) *Reinventing Anthropology*, Roy Wagner's (1975) *The Invention of Culture*, and eventually Adam Kuper's (1988) *The Invention of Primitive Society: Transformations of an Illusion*. But each field experienced it in its own way, questioning old concepts and assumptions, experimenting with new research methods and new writing styles, and sometimes doubting its mission or its very right to exist.

Indeed, in 2000 Carlos Antonio Aguirre Rojas argued that, since the late 1960s, "it has been apparent that the entire 'system of branches of knowledge' regarding the social domain, which dated from 1870 to 1968, has entered into a total and irreversible crisis":

> Established in the last third of the nineteenth century, and having been deployed during the first half of the twentieth century, this particular "episteme" regarding the social domain—which conceived the latter as a sum or aggregate of spaces, segmented, distinct, and even autonomous among one another; spaces that in turn corresponded to the different and equally autonomous social sciences or disciplines—was progressively questioned.
>
> (2000: 750)

There have been many reasons for this lack of confidence, some healthy, some maybe less so. Key to all of them is the changing nature of the social reality that the social sciences purported to describe and explain. Paradigms forged in the mid-1800s no longer entirely fit the globalized, post-modern social world. Even more, probably, the (re)appearance of other ways of thinking about—and living in—the world compelled social scientists to contemplate their own knowledge claims and knowledge-making practices. For instance, as Linda Tuhiwai Smith, whose quote opens the present chapter, insists, indigenous peoples have become tired of being "researched" by Western scholars for the benefit of Western scholarship. Smith, a Maori or indigenous New Zealand woman and academic, echoes a sentiment felt by most of the world's native peoples, most bluntly and even angrily expressed by Vine Deloria, a Native American intellectual, whose own books bear titles like *Custer Died for Your Sins* and *Red Earth, White Lies*. But it was not only indigenous people who refused to hold still while the Western academy studied them. The poor, non-white peoples, women, people of non-conventional sexuality, and many others demanded not only the right to be heard—the right to be treated as a knowledge-bearing and knowledge-creating community—but also the right to conduct their own research, on their own terms and in their own interests.

Other sources too began to be seen, or to assert themselves, as valid things to know and valid ways of knowing. Non-Western civilizations such as China, India, or Islam staked their claims as epistemic cultures (see Chapter 1), even challenging the hegemony of Western science. Religion and the arts and humanities likewise voiced their displeasure in being shunted aside in favor of science and social science. At the extreme, the very possibility of knowledge was sometimes disputed, and knowledge was more and more seen as perspectival (that is, *somebody's* knowledge) and "interested" (that is, shaped by *somebody's* interests) instead of universal, neutral, and objective.

Finally, as we will see shortly, the boundaries between the received social sciences also began to waver, since they were certainly never "real" and were becoming increasingly inadequate and arbitrary. Aguirre Rojas further observed "the proliferation and multiplication" of "projects to defend and promote a 'multi,' 'pluri,' 'trans,' or 'inter' disciplinarity" in the social sciences (and sometimes beyond them, to include natural science or art and humanities), even if more than occasionally "the core itself is left untouched regarding the division of social knowledge into 'disciplines'" (751).

In this chapter we will examine the limits of and the challenges to the knowledge-construction and the intellectual habits of the standard social sciences. As we stated in the first chapter and demonstrated in every chapter, the perspectives of modern social science were only formulated in the nineteenth century and settled in the twentieth, which means that they are relatively new and thus hardly natural or inevitable. The social sciences as we have known them have produced some valuable understanding of the world. However, just as knowledge-traditions had to be rethought in order to invent today's social sciences, so the young knowledge-traditions of today's social sciences may have to be, and are currently being, rethought as the foundations for tomorrow's knowledge.

Rethinking and Unthinking the Social Sciences

Citizens of the twenty-first century are probably familiar with, even actively engaged in, the ongoing rethinking of their ideas, practices, and institutions. Organizations like schools and corporations are constantly asked to assess themselves, to critique their current "best practices" and adapt to changing markets, audiences, students, consumers, and societies. Individually we are encouraged to "think outside the box"—when most of us were not aware we were inside a box—and to "push the envelope" and shift paradigms.

The social sciences have gone through such soul-searching too, with friends and enemies inside and outside of the social sciences telling them that they must change. One of the most articulate and tireless advocates of re-envisioning the social sciences has been the don of "world systems" theory, Immanuel Wallerstein. In his provocatively named essay "Anthropology, Sociology, and Other Dubious Disciplines," he declared that social science as a set of "intellectual arenas" that were settled in the late 1800s and early 1900s "has outlived its usefulness and is today a major obstacle to serious intellectual work"; already he perceived "cracks in the structures of knowledge that make them less solid than most participants imagine" (2003: 453).

As he put it in an earlier essay, "when the dust settled by about 1950, there appeared to be five generally accepted 'branches' of the study of social processes. These bore the names of anthropology, economics, history, political science, and sociology. A sixth and far weaker contender (measured quantitatively) was geography" (1987: 1–2). These six departments, plus psychology, have been precisely the subject of the present book. He proposed that the Big Three of economics, political science, and sociology "reflected the basic assumption that . . . collective human activity occurred in three different arenas, or at three different levels—the economy (or the market), the State (or the polity), and the society (or the culture)"; additionally, "Since these three fields were presumed to deal with timeless processes, but in practice discussed primarily current (or recent) processes, a separate field of history became necessary as the field of study of *past* events" (2). Anthropology was charged with studying the leftovers of this intellectual division of labor, the "others" in non-modern and non-Western societies.

Moreover, Wallerstein opined that the social sciences were and always had been "three things simultaneously" (2003: 453). They were of course and necessarily "intellectual categories—modes of asserting that there exists a defined field of study with some kind of boundaries." But categories, we recognize, are human creations, and their boundaries are always artificial, negotiable, and ultimately flimsy. Second, the social sciences, as we have discussed in some chapters, are "institutional structures that since the late nineteenth century have taken on ever more elaborate forms. There were and are departments in universities with disciplinary names" with all sorts of processes of self-perpetuation such as degree programs, endowed chairs, publishers, prizes, and "bookstore shelvings with disciplinary names" (453). Finally and most interestingly, the various social sciences disciplines "are cultures. The scholars who claim membership in a disciplinary grouping share for the most part certain experiences and exposures": "They have often read the same 'classic' books. They participate in well-known traditional debates that are often different from those of neighboring disciplines. The disciplines seem to favor certain styles of scholarship over others, and members are rewarded for using the appropriate style" (453).

To be sure, this culture, this *epistemic* culture, changes over time and contains disagreements and divergences at any given time, but individuals who violate it often are treated as "failed" scholars and do not receive teaching positions and publishing contracts.

In his 1987 paper, Wallerstein specified some of the features of the dominant culture of social science (which he called "the liberal-Marxist consensus"). One of these traits was the notion of *progress*, that the human social world was moving, or could be made to move with sufficient knowledge and energy, in a better direction. The second trait or theme was *increasing integration*, that societies were evolving "from the small to the large, from the simple to the complex, from the part to the whole" (1987: 5). Ideally and actually, people would be united politically and culturally in ever-expanding—and ever-improving—communities, characterized by cultural homogeneity and institutional rationality. The third shared premise was *scientificity*, the simple but profound claim that society and its processes were "knowable" through the application of the scientific method. Fourth was "the belief that the basic social unit within which social activity occurs is *the state/society*" (7, emphasis added); that is, it was within a system of states and/or discrete societies that humans would achieve progress, integration, and scientific knowledge and control of their own lives.

As events in the late-twentieth and early-twentieth centuries have proven, the predictions and dreams of the social sciences have not quite come to pass. We have not woken up from history, our states are neither stable nor peaceful, our institutions are not particularly rational (and often fail altogether), and it is difficult to tell which way progress lies. In his 1987 essay and his 1991 book on the subject, Wallerstein insisted that the social sciences as we know them are exhausted, perhaps even beyond salvaging.

Opening the Social Sciences: The Report of the Gulbenkian Commission on the Restructuring of the Social Sciences

No system of thought as well-entrenched as the social sciences will be dismantled and reinvented via an essay or a book or two, no matter how grumpy. Just as the social sciences were institutionalized into existence, they would have to be institutionalized out of existence. One concrete step in this direction was the Gulbenkian Commission on the Restructuring of the Social Sciences, which issued its report in 1996. Wallerstein was a member of the distinguished panel of social scientists, natural scientists, and philosophers who reviewed the history and current status of the social sciences and asked, "What kind of social science shall we now build?" The panel determined that the social sciences as we have inherited them struggle under three binary oppositions— between the past and the present, between the idea of the civilized or modern (roughly the Western) world and the traditional or pre-modern (roughly the non-Western) world, and between the inclination toward the general and universal (that is, the discovery of "social laws") and toward the specific and local (that is, the description and understanding of particular times and places). They endorsed the notion of "opening" the social sciences, specifically opening the boundaries that currently isolate disciplines, opening the university to the wider society, opening the wall that divides humans from nature, and opening the thought-processes of scholars to transcend the concepts of "state" and "economy" and "culture" and to outgrow the alleged objectivity and positivism of today's social (and natural) sciences.

Instead of merely rethinking them, he demanded that we "unthink" them, literally forget them and start over again.

If "we are prisoners of dubious assumptions that are little discussed and deeply held and which disappear and reappear in a thousand avatars" (Wallerstein 1987: 11), what exactly did Wallerstein suggest to replace the existing social sciences? He offered five specific possible steps toward or versions of a new type of social science:

1. use the concept of "historical system" instead of "society" to convey the sense that each social system "exists in specific time" and "in specific but malleable space" (9)
2. do away with the dichotomy of traditional-versus-modern (in classical sociology, *Gemeinschaft* versus *Gesellschaft* or community versus society [see Chapter 6])
3. overthrow the assumption that there are distinct autonomous "arenas" or domains of society like economy, polity, and culture
4. reject the idea that "culture" is "the residue of pastness" and with it the dichotomy of past-versus-present: "Maybe all is present, nothing is past within the framework of a living system," and "the past is so frequently and so rapidly reformulated and revised that it seems almost evanescent at times" (10) and is definitely a construction of the present
5. rethink science itself, which has so far been the analysis ("taking-apart") of complex systems in search of simple, even elementary, bits, basic laws, and linear processes. A newly-formulated science of society "may inversely look towards the elaboration of complex, dense interpretative schema, in which case our methodologies must inevitably be quite different, and in which case we may have to reopen the assumption that there are 'two cultures'—science and art" (10–11).

If we and Wallerstein could summarize his recommendations in two points, they would be *particularity* and *multiplicity*. "First, virtually all statements [about societies] should be made in the past tense. To make them in the present tense is to presume universality and eternal reality" (2003: 458) rather than recognizing the unique contingent nature of each society. Second, he urges us to adopt "a culture of plurals. Most concepts are plural concepts —civilizations, cultures, economies, families, structures of knowledge, and so on"; "almost all conceptual terms are defined in multiple ways" (458), including the very idea of *knowledges* in the first place.

Alternatives to the Social Sciences: Non-Western Knowledge

As noted by the Gulbenkian Commission and other critics, especially since the crisis days of the late-twentieth century, and as is evident from glancing back at the discussion in the previous chapters, the established social sciences are fundamentally Western. They developed out of the Western intellectual tradition (namely, out of philosophy and Christian theology), take their terms and concepts more or less for granted from Western language and culture, and offer Western society and history as the template for all human organization. When social science was only done *by* Western scholars and *for* Western scholars, this perspective was at least understandable, if not forgivable. But as Michael Burawoy asked in his retort to the Gulbenkian Commission, we have no choice today but to confront two questions: "knowledge for whom?; and knowledge for what?" (2007: 138). These queries apply not only to the disciplinary social sciences but to the very idea of knowledge as such.

Recent research by Sébastien Mosbah-Natanson and Yves Gingras shows that, more than a century into their histories, the social sciences are still heavily dominated by Western individuals and institutions. In short, "the centrality of the two major regions that are North America and Europe is largely unchallenged . . . despite the growing development of Asian social sciences" (2013: 1). The authors calculated the productivity of different regions in terms of the number of social science publications, the amount of collaboration between scholars, and the citation of research in the work of other scholars. For instance, they discovered that more than half (51.5 percent) of all social science journals were based in Europe during the first decade of the twenty-first century, with more than one-third (36.5 percent) based in North America and a paltry 12 percent emanating from the rest of the world. In terms of sheer production of social science knowledge, North America was the leader in published social science articles, with 126,461 in the decade between 2000 and 2009. Europe followed not far behind with 103,627, but the entire continent of Asia produced only 26,105, Latin America 5,764, and Africa a measly 4,885.

Not surprisingly or unjustifiably, non-Western scholars (and some Western ones) have critiqued the established social sciences for "hearing only the voices of Western Europe," calling for "emancipation from generations of silence and emancipation from seeing the world in one color" (Gupta and Lincoln 2005: 212). As early as 1971, Mexican thinker Rodolfo Stavenhagen urged a "decolonializing" of the social sciences. Malaysian sociologist Syed Hussein Alatas went still further, declaring that Asians (and by implication other non-Western peoples) who followed or were impacted by social science suffered from a "captive mind," which he defined as the "uncritical and imitative mind dominated by an external source, whose thinking is deflected from an independent perspective" (1974: 692). As his son Syed Farid Hussein Alatas explicated, this captive mind "is trained almost entirely in the Western sciences, reads the works of Western authors and is taught predominantly by Western teachers, whether in the West itself or through their works available in local centers of education" (2014: 288–9).

One of the most-commented instances of colonization by Western social scientists, as well as arts and humanities scholars, is so-called *orientalism* or how Westerners see and understand "the East" (which includes everything from the Middle East and Muslim world to the Far East and China). "Orientalism" was most powerfully attacked in Edward Said's 1978 book by that title, in which he insisted that Western scholars and the Western public perceive "the Orient" as a homogenous "other" that is the total opposite of the modern, rational West. The Orient is viewed, and condemned, as backward, anti-modern, anti-democratic, irrational and fanatical, patriarchal and yet effeminate—in short, lacking in all of the ways in which the West feels superior.

One way to redress the imbalance of voices in the social sciences is for non-Westerners to do their own social science; given their sheer numerical dominance of the world's population, non-Western scholars could and should outpace the productivity of social science books and papers. This achievement alone would help bring about the goal that Indian historian Dipesh Chakrabarty (2007) called "provincializing Europe." Provincializing does not mean rejecting and certainly not demonizing; it merely means returning Europe and the West to its proper proportion in the world, as one part of and perspective on the world rather than the hegemonic part and the monopolistic perspective (Gupta and Lincoln's one voice and one color).

To be sure, more Africans, Asians, Indians, and Latin Americans study and practice social science than ever before. But provincializing the West does not mean simply absorbing more non-Westerners into the Western social scientific project. That is, non-Westerners can and increasingly want to do not just *more* social science but *different* social science. For example, William Mikulas champions "integrating the world's psychologies" to generate what he labels a "conjunctive psychology" that "draws from all the world's psychologies and health systems, including Western psychology, Buddhist psychology, the yogic sciences, *Ayurveda*, Chinese medicine, and Native American wisdom and practices" (2006: 100). This would also have the effect of questioning the standard notion of psychological normality, which largely describes "a Western White male" (93). One concrete difference mentioned by Mikulas is that in "most of Asia and the Middle East, individualistic self-actualization is a sign of mental illness and/or immorality, and it is not highly valued among many Western women and non-White minorities" (94). "Integrating the world's psychologies," he judges, "requires developing a perspective that is superordinate to, and free from, gender/cultural biases" (94). Likewise, there is a movement in anthropology to recognize the diversity of local anthropological practices and traditions, that is, to recognize the diversity of "world anthropologies" (see e.g. Ribeiro and Escobar 2006).

Other thinkers like Hasan Dzilo (2012) have considered or advocated the "Islamization of knowledge," while John Whalen-Bridge (2006) has pondered the Buddhist notion of knowledge-as-enlightenment in relation to familiar claims to knowledge.

Meanwhile, the economic ascendance and vast population of China has led to the emergence of a distinctly Chinese social science. Of course, many

Psychology the Islamic Way

Not all Muslims understand psychology in the same way, nor do they all import religion into psychology to the same degree. To claim otherwise would be to perpetrate the very orientalism that Edward Said warned against. Nevertheless, it is possible to conceive a psychology from an overtly Islamic perspective, and Aisha Utz has done just that. Much of it would be unrecognizable to Western psychologists and would even be dismissed as religious doctrine, which does not "count" as psychological knowledge (or often as knowledge at all). The first chapter begins with a quotation from the *Qur'an*: "Indeed, We sent down to you the book for the people in truth. So whoever is guided—it is for [the benefit of] his soul; and whoever goes astray only goes astray to its detriment." While this may sound totally foreign to the thrust of modern psychology, recall that "psyche" has meant "soul" in the Western tradition too and that for much of Western history psychology was enmeshed with Christian theology (see Chapter 5). At any rate, Utz then asserts that "Islam, as a way of life, outlines a comprehensive model of the human being that incorporates the spiritual, psychological, emotional, and social aspects," which makes it possible and important to construct "the Islamic perspective on psychology, mental health, and well-being" (2011: 25). Many of the topics of the book would be acceptable to Western psychologists, such as personality, emotions, social psychology, consciousness, dreaming, lifespan development, and mental illness. Others, however, do not appear in conventional psychology texts, including "Satan, Jinn, and Humans" and "Forces Working on the Heart and Soul." And every topic is refracted through an Islamic lens, with doctrinal statements, lines from scripture, and interpretations from religious scholars. The final chapter discusses "The Benefits of Worship for Humans" which might appear in a text on the psychology of religion but hardly in an introductory psychology book. Utz's treatise ends with the admonition that Islamic psychology "is simply what life is truly about. We either elevate ourselves spiritually through our beliefs and the choices that we make, thus attaining the rewards and good pleasure of Allah, or we reject the guidance, debasing ourselves and thus earning the wrath of Allah" (330). Fortunately, she also assures us that the "research of secular psychologists, despite all their efforts to avoid a religious foundation, actually substantiates the truth of Islam" (26).

Chinese scholars have been trained in and have become practitioners of Western-style social science, including a growing number of Chinese psycho-analysts, educated by German professionals. At the same time, Chinese sociologists and anthropologists have been developing a specifically Chinese variation of those disciplines, based on the premise of *Zhongguohua* or Sinicization (i.e., Chinese-making) or nationalization of the fields. According to Arif Dirlik, writing in a volume on contemporary Chinese social thought, *Zhongguohua* reflects "the necessity of bringing the social realities and problems of Chinese society into social science work" (2012: 27). Another Chinese term, *bentuhua*, "refers to concrete grounding in place in both social and cultural terms" (28), that is, addressing particular issues and problems of significance to Chinese scholars.

For instance, in the same volume Wang Jianmin (2012a) notes, just as European social scientists were focused on their colonies and American experts were preoccupied with their neighboring native peoples, in China sociological and anthropological interest has tended toward the *minzu* or "ethnic minorities within China"; this orientation perpetuates the notion of anthropology or ethnology as the study of the "other," in this case the other to the Han Chinese majority and "norm." In a second essay in the volume, Wang further identifies regional differences within China, producing different styles of social science. In particular, the southeast and southwest parts of the sprawling country have each spawned a distinct anthropological tradition that is not entirely amenable or relevant to the other: the "anthropology of the southeast has simply repeated the study of Han cultural pattern, and the anthropology of the southwest has merely reiterated the 'autonomy' or 'ethnicity' of the minority nationalities" (2012b: 185). At the same time, asserting their cultural and political separateness from the mainland, Taiwanese social scientists have practiced a sort of *Taiwanhua* or Taiwanization of their discipline, posing specifically Taiwanese questions and doing specifically Taiwanese research.

Naturally, just as the West has its disciplinary heroes, so China does too. Sun Benwen is celebrated as the father of Chinese sociology, for aiming "to make large-scale generalizations about society or create a universal theory of society" (Li 2012b: 79). Like her counterpart Harriet Martineau, China produced a prominent female sociologist in Lei Jieqiong who attended to issues relevant to women. Huang Wenshan was influenced by Franz Boas and imported the modern anthropological concept of culture to China, not only to build anthropology but to strengthen the country that had been weakened by colonialism and foreign intervention. Like other social scientists in China (and, truth to be told, in the West), the goal was as much political as intellectual, in this case "to regenerate China" (Li 2012a: 123) and to prevent "the loss of Chineseness in the areas of politics, social organization, and spirit" (127). Ultimately, then, for Huang and many others, the founding of Chinese social science "belonged to a grandiose scheme of nation-building in twentieth-century China" (131).

A similar analysis could be performed on uniquely Indian or African or Latin American, etc. social sciences, showing how professionals in those countries have made the disciplines their own. Social thought and social theory have been effectively nationalized and indigenized repeatedly, but then, as Allen Chun reminds us, "When has theory not been indigenous?"; indeed, "social science as we know it today is itself an abstraction rooted in concrete and local social experience" (2012: 277)—that is, standard social science is *the indigenous social science of the modern West, promoted as if it were universal in time and place.*

Alternatives to the Social Sciences: The Feminist Perspective

It will be recalled that William Mikulas castigated the social sciences as the study of the "Western White male," and peering back at the chapters of this book, it is painfully obvious how few women were allowed to contribute to Western social thought until the twentieth century. The nationalization of the various disciplines has gone a long way to remedying the overemphasis on white Westerners, but feminist thought and research has profoundly challenged the hegemony of males—while questioning the very universality and stability of gender categories and, by extension, of nearly all received categories.

Although feminism, as a social movement and as an intellectual tradition, was already well underway, a moment of singular significance was the 1982 publication of Carol Gilligan's *In a Different Voice*. Subtitled "Psychological Theory and Women's Development," she argued devastatingly that psychologists had implicitly (and often explicitly) adopted "male life as the norm" and so "tried to fashion women out of a masculine cloth" (1993: 6). This problem is apparent at least as early as Freud's psychoanalysis, which (oddly, based mostly on therapy with women) offered a model of psychological functioning and psychological development firmly founded on male experience. She also charged Jean Piaget with taking the male perspective as typical or ideal, Piaget claiming that "the legal sense," which is "essential to moral development, 'is far less developed in little girls than in boys'" (10). As one final example, even Erik Erikson's lifespan development model was suited to men more than to women.

Because male and female ways of thinking and behaving, indeed *of knowing*, differ, and because male ways have been institutionalized as the "normal" ones, female styles have necessarily been labeled as "abnormal," as pathological or at least less mature. Virginia Woolf said so as long ago as 1929 in her famous *A Room of One's Own*, where she wrote, "It is obvious that the values of women differ very often from the values which have been made by the other sex," and "it is the masculine values that prevail" (1929: 76). Shortly before Gilligan's work, Nancy Chodorow had rightly insisted that the difference between male and female development and psychology "does not mean that women have 'weaker' ego boundaries than men or are more prone to psychosis" but rather that "girls emerge from [childhood] with a basis for 'empathy' built into their primary definitions of self in a way that boys do not" (1978: 167).

> Girls emerge with a stronger basis for experiencing another's needs or feelings as one's own (or of thinking that one is so experiencing another's needs and feelings). Furthermore, girls do not define themselves in terms of the denial of preoedipal relational modes to the same extent as do boys. From very early, then, because they are parented by a person of the same gender . . . girls come to experience themselves as less differentiated than boys, as more continuous with and related to the external object-world and as differently oriented to their inner object-world as well.
>
> (167)

The upshot of this research, as Gilligan stressed, was that academic psychology (and arguably every social science) had a profound but invisible male bias that not only ignored but pathologized the thoughts, behaviors, experiences, and values of half of the species. Gilligan concluded that there is a pressing need "to delineate *in women's own terms* the experience of their adult life. My own work in that direction indicates that the inclusion of women's experience bring to developmental understanding a new perspective on relationships that changes the basic constructs of interpretation" (1993: A173).

While Gilligan and her colleagues have been criticized for simplifying and essentializing women's psychology (that is, assuming that all women are relational rather than rational and that this quality is *natural* to women), the wider implication of this thinking is serious and certainly true: *knowledge is gendered*. As Elizabeth Anderson (2012) states, feminism and women's studies illustrate

> the ways in which gender does and ought to influence our conceptions of knowledge, the knowing subject, and practices of inquiry and justification. It identifies ways in which dominant conceptions and practices of knowledge attribution, acquisition, and justification systematically disadvantage women and other subordinated groups, and strives to reform these conceptions and practices so that they serve the interests of these groups.

Of course, the dominance of male (or male-associated) knowledge and ways of knowing has immediate negative consequences for women, including

> (1) excluding them from inquiry, (2) denying them epistemic authority, (3) denigrating their "feminine" cognitive styles and modes of knowledge, (4) producing theories of women that represent them as inferior, deviant, or significant only in the ways they serve male interests, (5) producing theories of social phenomena that render women's activities and interests, or gendered power relations, invisible, and (6) producing knowledge

(science and technology) that is not useful for people in subordinate positions, or that reinforces gender and other social hierarchies.

But the implications are much wider and reverberate to the very roots of the social sciences and to science as a whole. For instance, Anderson posits that "a central concept of feminist epistemology" is the "situated knower, and hence situated knowledge: knowledge that reflects the particular perspectives of the subject." "What is known," she contends, "and the way that it is known, thereby reflects the situation or perspective of the knower." If this is so—and it is likely that it is—then the fact that men and women bring different life-experiences, different psychologies, and different embodied realities to moments of knowing suggests that their knowledge will diverge. Further, since society assigns people to different gendered statuses, roles, and norms and furnishes them with gendered skills, it is almost inevitable that men and women will "tend to represent the world in different terms, in virtue of their gendered interests, attitudes, emotions, and values, and perhaps also (although this is a matter of controversy among feminist theorists) in virtue of different cognitive styles."

Feminist scholars have not been slow to consider the impact on social science. In their introduction to a special volume of the journal *Signs* dedicated to "New Feminist Approaches to Social Science Methodologies," Sandra Harding and Kathryn Norberg claim that from "the early days of the women's movement of the 1970s, feminists have tried to intervene in the ways that the social sciences think about and do research. They have attempted to transform the methodologies and epistemologies of their disciplines" (2005: 2009). Operating from the premise of the "situated knower," they, like other scholars, have argued that "value-free research is an unachievable ideal" (2009) and that in fact the social sciences have never been value-free: they have always been saturated in male values and therefore in male power. Therefore, Harding and Norberg conclude, "the social sciences, while claiming to do impartial research, construct the 'conceptual practices of power,'" including "the power to control relations between men and women" and ultimately to control and define women (2009).

Fortunately, for them as for members of many other excluded categories (non-white, non-heterosexual, non-abled, non-rich, etc.), the feminist perspective has not only pointed out the limitations and injustices of standard knowledge but has "also pointed the way to possible solutions to controversies about relations between knowledge and power. They have insisted on the adoption of research principles and practices that are both intellectually alert to and sensitive about what disadvantaged groups want to know" (2011). More, they have resisted the alleged neutrality of the academy, confronting Michael Burawoy's question of "knowledge for what?" Feminist scholars, according to Harding and Norberg, "have insisted that their research projects have practical implications for the improvement of women's lives" by, among other things, "producing a liberatory, transformative subjectivity in an oppressed or marginalized group" as well as producing "knowledge that such a group desires" (2011). In a word, knowledge is not disinterested knowledge-for-knowledge-sake but is a "pedagogy of the oppressed" (Freire 1970) intended to inform for the purpose of transforming.

As the work of Chodorow and Gilligan indicates, feminism has probably had the greatest impact on psychology among the social sciences. Jean Baker Miller's 1976 *Toward a New Psychology of Women* helped shift the paradigm of the discipline away from what Raewyn Connell (1995) famously called "hegemonic masculinity." Looking back on Miller's contribution thirty years later, Christina Robb, in her aptly titled *This Changes Everything: The Relational Revolution in Psychology*, praises her predecessor for demonstrating "that what male psychologists had labeled women's weaknesses—hypersensitivity, merging, dependency needs—could be seen as strength: authenticity, empathy, a drive to connect, and the skills to stay connected" (2007: x). More deeply, Robb finds that Miller maintained that hegemonic masculinity, like all cultural hegemonies, was defensive about its power over knowledge and over people:

> there is a whole category of knowledge that the dominant people in any society spend an enormous amount of energy trivializing, demonizing, and ignoring—knowledge about the effects of their domination on subordinates, knowledge about what subordinates know about them, knowledge about human experiences they see only in subordinates and not in themselves—because these experiences (empathy, tenderness, mutuality, and respect) make it hard to dominate people. So it makes sense that subordinates know more about dominants and about themselves than dominants know about themselves or subordinates.
>
> (xviii)

Surely then, the effects of sexism on social knowledge are as serious and as wide-ranging as the political and personal effects.

Accordingly, the volume of psychological writing representing the feminist challenge to standard psychology is truly impressive. In 1998 Mari Jo Buhle published *Feminism and Its Discontents: A Century of Struggle with Psychoanalysis*, the title of which parodies the name of a classic book by Freud. Other examples include Jill Morawski's 1994 *Practicing Feminisms, Reconstructing Psychology: Notes on a Liminal Science*, Rhoda Unger's 1998 *Resisting Gender: Twenty-Five Years of Feminist Psychology*, Thomas Teo's 2005 *The Critique of Psychology: From Kant to Postcolonial Theory*, and more journal articles and entire journals than can be counted.

However, the effect of feminism has been felt throughout the social sciences. Economics has been another area for obvious gender contestation and rethinking. In 1970 Ester Boserup wrote *Woman's Role in Economic*

Development, which pioneered the research on the impact of economic-growth policies in poor countries. Marilyn Waring contributed *If Women Counted: A New Feminist Economics* in 1988, and Marianne Ferber gave us *Women in the Labor Market* in 1998 as well as two collected volumes, 1993's *Beyond Economic Man: Feminist Theory and Economics* and 2003's *Feminist Economics Today: Beyond Economic Man*, both co-edited with Julie Nelson. Reflecting interest in economic issues relevant to women, Nancy Fobre published *Who Pays for the Kids? Gender and the Structures of Constraint* in 1994, *The Invisible Heart: Economics and Family Values* in 2001, *Family Time: The Social Organization of Care* in 2004, and most recently *Greed, Lust, and Gender: A History of Economic Ideas* in 2009. There is even a journal specifically dedicated to *Feminist Economics* and an International Association for Feminist Economics.

As in psychology, the feminist approach to economics critiques the "unquestioned and unexamined masculinist values . . . deeply embedded in the theoretical and empirical aspects" of the discipline (Barker 2005: 2189). This critique reaches from specific topics in economics "such as the division of labor by gender, race, and nation; women's position and status in labor markets; the importance of social reproduction; and the increasing disparities of wealth and income that accompany globalization" (2189) to more general challenges to the rationality, individualism, and competitiveness assumed by standard economic thinking. One of the most interesting and important angles in feminist economics has been the analysis of "women's work," both in the sense of examining why work is divided by gender and in the sense of taking women's work—especially unpaid work—seriously as an economic matter. Some results have been concepts like "social reproduction" or the labor that goes into maintaining and perpetuating society (from child birth and child care to cooking and cleaning) and "caring labor" or "emotional labor" (all of the formal and informal ways that women provide for the physical and emotional needs of others, from mothering and nursing to sex work).

Reasonably, there is a feminist politics—indeed, feminism is largely based on the slogan, "the personal is the political"—which likewise expresses "skepticism toward a body of knowledge that, while it claims to be universal and objective, is in reality based on knowledge primarily from men's lives" (Tickner 2005: 2177). By the early 1990s feminist political scientists pushed against "the masculinist biases of the core assumptions and concepts of the field and demonstrated how the theory and practice of international relations is gendered"; since then they have "investigated a variety of empirical cases, making gender and women's lives visible" (2178). Others, like Charlotte Hooper in her 2001 *Manly States: Masculinity, International Relations, and Gender Politics*, have discussed how the entire global political system is defined and controlled by men.

Anthropology went through its own gender revolution in the 1970s, with such pivotal works as Rayna Reiter's 1975 *Toward an Anthropology of Women*, which condemned the male bias in the discipline; Michelle Rosaldo and Louise Lamphere's 1974 *Woman, Culture, and Society*; and Frances Dahlberg's 1981 *Woman the Gatherer*. There has even been a lively feminist rejoinder to geography, in the form of, for example, Linda McDowell's 1999 *Gender, Identity, and Place: Understanding Feminist Geographies*, Lynda Johnston and Robyn Longhurst's 2010 *Space, Place, and Sex: Geographies of Sexualities*, and Linda McDowell and Joanne Sharp's 1997 *Space, Gender, Knowledge: Feminist Readings* with sections on "body maps," "gendering everyday space," "gendering work," and "gender, nation, and inter-national relations."

It is worth noting that even the natural sciences have not escaped the feminist critique. A few examples include Ruth Bleier's 1986 *Feminist Approaches to Science*, Sharyn Clough's 2003 *Beyond Epistemology: A Pragmatist Approach to Feminist Science Studies*, Angela Creagers, Elizabeth Lunbeck, and Londa Schiebinger's 2001 *Feminism in Twentieth-Century Science, Technology, and Medicine*, Donna Haraway's 1991 very influential *Simians, Cyborgs, and Women: The Reinvention of Nature*, and Evelyn Fox Keller and Helen Longino's 1996 *Feminism and Science*. Alison Adam (1993) even suggested applications for feminism to the field of artificial intelligence and used the term "successor science" for what the next generation of sciences will look like after they have been transformed by feminism. Truly, there is no branch of knowledge or of research that is not gendered in some way, including philosophy, the arts, and all of the humanities.

Alternatives to the Social Sciences: Crossing Disciplines and Inventing Disciplines

Two of the main challengers to the classical social sciences, as just explored, have been non-Western peoples and women, two groups—comprising the majority of the human race—who have historically been outside the professional disciplines. However, another source of pressure has come from inside the disciplines, from individuals and institutions testing and questioning the boundaries of social science as they currently exist. A fourth and in the end the ultimate challenger to the social sciences as we know them is social reality itself, which is more complex and more interrelated than any disciplinary boundaries can ever represent.

One of the main points of this book has been that the contemporary social sciences are remarkably young and that until very recently they formed a relatively undifferentiated body of philosophical and moral thought. The greatest thinking in Western intellectual history straddled disciplinary lines, like Hobbes or Locke or Kant; even at the turn of the twentieth century, figures like Durkheim or Weber or Boas or Freud often contributed to more than one discipline. Ironically but not unreasonably, almost as soon as the modern social sciences were defined, they began to outgrow their disciplinary boundaries.

One outcome is the proliferation of many new or hybrid disciplines and departments, as well as specialist subdisciplines and subdepartments. Among the more common and influential new/hybrid social sciences are:

- Womens' Studies
- African American or Black Studies
- Hispanic Studies
- Cultural Studies
- Postcolonial Studies

It is apparent that these fields overlap with the classic social sciences, sometimes even sharing faculty members, but they also have built their more or less distinct literatures, degree-granting processes, and institutional structures (e.g. journals, conferences, teaching positions, and so on). And there are many others, from Sound Studies (with its *Journal of Sonic Studies*) to Decision Sciences (with its journals *Decision Sciences* and *Decision Sciences Journal of Innovative Education*), not to mention unified or inter-disciplinary social science initiatives (see for instance thesocialsciences.com and the journal *Interdisciplinary Social Sciences: Annual Review*).

One of the striking developments in the academy in the late-twentieth and twenty-first centuries was the rise of interdisciplinary and transdisciplinary research programs, conceptual tools, and knowledges or ways of thinking. Some of these interdisciplinary efforts are rather straightforward combinations of existing disciplines, such as cross-cultural psychology, political geography, or, as we saw in a previous chapter, behavioral economics; some reach beyond the social sciences to include natural sciences or arts and humanities, like neuroanthropology, medical sociology, or art therapy. Such programs do not necessarily threaten the integrity of the standard disciplines; in fact, interdisciplinary work, almost by definition (inter-disciplinary or "between disciplines"), implies the collaboration of discrete disciplines that retain their discreteness. However, simply bringing any two or more categories together can have the effect of altering the contents of and weakening the boundaries between the categories.

Any topic can be examined and probably should be examined from multiple disciplinary perspectives (as we have done in this book with terrorism), since each perspective has something to offer but none has a monopoly on knowledge. A more radical challenge to the stability of established disciplines is a *transdisciplinary* approach, or what has been called *transdisciplinarity*. The "trans" in transdisciplinarity means to cross or transgress boundaries and, in the process, at least potentially to contest or erase those boundaries. (The same can be said for "transsexuality," in which individuals not only cross sexual identities, from male to female or vice versa, but sometimes reject the reality or validity of sexual categories or identities altogether.) Transdisciplinary offers (or threatens) to *trans*form the disciplines, literally to change their very form. Interestingly, both social science and natural science have adopted transdisciplinary approaches to an extent. For instance, the Washington University School of Medicine in St. Louis has a Transdisciplinary Research on Energetics and Cancer Center, which explains that transdisciplinary research "is, essentially, team science. In a transdisciplinary research endeavor, scientists contribute their unique expertise but work entirely outside their own discipline. . . . Transdisciplinary research allows investigators to transcend their own disciplines to inform one another's work, capture complexity, and create new intellectual spaces" (www.obesity-cancer.wustl.edu/en/About/What-Is-Transdisciplinary-Research). The website goes on to contrast interdisciplinary and transdisciplinary action:

- Interdisciplinary: "Researchers interact with the goal of transferring knowledge from one discipline to another. Allows researchers to inform each other's work and compare individual findings."
- Transdisciplinary: "Collaboration in which exchanging information, altering discipline-specific approaches, sharing resources and integrating disciplines achieves a common scientific goal."

Significantly, transdisciplinary thinking has progressed to the point where Transdisciplinary Studies departments and programs exist (as at Claremont Graduate University or Texas Tech University) and a *Handbook of Transdisciplinary Research* has been produced, which declares that trandisciplinary "orientations in research, education, and institutions try to overcome the mismatch between knowledge production in academia and knowledge requests for solving societal problems" (Hirsch Hadorn et al. 2008: 3).

One of the earliest and most promising, yet highly controversial, attempts to construct a new transdisciplinary science of human behavior was *sociobiology*, an overt composite of sociology and biology. Launched by Edward O. Wilson's treatise *Sociobiology: The New Synthesis* (1975), the proposed new field was based on the notion that human behavior could best, indeed only, be understood as a product of physical, literally genetic, processes. In an abridged version of his tome, Wilson defined sociobiology as "the systematic study of the biological basis of all social behavior" (4), not only human but all social species. So far lacking a biological and evolutionary component but ultimately dependent upon biology and evolution, he argued that

> sociology and the other social sciences, as well as the humanities, are the last branches of biology waiting to be included in the Modern Synthesis. One of the functions of sociobiology, then, is to reformulate the foundations of the social sciences in a way that draws these subjects into the Modern Synthesis.

(4)

The Charter of Transdisciplinarity, 1994

At the first World Congress of Transdisciplinarity convened in Portugal, the participants adopted a charter propounding the importance of thinking and researching across the standard disciplines. It read, in part:

"Whereas, the present proliferation of academic and nonacademic disciplines is leading to an exponential increase in knowledge which makes a global view of the human being impossible;

"Whereas, only a form of intelligence capable of grasping the cosmic dimension of the present conflicts is able to confront the complexity of our world and the present challenge of the spiritual and material self-destruction of the human species;. . . .

"Article 1: Any attempt to reduce the human species by formally defining what a human being is and subjecting the human being to reductive analyses within a framework of formal structure, no matter what they are, is incompatible with the transdisciplinary vision.

"Article 2: The recognition of the existence of different levels of reality governed by different types of logic is inherent in the transdisciplinary attitude. Any attempt to reduce reality to a single level governed by a single form of logic does not lie within the scope of Transdisciplinarity.

"Article 3: Transdisciplinarity complements disciplinary approaches. It occasions the emergence of new data and new interactions from out of the encounter between disciplines. It offers a new vision of nature and reality. Transdisciplinarity does not strive for mastery of several disciplines but aims to open all disciplines to that which they share and to that which lies beyond them.

"Article 5: The transdisciplinary vision is resolutely open insofar as it goes beyond the field of the exact sciences and demands their dialogue and their reconciliation with the humanities and the social sciences as well as with art, literature, poetry, and spiritual experience.

"Article 10: No single culture is privileged over any other culture. The transdisciplinary approach is inherently transcultural."

Wilson then proceeded to apply biological concepts to complex human social behaviors including communication, aggression, dominance systems, sex, parenting, territoriality, roles and castes, and "moral" action like altruism.

Not surprisingly, Wilson's claims generated a lot of debate, not least because he was attributing more sublime (and for many people "spiritual") aspects of humanity to baser material/biological causes. He was by no means the first thinker to do so: Freud regarded most of the "higher" dimensions of human life, such as art and religion, as expressions of "lower" instincts and drives, especially sexual ones.

As Wilson's subtitle suggests, he was pursuing a sort of "unified theory" of human (and other species') social life, akin to the search for the grand unified theory among physicists that will finally bring together all physical forces and particles. And despite the early objections, Wilson persisted in this quest, publishing in 1998 his *Consilience: The Unity of Knowledge*. Like the word "convergence" that is sometimes used to describe the coming-together of all media and technologies (which are themselves conduits for and structures of knowledge), Wilson saw consilience as the solution to the "ongoing fragmentation of knowledge and resulting chaos in philosophy," which are "not reflections of the real world but artifacts of scholarship" (1998: 8). Consilience was, in a word, "the key to unification" (8) not only of the social sciences but of all human knowledge endeavors. Indeed, if and when it should succeed, he opined, "the enterprises of culture will eventually fall out into science, by which I mean the natural sciences, and the humanities, particularly the creative arts. These domains will be the two great branches of learning in the twenty-first century" (12).

> The social sciences will continue to split within each of its disciplines, a process already rancorously begun, with one part folding into or becoming continuous with biology, the other fusing with the humanities. Its disciplines will continue to exist but in radically altered forms. In the process the humanities, ranging from philosophy and history to moral reasoning, comparative religion, and interpretation of the arts, will draw closer to the sciences and partly fuse with them.
>
> (12)

If this seems like an odd prediction, Wilson went on to make some scathing comments about the social sciences, which he acknowledged had grown out of the Western Enlightenment but had succumbed to the "fragmentation of expertise" (39). In a later chapter committed entirely to the social sciences, he compared them unfavorably to the natural sciences, accusing them of a lack of "coherent foundation" and of unproductive "tribal loyalty": "For the most part, anthropologists, economists, sociologists, and political scientists fail to understand and encourage one another" (182). He went so far as to condemn the founding fathers of the various social sciences—"most notably Émile Durkheim, Karl Marx, Franz Boas, and Sigmund Freud"—

for practicing willful ignorance of natural science and attempting "to isolate their nascent disciplines from the foundational sciences of biology and psychology" (184).

It is of course not entirely true that the great early social scientists were ignorant of and hostile to the natural sciences, and some like Boas and Freud began as natural scientists and used their natural-science background profitably in their social science. Also, psychology has at least as problematic a history as any social science, and even biology was invented in relatively modern times. Even so, Wilson did see four "bridges across the divide" of the social and natural sciences, specifically:

- Cognitive neuroscience
- Human behavioral genetics
- Evolutionary biology
- Environmental sciences

(192)

A particularly promising candidate for a sort of consilience or integration of the social sciences and of social science with natural science is a version of cognitive neuroscience sometimes referred to as *evolutionary psychology* or *cognitive evolution*, which is (wittingly or not) carrying on Wilson's program for a biological and historical/evolutionary basis for complex social behaviors. In a recent article on this "new thinking" about human nature and action, Cecilia Heyes explains that the program of cognitive evolutionary theory "integrates findings from anthropology, archaeology, economics, evolutionary biology, neuroscience, philosophy, and psychology" (2012: 2091) to account for everyday behavior as well as "art, architecture, music and dance" not to mention sports, war, religion, and all of humanity's high and low achievements.

Although this disciplinary consilience is relatively new, the basic ideas behind evolutionary psychology are not new; rather, they trace back to the observations and predictions of Darwin, who noticed that animals have emotions and social behaviors and expected evolution to illuminate both ours and theirs. In fact, we might say that, if each social science (and natural science) discipline is a paradigm or epistemic culture, then the master paradigm or epistemic culture of all social (and natural) sciences is evolution and has been for a century and a half. We can understand, then, why Armin Geertz characterized the position of cultural evolutionary theory in these terms: "We are intelligent apes that are highly emotional, easily spooked, very superstitious, extremely sensitive to social norms and virtual realities, and equipped with nervous systems that are vulnerable to influence from conspecifics and their symbolic worlds" (2013: 19).

To make a long story short, evolutionary psychology posits that our human bodies—and especially our brains—evolved over millennia to have certain features that are (a) continuous with our pre-human ancestry and

(b) adaptive, since they have been selected over long periods of time in an environment that included social interaction and human creations like tools and language. These circumstances hardwired certain traits into our nature, including intense concern for the actions and opinions of other members of our group, emotional bonds, imagination and memory (the capacity to acquire and retain learned ideas and behaviors or "culture"), and therefore a fundamental orientation to the minds of others. Some scholars have called this orientation "agentive thinking," "theory of mind," or, in the words of Justin Barrett (2004), "hyperactive agency detection," that is, the tendency to attribute mind or personal/human qualities not only to other people but to non-human entities like animals, natural phenomena, and even "super-natural" phenomena. Thus, cognitive evolutionary theory finds the cause of sophisticated human ideas and institutions like morality, religion, and organized violence in our evolved mental and social tendencies.

Alternatives to the Social Sciences: Traditional or Indigenous Knowledge

If there is any class of people and societies that have been rendered voiceless, ignored and discounted, and literally colonized more than others, it is the traditional or indigenous peoples of the world. Often (but not always) living in small groups in remote places, with languages and cultures that are foreign to the dominant nations, they have frequently been dismissed as "primitive," more than occasionally enslaved and killed, and gawked at and probed (that is, "researched") in their homelands and in museums, traveling shows, and human zoos (see Chapter 7). Certainly, their knowledge has generally been scoffed at, if they were believed to possess any knowledge at all.

In recent decades, partly because modern urban societies have become interested in what they might know, and partly because these indigenous groups have demanded respect for their knowledge, "indigenous know-ledge"—also referred to as "traditional knowledge," "folk knowledge," "local knowledge," or "traditional environmental/ecological knowledge" (TEK)—has become a subject of serious consideration. In their handbook on traditional knowledge and intellectual property, Stephen Hansen and Justin VanFleet define traditional knowledge as

> the information that people in a given community, based on experience and adaptation to a local culture and environment, have developed over time, and continue to develop. This knowledge is used to sustain the community and its culture and to maintain the genetic resources necessary for the continued survival of the community.
>
> Traditional knowledge includes mental inventories of local biological resources, animal breeds, and local plant, crop and tree species. . . . [It] also encompasses belief systems that play a fundamental role in

a people's livelihood, maintaining their health, and protecting and replenishing the environment.

(2003: 3)

They add that traditional knowledge "is collective in nature and is often considered the property of the entire community, and not belonging to any single individual within the community. It is transmitted through specific cultural and traditional information exchange mechanisms, for example, maintained and transmitted orally through elders or specialists (breeders, healers, etc.), and often to only a select few people within a community" (3).

It can be seen that in many ways traditional knowledge does not conform to the standard (that is, academic Western) model of "knowledge." It is or was typically oral rather than written, local rather than universal, practical rather than theoretical, and it concerned matters that were either trivial to "knowledge" (such as plants and animals) or were actively excluded from the category of "knowledge" completely (such as religious belief). Who produces traditional knowledge, where it is stored, and how it is transmitted also put it at odds with Western standards of knowledge. Hansen and VanFleet say that traditional knowledge, instead of being produced by scholars, stored in universities and books, and transmitted by writing and formal teaching, tends to be located in

- "daily activities"
- "spiritual and religious activities"
- "folklore, songs, poetry, and theater"
- "community records," mostly "word of mouth" but also cultural "form of record keeping" like "maps, boundary markers (trees, poles, stones, etc.), drawings, paintings, or carvings"
- "people working with the community, such as NGO researchers, academics, scientists, and development specialists who may have been collecting" such knowledge
- "secondary sources such as journal articles and books, unpublished documents, databases, videos, photos, museums, and exhibits."

(41)

Little wonder, according to Paul Nadasdy, scientists and other Western elites have often felt that "the two types of knowledge are incommensurable. In contrast to traditional knowledge, which is assumed to be qualitative, intuitive, holistic, and oral, science is seen as quantitative, analytical, reductionist, and literate" (1999: 2).

An example of traditional/indigenous knowledge, which seems particularly incommensurable to Western minds, but which proved to have some utility emerges from a mapping project in Chile. What could be more "objective" and "scientific" than mapping? Yet, recall that Western maps

Is There Such a Thing as "Indigenous Knowledge"?

The idea of traditional or indigenous knowledge compels us to contemplate the very idea of "knowledge." Kai Horsthemke from the University of Witwatersrand in South Africa, while no enemy of indigenous people, contends that the notion of "indigenous knowledge" as distinct from any other kind of knowledge is incoherent, resting on "at best an incomplete, partial or, at worst, questionable understanding or conception of knowledge" and that even "as a tool of anti-discrimination and anti-repression discourse, 'indigenous knowledge' is largely inappropriate" (2008: 129). The category of indigenous knowledge, he argues, is more political than intellectual, more about what it is "meant to achieve" than about the fact or quality of knowledge-claims. His basic assertion is that, "Insofar as the term 'indigenous' makes sense, it is not a matter of 'knowledge,' strictly speaking, but rather of 'indigenous skills/practices' or 'indigenous beliefs.' Insofar as the term 'knowledge' is plausible in this context, it cannot be 'indigenous,' 'local,' and so forth. It is 'knowledge' per se" (135–6). In other words, taking his second objection first, he insists that knowledge is knowledge: there may be things that "they" know that "we" do not (yet), but that does not make it a different kind of knowledge. His initial complaint is more serious and speaks to the issue of what "counts" as knowledge. Are, for instance, skills and practices "knowledge"? There is no reason in principle why "practical" knowledge should be rejected as knowledge; surely knowing how to bake a cake or program a computer is knowledge. Are "beliefs" knowledge? That is a thornier question, since beliefs, especially religious ones, are usually treated as cultural ideas at best and as errors at worst. On the other hand, a common (and, I hold, mistaken) philosophical definition of knowledge is "justified true belief," in which case knowledge is a subtype of belief. But that delivers us to the problem of "truth"—and whether "truth" is a necessary feature of knowledge and *whether "truth" is a preoccupation of Western thinking but not of all thought-systems.*

have conventionally reflected Western political and cultural interests and beliefs rather than being culture-free. Irène Hirt describes a project to map Mapuche territory in southern Chile between 2004 and 2006, which could not disregard "Mapuche behavior and ways of being" (2012: 105). Consequently, the project became an exercise in what has come to be called *social cartography*, which in the Mapuche case meant respecting the spirits of the land and embedding spiritual knowledge in the map. For the Mapuche, as for many indigenous peoples, mapping requires "a holistic conception of territory as composed of tangible and intangible spheres in which the living and the dead, human and non-human beings, all interact and are given similar agency" (107). So, a worthwhile map of Mapuche country must include "the ancestral boundaries" as well as "the sacred sites and sites of cultural and historical significance" (111). And where does much of this knowledge come from? For the Mapuche, the answer is *dreams*. In their dreams, the people meet and consult with spirits; creating a Mapuche-sensitive map "made the spirits actors in the full sense of the word, involving them in the project in the same way as their human peers. Dreamers would get in touch with the *ngen* (spirits) or *newen* (powers) of the territory" (115). But as Chilean anthropologist Roberto Morales is quoted as saying, "Actually, isn't dreaming a sort of GPS for the Mapuche?" (113).

Significantly, the message of traditional/indigenous knowledge resonates with the message of feminist critiques of Western knowledge. For instance, feminism tends to stress that knowledge and the knower are "situated," and traditional knowledge is generally socially and geographically local: it is something that *someone or some group* knows, and it is often about *some place*. Also, feminism insists that knowledge is "for something," and traditional knowledge is widely recognized as knowledge *for* the local people who possess it, to help them live their lives and to preserve their identity and their culture.

Many people, indigenous and non-indigenous, have become champions of traditional knowledge, none perhaps more eloquent or passionate than Linda Tuhiwai Smith, whose words opened this chapter. She, as an indigenous woman, has been particularly critical of the colonization of indigenous societies and knowledge systems, reminding us that "primitive" or non-Western societies were often the sites where the social sciences honed their concepts. Native and Eastern peoples were "studied," "collected," and often carried off for further examination. This is why she is so suspicious of "research," asking reasonably enough, "Whose research is it? Who owns it? Whose interests does it serve? Who will benefit from it? Who has designed its questions and framed its scope. Who will carry it out? Who will write it up? How will its results be disseminated?" (2012: 10).

As an academic herself, Smith is not opposed to research. Rather, like the Chinese discussed before, she wants to indigenize the social (and natural) sciences, to make them reflect the knowledge and the interests of indigenous people as well as those of Westerners. She wants to rethink social science research "with a view to *re*writing and *re*righting our position" (29), which means upending some venerable assumptions in Western thought, such as the assumption that there is a single universal history of humankind, that humans can be divided into binaries like "modern" and "traditional," that science is "an innocent neutral discipline," and that the goal of all human development is "the self-actualizing human subject" (30).

She and others like her, then, have begun the process of rethinking and unthinking the social sciences, as Wallerstein advocated earlier. She gives, for example, a list of twenty-five "indigenous projects" that indigenous people could conduct with or without Western scholars, focusing on such issues as land claiming, storytelling and oral testimony, cultural survival and revitalization, networking, protecting, returning artifacts and human remains, democratizing, and creating and representing (e.g. making their own studies, books, films, exhibits, and art).

For such purposes, a great number of resources and institutions have been established, just one example of which will have to suffice. In 2005 the First Nations Center National Aboriginal Health Organization (Canada) produced a guidebook or "toolkit" called *Sacred Ways of Life: Traditional Knowledge*. Opening with a prayer of thanksgiving, the document compares Western and indigenous styles of thought and then offers guidance on matters of law (e.g. intellectual property and bio-piracy or "the misuse of knowledge and biological resources from communities" [Crowshoe 2005: 4]) and organization, such as forming a "First Nations research committee," developing and enforcing local regulations on research, founding their own curriculum and training programs, setting codes of conduct for traditional healers, and of course preserving native languages. Ironically, the National Aboriginal Health Organization was discontinued in 2012 due to lack of funding from the Canadian government. Neither indigenous health nor indigenous knowledge is yet adequately respected and protected.

Conclusion: The Future of Social Sciences

A century ago, the social sciences did not yet exist in their current form: Malinowski, Sauer, Schmitt, Spengler, and Toynbee had not published their ideas, Freud's most innovative work lay in the future, and Durkheim's seminal study of religion had only appeared (in French) four years prior. Despite their shared roots in Western intellectual history and their shared ambition to be scientific, the developmental course of the social sciences through the twentieth century was by no means predetermined and inevitable, and as soon as disciplinary boundaries solidified they began to crumble. In other words, there is no necessary reason why the social sciences settled as they did, and there is no necessary reason why that settlement should endure a century from now.

During their short lives, the social sciences have been convulsed by many crises and "turns," as events in the world and conceptual innovations inside and outside the social sciences have invited or compelled new ways of thinking. Along the way, social scientists have realized that they are not so much studying the economy or the political system or culture as the process of thinking itself and the social construction of knowledge. They have accordingly, and positively, become more reflexive about their own ways of knowing. They have also become more aware of their public role, as evinced by the change in wording in the American Anthropological Association's mission statement in 2012: instead of describing its purpose as advancing "anthropology as the *science* that studies humankind," the organization repurposed itself "to advance public understanding of humankind" through "the dissemination of anthropological knowledge, expertise, and interpretation." At the same time, while many social sciences have long been practical and even policy-oriented, more of them have accepted the mantle of "applied" or "engaged" or "public" research.

The social sciences can change because they are human creations, and they must change because of the changing nature of society itself. For instance, once veering away from while imitating the natural sciences, the social sciences are again converging with natural science. Further, the social sciences do not hold a monopoly on their concepts and methods or even their institutions. For instance, an increasing number of corporations operate their own "universities," teaching courses and granting degrees that are tailored to the needs of their industry or their particular company. These programs appear at a moment when the traditional university—also a recent invention—struggles with funding, enrollment, and competition from online and for-profit education. The social sciences do not even own social research: in a recent article in *Harvard Business Review*, Michael Schrage (2015) argues, "Tomorrow's most important discoveries into why people do what they do will most likely come from business innovation than university research. The best and most rigorous social science experiments will be done for profit."

Add to these threats or opportunities the critiques from feminism, non-Western cultures, inter- and transdisciplinary perspectives, and indigenous peoples, and it becomes clear that the social sciences are under intense pressure to re-examine themselves. And they have risen to the occasion, as in the 2014 Cornell University workshop "The Future of the Social Sciences" (see www.youtube.com/watch?v=TZjBzTrJEgo for the introductory session, with links to subsequent sessions). These and other efforts have embraced Wallerstein's challenge to rethink or unthink social science as we know it—and not only to learn more about knowing in the process but to contribute to future ways of knowing.

Bibliography

Abu-Lughod, Lila. 1991. "Writing Against Culture." In Richard Fox, Ed. *Recapturing Anthropology: Working in the Present*. Santa Fe, NM: School of American Research Press, 137–62.

Adam, Alison. 1993. "Gendered Knowledge—Epistemology and Artificial Intelligence." *AI & Society* 7: 311–22.

Aguirre, Rojas and Carlos Antonio. 2000. "Rethinking Current Social Sciences: The Case of Historical Discourses in the History of Modernity." *Journal of World-Systems Research* 6(3): 750–66.

Alatas, Syed Farid. 2014. "The Problem of Academic Dependency: Latin America and the Malay World." In *Post-Regionalism in the Global Age: Multiculturalism and Cultural Circulation in Asia and Latin America*. Rio de Janeiro: Academy of Latinity, 273–308.

Alatas, Syed Hussein. 1974. "The Captive Mind and Creative Development." *International Social Science Journal* 36(4): 691–9.

Alatout, Samer. 2009. "Walls as Technologies of Government: The Double Construction of Geographies of Peace and Conflict in Israeli Politics, 2002–Present." *Annals of the Association of American Geographers* 99(5): 956–68.

Allport, Gordon. 1979 [1954]. *The Nature of Prejudice*. Reading, MA: Addison-Wesley Publishing Company.

Ammerman, Nancy T. 1987. *Bible Believers: Fundamentalists in the Modern World*. New Brunswick, NJ and London: Rutgers University Press.

Anderson, Elizabeth. 2012. "Feminist Epistemology and Philosophy of Science." In Edward N. Zalta, Ed. *The Stanford Encyclopedia of Philosophy*. http://plato.stanford.edu/archives/fall2012/entries/feminism-epistemology, accessed April 23, 2014.

Anderson, Jon. 2015. *Understanding Cultural Geography: Places and Traces*, 2nd ed. Abingdon, UK and New York: Routledge.

Anderson, Kay, Mona Domosh, Steve Pile, and Nigel Thrift, Eds. 2003. *Handbook of Cultural Geography*. London: Sage.

Arefi, Mahyar. 1999. "Non-Place and Placelessness as Narratives of Loss: Rethinking the Notion of Place." *Journal of Urban Design* 4(2): 179–93.

Ariely, Dan. 2008. *Predictably Irrational: The Hidden Forces that Shape Our Decisions*. New York: HarperCollins.

Atran, Scott. 2004. "Mishandling Suicide Terrorism." *The Washington Quarterly* 27(3): 67–90.

——. 2010. *Talking to the Enemy: Religion, Brotherhood, and the (Un)Making of Terrorists*. New York: HarperCollins.

Augé, Marc. 1995 [1992]. *Non-Places: Introduction to an Anthropology of Supermodernity*. John Howe, trans. London and New York: Verso.

Ayres, Thomas. 2000. *That's Not in My American History Book*. Lanham, MD: Taylor Trade Publishing.

Bahn, Paul. 1996. *Archaeology: A Very Short Introduction*. Oxford and New York: Oxford University Press.

Bandura, Albert. 1990. "Mechanisms of Moral Disengagement." In W. Reich, Ed. *Origins of Terrorism: Psychologies, Ideologies, Theologies, States of Mind*. Cambridge: Cambridge University Press, 161–91.

Barker, Drucilla K. 2005. "Beyond Women and Economics: Rereading 'Women's Work.'" *Signs* 30(4): 2189–2209.

Barrett, Justin L. 2004. *Why Would Anyone Believe in God?* Lanham, MD: AltaMira Press.

Baumeister, Roy. 2001. *Evil: Inside Human Violence and Cruelty*. New York: Barnes & Noble Books.

Benmelech, Efraim and Claude Berrebi. 2007. "Human Capital and Productivity of Suicide Bombers." *Journal of Economic Perspectives* 21(3): 223–38.

Benmelech, Efraim, Claude Berrebi, and Esteban F. Klor. 2012. "Economic Conditions and the Quality of Suicide Terrorism." *The Journal of Politics* 74(1): 113–28.

Bennell, Craig and Shevaun Corey. 2007. "Geographic Profiling of Terrorist Attacks." In R. N. Kocsis, Ed. *Criminal Profiling: International Theory, Research, and Practice*. Totowa, NJ: Humana Press, 189–203.

Bensaude-Vincent, Bernadette and Isabelle Stengers. 1997. *A History of Chemistry*. Cambridge, MA: Harvard University Press.

Bergesen, Albert J. and Omar Lizardo. 2004. "International Terrorism and the World-System." *Sociological Theory* 22(1): 38–52.

Berlin, Isaiah. 1976. *Vico & Herder: Two Studies in the History of Ideas*. New York: Viking Press.

Bernstein, Basil. 1975. *Class, Codes, and Control, volume III: Towards a Theory of Educational Transmissions*. London: Routledge & Kegan Paul.

Binford, Lewis R. 1962. "Archaeology as Anthropology." *American Antiquity* 28(2): 217–25.

Blaug, Mark. 1992. *The Methodology of Economics, or How Economists Explain*, 2nd ed. Cambridge and New York: Cambridge University Press.

Blaydes, Lisa, Justin Grimmer, and Alison McQueen. 2013. "Mirrors for Princes and Sultans: Advice on the Art of Governance in the Medieval Christian and Islamic Worlds." Paper presented to Association for Analytic Learning about Islam and Muslim Societies, Princeton University, NJ, October 18, 2013.

Blumer, Herbert. 1939. "Collective Behavior." In Robert E. Park, Ed. *An Outline of the Principles of Sociology*. New York: Barnes and Noble, Inc., 221–80.

——. 1969. *Symbolic Interactionism: Perspective and Method*. Englewood Cliffs, NJ: Prentice-Hall.

Boas, Franz. 1887. "The Study of Geography." *Science* 9(210): 137–41.

——. 1901. "The Mind of Primitive Man." *The Journal of American Folklore* 14(52): 1–11.

——. 1912. "Changes in the Bodily Form of Descendants of Immigrants." *American Anthropologist* 14(3): 530–62.

Bonnett, Alastair. 1997. "Geography, 'Race,' and Whiteness: Invisible Traditions and Current Challenges." *Area* 29(3): 193–9.

Bourdieu, Pierre. 1977. *Outline of a Theory of Practice*. Cambridge: Cambridge University Press.

Braudel, Fernand. 1981 [1979]. *Civilization and Capitalism, 15th–18th Century, Volume I: The Structure of Everyday Life*. Sian Reynolds, trans. New York: Harper & Row.

Brown, Marilyn A. 1982. "Modelling the Spatial Distribution of Suburban Crime." *Economic* I 58(3): 247–61.

Brubaker, Rogers and David D. Laitin. 1998. "Ethnic and Nationalist Violence." *Annual Review of Sociology* 24: 423–52.

Burawoy, Michael. 2007. "Open the Social Sciences: To Whom and For What?" *Portuguese Journal of Social Science* 6(3): 137–46.

Burgess, Ernest and Harvey Locke. 1945. *The Family: From Institution to Companionship*. New York: American Book Company.

Burke, Edmund. 1790. *Reflections on the Revolution in France*. http://socserv2. mcmaster.ca/~econ/ugcm/3ll3/burke/revfrance.pdf, accessed July 20, 2015.

Burnham, Peter, Karin Gilland Lutz, Wyn Grant, and Zig Layton-Henry. 2008. *Research Methods in Politics*, 2nd ed. Basingstoke, UK and New York: Palgrave Macmillan.

Byrd, Michael D. 2001. "Back to the Future for Higher Education: Medieval Universities." *Internet and Higher Education* 4: 1–7.

Canby, William. 1870. "The History of the Flag of the United States." www. ushistory.org/betsy/more/canby.htm, accessed July 28, 2015.

Canterbury, E. Ray. 2001. *A Brief History of Economics: Artful Approaches to the Dismal Science*. Singapore, NJ , London, and Hong Kong: World Scientific.

Carlyle, Thomas. 1906 [1841]. *On Heroes, Hero-Worship, and the Heroic in History*. Henry David Gray, Ed. New York: Longmans, Green, and Co.

Chakrabarty, Dipesh. 2007 [2000]. *Provincializing Europe: Postcolonial Thought and Historical Difference*. Princeton, NJ and Oxford: Princeton University Press.

Cherry, John F. 2005. "Survey." In Colin Renfrew and Paul Bahn, Eds. *Archaeology: The Key Concepts*. Abingdon and New York: Routledge, 186–9.

Chodorow, Nancy J. 1978. *The Reproduction of Mothering*. Berkeley and Los Angeles, CA: University of California Press.

Chomsky, Noam. 1959. "Review of *Verbal Behavior* by B. F. Skinner." *Language* 35(1): 26–58.

Chun, Allen. 2012. "From Sinicization to Indigenization in the Social Sciences: Is That All There Is?" In Arif Dirlik, Guannan Li and Hsiao-pei Yen, Eds. *Sociology and Anthropology in Twentieth-Century China: Between Universalism and Indigenism*. Hong Kong: The Chinese University Press, 255–82.

Cialdini, Robert B. 2001. *Influence: Science and Practice*, 4th ed. Boston, MA and London: Allyn and Bacon.

Cochrane, James L. 1970. *Macroeconomics Before Keynes*. Glenview, IL: Scott, Foresman and Company.

Collingwood, R.G. 1946. *The Idea of History*. New York: Oxford University Press.

Collins, Randall and Michael Makowsky. 1993. *The Discovery of Society*, 5th ed. New York: McGraw-Hill.

Comte, Auguste. 1855. *The Positive Philosophy of Auguste Comte*. Harriett Martineau, trans. New York: Calvin Blanchard.

Connell, Raewyn W. 1995. *Masculinities*. Berkeley, CA and Los Angeles, CA: University of California Press.

Cosgrove, Denis. 1983. "Towards a Radical Cultural Geography: Problems of Theory." *Antipode* 15(1): 1–11.

——. 1984. *Social Formation and Symbolic Landscape*. London: Croom Helm.

Costandi, Mo. 2006. "The Incredible Case of Phineas Gage." https://neurophilosophy.wordpress.com/2006/12/04/the-incredible-case-of-phineas-gage, accessed July 20, 2016.

Crenshaw, Martha. 2000. "The Psychology of Terrorism: An Agenda for the 21st Century." *Political Psychology* 21(2): 405–20.

Crombie, Alistair. 1994. *Styles of Scientific Thinking in the European Tradition*. London: Gerald Duckworth.

Crowshoe, Chelsea. 2005. *Sacred Ways of Life: Traditional Knowledge*. Ottawa, Canada: First Nations Center National Aboriginal Health Organization.

Dash, Mike. 2002. *Batavia's Graveyard: The True Story of the Mad Heretic Who Led History's Bloodiest Mutiny*. New York: Three Rivers Press.

Datta, Ayona. 2015. "New Urban Utopias of Postcolonial India: 'Entrepreneurial Urbanization' in Dholera Smart City, Gujarat." *Dialogues in Human Geography* 5(1): 3–22.

Debaene, Vincent. 2014. *Far Afield: French Anthropology between Science and Literature*. Justin Izzo, trans. Chicago, IL and London: The University of Chicago Press.

Deloria, Jr., Vine. 1969. *Custer Died For Your Sins: An Indian Manifesto*. New York: Avon Books.

Diamond, Jared. 1999 [1997]. *Guns, Germs, and Steel: The Fates of Human Societies*. New York: W.W. Norton.

Diebold, Francis X. 2015. *Econometrics: Streamlined, Applied, and e-Aware*. Philadelphia, PA: University of Pennsylvania.

Diriwachter, Rainer. 2004. "*Völkerpsychologie*: The Synthesis that Never Was." *Culture & Psychology* 10(1): 85–109.

Dirlik, Arif. 2012. "*Zhongguohua*: Worlding China—The Case of Sociology and Anthropology in 20th-Century China." In Arif Dirlik, Guannan Li and Hsiao-pei Yen, Eds. *Sociology and Anthropology in Twentieth-Century China: Between Universalism and Indigenism*. Hong Kong: The Chinese University Press, 1–39.

Domosh, Mona, Roderick Neumann, Patricia Price, and Terry Jordan-Bychkov. 2012. *The Human Mosaic*, 12th ed. New York: W.H. Freeman.

Druckman, James N. and Arthur Lupia. 2012. "Experimenting with Politics." *Science* 335 (March 9): 1177–9.

Drysdale, John P. and Susan Hoecker-Drysdale. 2007. "The History of Sociology: The North American Perspective." In Clifton D. Bryant and Dennis L. Peck, Eds. *21st Century Sociology: A Reference Handbook*. Thousand Oaks, CA: Sage Publications, 28–44.

Durkheim, Émile. 1951 [1897]. *Suicide: A Study in Sociology*. John A. Spaulding and George Simpson, trans. New York: The Free Press.

——. 1982 [1895]. *The Rules of Sociological Method*. Steven Lukes, Ed. New York: The Free Press.

——. 1995 [1912]. *The Forms of Religious Life*. K. Fields, trans. New York: The Free Press.

Dzilo, Hasan. 2012. "The Concept of 'Islamization of Knowledge' and its Philosophical Implications." *Islam and Christian–Muslim Relations* 23(3): 247–56.

Ekinsmyth, Carol and Pamela Shurmer-Smith. 2002. "Humanistic and Behavioural Geography." In Pamela Shurmer-Smith, Ed. *Doing Cultural Geography*. Malden, MA and Oxford: Blackwell, 19–27.

Elden, Stuart. 2009. "Reassessing Kant's Geography." *Journal of Historical Geography* 35: 3–25.

Engels, Friedrich. 1942 [1884]. *The Origin of the Family, Private Property, and the State*. Eleanor Burke Leacock, Ed. New York: International Publishers.

Ergang, Robert Reinhold. 1931. *Herder and the Foundations of German Nationalism*. New York: Columbia University Press.

Fleck, Ludwik. 1979 [1935]. *Genesis and Development of a Scientific Fact*. Thaddeus J. Trenn and Robert K. Merton, Eds. Fred Bradley and Thaddeus J. Trenn, trans. Chicago, IL and London: The Chicago University Press.

Foucault, Michel and Jay Miskowiec. 1986. "Of Other Spaces." *Diacritics* 16(1): 22–7.

Frei, Hans W. 1974. *The Eclipse of Biblical Narrative: A Study in Eighteenth and Nineteenth-Century Hermeneutics*. New Haven, CT: Yale University Press.

Freire, Paulo. 1970 [1968]. *Pedagogy of the Oppressed*. Myra Ramos, trans. New York: Continuum Publishing.

Friedman, Milton. 1962. *Capitalism and Freedom*. Chicago, IL and London: The University of Chicago Press.

Friedman, Thomas. 2005. *The World is Flat: A Brief History of the Twenty-First Century*. New York: Farrar, Straus, and Giroux.

Furay, Conal and Michael J. Salevouris. 2009. *The Methods and Skills of History: A Practical Guide*, 3rd ed. Malden, MA and Oxford: Wiley-Blackwell.

Garraghan, Gilbert J. 1946. *A Guide to Historical Method*. New York: Fordham University Press.

Garson, John George and Charles Hercules Read, Eds. 1899. *Notes and Queries on Anthropology, or A Guide to Anthropological Research for the Use of Travellers and Others*, 3rd ed. London: The Anthropological Institute.

Geary, Patrick J. 2002. *The Myth of Nations: The Medieval Origins of Europe*. Princeton, NJ: Princeton University Press.

Geertz, Armin. 2013. "Whence Religion? How the Brain Constructs the World and What This Might Tell Us About the Origins of Religion." In Armin Geertz, Ed. *Origins of Religion, Cognition, and Culture*. Durham, UK and Bristol, CT: Acumen, 17–70.

Germain, Marie-Line. 2006. *Development and Preliminary Validation of a Psychometric Measure of Expertise: The Generalized Expertise Measure (GEM)*. Unpublished doctoral dissertation. Miami, FL: Barry University.

Giddens, Anthony. 1989. *Sociology*. Cambridge: Polity.

Gilligan, Carol. 1993 [1982]. *In a Different Voice: Psychological Theory and Women's Development*. Cambridge, MA and London: Harvard University Press.

Gleitman, Henry, James Gross, and Daniel Reisberg. 2011. *Psychology*, 8th ed. New York: W.W. Norton & Company.

Gold, David. 2004. "The Economics of Terrorism." *Columbia International Affairs Online (CIAO) Case* Studies. www.isn.ethz.ch/Digital-Library/Publications/Detail/?id=10698&lng=en, accessed March 20, 2014.

Gordon, David. 2000. *An Introduction to Economic Reasoning.* Auburn, AL: Ludwig von Mises Institute.

Gorzycki, Meg and Linda Elder. 2011. *A Thinker's Guide to Historical Thinking: Bringing Critical Thinking Explicitly to the Heart of Historical Study.* Tomales, CA: The Foundation for Critical Thinking.

Gracey, Harry L. 1968. "Learning the Student Role: Kindergarten as Academic Boot Camp." In Dennis Wrong and Harry L. Gracey, Eds. *Readings in Introductory Sociology.* New York: Macmillan, 63–71.

Gramsci, Antonio. 1971. *Selections from the Prison Notebooks of Antonio Gramsci.* Quintin Hoare and Geoffrey Nowell Smith, trans. and Ed. London: Lawrence and Wishart.

Gregory, Derek, Ron Johnston, Geraldine Pratt, Michael J. Watts, and Sarah Whatmore. 2009. *Dictionary of Human Geography,* 5th ed. Malden, MA and Oxford: Wiley-Blackwell.

Grenz, Stanley J., David Guretzki, and Cherith Fee Nordling. 1999. *Pocket Dictionary of Theological Terms.* Downers Grove, IL: InterVarsity.

Griffin, Miriam. 2005 [2000]. "Seneca and Pliny." In Christopher Rowe and Malcolm Schofield, Eds. *The Cambridge History of Greek and Roman Political Thought.* Cambridge: Cambridge University Press, 532–58.

Grigsby, Ellen. 2009. *Analyzing Politics: An Introduction to Political Science,* 4th ed. Belmont, CA: Wadsworth/Cengage Learning.

Gupta, Ego G. and Yvonna S. Lincoln. 2005. "Paradigmatic Controversies, Contradictions, and Emerging Confluences." In Norman K. Denzin, Ed. *The Sage Handbook of Qualitative Research,* revised 2nd ed. London and New Delhi: Sage Publications, 191–215.

Hacker, Frederick J. 1976. *Crusaders, Criminals and Crazies: Terror and Terrorism in our Time.* New York: Norton.

Hacking, Ian. 2002. "'Style' for Historians and Philosophers." In Ian Hacking, Ed. *Historical Ontology.* Cambridge, MA: Harvard University Press, 178–99.

Haller, Jr. John S., 1971. *Outcasts from Evolution: Scientific Attitudes of Racial Inferiority, 1859–1900.* Carbondale, IL and Edwardsville, IL: Southern Illinois University Press.

Hallowell, A. Irving. 1967 [1955]. *Culture and Experience.* New York: Schocken Books.

Halsall, Paul. 1997. "Modern History Sourcebook: Maximilien Robespierre: Justification of the Use of Terror." http://legacy.fordham.edu/halsall/mod/robespierre-terror.asp, accessed June 23, 2016.

Hamilton, H.C. and W. Falconer. 1854. *The Geography of Strabo,* volume 1. London: Henry G. Bohn.

Hamm, Mark S. 2013. *The Spectacular Few: Prisoner Radicalization and the Evolving Terrorist Threat.* New York and London: New York University Press.

Hansen, Stephen A. and Justin W. VanFleet. 2003. *Traditional Knowledge and Intellectual Property: A Handbook on Issues and Options for Traditional Knowledge Holders in Protecting their Intellectual Property and Maintaining Biological Diversity.* New York: American Association for the Advancement of Science.

Harding, Sandra and Kathryn Norberg. 2005. "New Feminist Approaches to Social Science Methodologies: An Introduction." *Signs* 30(4): 2009–2015.

Harley, J.B. 1988. "Maps, Knowledge, and Power." In Denis Cosgrove and Stephen Daniels, Eds. *The Iconography of Landscape*. Cambridge: Cambridge University Press, 277–312.

Harris, Marvin. 1968. *The Rise of Anthropological Theory*. New York: Thomas Y. Crowell Company.

Hartog, François. 2000. "The Invention of History: The Pre-History of a Concept from Homer to Herodotus." *History and Theory* 39(3): 384–95.

Hassan, Faridah Hj. 2006. "Ibn Khaldun and Jane Addams: The Real Father of Sociology and the Mother of Social Works." www.uned.es/congreso-ibn khaldun/pdf/04%20Faridah%20Hj%20Hassan.pdf, accessed March 31, 2014.

Hastrup, Kirsten. 1995. *A Passage to Anthropology: Between Experience and Theory*. London: Routledge.

Hayek, Friedrich A. 1976. *Law, Legislation, and Liberty, Volume 2: The Mirage of Social Justice*. Chicago, IL and London: The University of Chicago Press.

Hergenhahn, B.R. 2000. *Introduction to the History of Psychology*, 4th ed. Belmont, CA: Wadsworth Publishing.

Herodotus. 1972 [1954]. *The Histories*. Aubrey de Sélincourt, trans. London and New York: Penguin.

Hesiod. 1914. *Works and Days*. Hugh G. Evelyn-White, trans. Cambridge, MA: Harvard University Press.

Heyes, Cecilia. 2012. "New Thinking: The Evolution of Human Cognition." *Philosophical Transactions of the Royal Society B* 367: 2091–2096.

Hirsch Hadorn, Gertrude, Holger Hoffmann-Riem, Susette Biber-Klemm, Walter Grossenbacher-Mansuy, Dominique Joye, Christian Pohl, Urs Wiesmann, and Elisabeth Zemp, Eds. 2008. *Handbook of Transdisciplinary Research*. Dordrecht, Netherlands: Springer Science + Business Media B.V.

Hirt, Irène. 2012. "Mapping Dreams/Dreaming Maps: Bridging Indigenous and Western Geographical Knowledge." *Cartographica* 47(2): 105–20.

Hix, Simon and Matthew Whiting. 2012. *Introduction to Political Science PS1 172*. London: University of London.

Hobbes, Thomas. 1651. *Leviathan or the Matter, Form, and Power of a Commonwealth Ecclesiastical and Civil*. Hamilton, Canada: McMaster University Archive of the History of Economic Thought.

Hodder, Ian. 2005. "Post-Processual and Interpretive Archaeology." In Colin Renfrew and Paul Bahn, Eds. *Archaeology: The Key Concepts*. Abingdon, UK and New York: Routledge, 155–9.

Hoge, John D., Thomas A. Lucey, and Laura E. Pinto. 2013. *Effective Elementary Social Studies*. Athens, GA: Digitaltextbooks.biz.

Horsthemke, Kai. 2008. "The Idea of Indigenous Knowledge." *Archaeologies: Journal of the World Archaeological Congress* 4(1): 129–43.

Huffman, Karen. 2012. *Psychology in Action*, 10th ed. Hoboken, NJ: John Wiley & Sons, Inc.

Huizinga, Jan. 1954 [1924]. *The Waning of the Middle Ages: A Study of the Forms of Life, Thought, and Art in France and the Netherlands in the Dawn of the Renaissance*. New York: Anchor Books.

Hülsmann, Jörg Guido. 2008. *The Ethics of Money Production*. Auburn, AL: Ludwig von Mises Institute.

Huntington, Samuel P. 1993. "The Clash of Civilizations?" *Foreign Affairs* 72 (summer): 22–49.

——. 1996. *The Clash of Civilizations and the Remaking of World Order*. New York: Simon & Schuster.

Iggers, Georg G. 1995. "Historicism: The History and Meaning of the Term." *Journal of the History of Ideas* 56(1): 129–52.

Ingold, Tim. 1992. "Editorial." *Man* 27(4): 693–6.

Intriligator, Michael D. 2010. "The Economics of Terrorism." *Economic Inquiry* 48(1): 1–13.

Jackson, Peter, Ed. 1987. *Race & Racism: Essays in Social Geography*. London: Allen & Unwin.

——. 2012. "Overview of Social and Cultural Geography." www.rgs.org/NR/rdon lyres/EBFC85E8-E8A3-4477-91B7-463F19161CEF/0/Benchmarking_Review_ of_UK_social_and_cultural_geography_April2012.pdf, accessed January 18, 2016.

Jackson, Richard. 2007. "The Core Commitments of Critical Terrorism Studies." *European Political Science* 6(3): 244–51.

Jain, T.R. and O.P. Khanna. 2007. *Economic Concepts and Methods*. New Delhi: V. K. (India) Enterprises.

Janoski, Thomas. 2014. "Citizenship in China: A Comparison of Rights with the East and West." *Journal of Chinese Political Science* 19: 365–85.

Jaynes, Julian. 1976. *The Origin of Consciousness in the Breakdown of the Bicameral Mind*. Boston, MA: Houghton Mifflin Company.

Johnson, Doyle Paul. 2008. *Contemporary Sociological Theory: An Integrated Multi-Level Approach*. New York: Springer Science + Business Media.

Kant, Immanuel. 2006 [1798]. *Anthropology from a Pragmatic Point of View*. Robert B. Louden, trans. and Ed. Cambridge and New York: Cambridge University Press.

Kaplan, Jeffrey. 2010. *Terrorist Groups and the New Tribalism: Terrorism's Fifth Wave*. Abingdon, UK and New York: Routledge.

Klein, Naomi. 2007. *The Shock Doctrine: The Rise of Disaster Capitalism*. New York: Picador.

Kliot, Nurit and Igal Charney. 2006. "The Geography of Suicide Terrorism in Israel." *GeoJournal* 66(4): 353–73.

Knorr-Cetina, Karin. 1999. *Epistemic Cultures: How the Sciences Make Knowledge*. Cambridge, MA: Harvard University Press.

Kobayashi, Audrey. 2009. "Geographies of Peace and Armed Conflict: Introduction." *Annals of the Association of American Geographers* 99(5): 819–26.

Kruglanski, Arie W. and Shira Fishman. 2006. "The Psychology of Terrorism: 'Syndrome' versus 'Tool' Perspectives." *Terrorism and Political Violence* 18(2): 193–215.

Kuhn, Thomas S. 1970 [1962]. *The Structure of Scientific Revolutions*, 2nd ed. Chicago, IL: The University of Chicago Press.

Kuper, Adam. 1988. *The Invention of Primitive Society: Transformations of an Illusion*. London: Routledge.

Landmann, Michael. 1974. *Philosophical Anthropology*. David J. Parent, trans. Philadelphia, PA: The Westminster Press.

Laqueur, Walter. 1987. *The Age of Terrorism*. Boston, MA and Toronto, Canada: Little, Brown and Company.

Latour, Bruno. 1987. *Science in Action: How to Follow Scientists and Engineers Through Society*. Cambridge, MA: Harvard University Press.

Le Billon, Philippe. 2008. "Diamond Wars? Conflict Diamonds and Geographies of Resource Wars." *Annals of the Association of American Geographers* 98(2): 345–72.

LeDoux, Joseph. 2002. *Synaptic Self: How Our Brains Become Who We Are*. New York: Penguin Books.

Leepson, Marc. 2006. *Flag: An American Biography*. New York: Thomas Dunne Books.

Lemke, Thomas. 2007. "An Indigestible Meal? Foucault, Governmentality, and State Theory." *Distinktion: Scandinavian Journal of Social Theory* 8(2): 43–64.

Leroi-Gourhan, André. 1964. *Gesture and Speech*. Cambridge, MA: Massachusetts Institute of Technology Press.

Levy, Leonard. 1993. *Blasphemy: Verbal Offense against the Sacred, from Moses to Salman Rushdie*. New York: Knopf.

Lewis-Williams, J. David. 2002. *The Mind in the Cave: Consciousness and the Origins of Art*. London: Thames & Hudson.

Li, Guannan. 2012a. "Cultural Policy and Culture under the Guomindang: Huang Wenshan and 'Culturology.' " In Arif Dirlik, Guannan Li and Hsiao-pei Yen, Eds. *Sociology and Anthropology in Twentieth-Century China: Between Universalism and Indigenism*. Hong Kong: The Chinese University Press, 109–37.

——. 2012b. "The Synthesis School and the Founding of 'Orthodox' and 'Authentic' Sociology in Nationalist China: Sun Benwen's Sociological Thinking and Practice." In Arif Dirlik, Guannan Li and Hsiao-pei Yen, Eds. *Sociology and Anthropology in Twentieth-Century China: Between Universalism and Indigenism*. Hong Kong: The Chinese University Press, 63–87.

Liakos, Antonis. 2007. "Utopian and Historical Thinking: Interplays and Transferences." *Historein* 7: 20–57.

Liddell, Henry George and Robert Scott. 1940. *A Greek-English Lexicon*. www. perseus.tufts.edu/hopper/text?doc=Perseus%3Atext%3A1999.04.0057%3Aentry %3D%2384506&redirect=true, accessed March 10, 2014.

Limerick, Patricia. 1987. *The Legacy of Conquest: The Unbroken Past of the American West*. New York: W.W. Norton & Company.

——. 2000. *Something in the Soil: Legacies and Reckoning in the New West*. New York: W. W. Norton & Company.

Lloyd, Sharon A. and Susanne Sreedhar. 2014. "Hobbes's Moral and Political Philosophy." In Edward N. Zalta, Ed. *The Stanford Encyclopedia of Philosophy* (Spring 2014 Edition). www.plato.stanford. edu/archives/spr2014/entries/hobbes-moral, accessed March 11, 2014.

Llussa, Fernanda and José Tavares. 2006. "Economics and Terrorism: What We Know, What We Should Know, and the Data We Need." *Proceedings of the 10th Annual International Conference on Economics and Security*, 187–248.

Locke, John. 1796 [1690]. *An Essay Concerning Human Understanding*. London: T. Longman.

Lorimer, Hayden. 2005. "Cultural Geography: The Busyness of Being 'More-than-Representational.' " *Progress in Human Geography* 29(1): 83–94.

Loza, Wadgy. 2007. "The Psychology of Extremism and Terrorism: A Middle-Eastern Perspective." *Aggression and Violent Behavior* 12: 141–55.

Lukes, Steven. 1971. *Power: A Radical View*. Basingstoke, UK: Palgrave Macmillan.

McAfee, R. Preston. 2006. *Introduction to Economic Analysis*. Pasadena: California Institute of Technology.

McBride, Marissa F. and Mark A. Burgman. 2012. "What is Expert Knowledge, How is Such Knowledge Gathered, and How Do we Use it to Address Questions of Landscape Ecology?' In Ajith H. Perera, C. Ashton Drew, and Chris J. Johnson, Eds. *Expert Knowledge and Its Application to Landscape Ecology*. New York: Springer, 11–37.

McCallum, Cecilia. 1996. "The Body that Knows: From Cashinahua Epistemology to a Medical Anthropology of Lowland South America." *Medical Anthropology Quarterly* 10(3): 347–72.

McColl, Robert W. 1969. "The Insurgent State: Territorial Bases of Revolution." *Annals of the Association of American Geographers* 59(4): 613–31.

McDermott, Rose. 2002. "Experimental Methods in Political Science." *Annual Review of Political Science* 5: 31–61.

Mackinder, H. J. 1904. "The Geographical Pivot of History." *The Geographical Journal* 170(4): 298–321.

McKinley, James C. 2010. "Texas Conservatives Win Curriculum Change." *New York Times* (March 12). www.nytimes.com/2010/03/13/education/13texas.html?hpw=&pagewanted=print, accessed March 12, 2010.

Mankiw, N. Gregory. 2000. *Principles of Microeconomics*, 2nd ed. San Diego, CA: Harcourt Brace.

——. 2009. *Brief Principles of Macroeconomics*, 5th ed. Mason, OH: South-Western, Cengage Learning.

Mannheim, Karl. 1952. "The Problem of Generations." In Paul Keckemeti, Ed. *Essays on the Sociology of Knowledge*. London: Routledge & Kegan Paul, 276–322.

Martineau, Harriet. 1837. *Society in America*. London: Saunders and Otley.

Marx, Karl. 1977. *Karl Marx: Selected Writings*. D. McLellan, Ed. Oxford: Oxford University Press.

Menzies, Gavin. 2003 [2002]. *1421: The Year China Discovered America*. New York: William Morrow.

Merton, Robert K. 1957. *Social Theory and Social Structure*. Glencoe, IL: Free Press.

Michaels, David. 2008. *Doubt is Their Product: How Industry's Assault on Science Threatens Your Health*. Oxford and New York: Oxford University Press.

Mikulas, William J. 2006. "Integrating the World's Psychologies." In L. Hoshmand (Ed.) *Culture, Psychotherapy, and Counseling: Critical and Integrative Perspectives*. Thousand Oaks, CA: Sage Publications, 91–113.

Miller, Laurence. 2006. "The Terrorist Mind II. Typologies, Psychopathologies, and Practical Guidelines for Investigation." *International Journal of Offender Therapy and Comparative Criminology* 50(3): 255–68.

Mills, C. Wright. 1956. *The Power Elite*. New York: Oxford University Press.

——. 2000 [1959]. *The Sociological Imagination*, 40th anniversary ed. Oxford and New York: Oxford University Press.

Moeran, Brian. 2014. *The Business of Creativity: Toward an Anthropology of Worth*. Walnut Creek, CA: Left Coast Press.

Moghaddam, Fathali M. 2005. "The Staircase to Terrorism: A Psychological Exploration." *American Psychologist* 60(2): 161–9.

——. 2006. *From the Terrorists' Point of View: What They Experience and Why They Come to Destroy*. Westport, CT: Praeger.

Morgan, Lewis Henry. 1877. *Ancient Society, or Researches in the Lines of Human Progress from Savagery, through Barbarism to Civilization*. New York: Henry Holt and Company.

Mosbah-Natanson, Sébastien and Yves Gingras. 2013. "The Globalization of Social Sciences? Evidence from a Quantitative Analysis of 30 Years of Production, Collaboration, and Citations in the Social Sciences (1980–2009)." *Current Sociology* (online): 1–21.

Nadasdy, Paul. 1999. "The Politics of TEK: Power and the 'Integration' of Knowledge." *Arctic Anthropology* 36(1/2): 1–18.

National Counterterrorism Center. 2011. *2010 Report on Terrorism*. Washington, DC: Office of the Director of National Intelligence.

Oberschall, Anthony. 2004. "Explaining Terrorism: The Contribution of Collective Action Theory." *Sociological Theory* 22(1): 26–37.

Pape, Robert A. and James K. Feldman. 2010. *Cutting the Fuse: The Explosion of Global Suicide Terrorism and How to Stop It*. Chicago, IL and London: The University of Chicago Press.

Pearlstein, Richard M. 1991. *The Mind of the Political Terrorist*. Wilmington, DE: Scholarly Resources Inc.

Pentland, Alex. 2014. *Social Physics: How Good Ideas Spread—The Lessons from a New Science*. New York: Penguin.

Perera, Ajith A., C. Ashton Drew, and Chris J. Johnson. 2012. "Experts, Expert Knowledge, and Their Roles in Landscape Ecological Applications." In Ajith H. Perera, C. Ashton Drew, and Chris J. Johnson, Eds. *Expert Knowledge and Its Application to Landscape Ecology*. New York: Springer, 1–10.

Perkins, Chris. 2010. "Mapping and Graphicacy." In Nicholas Clifford, Shaun French, and Gill Valentine, Eds. *Key Methods in Geography*, 2nd ed. London and Thousand Oaks, CA: Sage, 350–73.

Perry, John A. and Erna K. Perry. 2012. *Contemporary Society: An Introduction to Social Science*, 13th ed. Boston, MA: Pearson.

Pew Research Center. 2014. "2014 Party Identification Detailed Tables." www.people-press.org/2015/04/07/2014-party-identification-detailed-tables, accessed December 16, 2015.

Piketty, Thomas. 2014 [2013]. *Capital in the Twenty-First Century*. Arthur Goldhammer, trans. Cambridge, MA: Harvard University Press.

Pinney, Christopher. 2011. *Photography and Anthropology*. London: Reaktion Books.

Porter, Theodore M. and Dorothy Ross. 2003. "Introduction: Writing the History of Social Science." In Theodore M. Porter and Dorothy Ross, Eds. *The Cambridge History of Science, vol. 7 The Modern Social Sciences*. Cambridge and New York: Cambridge University Press, 1–10.

Post, Jerrold M. 2005. "The Psychological and Behavioral Bases of Terrorism: Individual, Group, and Collective Contributions." *International Affairs Review* 14(2): 195–203.

Proctor, Robert N. 2008. "Agnotology: A Missing Term to Describe the Cultural Production of Ignorance (and Its Study)." In Proctor, Robert N. and Londa Schiebinger, Eds. *Agnotology: The Making & Unmaking of Ignorance*. Stanford, CA: Stanford University Press, 1–33.

Qureshi, Sadiah. 2011. *Peoples on Parade: Exhibitions, Empire, and Anthropology in Nineteenth-Century Britain*. Chicago, IL and London: The University of Chicago Press.

Radcliffe-Brown, A.R. 1957. *A Natural Science of Society*. Glencoe, IL: The Free Press.

Rapoport, David C. 2004. "The Four Waves of Modern Terrorism." In Audrey Kurth Cronin and J. Ludes, Eds. *Attacking Terrorism: Elements of a Grand Strategy*. Washington, DC: Georgetown University Press, 46–73.

Regan, Richard J. 1996. *Just War: Principles and Cases*. Washington, DC: The Catholic University Press.

Renfrew, Colin and Ezra B.W. Zubrow, Eds. 1994. *The Ancient Mind: Elements of Cognitive Archaeology*. Cambridge and New York: Cambridge University Press.

Ribeiro, Gustavo Lins and Arturo Escobar, Eds. 2006. *World Anthropologies: Disciplinary Transformations within Systems of Power*. Oxford and New York: Berg.

Richardson, Louise. 2006. *What Terrorists Want: Understanding the Enemy, Containing the Threat*. New York: Random House.

Riley, Alexander Tristan. 2010. *Godless Intellectuals? The Intellectual Pursuit of the Sacred Reinvented*. New York and Oxford: Berghahn.

Ritzer, George. 2013. *Introduction to Sociology*. Los Angeles, CA and London: Sage Publications.

Robb, Christina. 2007. *This Changes Everything: The Relational Revolution in Psychology*. New York: Farrar, Straus, and Giroux.

Robbins, Lionel. 1935. *An Essay on the Nature and Significance of Economic Science*. London: Macmillan and Co.

Rock, John C. n.d. "The Geographic Nature of Terrorism." http://ontology.buffalo.edu/smith/courses01/papers/rock(geo).pdf, accessed April 17, 2014.

Romer, Christina D. and David H. Romer. 2007. "The Macroeconomic Effects of Tax Changes: Estimates Based on a New Measure of Fiscal Shocks." *Working Paper 13264*. Cambridge, MA: National Bureau of Economic Research.

Rousseau, Jean-Jacques. 1923 [1762]. *The Social Contract and Discourses*. G.D.H. Cole, trans. London and Toronto, Canada: J. M. Dent and Sons.

Ruby, C.L. 2002. "The Definition of Terrorism." *Analyses of Social Issues and Public Policy* 2(1): 9–14.

Sack, R.D. 2004. "Place-making and Time." In T. Mels, Ed. *Reanimating Places: Re-Materialising*. Aldershot, UK: Ashgate, 243–53.

Said, Edward W. 1978. *Orientalism*. New York: Vintage Books.

Sauer, Carl O. 1925. "The Morphology of Landscape." *University of California Publications in Geography* 2(2): 19–53.

Scahill, John H. 1993. "Meaning-Construction and Habitus." http://archive.is/8s DNC, accessed February 25, 2014.

Schlanger, Nathan. 2005. "The *Chaîne Opératoire*." In Colin Renfrew and Paul Bahn, Eds. *Archaeology: The Key Concepts*. Abingdon, UK and New York: Routledge, 18–23.

Schlottmann, Antje and Judith Miggelbrink. 2009. "Visual Geographies: An Editorial." *Social Geography* 4: 1–11.

Schmitt, Carl. 2007 [1995]. *The Concept of the Political*. George Schwab, trans. Chicago, IL and London: The University of Chicago Press.

Schneider, Anne and Helen Ingram. 1993. "Social Construction of Target Populations: Implications for Politics and Policy." *The American Political Science Review* 87(2): 334–47.

Schrage, Michael. 2015. "Why the Future of Social Science is With Private Companies." *Harvard Business Review*. https://hbr.org/2015/09/why-the-future-of-social-science-is-with-private-companies, accessed January 26, 2016.

Schumpeter, Joseph A. 2006 [1954]. *History of Economic Analysis*. Elizabeth Boody Schumpeter, Ed. London: Routledge.

Schutz, Alfred. 1954. "Concept and Theory Formation in the Social Sciences." *The Journal of Philosophy* 51(9): 257–73.

Sewall, Gilbert T. 2004. *World History Textbooks: A Review*. New York: American Textbook Council.

Shiraev, Eric. 2011. *A History of Psychology: A Global Perspective*. Thousand Oaks, CA: Sage Publications.

Shively, W. Phillips. 2009. *The Craft of Political Research*, 7th ed. Upper Saddle River, NJ: Pearson Education.

Shurmer-Smith, Pamela. 2002a. "Introduction." In Pamela Shurmer-Smith, Ed. *Doing Cultural Geography*. Malden, MA and Oxford: Blackwell, 1–7.

——. 2002b. "Methods and Methodology." In Pamela Shurmer-Smith, Ed. *Doing Cultural Geography*. Malden, MA and Oxford: Blackwell, 95–8.

Simons, Anna and David Tucker. 2007. "The Misleading Problem of Failed States: A 'Socio-Geography' of Terrorism in the Post-9/11 Era." *Third World Quarterly* 28(2): 387–401.

Slotkin, J.S., Ed. 1965. *Readings in Early Anthropology*. London: Methuen & Co.

Sluka, Jeffrey A. 2009. "The Contribution of Anthropology to Critical Terrorism Studies." In Richard Jackson, Marie Breen Smyth, and Jeroen Gunning, Eds. *Critical Terrorism Studies: A New Research Agenda*. Abingdon, UK and New York: Routledge, 138–55.

——. 2010. "The Ruatoki Valley 'Antiterrorism' Police Raids: Losing 'Hearts and Minds' in Te Urewera." *Sites* 7(1): 44–64.

Smelser, Neil J. 1962. *Theory of Collective Behavior*. New York: The Free Press.

Smith, Adam. 1776. *An Inquiry into the Nature and Causes of the Wealth of Nations*. www.ifaarchive.com/pdf/smith_-_an_inquiry_into_the_nature_and_causes_of_the_wealth_of_nations%5B1%5D.pdf, accessed July 20, 2016.

Smith, Linda Tuhiwai. 2012. *Decolonizing Methodologies: Research and Indigenous Peoples*, 2nd ed. London and New York: Zed Books.

Smithson, Michael. 1989. *Ignorance and Uncertainty: Emerging Paradigms*. New York: Spring-Verlag.

Solot, Michael. 1986. "Carl Sauer and Cultural Evolution." *Annals of the Association of American Geographers* 76(4): 508–20.

Spengler, Oswald. 1926 [1918]. *The Decline of the West, vol. 1 Form and Actuality*. Charles Francis Atkinson, trans. New York: Alfred A. Knopf.

Springer, Simon. 2014. "Why a Radical Geography Must Be Anarchist." *Dialogues in Human Geography* 4(3): 249–70.

Stark, Rodney, and Laurence Iannaccone. 1994. "A Supply-Side Reinterpretation of the 'Secularization' of Europe." *Journal for the Scientific Study of Religion* 33(3): 230–52.

Stark, Werner. 1976. "The Theoretical and Practical Relevance of Vico's Sociology for Today." *Social Research* 43(4): 818–25.

Stavenhagen, Rodolfo. 1971. "Decolonializing Applied Social Sciences." *Human Organization* 30(4): 333–57.

Stedman Jones, Susan. 2013. "Durkheim, Anthropology, and the Question of the Categories in *Les Formes Élémentaires de la Vie Religieuse*." In Susan L. Hausner, Ed. *Durkheim in Dialogue: A Centenary Celebration of the Elementary Forms of Religious Life*. New York and Oxford: Berghahn, 143–64.

Stump, Jacob L. and Priya Dixit. 2012. "Toward a Completely Constructivist Critical Terrorism Studies." *International Relations* 26(2): 199–217.

Swidler, Ann and Jorge Arditi. 1994. "The New Sociology of Knowledge." *Annual Review of Sociology* 20: 305–29.

Tajfel, Henri. 1978. *Differentiation between Social Groups*. London: Academic Press.

——. 1981. *Human Groups and Social Categories: Studies in Social Psychology*. Cambridge: Cambridge University Press.

Task Force of the National Council for the Social Studies. 1994. *Expectations of Excellence: Curriculum Standards for Social Studies*, Bulletin 89. Washington, DC: National Council for the Social Studies.

Thrift, Nigel. 2007. *Non-Representational Theory: Space, Politics, Affect*. Abingdon and New York: Routledge.

Tickner, J. Ann. 2005. "Gendering a Discipline: Some Feminist Methodological Contributions to International Relations." *Signs* 30(4): 2173–2188.

Tobler, W.R. 1970. "A Computer Movie Simulating Urban Growth in the Detroit Region." *Economic Geography* 46 (supplement): 234–40.

Toynbee, Arnold. 1946. *A Study of History*, abridgement of volumes I-VI. Dorothea Grace Somervell, Ed. New York and Oxford: Oxford University Press.

——. 1962. *A Study of History: The Growths of Civilizations*, volume 3. New York: Oxford University Press.

Tuckness, Alex. 2012. "Locke's Political Philosophy." In Edward N. Zalta, Ed. *The Stanford Encyclopedia of Philosophy* (Winter 2012 Edition). http://plato. stanford.edu/archives/win2012/entries/locke-political, accessed March 11, 2014.

Turk, Austin T. 2004. "Sociology of Terrorism." *Annual Review of Sociology* 30, 271–86.

Tversky, Amos and Daniel Kahneman. 1974. "Judgment under Uncertainty: Heuristics and Biases." *Science* 185(4157): 1124–1131.

Tylor, E.B. 1958 [1871]. *Primitive Culture*. New York: Harper Torchbooks.

US Army TRADOC. 2007. *A Military Guide to Terrorism in the Twenty-First Century*. Fort Leavenworth, KS: US Army Training and Doctrine Command.

Utz, Aisha. 2011. *Psychology from the Islamic Perspective*. Riyadh, Saudi Arabia: International Islamic Publishing House.

van Schendel, Willem. 2002. "Geographies of Knowing, Geographies of Ignorance: Jumping Scale in Southeast Asia." *Environment and Planning D: Society and Space* 20: 647–68.

Van Sickle, John V. and Benjamin A. Rogge 1954. *Introduction to Economics*. New York, Toronto, Canada, and London: D. Van Nostrand Company.

Villanueva, Maria and Carmen Gonzalo. 2000. "Maps, Values, and Representations: Deconstructing Eurocentrism among European Primary Teachers." *International Research in Geographical and Environmental Education* 9(1): 61–6.

Von Humboldt, Alexander. 1864 [1845]. *Cosmos: A Sketch of a Physical Description of the Universe*. E.C. Otté, trans. London: Henry G. Bohn.

Wallerstein, Immanuel. 1987. "Should We Unthink the Nineteenth Century Social Science?" Paper presented to the International Meeting of Social and Human Scientists, Paris, December 14–18, 1987.

——. 1991. *Unthinking Social Science: The Limits to Nineteenth-Century Paradigms*. Cambridge, MA: Polity Press in association with Basil Blackwell.

——. 2003. "Anthropology, Sociology, and Other Dubious Disciplines." *Current Anthropology* 44(4): 453–65.

Wang Jianmin. 2012a. "Academic Universality and Indigenization: The Case of Chinese Anthropology." In Arif Dirlik, Guannan Li and Hsiao-pei Yen, Eds. *Sociology and Anthropology in Twentieth-Century China: Between Universalism and Indigenism*. Hong Kong: The Chinese University Press, 41–61.

——. 2012b. "Southeast and Southwest: Searching for the Link Between Research Regions." In Arif Dirlik, Guannan Li and Hsiao-pei Yen, Eds. *Sociology and Anthropology in Twentieth-Century China: Between Universalism and Indigenism*. Hong Kong: The Chinese University Press, 161–90.

Watson, John B. 1913. "Psychology as the Behaviorist Views It." *Psychological Review* 20: 158–77.

Watson, Robert I. 1978. *The Great Psychologists*, 4th ed. Philadelphia, PA: J.B. Lippincott Company.

Weber, Max. 1919. *Politics as a Vocation*. 1919. http://www2.southeastern.edu/Academics/Faculty/jbell/weber.pdf, accessed March 12, 2014.

——. 1949. *On the Methodology of the Social Sciences*. Edward A. Shils and Henry A. Finch, trans. and Eds. Glencoe, IL: The Free Press.

——. 1968. *Economy and Society: An Outline of Interpretive Sociology*. New York: Bedminster Press.

——. 1997. *The Theory of Social and Economic Organization*. New York: The Free Press.

Werlen, Benno. 1993 [1988]. *Society, Action, and Space: An Alternative Human Geography*. London and New York: Routledge.

Whalen-Bridge, John. 2006. "Enlightenment (Zen Buddhist)." *Theory, Culture, & Society* 23(2–3): 179–80.

Wheelwright, Philip, Ed. 1966. *The Presocratics*. New York: The Odyssey Press.

Wiedemann, Thomas. 2005 [2000]. "Reflections of Roman Political Thought in Latin Historical Writing." In Christopher Rowe and Malcolm Schofield, Eds. *The Cambridge History of Greek and Roman Political Thought*. Cambridge: Cambridge University Press, 517–31.

Wilkinson, Toby A.H. 2000. *Royal Annals of Ancient Egypt: The Palermo Stone and its Associated Fragments*. London: Kegan Paul.

Wilson, Edward O. 1975. *Sociobiology: The New Synthesis*. Cambridge, MA: Harvard University Press.

——. 1998. *Consilience: The Unity of Knowledge*. New York: Alfred A. Knopf.

Winch, Peter. 2003 [1958]. *The Idea of a Social Science and its Relation to Philosophy*, 2nd ed. London: Routledge.

Wirth, Louis. 1938. "Urbanism as a Way of Life." *The American Journal of Sociology* 44(1): 1–24.

Wolf, Eric R. 1964. *Anthropology: Humanistic Scholarship in America*. Englewood Cliffs, NJ: Prentice-Hall.

Woolf, Virginia. 1929. *A Room of One's Own*. New York: Harcourt, Brace, and World.

Woolridge, Jeffrey M. 2013. *Introductory Econometrics: A Modern Approach*, 5th ed. Mason, OH: South-Western, Cengage Learning.

Zimbardo, Philip. 2000. "The Psychology of Evil." *Psi Chi* 5, 16–19.

Zinn, Howard. 1980. *A People's History of the United States*. New York: Harper & Row.

Index